15.95

This textbook considers the methods used by governments to change the environment within which agricultural production takes place: by influencing the prices of farm inputs and outputs, by modifying agricultural institutions, and by promoting new technologies in agriculture.

The book is organised around a central set of eight policy chapters, covering topics of price policy, marketing policy, input policy, credit policy, mechanisation policy, land reform policy, research policy and irrigation policy. These chapters are preceded by material covering the nature of policy, in the context of the market versus state debate, and the principles used by economists to undertake agricultural policy analysis. They are followed by chapters that examine the status of women in agricultural policy, and that summarise aspects of food policy not covered in the main chapters.

This book is designed for undergraduate and graduate students taking courses related to agricultural policy, agricultural economics, or rural development in developing countries. It will also be accessible to the non-specialist reader who wishes to obtain an overview of the individual policy topics covered.

Agricultural policies in developing countries

WYE STUDIES IN AGRICULTURAL AND RURAL DEVELOPMENT

Solving the problems of agricultural and rural development in poorer countries requires, among other things, sufficient numbers of well-trained and skilled professionals. To help meet the need for topical and effective teaching materials in this area, the books in the series are designed for use by teachers, students and practitioners of the planning and management of agricultural and rural development. The series is being developed in association with the innovative postgraduate programme in Agricultural Development for external students of the University of London.

The series concentrates on the principles, techniques and applications of policy analysis, planning and implementation of agricultural and rural development. Texts review and synthesise existing knowledge and highlight current issues, combining academic rigour and topicality with a concern for practical applications. Most importantly, the series provides simultaneously a systematic basis for teaching and study, a means of updating the knowledge of workers in the field, and a source of ideas for those involved in planning development.

Agricultural Policies in Developing Countries

FRANK ELLIS

School of Development Studies, University of East Anglia

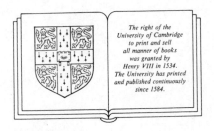

CAMBRIDGE UNIVERSITY PRESS

Cambridge

New York   Port Chester   Melbourne   Sydney

Published by the Press Syndicate of the University of Cambridge
The Pitt Building, Trumpington Street, Cambridge CB2 1RP
40 West 20th Street, New York, NY 10011-4211, USA
10 Stamford Road, Oakleigh, Victoria 3166, Australia

First published 1992

Printed in Great Britain at the University Press, Cambridge

A catalogue record of this book is available from the British Library

Library of Congress cataloguing in publication data

Ellis, Frank.
    Agricultural policies in developing countries / by Frank Ellis.
        p.   cm.
    Includes bibliographical references and index.
    ISBN 0-521-40004-X. – ISBN 0-521-39584-4 (pbk).
    1. Agriculture and state – Developing countries.   I. Title.
    HD1417.E45   1992
    338.1'8'091724–dc20   91-18837   CIP

ISBN 0 521 40004 X hardback
ISBN 0 521 39584 4 paperback

PN

To Jane, Clare and Josie again

Contents

Contents xi

Preface

This textbook is based on courses that I teach at undergraduate and postgraduate levels on the agricultural policies of developing countries. In this subject area there tends to be a lack of suitable teaching material for students located in the middle ground between purely descriptive accounts of policies, on the one hand, and technical treatments requiring an advanced grasp of neoclassical policy analysis, on the other hand. This book attempts to make a contribution towards filling this gap.

Writing a textbook on policies is a risky enterprise. Policy discussion is prone to sudden and sweeping changes of fashion. A topic or an approach that seemed to be exercising everyone's interest yesterday is suddenly of little or no interest today. For example, the current emphasis of agricultural policy discussion is heavily oriented towards structural adjustment policies in an African context. Many policy topics have come to be viewed through a structural adjustment lens.

This book tries to avoid too close adherence to policy perspectives that may prove ephemeral when fashion changes. It adopts a fairly conventional approach to agricultural policies, defining them as sectoral policies aimed at influencing the inputs, outputs, and technology of farm household production in developing countries. The book is organised around a central set of eight policy chapters, covering the topics of price policy, marketing policy, input policy, credit policy, mechanisation policy, land reform policy, research policy, and irrigation policy. These chapters incorporate many ideas and situations that reflect contemporary policy concerns, but they are not dominated by any single preoccupation regarding the point of entry into policy discussion.

The book is designed for selective use, according to the interests or study assignments of the reader. The first part of the book contains chapters on the framework and methodology of the partial equilibrium analysis of policies. These chapters can be regarded as optional by readers who are more interested in the policies themselves than in their economic analysis. The book also contains themes that cut across the material of the central policy chapters. Two of these – the gender dimension of agricultural policy, and food security – are given treatment of their own in the final part of the book.

Inevitably, the content of a book like this reflects the experiences and research interests of its author. Since the book was conceived and written while I was working on food policy issues in Indonesia, some of its examples and material reflect that personal context. Other material reflects periods living in Tanzania, Fiji, and Panama, which may help to explain (or to excuse) the examples used for illustrative purposes in some chapters. Lastly, the book was conceived in part as a companion volume to the author's earlier book in this series, *Peasant Economics*. It therefore reflects a continuing interest in the household and intra-household implications of state policies towards peasants.

Acknowledgements

Many people supported the idea of writing this book and the work that has gone into its preparation. Early ideas arose in conversations in Jakarta with Steve Tabor, who made a valuable contribution to the first outline, and later provided penetrating comments on the drafts of some chapters. In different ways and at different points in time Peter Timmer, Scott Pearson, and Henry Bernstein also provided the encouragement necessary for me to embark, with some misgiving, on such a formidable writing task.

For making comments of detail on individual chapters I thank Tony Barnett, Robert Bates, Steve Biggs, Priscilla Magrath, Richard Palmer-Jones, Scott Pearson, Sharon Truelove, and John Wyeth. The entire text was read by Hassan Hakimian who did an excellent job correcting theoretical, technical and stylistic errors. I am most grateful to him for the time and attention to detail that he devoted to this task. Thanks are also due to Sharon Truelove and Imogen Kirk for providing research assistance at particular points in the writing process. Needless to say, any errors of interpretation or expression remain entirely my own responsibility.

During the period immediately prior to writing the book, I was fortunate to be working in Indonesia in a technical assistance project related to food security. The book has gained much from my experience on that project, from collaboration with my Indonesian colleagues, and from a continued association with the project since my return to England. A special note of thanks is due to John Conway, the project manager, for providing such an encouraging work environment during this period.

Norwich   FE
June 1991

PART I

Agricultural policy analysis

1

Market, state and policy

Overview

This book is about agricultural policies in developing countries. It is concerned with the methods used by governments to change the environment within which agricultural production takes place: by altering the prices of farm inputs and outputs, by changing the institutions in which farm input and output markets operate, or by promoting new technologies in agriculture.

The book has a particular emphasis, which is on policies affecting peasant production. This means that it focuses on policies for small farmers, mainly engaged in crop production. However, many of the policies examined in the book are sectoral in scope, and they therefore have an impact across many different types of agricultural production.

There are many ways in which a book on agricultural policies could be organised. The approach here focuses on the relationship of policy to the inputs and outputs of the farm system. This provides a direct connection between decisions taken far away in capital cities, and the influence of those decisions down on the farm. The core of the book consists of a set of eight chapters, which are delineated according to the following interaction between policy decisions and farm production:

Price policy
Policies designed to influence the level and stability of the prices received by farmers for *farm outputs*.

Marketing policy
Policies concerned with the transfer of *farm outputs* from the farm gate to the domestic consumer, or to ports of exportation.

Input policy
Policies designed to influence the prices and delivery systems of purchased *variable inputs* used in farm production.

Credit policy
Policies related mainly, but not exclusively, to the provision of *working capital* for the purchase of variable inputs used in farm production.

Mechanisation policy
Policies that affect the pace and direction of the adoption of mechanical technologies, or farm *fixed capital*, by farmers.

Land reform policy
Policies that seek to alter the ownership distribution or conditions of access to *land as a resource* in farm production.

Research policy
Policies concerned with the generation and diffusion of *new technology* designed to increase the productivity of resources in farm production.

Irrigation policy
Policies concerned with the provision of *water as a resource* in farm production, often involving large-scale public investment in the *infrastructure* of farm production.

These policies are all defined as *sectoral policies*. They aim to influence the social and economic development of the agricultural sector, as distinct from the rural economy at large, which contains many other types of activity in addition to farm production. Policies that affect the entire economy are not covered in this book except in so far as they influence the working of the policies already listed. Such economy-wide policies include exchange rate policy, monetary policy, and fiscal policy. They are referred to as *macro policies* or macroeconomic policies in this book.

The agricultural policies examined in the book involve three main categories of state economic intervention. First, there is intervention in *price* levels and trends for farm outputs and farm inputs. Second, there is intervention in the *institutions* involved, either in the marketing of agricultural commodities or in the delivery of farm inputs or technology. Third, there is intervention in *technology* creation and its transmission to farmers. These three categories are sometimes referred to as price policies, institutional policies, and technology policies respectively. The term price policies in this context refers to a wider set of price interventions than just output price policy, which is listed above as the first of the core policy topics of this book. Output price policy is a subset of this wider category of price interventions.

The literature on agricultural policy in developing countries often poses a contrast between price policies and technology policies, while ignoring institutional policies. The aim is usually to argue that technology policies are a superior type of state intervention compared to price policies. In reality, these two types of policy are often closely entwined. Moreover, institutional policies tend to cut across both price and technology policies. The relative success of these categories of policy at achieving specified goals is examined on a continuing basis throughout the book.

The book contains two other main components in addition to the central part. The first of these, covered in this and the next two chapters, is concerned with the context and concepts of agricultural policy analysis, treated as a branch of applied welfare economics. The aims of this component are to provide the reader with (i) working definitions of policy-related concepts such as market, state, policy, and social welfare, (ii) a framework within which to locate the economic approach to policy analysis, and (iii) the main concepts of policy analysis that are widely encountered in the economics literature on agricultural policy.

The second additional component covers policy concerns that do not fit into the central scheme of the book as described so far. One of these is the impact of the various agricultural policies on women in farm households. This aims to provide a gender dimension to the discussion of agricultural policies. The other is the topic of food security and food policy. Food security cuts across other policies described in this book but also involves important aspects that do not feature in the coverage of general agricultural policies. The gender dimension and the food security dimension are examined in the penultimate two chapters of the book.

Aside from gender and food security, there are two further cross-cutting themes that inform the approach to policy in this book. One of these is a state versus market theme, which concerns the scope and limitations of state action in the economy and the division of economic roles between the state and private markets. The second is a peasant farmer theme, which recognises that peasant households possess special economic characteristics that make them interact with state policies in ways that may differ from farmers operating in fully formed and competitive markets.

In summary, the core of this book consists of a set of eight chapters covering the topics of price policy, marketing policy, input policy, credit policy, mechanisation policy, land reform policy, research policy, and irrigation policy in developing countries. These chapters are supported, in the first part of the book, by an exposition of the concepts and methods of agricultural policy analysis, and, in the second part of the book, by cross-cutting themes of gender and food security. Additional cross-cutting themes of state versus market and peasant household production inform the development of the argument throughout the book.

The remainder of this chapter has three preliminary purposes. The first is to clarify some terms related to agricultural policies: market, policy, government and state. The second is to provide a summary of relevant aspects of the state versus market debate in development economics. The third is to consider special features of peasant production that influence the way policies work at farm level in developing countries.

Market, policy and state

Policies are typically thought of as types of state intervention in the market economy. For example, when someone refers to 'credit policy' this evokes an image of government involvement in the provision of credit to farmers. The government does this in order to substitute for, or modify, the ways farmers obtain credit in the absence of state intervention. This commonsense picture of policies is broadly correct. In the following paragraphs, the various elements of this picture – market, policy, government and state – are defined and discussed in more detail.

Market

The term 'market' as used by economists has a different meaning from ordinary usage. It does not mean literally the physical place in which commodities are sold or purchased (as in 'village market'), nor does it mean the stages that a commodity passes through between the producer and the consumer (as in 'marketing channels'). Rather it refers in an abstract way to the purchase and sale transactions of a commodity and the formation of its price. Used in this way, the term refers to the countless decisions made by producers of a commodity (the supply side of the market) and consumers of a commodity (the demand side of the market) which taken together determine the price level of the commodity.

Definition

The market refers to production and consumption decisions by households and individuals, the combined effects of which result in the determination of a market price for a commodity.

This definition indicates that the term market is detached from any particular geographical coverage. The geographical scope of the term depends on the context in which it is being used. It may refer to the local situation in some part of the rural economy, for example the market for cassava in southern Tanzania, or it can refer to the country as a whole, the region, or the international economy. Thus the expression 'world market' refers to the process of price formation at an international level for traded agricultural commodities.

Markets work in different ways according to the number and size of participants on each side of the market, the adequacy of information flows between buyers and sellers, and the physical infrastructure (roads, railways, etc.) by which commodities are moved. Economists use the term 'competitive market' to describe a situation in which there are numerous buyers and sellers, each too small on their own to influence directly the market price.

The terms 'imperfect market' or 'market failure' mean that some ingredients of the competitive situation are absent. For example, a single very large buyer or seller can directly influence the market price by purchase or sale decisions, a condition known as monopoly. Information about prices and their trends may be unevenly distributed, favouring some market participants above others. Markets may be fragmented due to poor transport and communications, or they may be absent due to high transaction costs, information failures, and other reasons.

Policy

There is no single definition of the term 'policy' that is used by all writers. However, economists usually think of policies as the goals and methods adopted by governments in order to influence the level of economic variables like prices, incomes, national income, the exchange rate and so on. 'Policy' as a general term therefore implies state intervention in the economy, while 'policies' are the specific types of intervention such as, for example, producer price policy, exchange rate policy, credit policy, or research policy.

This definition is adequate in so far as it goes, but in some ways it is restrictive of the courses of action open to government because it does not allow non-intervention as a policy option. Given that there are doubts, described below, about the efficacy of many types of state intervention, it becomes relevant to include non-intervention decisions as well as intervention decisions under the scope of policy. One of the many dictionary definitions of policy is 'the art of government', and we may presume that part of such an art might be to make informed judgements about whether intervention is necessary at all, in addition to the appropriate degree of intervention when it occurs.

Definition
Policy is defined as the course of action chosen by government towards an aspect of the economy, including the goals the government seeks to achieve, and the choice of methods to pursue those goals.

Government and state
Policies are adopted by governments, but tend to be formulated and implemented by the state or agencies of the state. The term 'government' refers to the group of people who are (at least nominally) in charge of running a country at any particular moment of time; while the term 'state' refers to the whole apparatus of public institutions and bureaucracies – the civil service and the armed forces – through which government exercises its rule. Another way of posing this distinction is to say that governments are concerned with political decision making, while states are concerned with administration and enforcement of decisions. Governments change – rather frequently in some countries – but the state tends to be more enduring in size and scope over lengthy periods of history. Organisations, such as marketing boards, that are wholly-owned by the state, but that supposedly make independent operating decisions, are usually called 'parastatals'.

Definitions
The government is defined as the group of people in charge of running a country, and who are responsible for making policy decisions. The state is defined as the whole set of public institutions responsible for the administration and enforcement of policy decisions.

State versus market
The 'state' is often counterposed to the 'market', the latter referring to the outcome of the myriad of economic decisions that are made independently by producers and consumers. A growing literature in

development economics contrasts the idea of 'market failure' (meaning the adverse impact on society of imperfect or non-working markets) with that of 'state failure' (meaning the adverse impact on society of inefficiencies and improprieties on the part of government and the state). This distinction has become central to debates about the role of the state in economic development, and therefore provides relevant background to the later exposition of agricultural policies.

During most of the period from the 1950s to the 1980s an implicit assumption of all major perspectives on development was that the state had a central role to play in accelerating the pace of economic growth, modifying its outcomes for different groups of people (e.g. by measures for ensuring a more equal distribution of income), or by carrying out tasks that by their nature would be unlikely or impossible for the private sector to carry out (e.g. provision of social services such as health and education, or investment in public infrastructure such as roads and communications). States varied in the degree to which they decided to modify or supplant the working of the market: some governments chose to replace markets almost entirely by state-led forms of production and exchange, others opted for co-existence of market and state in many different guises.

Development economists did not in general have too much quarrel with these state interventions. The inability of private markets to deliver all the ingredients of development, taken together with the non-working or imperfection of many markets, provided a well-known set of 'market failures' that state action was considered necessary to overcome. These 'market failures' are listed as follows (Stiglitz, 1986a: 90; Killick, 1989: 25):

(a) *failures of competition*: the existence of various types of monopoly power in the economy, for example the existence of localised trading monopolies in the supply of consumer goods to rural areas or in the purchase of crops from farmers;

(b) *failures of provision*: the existence of a class of goods and services that private operators are not prepared to supply because once they are made available it is impossible exclude individuals from making free use of them ('public goods' such as street lighting, police force, national defence, and public roads);

(c) *externalities*: costs that are not incurred by the private operator but represent disbenefits to other members of the community, such as the impact on downstream river users of pollution by a private industrial plant (negative externality), or benefits that do not accrue to the private operator but represent gains to society, such as the beneficial impact of higher education on the level of skills in the country (positive external-ity);

  (d) *common property resources*: resources of communal access (e.g. forests for firewood) where the private cost of using more of the resource is lower than the social cost incurred by the community as a whole, resulting in over-exploitation and possible permanent damage to the resource;

  (e) *incomplete markets*: where markets fail to produce commodities or services for which there is a private demand at prices above production cost, due to transaction cost and moral hazard problems (the credit market, with high risk of default and high cost of enforcing repayment, is a good example);

  (f) *failures of information*: a tendency to under-produce the type of information to which everyone should have access if markets are to work well (e.g. information on prices and technologies);

  (g) *macroeconomic problems*: problems that can only be handled by a central authority, for example, money supply, inflation, exchange rate, taxation and so on;

  (h) *poverty and inequality*: the market outcome may result in a degree of inequality or an incidence of poverty that is regarded as socially unacceptable by the majority of people in society.

  The view that state interventions are effective in overcoming these 'market failures' is based on the critical assumption that government and state 'act benevolently to secure the public interest' (Dearlove, 1987: 5), or, as summarised by Killick (1989: 14), 'the general presumption was that the state was benign in its intentions, with the theory of policy centred around the question of how best the state could maximise social welfare'. It is this assumption that has been called into question in much recent writing, resulting in the identification of 'state failures', which some would argue are more detrimental in their impact on the material well-being of people in society than the market failures which they purport to overcome.

  State failure can take many different forms. Particular emphasis has been placed on the pervasive inefficiency and impropriety of state institutions in many developing countries, and the descriptions that have been used to capture these facets include mismanagement, malpractice, overstaffing, nepotism, bribery, corruption, personal fortune seeking, and so on. These factors lead to the state sometimes being characterised as a 'parasitic' or 'predatory' state rather than as a 'benign' or 'beneficial' state.

Several different explanations have been advanced to explain the causes of these and other attributes of 'state failure'. The *first* approach emphasises the absence in postcolonial societies of a viable capitalist class, causing the state and its agencies to fill the ensuing vacuum. This is said to place the state in an inherently contradictory and unstable position since its bureaucratic roles are at odds with its involvement in direct productive activity. Variants of this explanation include interpreting the state as:

(a) a 'comprador' class mediating between foreign and domestic capital, and exacting 'fees' for services rendered in this role (Beckman, 1988);

(b) a 'bureaucratic' class, which has to plunder the private sector for its own renewal and expansion (Shivji, 1976; Brett, 1986);

(c) a 'rootless' class, which remains fatally entangled in peasant-style relations of patronage and kinship, described as the 'economy of affection' (Hyden, 1980; 1983).

A *second* approach derives from the neoclassical school of political economy known as public choice theory (e.g. Colander, 1984). This stresses the self-interest motivation of government officials and state employees, which can only be curbed by a political system that allows the population many and diverse ways of vetoing the actions of people in state positions. A pluralistic democracy is considered to satisfy this condition to some degree, even if it does so imperfectly. Where this is absent, the state can essentially act as a monopoly agency unrestrained by public accountability. This monopoly power enables state functionaries to maximise the surplus accruing to themselves. Bates (1981) on agricultural price and marketing interventions in Africa is regarded as a classic work in this tradition.

A *third* approach sees the state as operating on the basis of patrimonial or 'personal rule' systems in which personal loyalty, patron–client relations, nepotism, reward and coercion override and replace the rule of law (Jackson & Rosberg, 1984; Sandbrook, 1986). The weaker the popular credibility of the person in power the more that person has to resort to 'personal rule' mechanisms to stay in power. Meanwhile, with state officials operating in varying degrees outside the law, a mockery is made of the orthodox idea of the bureaucracy as a neutral, efficient, specialised, and rational administrative agency.

While there are different explanations of the causes of state failure, there is little disagreement regarding its symptoms and its detrimental side-effects. The following list of 'state failures' may be placed in contrast to the list of 'market failures' set out above:

(a) *information failure*: it is almost always wrong to assume that state officials have any clearer idea of the market in which they are intervening than private sector operators in that market;

(b) *complex side effects*: the state has no way of predicting accurately the secondary and tributary effects of actions carried out on a particular economic problem;

(c) *second-best theory*: when several market failures are present, state action to correct any single one of them may result in a worse outcome for society than no action at all (this stems from a rather abstract argument in welfare economics, which cannot be treated in detail here) – see definition provided by Bohm (1987);

(d) *implementation failures*: even if a policy is correctly designed to increase social welfare, the predicted gains may be lost in poor and inept implementation;

(e) *motivation failures*: state officials are often paid very low wages, sometimes even below their needs of subsistence, meaning that secondary sources of income may be essential for their livelihood;

(f) *rent-seeking*: state action that involves artificially restricting the supply of a good or service, or making its availability conditional on the issue of a licence, can lead to bribery and malpractice by those seeking to capture the rents to be gained by being allocated a share of the restricted commodity (Krueger, 1974). The methods used by individuals in order to get access to state licences, etc. have also been called directly unproductive profit-seeking activities or DUPs (Bhagwati, 1982).

A number of useful summary points on the 'market failure' versus 'state failure' issue are made by Killick (1989). A *first* point is that the size of the state is less at issue than the role and scope of its actions. Developing countries do not in general possess states that are larger in their share of Gross Domestic Product (GDP) than the state in industrial countries. A *second* point is that price intervention is likely to have more distorting side-effects, and less predictable outcomes, than non-price interventions such as irrigation schemes, rural roads, agricultural research, or farmer information systems. A *third* point is that price interventions where they do occur should be narrowly focused and finely targeted at the distortion they are designed to remove, not widely and indiscriminately applied to entire markets or sets of markets. A *fourth* point is that policies that operate with or through markets are more likely to succeed than policies of control or command that attempt to replace markets.

A major swing towards policies of minimal state intervention in markets occurred in the 1980s. This was a decade when economists with strong free-market ideas gained ascendancy as advisors to industrial-country governments and to international agencies. However, it seems likely that the pendulum of economic opinion may swing again at some point partly back towards recognising beneficial roles for the state in economic development.

A view is also emerging that redefining the role of the state is not just about the alleged superiority of free-market outcomes. It is more relevantly about giving people greater control over their own lives, and fostering an economic and political diversity so that it becomes more difficult for any single institution to have such a large impact on peoples' lives and livelihoods.

Peasants and policies

The purpose of the term 'peasant' is to capture the situation of a type of farm family that is neither fully committed to production for sale in the market, nor confronted with competitive markets in all the inputs and outputs of the farm (Ellis, 1988a: 1–15).

The majority of farm households in developing countries maintain a significant, if somewhat varying, degree of autonomy from the market, as typified by the share of farm output that is consumed as family subsistence rather than sold in the market. Likewise, many such farm households confront incomplete or imperfect markets for their inputs or outputs. Sometimes markets exist but work defectively due to lack of information (Stiglitz, 1986b).

This dual character of peasant agriculture – the ability to disengage in varying degrees from market relations, and the imperfect nature of the markets themselves – is relevant for policy discussion for several reasons. *First*, a great many agricultural policies in developing countries are designed either to reduce the relative autonomy of peasants, or to overcome the imperfections in input and output markets that they confront. *Second*, the ability of peasants to disengage from the market gives them some capacity to evade state actions that are perceived as disadvantageous. *Third*, the effectiveness of policies in achieving stated goals may differ between peasant households and commercial family farmers.

The last of these points requires further elaboration. The peasant household is a joint consumption–production unit, which experiences difficult trade-offs between alternative goals. For example, four such goals might be (i) higher farm output, (ii) increased cash for buying consumer goods, (iii) greater food security, and (iv) less family labour time in farm work. Some of these goals conflict and some are complementary, but they cannot all be satisfied simultaneously. For example, the first objective is likely to conflict with the last objective, unless there is a market for hired wage labour that can substitute for family labour on the farm.

Economists have developed several models to describe these trade-offs in the decision-making of the peasant household (Ellis, 1988a: Chs. 4–7). A general conclusion is that the reaction of the peasant household to an exogenous change – like an increase in output price – is likely to differ from that of a farm enterprise concerned with the single purpose of profit maximisation in a market economy. Empirical studies of peasant household decision making confirm these differences (Singh *et al.*, 1986: Ch. 1).

The special features of peasant production constitute an important cross-cutting theme in this book. The reactions of peasant households to state agricultural policies vary widely according to local circumstances of place and history so that it is not always possible or valid to deduce consequences of general applicability. Nevertheless, it is useful to identify the aspects of different policies that are especially sensitive to trade-offs in the decision-making of peasant households.

Summary
1. This chapter provides an overview of the book as a whole. The book is organised around a central set of eight policy chapters, covering the topics of price policy, marketing policy, input policy, credit policy, mechanisation policy, land reform policy, research policy, and irrigation policy in developing countries. These eight chapters are supported, on the one hand, by an exposition of the concepts and methods of agricultural policy analysis, and, on the other hand, by four cross-cutting themes – gender, food security, state versus market, peasants – the first two of which are also the subject of separate chapters.
2. Markets are defined in their economic sense as the outcome of decisions by producers and consumers, the combined effect of which is the determination of a market price for a commodity. The economic 'ideal' is the competitive market in which there are

many buyers and sellers, none of whom can singly influence the
market price, and in which relevant information is freely available to all participants.

3. Policies are defined as the courses of action by which governments seek to influence the outcome of economic events. Policies include goals set by governments, as well as the methods
chosen to pursue those goals.

4. The terms 'government' and 'state' are defined. Government is
defined as the group of people who rule a country, and who are
responsible for making policy decisions. The state is defined as
the whole set of public institutions responsible for the administration and enforcement of policy decisions.

5. 'Market failure' is counterposed and contrasted to 'state failure'.
Market failure may result from monopoly, non-provision (of
public goods), externalities, common property resources, transaction costs, moral hazard, and insufficient information. State
failure may occur due to defective information, unpredicted
side-effects, second-best outcomes, poor implementation, poor
motivation, impropriety and inefficiency.

6. The occurrence of widespread – even catastrophic – 'state failure' is nowadays a widely recognised and debated feature of the
development process in some countries and regions. This encompasses not just minor instances of inefficiency and bureaucratic
mismanagement, but personal rule systems, coercion, nepotism,
over-staffing, income-seeking, bribery, and so on.

7. These perceptions of state failure have resulted in policies of
minimal state intervention being promoted in many countries.
However, the pendulum of opinion regarding the advisability of
reliance on free markets is likely to swing back to some degree
towards recognition of legitimate economic roles for the state.
Beyond the purely economic issue of markets, the reduction of
the role of the state is also about economic and political diversity,
giving people more options from which choices can be made.

8. Peasants are defined as farm households only partially integrated
into imperfect or incomplete markets. The dual aspect of this
definition is the semi-subsistence basis of peasant survival and
the imperfect nature of the markets for farm outputs and inputs.
The relevance of this definition for policy is threefold, consisting
of (i) the aim of many agricultural policies to reduce the relative
autonomy of peasants and to overcome imperfections in input

and output markets, (ii) the ability of peasants to disengage from the market, enabling them to evade the sometimes negative effects of state action, and (iii) the unpredictability of policy outcomes at household level given the trade-offs between goals in household decision-making.

Further reading

An excellent summary of the state-versus-market debate in development economics is provided by Killick (1989). The evolution of ideas concerning policy and the state with respect to Africa during the 1980s can be traced in several issues of the *IDS Bulletin*, published by the Institute of Development Studies, Sussex University, UK (see Mars & White, 1986; Dearlove & White, 1987; Roberts, 1987; Brett, 1988). The 'personal rule' theory of state and economic decline is set out in Jackson & Rosberg (1984) and Sandbrook (1986). Bates (1981) remains relevant as an important early contribution to the contemporary state failure literature. The economic study of peasants and farm household decision-making is set out in full in Ellis (1988a), and an additional useful source in this area, although more difficult in its level of economics, is Singh *et al.* (1986).

Reading list

Bates, R.H. (1981). *Markets and States in Tropical Africa*. University of California Press.

Brett, E.A. (ed.) (1988). Adjustment and the State: The Problem of Administrative Reform. *IDS Bulletin*, **19**, No. 4, October.

Dearlove, J. & White, G. (eds) (1987). The Retreat of the State? *IDS Bulletin*, **18**, No. 3.

Ellis, F. (1988a). *Peasant Economics: Farm Households and Agrarian Development*. Cambridge University Press.

Jackson, R.H. & Rosberg, C.G. (1984). Personal Rule: Theory and Practice in Africa. *Comparative Politics*, **16**, No. 4.

Killick, T. (1989). *A Reaction Too Far: Economic Theory and the Role of the State in Developing Countries*. Overseas Development Institute.

Mars, T. & White, G. (eds) (1986). Developmental States and African Agriculture. *IDS Bulletin*, **17**, No. 1.

Roberts, H. (ed.) (1987). Politics in Command? *IDS Bulletin*, **18**, No. 4.

Sandbrook, R. (1986). The State and Economic Stagnation in Tropical Africa. *World Development*, **14**, No. 3.

Singh, I., Squire, L. & Strauss, J. (eds) (1986). *Agricultural Household Models*. Baltimore: Johns Hopkins.

2

Policy analysis: Framework

Objectives, constraints, instruments

This chapter has three main purposes. The first is to describe the framework commonly used by economists to organise ideas about state agricultural policies. The second is to examine critically the process of policy formulation and implementation typically associated with this framework. The third is to provide a simplified guide to concepts in applied welfare economics that are widely used by economists in the discussion of policies.

Of particular importance with respect to the last purpose is to clarify the meaning attached by economists to the term 'social welfare'. This term has already been encountered in the first chapter of the book, and is also used from early in the present chapter. Its short definition is 'the material well-being of society as a whole'. A more precise description in economic terms is deferred to the third section of this chapter.

The framework for policy analysis utilised in this book loosely follows the so-called 'theory of economic policy' elaborated originally by Tinbergen (1952; 1956). According to this approach the goal of government is to maximise social welfare, and it chooses 'target variables' which it sets out to achieve (e.g. income per capita, or hospital patients per bed, or grain stores per district) in pursuit of this overall goal. The task of policy is then to select the best 'instruments' to achieve the selected targets, given (i) constraints (e.g. of state resources or administrative capacity), (ii) the existence of certain factors over which the policy maker may not have control (e.g. the climate), and (iii) side-effects which, if they are detrimental, must obviously be minimised.

These components of the Tinbergen framework are illustrated in Figure 2.1. As originally conceived this framework was considered suitable for formulation as a mathematical model. Its major components are the same as those found in linear programming type models. The framework is not, however, used in that way in this book. Rather, it is used informally as a way of organising the descriptive components of a policy topic.

The Tinbergen framework is also referred to in the policy literature as the 'objectives–constraints–instruments' approach to policy analysis (Timmer & Falcon, 1975: 396–400; Monke & Pearson, 1989: Ch. 1). Its chief components are discussed in more detail in the following paragraphs.

Objectives

The objectives of agricultural policy interventions can be diverse and numerous. They may involve considerations of political and social stability, integration of the national economy, increased food security, increased export earnings, prevention of malnutrition, economic growth, employment generation, and so on. They may be local in scope (e.g. to raise the incomes of a particular group of small poor farmers), provincial in scope (e.g. to improve fertilizer delivery in X region), or nationwide in scope (e.g. to overcome a balance of payments deficit).

The basic theory underlying the economic analysis of agricultural policies initially stands back from and greatly simplifies this myriad of potential goals. It is assumed that most social objectives fall into two main

Figure 2.1. Tinbergen framework of policy analysis. Source: adapted from Thorbecke & Hall (1982: 9).

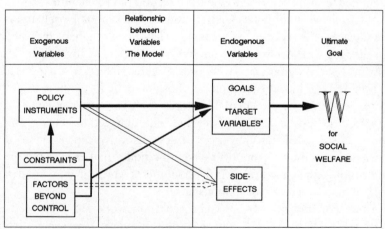

categories: goals of *economic growth* and goals of improved *income distribution*. These two types of goal are also sometimes called *efficiency* and *equity* goals respectively. However, this involves some oversimplification because growth is a dynamic concept while efficiency is a static concept.

In neoclassical economics *efficiency* refers to making the economic optimum use of a given set of national resources, i.e. achieving the highest level of material welfare for the consumers of society as a whole, for a given set of prices in resource and output markets. Growth can occur either by moving from a less efficient to a more efficient use of existing resources, or by increasing the productivity of resources so that more output can be obtained from a given level of resources.

Equity, by contrast, refers to the distribution of this total output between individuals or social groups within the society. It is a standard finding of welfare economics that whereas efficiency is an objective phenomenon – a unique most efficient outcome can be specified for a given initial income distribution; equity is a subjective phenomenon – decisions about income distribution require value judgments about the 'fairness' or otherwise of the outcome for different groups of people.

In general, there are as many potential efficient states of the economy as there are initial income distributions. It does not follow, unfortunately, that all one needs to do is to start with a more equal income distribution and then proceed to make the economy as efficient as possible with that distribution. The efficient outcome for an equal distribution may be at a lower level of total material welfare than for a less equal one. Thus efficiency objectives and equity objectives may, and often in practice do, conflict with each other.

One function of policy analysis is to try to quantify both the efficiency and equity results of choosing one policy instrument rather than another in pursuit of a particular objective. This applies whether the goal itself is efficiency or equity orientated. Thus policy instruments designed to increase output (efficiency goals) always have effects of varying importance on income distribution. Likewise, policy instruments designed with income distribution objectives in mind (equity goals) always have direct or indirect effects on output, and these need to be quantified if it is possible to do so.

Constraints

The constraints involved in pursuing a particular objective or set of objectives vary according to the scope and nature of the policy problem under consideration. Some constraints are highly policy specific. For example, if price instability is regarded as a constraint on increased small farm output, then instruments for stabilising farm prices will be the focus of the policy analysis. Similarly, lack of water as a constraint would be associated with irrigation policies; proneness of a crop to infestation with a particular pest would be associated with research policy on pest-resistant crop varieties, and so on.

Other constraints may be more general in scope. The climate, rainfall, soils and other natural resource features of a region or country are evident constraints on what can be achieved for agricultural production at a specified point in historical time. In the economic sphere, the availability of foreign exchange, the size of the government budget, the international prices of farm outputs and inputs, may all act as limitations on goals and policy options. In the political sphere, considerations of national security, the stability of the government in power and the basis of its political support in society, and rivalry between factions or between different branches of the bureaucracy, are other factors that may circumscribe policy choice.

In applied welfare economics the existing availability of *resources* and the current *technology* of production are regarded as the most basic constraints on what is feasible for an economy. The latter strongly influences the former, since new technologies can both improve the productivity of existing resources and make use of resources that may previously have been idle. Thus a most important class of policies are those that seek to accelerate technological change directly (as in agricultural research policy) or indirectly (as in education and training policy).

Instruments

Policy instruments, as the methods of state intervention, are devised with both objectives and constraints in view. If constraints are in some sense absolute (e.g. the average temperature and rainfall in a particular location) then instruments may be designed to get round the constraint (e.g. by growing a different type of crop, more appropriate to the climate and rainfall). However, if a constraint is only relative (e.g. shortage of foreign exchange), it may be part of the policy to alleviate the constraint in addition to pursuing some other ultimate goal.

It is possible, though rare, that a single policy instrument may accomplish more than one objective. For example, if maize is the staple diet, and all maize farmers are poor, then increasing the price of maize may accomplish both growth (increased output of maize) and equity (improved income distribution) goals. More commonly, however, there are several potential policy instruments that separately or together can contribute to the stated objectives, and the task of agricultural policy analysis is to assess the advantages and disadvantages – the benefits and costs – of the alternative policy instruments available.

Some authors have developed quite complex systems of agricultural policy classification according to goals, types of policy instrument, and other criteria (McCalla & Josling, 1985: 107–9; Colman & Young, 1989: 168–72). Policy instruments can be categorised according to:

(a) whether efficiency or equity is their prime objective;
(b) whether they operate at farm, market, consumer or border points in the agricultural marketing chain;
(c) whether they are instruments that operate on prices, institutions, or technology;
(d) whether they are agriculture specific or general in scope and effect (like exchange rate policy, or minimum wage legislation);
(e) whether they are commodity market policies (e.g. a coffee input subsidy), trade policies (tariffs, quotas, export taxes), or macroeconomic policies (exchange rate, interest rate, money supply, etc.).

As already established in the previous chapter, policy instruments are grouped in this book according to the particular impact they are designed to have on the small-farm system. This approach cuts across the various different classifications set out above because more than one type of instrument, operating at more than one level in the economic system, and with different impacts on efficiency and equity, may operate on the same facet of the farm as a production system.

The advantage of this approach is that a wide variety of different instruments, which affect each particular variable confronting the farm household (e.g. the farm-gate price of marketed supply), can be reviewed and compared under one heading. This does not mean that other distinctions between policy instruments are regarded as unhelpful or unimportant. On the contrary, the distinctions between (i) instruments for efficiency versus equity; (ii) instruments of commodity, trade and macroeconomic policies; and (iii) price versus non-price policy instruments are found to be useful in many different contexts later in the book.

Policy as a linear process: A critical view

The Tinbergen framework gives rise to a conventional approach to the process of policy decision making. This can be described as the linear policy model, or *linear policy cycle*, and it is illustrated in Figure 2.2. According to this, policy formulation and implementation is a linear process in two phases. The first phase is concerned with policy formulation and the second phase with policy implementation.

The first phase begins with a statement by a policy-maker concerning a goal that the government wishes to achieve (e.g. the Minister of Agriculture declares that maize output should grow by 10 per cent next year). The next step is the technical and economic analysis that generates a number of alternative ways that this target can be reached (e.g. by raising the price of maize, or lowering the price of fertilizer, or extending a maize irrigation scheme to a new area). The costs and benefits of the alternative policies are calculated and the array of alternative policies is placed before the Minister for decision. The Minister chooses the 'best' alternative policy taking into account its net social benefits, its administrative feasibility, and any constraints or side-effects that may be relevant to its implementation.

Figure 2.2. The linear policy cycle model.
Source: Clay and Schaffer (1984: 4).

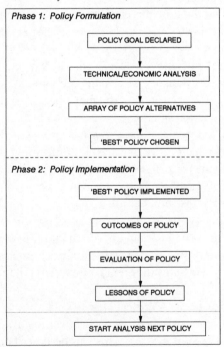

In the second phase the best policy is implemented (e.g. the price of fertilizer is subsidised). The policy eventually results in outcomes that can be measured (maize output increases, but only by 5 per cent). An evaluation exercise is carried out which reveals the strengths and weaknesses of the policy, and suitable adjustments are made to its future operation. Work begins on the next set of policies requiring formulation. The policy cycle starts again.

This is evidently a caricature of real policy processes. Nevertheless, it is the model that is implicitly or explicitly assumed in a great number of cases. Its key assumptions are (i) that governments are genuinely concerned with maximising social welfare, and (ii) that the state apparatus operates as an entirely neutral – objective, technical, competent – body for its roles in the policy cycle. The model helps to explain what is commonly meant by the expression 'agricultural policy analysis'. The policy analysis in the model is the technical and economic work that considers alternative policy instruments, assesses and compares them in terms of net benefits, and, at a later stage, evaluates the impact of the chosen policy and infers lessons for the future from its implementation.

The linear policy model has several weaknesses. Some of these are to do with the naivety of its assumptions about the politics of policy decisions, and about the goals of government leaders; some impinge on the 'state failure' problems listed in the previous chapter; some are more workaday problems concerning the validity of the linear sequence itself. With respect to the latter group of problems, the following defects of the linear model are identified (see also Clay & Schaffer, 1984: Ch. 1):

(a) the separation of policy formulation and policy implementation, allowing those involved in one to blame those involved in the other for policy failure;
(b) the lack of participation and feedback, creating plenty of excuses or 'escape-hatches' for failure;
(c) the implied top-down orientation of policies;
(d) data are often too sparse or too inaccurate to support the analysis proposed;
(e) policy analysts are constrained by the institutional circumstances in which they find themselves and can rarely, if ever, be considered entirely objective;
(f) external aid agencies often override domestic decisions by having already allocated resources for donor preferred projects.

The policy cycle may be compromised still further if one or other of its main assumptions is breached: for example, if government ministers are more concerned with the size of their Swiss bank accounts than with social welfare, or if the various actors in the cycle are more concerned with the personal income-generating properties of the policies under review than with their objective impacts on society.

In summary, policies often seem to follow a format and a way of treating government decisions that correspond to a linear cycle of policy formulation and policy implementation. International agencies and foreign experts are especially prone to view policy processes in this way. The linear model assigns a specific role for policy analysis, which is to provide the objective, technical, basis upon which informed policy decisions can be made.

A healthy scepticism is required regarding this model, which embodies naive expectations regarding the goals of policy makers, the competence of civil servants, and the objectivity of policy analysts. A major defect of the model is its lack of mechanisms for participation and feedback by the supposed beneficiaries of policies.

Awareness of these problems does not preclude a useful role for policy analysis, though the nature of this role must undergo a shift in orientation. Rather than being regarded as the objective basis for identifying a single 'best' policy, the role changes such that 'policy analysts provide fuel for the on-going debate between those who wish to change policies and those who wish to maintain them' (Monke and Pearson, 1989: 12).

Concepts in applied welfare economics

This section of the chapter, as well as the whole of the next chapter, should be considered as optional by those readers who are more interested in the policies than the economics of policy analysis.

The limited purpose here is to explain certain key ideas deriving from applied welfare economics that will help the reader to interpret better the material of the next chapter and later policy chapters in the book. The concepts described briefly in this section are the Pareto optimum, the Pareto criterion, and the compensation criterion.

The cornerstone of welfare economics is the concept of the *Pareto optimum*. This is defined as a situation for society as a whole in which it is not possible to make one person better off without making another person worse off. If the possibility exists of increasing output in such a way that all people can be made better off with existing resources, or some people can be made better off without making others worse off, then improvements in social welfare can still be achieved and the situation is Pareto sub-optimal.

In the terminology of welfare economics, 'social welfare' means the total volume of material goods and services available for consumption in that society. An increase in social welfare always refers to material consumption, and to the final demand side of the economy, not to resources or to production *per se*. Since in an accounting sense the gross output and the gross income of a country are the same (the sum of output values equals the sum of payments made to the ultimate owners of resources), the Pareto optimum represents the maximum output (or income) of the economy and is the most *efficient* point of operation. From a viewpoint of policy, the idea of the Pareto optimum leads to the following Pareto criterion for policy formulation:

Definition
The Pareto criterion states that a policy change is socially desirable if as a result of the change either everyone can be made better off, or at least some people are made better off while no one is made worse off.

There are two important aspects of the Pareto optimum that arise in one guise or another in applied policy analysis. The first is that a situation of competitive equilibrium in a market economy is a Pareto optimum. A competitive equilibrium (see e.g. Laidler & Estrin, 1989: Ch. 26) exists when for a given set of clearing prices in all output and input markets (i) all consumers equate their relative marginal utilities between commodities to the relative prices they confront; (ii) all producers equate their relative marginal returns between outputs to the same set of relative prices; and (iii) all producers use inputs up to the point where marginal costs equal marginal returns. If this equilibrium were attained no adjustment could be made without causing an inefficiency making someone worse off. The competitive equilibrium is a *sufficient* but not a necessary condition for a Pareto optimum to exist.

The second aspect is that the Pareto optimum is not unique. It is defined only for the initial distribution of income with which it is associated. If the income distribution changes then a new Pareto optimum is defined. There are thus as many efficient states as there are different possible income distributions. The problem with this for policy is that there is no way of telling whether a different income distribution would result in a Pareto optimum at a higher or lower level of social welfare than the one it replaces.

Thus the definition of *efficiency* in an economy tells us nothing about *equity*. It is for this reason that income distribution is viewed by neoclassical economists as a normative (subjective) issue, which is in practice only resolved by society through its political processes.

The Pareto criterion turns out to be a too narrow principle on which to base policy choice, and one which would in effect cause policy paralysis. This is because it is difficult to find cases where some people can be made better off without making others worse off. If a new road is constructed, then road users benefit and those whose houses are destroyed lose. If taxes are raised to pay for schools then those who pay the taxes are worse off, and those who send their children to school are better off. Closer to the subject of this book, if the farm-gate price of a food staple is increased, then food surplus farmers gain and food consumers lose.

For this reason, policy analysis is seldom based on the Pareto criterion. Instead it obeys an alternative principle, known as the *compensation criterion*. The compensation criterion rests on the idea that a 'potential' welfare gain exists if, as the result of a policy action, the gainers gain more than the losers lose so that the gainers could potentially recompense the losers and still be better off:

Definition
The compensation criterion states that a policy change is potentially socially desirable if as a result of the change the gainers could compensate the losers so that no one ended up worse off.

The compensation criterion underlies the partial equilibrium analysis of policies to which we turn in the next chapter. Its central feature is that the compensation is only 'potential': it permits policies to go ahead whether or not compensation is actually enforced, and leaves it up to a separate political decision whether and how much compensation to pay. It thus obeys the spirit of the Pareto optimum idea of social welfare maximisation in that the outcome is such that the policy *could* potentially be implemented without making anyone worse off, but it leaves open whether the losers are actually compensated in this way. In practice, in fact, compensation for welfare losses from policy changes is rarely made, the exception in many countries being compensation for loss of property due to infrastructural developments like roads, power supplies, dams, and so on.

Summary
1. This chapter has three main purposes. The first is to set out the mainstream framework for the economic study of state agricultural policies. The second is to examine critically the linear policy model that arises from that framework. The third is to provide a

simple account of concepts in applied welfare economics that are widely used by economists in the discussion of policies.

2. The framework for organising ideas about policies called the Tinbergen model is described. This model identifies goals, constraints, instruments, and side-effects as the chief components of most kinds of policy topic. The framework tends to be referred to in the more recent literature as the 'objectives–constraints–instruments' approach to policy, and this is the designation that is used in this book.

3. While there may be many different objectives of agricultural policy, most of these fall into the two main categories of efficiency or equity objectives. Efficiency is about obtaining the economic optimum level of output of commodities and services from a given set of resources. Equity refers to the distribution of this total output between individuals or social groups within the society.

4. Constraints are also numerous, and vary in scope according to the breadth and time-scale of the problem under consideration. Some constraints pose major underlying limitations on what is feasible, such as the natural resources and climate of a country. Other constraints are related to less permanent limitations on state action, such as shortage of foreign exchange, government budgetary deficits, or adverse world price trends for exports. All constraints are relative to existing technology, since technological change can improve the productivity of existing resources or make new resources available.

5. Instruments are the methods chosen by governments in order to implement policies. It is possible for a single policy instrument to accomplish more than one objective, but it is more common for several instruments to be set to work in different ways on a set of policy goals. Policy instruments can be classified in various ways, but for this book what is relevant are the farm inputs or outputs upon which they are designed to have an impact.

6. An offshoot of the Tinbergen framework is a conventional view of policy as a linear process in two phases. This is described as the linear policy model or linear policy cycle, and the two phases are policy formulation and policy implementation. This model is shown to have important defects such as the separation of formulation and implementation, the lack of participation and feedback, undue reliance on often faulty data or information, and naivety about the goals of policy makers, the competence of

civil servants, and the objectivity of researchers. It is concluded that the role of policy analysis is less definitive than the linear model suggests, and must be seen as one amongst several forces acting on the decision-making process.

7. Some major concepts in welfare economics are briefly explained. These include the Pareto optimum, the Pareto criterion, and the compensation criterion. While the Pareto criterion insists that a policy change is only desirable if no one is made worse off by the change, the compensation criterion allows some people to be made worse off provided that the gains from the change are sufficient to permit the potential compensation of the losers. Only the potential for compensation is required, whether or not this compensation is paid is left open.

Further reading

The objective–constraints–instruments approach to policy is described in Timmer & Falcon (1975: 396–400), McCalla & Josling (1985: Ch. 5), and Monke & Pearson (1989: Ch. 1). For a useful coverage of the conventional approach to policy along the same lines see Killick (1981). The linear policy cycle and other relevant aspects concerning the conduct of public policy are discussed in Clay & Schaffer (1984: 1–12 and Chs. 9 & 10). A useful review of some of the features discussed in this chapter is also contained in Colman & Young (1989: Ch. 12). An accessible intermediate level account of welfare economics can be found in Laidler & Estrin (1989: Chs. 23–27).

Reading list

Clay, E.J. & Schaffer, B.B. (1984). *Room for Manoeuvre: An Exploration of Public Policy in Agriculture and Rural Development*. London: Heinemann.

Colman, D. & Young, T. (1989). *Principles of Agricultural Economics*. Cambridge University Press.

Killick, T. (1981). *Policy Economics: A Textbook of Applied Economics on Developing Countries*. London: Heinemann.

Laidler, D. & Estrin, S. (1989). *Introduction to Microeconomics*, 3rd edn. Oxford: Philip Allan.

McCalla, A.F. & Josling, T.E. (1985). *Agricultural Policies and World Markets*. London: Macmillan.

Monke, E.A. & Pearson, S.R. (1989). *The Policy Analysis Matrix for Agricultural Development*. Ithaca: Cornell University Press.

Timmer, C.P. & Falcon, W.P. (1975). The Political Economy of Rice Production and Trade in Asia. In *Agriculture in Development Theory*, ed. L.G. Reynolds, Ch. 14. London: Yale University Press.

3

Policy analysis: Economics

Scope and tasks of policy analysis

The purpose of this chapter is to set out the basic tools and concepts that are used by economists in order to assess the effects of proposed policy interventions. This is the task of economic policy analysis: to quantify the direct and indirect outcomes of policies, or policy instruments, so that alternatives can be compared and informed choices can be made between them.

The chapter may be considered as optional by readers who do not wish to cover the partial equilibrium approach to policy analysis. The content of later policy chapters can be understood, up to a point, without the concepts treated here, although some examples and arguments will inevitably as a result seem rather obscure.

The analysis of most policies has a *physical* (real) and a *valuation* (monetary) dimension. The physical dimension involves the need to estimate the physical resources and volume changes associated with a policy intervention such as output, supply, consumption or input use changes. As an example, a proposed policy to raise the market price of a staple food, like maize, has impacts on the volume of maize production, the quantity of maize that is sold in the market rather than retained for home consumption, the demand by farmers for variable inputs like fertilizers used in maize production, and the demand by consumers for maize flour.

The valuation dimension concerns the assessment of social welfare changes. In the maize example, the price rise causes a change in the aggregate value – price multiplied by quantity – for marketed maize and for purchased variable inputs. These changes imply social welfare gains and losses for different participants in the maize market. Farmers experience a welfare gain from the rise in the price of maize, while consumers experience a welfare loss. Whether there is an overall social welfare gain or loss from this policy change depends on factors that are described later in this chapter.

This example shows that even an apparently simple policy change has multiple effects. A rise in the price of a staple food, like maize, is likely to have effects that go beyond the immediate impact in the commodity market. It may have significant impacts on macroeconomic variables like consumer expenditure, wages, inflation and the exchange rate. The extent to which policy analysis needs to pursue impacts and side-effects in these directions depends on the nature and scale of the policy change being contemplated. In practice, limits of data, accuracy, and time often mean that only immediate impacts can be assessed.

There are no rigid boundaries circumscribing the aspects that might require examination in policy analysis. Colman & Young (1989: 284) provide a classification of policy impacts that is useful for describing the approximate range of concerns in agricultural policy analysis. Seven categories of policy effect are identified:

(a) price effects, meaning not just own price effects in a single market but also the impact on prices in closely related markets;

(b) production effects, including the quantities of outputs and inputs;

(c) consumption effects, meaning the demand impacts of the policy in affected markets;

(d) trade or balance of payments effects, including effects on imports, exports, foreign exchange reserves and the exchange rate;

(e) budget effects, meaning the impact on government tax receipts and public expenditure;

(f) income distribution effects, meaning the impact of policies on equity;

(g) social welfare effects, meaning the identification of the gainers and losers of policy interventions, as well as measurement of the overall impact on social welfare.

An exposition of the alternative methods available to tackle this entire range of policy effects and side-effects would require a substantial textbook in itself. This chapter, and most of this book, focuses on the direct impacts of policies in the markets most closely affected by policy changes. The method is called *partial equilibrium analysis*, in which only one market, or perhaps two or three closely related markets, are examined. This method is especially useful for examining the efficiency impact of policies, and their distributional effects in terms of broad categories of economic actors such as producers, consumers and the state. The method is not so useful for studying interpersonal income distribution effects for producers or consumers with differing income levels.

There is a wide class of policy problem that can be handled using partial equilibrium analysis. The earlier example of the maize market gives an indication of the analytical scope of this method. Its essential basis is the demand curve and the supply curve in the single commodity market affected by a policy change. The analysis can be expanded to include closely related markets, but the scope does not include intersectoral or economy-wide effects.

The chapter proceeds as follows. *First*, a brief revision of elasticity concepts is provided, with particular reference to the price and income elasticity of demand and the price elasticity of supply. *Second*, the welfare economics concepts of producer and consumer surplus are described and defined. *Third*, the concepts of producer and consumer surplus are applied, in a world price context, to several common types of agricultural policy intervention. *Fourth*, private, economic, and social prices are defined and compared in the context of their application to policy problems. *Fifth*, the chapter concludes by defining a set of summary measures used by economists to describe the efficiency effects of price policies.

Revision of elasticities

Space does not permit the coverage in this book of the standard economic theory of demand and supply, for which the reader should refer to an intermediate microeconomics textbook (e.g. Laidler & Estrin, 1989). However, one elementary economic concept, elasticity, is widely and routinely used in policy analysis, and therefore merits a brief exposition here.

As a general concept, elasticity refers to the way in which any variable, say, A, is affected by a change in the level of another variable, say, B. Since in most cases variables A and B have different units of measurement – e.g. bars of chocolate versus income in dollars per capita – the impact of one upon the other has to be stated independently of measurement units. This is done by calculating the *proportional* change in A associated with a given *proportional* change in B.

Elasticities can be expressed in several different ways as is illustrated by the following cases and examples:

(a) *First*, the simplest way of stating an elasticity is as a ratio of the percentage changes in the two variables:

$$\varepsilon_{A,B} = \frac{\text{percentage change in } A}{\text{percentage change in } B}$$

For example, if a 5 per cent fall in the demand for oranges (variable A) is brought about by a 10 per cent rise in the price of oranges (variable B), then $\varepsilon_{A,B} = -5/10 = -0.5$.

(b) *Second*, the relationship between variables A and B may be expressed in the form of an equation. The general form of such an equation is:

$$A = f(B)$$

This means that variable A is some function of variable B, for example the supply of pineapples is a function of the price of pineapples. In this case elasticity can be expressed as:

$$\varepsilon_{A,B} = \frac{dA}{A} \div \frac{dB}{B} = \frac{dA}{dB} \times \frac{B}{A}$$

where the symbol d represents a very small change in the variable, and the expressions dA/A and dB/B represent proportional changes. The expression dA/dB is the first derivative, measuring the slope, of the equation $A = f(B)$.

To provide an example, suppose that pineapple supply (A) is related to the pineapple price (B) in the form of a linear equation as follows:

$$A = 1900 + 0.2B$$

then, dA/dB = 0.2 (the constant slope of the linear supply curve). The value of the supply elasticity at a production level of 2000 pineapples and a price of 500 cents per pineapple is:

$$\varepsilon_{A,B} = \frac{dA}{dB} \times \frac{B}{A} = 0.2 \times (2000/500) = 0.8$$

In other words, if the supply curve for pineapples was represented by a linear equation as stated, then a 10 per cent rise in the pineapple price would cause an 8 per cent increase in pineapple supply, but only in the vicinity of the stated production and price levels.

An important aspect demonstrated in the above example is that if the relationship between the two variables is linear in form, then the elasticity changes for different absolute levels of either variable. For example, if the supply elasticity were measured where output is 4000 pineapples and price is 10500 cents, then its level would be 0.076 instead of 0.8. These figures are just illustrative, but the general point is made: elasticity changes along a linear demand or supply curve.

(c) A *third* expression for elasticity is encountered when the equation linking variables A and B is a power function of the general form:

$$A = \alpha B^\sigma$$

A function like this is linear in the logarithms of its variables, such that:

$$\log A = \log \alpha + \sigma \log B$$

An important mathematical property of this form of equation is that the power coefficient, σ, directly represents the proportional impact of variable B on variable A, and it is constant for all feasible levels of A and B. For this reason, as well as other reasons, economists often prefer to use power functions to represent the relationships between quantities, prices, and other variables. This mathematical form of the relationship between two economic variables is called the *constant elasticity* form.

An example can illustrate this. Suppose that the demand for rice (Q_D) is a function of its price (P) and income (Y), as in the equation:

$$Q_D = 35 \times P^{-0.2} \times Y^{0.15}$$

Here, the price elasticity of demand for rice is -0.2, irrespective of the quantity or price level of rice under discussion (within plausible ranges). The income elasticity of demand is likewise constant at 0.15.

There are several elasticity concepts that are widely prevalent in policy work. Some have already been mentioned. Note that the condition *ceteris paribus* is required for all types of elasticity. This means that in assessing the impact on one variable of a small change in another, all other influences are held constant. The main elasticities referred to in later chapters of the book are:

(a) *Price elasticity of demand*, defined as the percentage change in demand for a commodity resulting from a one per cent change in its price. Demand elasticities strictly have negative signs, but since it is sometimes taken as obvious that the quantity demanded and its price are inversely related, some authors choose to leave the minus sign out when quoting such elasticities.

(b) *Income elasticity of demand*, defined as the percentage change in demand for a commodity resulting from a one per cent change in income.

(c) *Price elasticity of supply*, defined as the percentage change in the supply of a commodity resulting from a one per cent change in its price.

(d) *Input elasticity of yield*, defined as the percentage change in crop yield per hectare resulting from a one per cent change in the physical quantity of a variable input like fertilizer.

(e) *Price elasticity of a variable input*, defined as the percentage change in demand for a variable input by farmers resulting from a one per cent change in its price.

The terms *elastic*, *unit elastic*, and *inelastic* are used to describe situations in which the elasticity has an absolute value (ignoring sign) of more than one, one, or less than one respectively. An elasticity value less than one means that the dependent variable (A) changes in level by a smaller percentage than the independent variable (B). An elasticity value equal to one means that both variables change by the same percentage. An elasticity value greater than one means that the dependent variable changes in level by a greater percentage than the independent variable.

One area of application for the various price elasticities is in exploring the effect of a price change on the total value ($P \times Q$) of the commodity under consideration. Taking the demand for a commodity as an example, the response of total expenditure on the commodity, $P \times Q$, to a price increase varies according to the absolute size of the demand elasticity as follows:

(a) Elastic demand ($\varepsilon_{A,B} > 1$), total expenditure falls when price increases, and rises when price decreases. For a price increase, this is because the fall in volume (Q) is more than proportionate to the rise in price (P), resulting in a lower combined value ($P \times Q$).

(b) Unit elastic demand ($\varepsilon_{A,B} = 1$), total expenditure stays the same when price changes, because an exactly offsetting proportional change in quantity occurs.

(c) Inelastic demand ($\varepsilon_{A,B} < 1$), total expenditure rises when price increases, and falls when the price decreases. For a price increase, this is because the fall in volume (Q) is less than proportionate to the rise in price (P), resulting in a higher combined value ($P \times Q$).

The reader may wonder where elasticity values for use in policy work come from. The answer is that they mainly come from statistical work aimed at estimating the coefficients of equations, such as those discussed above. The branch of economics most closely associated with estimating such equations is called econometrics. For a variety of reasons of data or technique, different econometric exercises often yield different values for even quite commonplace elasticities. It is unwise for the policy analyst to depend on a single elasticity estimate when calculating policy outcomes.

Producer and consumer surplus

Partial equilibrium analysis makes extensive use of two main concepts that permit the rather abstract notion of social welfare to be translated into something which can be measured and quantified in terms of money. These two concepts are *producer surplus* and *consumer surplus*. There is some debate within neoclassical economics concerning the theoretical soundness of these concepts, but with few exceptions this debate is ignored here. Producer surplus and consumer surplus are the only practical means so far devised by economists for measuring welfare changes. In development economics they are the foundation both for assessing the welfare implications of alternative policies and for the social cost–benefit analysis of development projects.

Producer surplus

The concept of producer surplus is illustrated graphically in Figure 3.1. The graph shows the market supply curve, *SS*, for a farm output. This could be any farm output such as maize, cassava, or beans. In this instance paddy is used as an example to illustrate the various facets of producer surplus. The price of paddy is given on the vertical axis; the quantity that farmers are prepared to supply at different market price levels over a given time period is shown on the horizontal axis. The supply curve is upward sloping: more of the commodity is supplied as its price rises.

For the exposition given here the market supply curve is treated as the marginal cost (MC) curve of the farm sector producing this commodity. The identity of the supply curve with the marginal cost curve for the individual farm firm is explained in Ellis (1988a: 25–7). With *SS* defined as a marginal cost curve, the area under this curve, such as area *b* in Figure 3.1, represents the total variable cost (TVC) incurred by farm households, when operating at a given point on the market supply curve. To see why this should be so, consider that marginal cost is the additional production cost incurred for each successive unit increase in output from zero upwards. Therefore, when MC is summed across all the units of output produced up to a given point such as Q_1 in Figure 3.1, this gives us the total variable costs of production incurred up to that point.

We begin with producers confronting a paddy price of $0.50/kg and producing 250 000 metric tons of paddy. Therefore, their total revenue (TR) from producing paddy is $P_1 \times Q_1$ = $500/metric ton $\times$ 250 000 metric tons = $125 million. More generally, producer gross returns can always be calculated by multiplying their total output by the ruling market price (i.e. $P \times Q$ at any point on the supply curve).

This total revenue divides between an area under the supply curve, area **b**, which represents the total variable cost (TVC) of producing the stated quantity, and an area above the supply curve but under the ruling market price, area **a**, which represents the *gross margin* obtained by selling Q_1 at price P_1. This gross margin, representing profit and payments to fixed factors of production such as land, capital, and family labour is called the *producer surplus*.

Definition
Producer surplus is defined as the area above the supply curve and below the price line of the corresponding firm or industry. (Just *et al.*, 1982: 54)

From a practical point of view, the supply curve does not need to be observed to calculate total producer surplus as so defined. Producer

Figure 3.1. The supply curve and producer surplus.

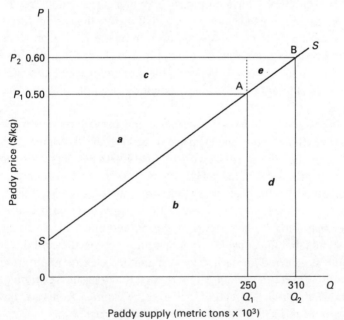

Paddy supply (metric tons x 10³)

surplus equals total revenue (gross farm income) minus total variable costs, and thus equals the gross margin for the farm household or for the group of farm households under consideration.

Now suppose that a policy change is contemplated that would seek to raise the producer price from \$0.50 to \$0.60 (a 20 per cent increase), say, by implementing a producer price support policy. This price increase has two major effects as shown in Figure 3.1: it has a *physical effect* in the form of higher output at Q_2, the precise size of this increase depending on the elasticity of supply in the region of the movement from A to B. It also has an *accounting effect* in the form of higher gross income, some of which is required to meet additional variable costs of production, area *d* in Figure 3.1, and some of which is an addition to the farmers' gross margin above variable costs, areas *c* and *e*.

In our example, it is assumed that the price rise from \$0.50 to \$0.60 per kg results in a supply increase from 250 000 to 310 000 metric tons. Thus gross revenue is increased from \$125 million to \$186 million. The change in the producer surplus (area *c* + *e* in Figure 3.1) consists of two components, the rectangular area *c*, which is measured by the price change times the original quantity supplied (\$100/metric ton $\times$ 250 000 metric tons = \$25 million), and the triangular area *e*, which in this simple example can be measured as one half the price change times the quantity change equals 1/2 $\times$ 60 000 = \$3 million. Thus the change in producer surplus resulting from this policy change is \$28 million.

This increase in producer surplus is a direct welfare *benefit* to the farm sector producing the crop for which a higher price is obtained. A price fall would, conversely, cause a loss in producer surplus and would count as a social *cost* of the price decline.

Even though we have stated this at the end of the previous chapter, it is worth repeating the sense in which these measurements are considered *social benefits* or *social costs*. The producer surplus measures the increase in income available for consumption on the part of the producers concerned. It therefore represents an improvement in their material welfare as *consumers* and, as such, it is defined as a welfare gain. The social welfare gain is never measured directly by the increase of gross output, an increase which involves additional resources and costs as well as net income gains. In policy economics it is always the ultimate *net* impact on the consumption possibilities of the society as a whole that counts as the welfare gain or loss.

Note that the key figure required in order to make the calculation of the change in producer surplus in Figure 3.1 is the price elasticity of supply.

The supply elasticity allows the new output level, Q_2, to be projected. From this, the change in producer surplus can be calculated using the rectangle, c, and the triangle, e, provided that the minor simplification is made that the supply curve is linear over the interval Q_1 to Q_2. The reason this simplification is stated as 'minor' is that in most practical cases the rectangle c (price change × old quantity) represents by far the largest proportion of the producer surplus change. In the above example it represented \$25 million/\$28 million or 90 per cent of the change. Therefore, small changes in the size of triangle e caused by alternative assumptions about the shape of the supply curve often have negligible effects on the orders of magnitude involved.

A few more examples of changes in producer surplus may be helpful in order to consolidate the understanding of this concept. The first of these refers to an improvement in overall farm technology. The second refers to a price subsidy on a variable input.

There are many types of agricultural development project that aim to increase output via a general improvement in the efficiency of resource use. A typical project may involve introducing a new, higher-yielding, variety to farmers, and supporting this with new inputs, better input delivery, credit for input purchase, and advice on how to obtain the best yields per hectare. The effect of such a project, if successful, is a new, more productive, farm technology. As shown in Figure 3.2, the supply curve shifts outwards to the right: farmers are prepared to supply more of the commodity at every price. A similar effect would occur if there was an agricultural project which caused a once-for-all expansion in the production area of a crop, even if the basic technology stays the same.

The impact of this type of production project is to increase output (from Q_1 to Q_2 in Figure 3.2) for a given market price. This assumes that farmers are price takers in the market, such as would be the case if their output was being exported to the world market. As before, the producer surplus is measured as the area above the supply curves and below the price line. It increases from area a before the project to the sum of areas $a + b + c$. The farmers have clearly gained from project implementation in this example.

In practical terms, the gains to farmers (area $b + c$) is composed of two components. One component (area b) represents cost saving at the old output level caused by improved resource efficiency. The other component (area c) is the new gross farm income minus the new variable costs incurred in the move to output Q_2. The total increase in producer surplus

– areas **b** + **c** – is in effect what is measured when the net benefit stream of an agricultural development project is calculated in cost–benefit analysis. The difference between policy and projects – in this particular context – is that the latter involves a capital sum, with which the discounted net benefit stream is compared, while the former involves only the comparative static measurement of before- and after-policy positions.

A policy proposal to subsidise the price of a variable farm input involves similar considerations and measurements. In this case, the effect of the subsidy is to reduce the marginal cost associated with each successive level of output so that the supply curve 'pivots' to the right as shown in Figure 3.3. Again, the increase in producer surplus is represented by areas **b** + **c**, with area **b** representing the cost saving on existing output caused by the input subsidy, while area **c** represents the addition to farmers' aggregate gross margin caused by the resulting supply expansion to Q_2.

The cost saving at old levels of input use (area **b**) is simply total existing input purchase by farmers multiplied by the proposed subsidy per unit. For example, if farmers were purchasing 20 000 tons of urea fertilizer at a price of $120/metric ton and this price were dropped to $100/metric ton,

Figure 3.2. Impact of new technology.

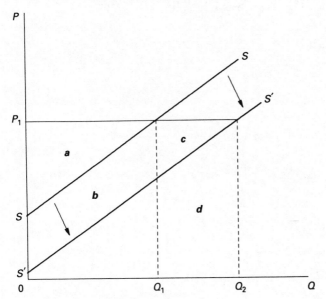

the cost saving at previous levels of use would be $20 \times 20\,000 = \$400\,000$. The new gross margin created by output expansion (area *c*) requires an estimate of the likely increase in input demand *and* its impact on yields per hectare. The two elasticities needed here are the fertilizer demand elasticity and the response elasticity of yield to fertilizer use. An example of the use of these elasticities to derive the full picture of the costs and benefits of an input subsidy is given in Chapter 6 (under the Section entitled 'Input subsidy versus price support: An example').

In the literature on producer surplus, the same concept is sometimes described as *rent*, or *quasi-rent* (see e.g. Mishan, 1988: Ch. 10). The reason for this is that as soon as we go behind producer surplus to consider who are the actual beneficiaries of this producer gross margin above variable cost, we are looking at payments to 'fixed' factors of production, i.e. to landowners (land rent), to fixed capital (returns on investment), and to family labour (net family income). Some economists consider producer surplus to be a bit of an illusion due to this feature. Since all income of this kind accrues in the end to the ultimate owners of resources, producer surplus in the sense of a net income or profit accruing to an entity called 'the enterprise' does not strictly exist.

Luckily for us the peasant farm household has the dual character of being both a farm enterprise and a consumption unit (Ellis, 1988a: 102–

Figure 3.3. Impact of an input price change.

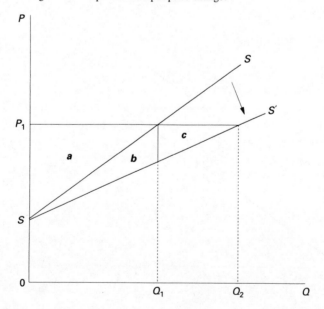

3). Thus for the majority of situations with which we are concerned, the returns to family labour and the producer surplus can for practical purposes be regarded as synonymous.

However, for policy problems where the focus is on the equity impact of a particular course of action, account should be taken of situations in which rent to landowners absorbs the producer surplus, leaving tenants at the same level of income as before the change takes place. This could easily occur where cash tenancy is widespread and land for farming is in very short supply. In the extreme case where the target farmers of a policy are all cash tenants and the supply of land is completely inelastic, an increase in producer surplus will entirely accrue to landlords in the form of higher rents per hectare of land (Just *et al.*, 1982: 50–1).

Consumer surplus

The equivalent measure to producer surplus on the demand side of the market is consumer surplus. Although the two types of surplus seem mirror images of each other on a graph, consumer surplus involves a logic and a set of possible problems that are different from those of producer surplus.

The concept of consumer surplus is introduced in Figure 3.4. This graph shows the market demand curve, *DD*, for an agricultural commodity like bananas, yams or wheat. For comparability with the previous section, rice is again used as an example of a commodity demanded by consumers. The price of rice is given on the vertical axis, the quantity that consumers would be prepared to buy at different price levels over any given time period is shown on the horizontal axis. The demand curve has a negative slope: more of the commodity is purchased by consumers as its price falls.

In Figure 3.4, assume that consumers are in equilibrium at point A on the market demand curve. At this point they have chosen to purchase 300 million kg of rice at a unit price of $0.50 per kg. Total consumer expenditure is thus given by $P_1 \times Q_1 = \$150$ million.

More generally, consumer expenditure can be calculated as the area under the demand curve bounded by the market price and the quantity purchased at the price (i.e. it is $P \times Q$ at any point on the demand curve).

In a sense these consumers are lucky. They are lucky that the price is not, for example, $1.00 per kg, when they would have incurred a total expenditure of $200 million, buying only 200 million kilos of rice. At the current price that quantity now only costs them $100 million, so they are saving $100 million over and above what they would have been *willing to pay* to buy 200 million kg of rice. This $100 million in savings – area *b* in Figure 3.4 – is called the *consumer surplus*, accruing to rice consumers due to the difference between what they would have been prepared to pay for the first 200 million tons of their rice consumption and what they actually pay at the ruling market price.

The example can of course be generalised with respect to any price above the ruling market place price. At a price of $2.00 per kilo consumers would not have been willing to buy any rice. However, thereafter they would have been willing to buy successively greater quantities of rice as the price goes down from $2.00 per kg towards the current market price of $0.50 per kg.

The area below the demand curve and above the ruling market price – area *a* + *b* + *c* in Figure 3.4 – is the total consumer surplus accruing to these consumers. This area represents the difference between what consumers would have been willing to pay for successive units of rice going from zero to 300 million kg, and what they actually pay at the ruling market price of $0.50 per kg. Put another way this area is the sum of what consumers *would have spent* on rice at successive prices going from $2.00 to $0.50 per kg, less what they actually spent at $0.50 per kg.

Figure 3.4. The demand curve and consumer surplus.

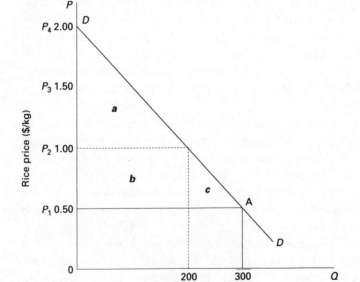

Rice demand (million kg)

Definition
Consumer surplus is defined as the area under the demand curve and above the price line. (Just *et al.*, 1982: 72)

Now assume that a policy change occurs that reduces the market price of rice from $0.50 to $0.40 (Figure 3.5). For example, the removal of a fixed tariff on rice imports might have this effect. Consumers now purchase 320 million kg rice at the new price of $0.40 per kg, giving a new consumer expenditure of $128 million. Consumers have clearly gained from this price change: they are consuming more rice at a lower price. Their total expenditure happens also to be less than it was before the price change, though this need not be the case (it occurs here because the demand curve in Figure 3.5 is inelastic in the vicinity of point A).

The gain to consumers is *not* measured by the change in their total expenditure on rice (which may go up or down depending on whether the price elasticity of demand is greater or less than unity). It is measured by the change in their consumer surplus that occurs as a result of the price change. The increase in consumer surplus is the area *d* + *e* in Figure 3.5, and it consists of two components. The first is the reduction in outlay for

Figure 3.5. Price change and consumer surplus.

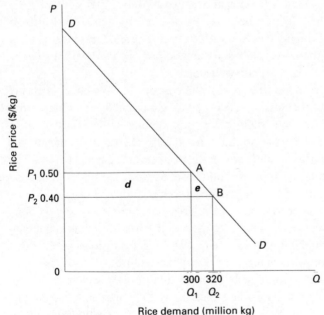

the old quantity of rice consumed (area *d*), and in this example equals $0.10 × 300 million kg = $30 million. The second is the sum of the amounts that consumers would have been willing to pay for successive increases in quantity as they moved from 300 to 320 million kg rice. This is given by the area of triangle *e* in Figure 3.5, which is equal to $\frac{1}{2}$ × $0.10 × 20 million kg = $1 million. The total consumer surplus, or social welfare gain, from the price fall is therefore $31 million.

A few more points can be made concerning this example in the measurement of consumer surplus. First, the impact of a price rise is simply to reverse the movement shown in Figure 3.5: if the movement were from $0.40 to $0.50, then areas *d* + *e* would represent a loss of consumer surplus and hence a fall in social welfare. Second, it is only the *change* in consumer surplus which is of interest to the policy analyst, not the total consumer surplus, which never needs to be estimated. Third, the major proportion of this change is given by rectangle *d* in Figure 3.5, i.e. the change in price multiplied by the old quantity demanded.

Fourth, the size of triangle *e* in Figure 3.5 depends on the *price elasticity of demand* for the commodity under consideration. As before, this can be obtained either from secondary sources or from econometric estimations of the demand function. From a practical viewpoint, triangle *e* is often likely to be so small as to make little difference to aggregate welfare measurements (in the example above it was only 3 per cent of total consumer surplus). This is because the demand for basic foodstuffs in most countries is highly inelastic with respect to price. Graphically, for a given point on the curve, inelastic demand is associated with a steeper slope, and hence a smaller size of triangle *e*.

Like producer surplus, the use of the concept of consumer surplus is not trouble free for assessing social welfare gains and losses. One source of difficulty arises potentially when price changes in several related markets are under consideration. Here, the size of consumer surplus will vary according to the order in which the markets are taken. This is called the 'path dependence' problem, and it stems from the underlying consideration – recognisable to the reader who has studied consumer theory – that the consumer response to a price change consists of both a substitution effect and an income effect. It turns out that consumer surplus is an unambiguous measure of welfare gains or losses only if the income effects of price changes are always zero (Just *et al.*, 1982: 73–7).

While this result seems to restrict the usefulness of consumer surplus, it has also been shown that income effects of price changes are of negligible importance (i) when the income elasticities of the commodities under consideration are low, and (ii) when the proportion of household income spent on a commodity is small (Willig, 1976). Alternatively, and in more complex types of analysis, knowledge of the income elasticity of demand for a commodity can be used to make suitable adjustments to consumer surplus measures. In the present context it is sufficient for the student to be aware that these difficulties exist and that this topic can be pursued, if desired, up to higher levels of complexity.

Single commodity market analysis

So far we have introduced producer surplus and consumer surplus on their own, as if they could be measured and their impact assessed in isolation one from the other. However, most types of policy change affect both the supply and demand side of a commodity market. They may also affect input markets on the production side and markets for closely related commodities – substitutes and complements – on the demand side. Moreover, a wide range of policies involve making domestic price levels (of inputs or outputs) diverge from world market prices.

Before turning to world price and trade aspects of these measures, it is useful first to review the case when both supply and demand sides of a commodity market are included in the analysis (in a domestic context not involving trade). Figure 3.6 does this for an example we have already

Figure 3.6. Policy effects in a commodity market.

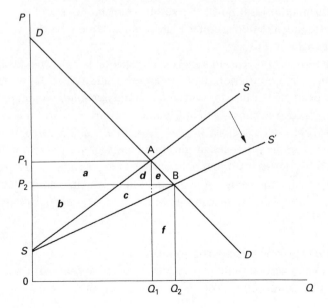

considered, the impact of a subsidy on a farm variable input that causes the supply curve to shift outwards.

Figure 3.6 displays the net welfare and income distribution effects of an input subsidy by combining both demand and supply curves. Before the subsidy, the domestic market is in equilibrium at point A with price P_1 and quantity Q_1. After the subsidy, the new equilibrium point is B, with price P_2 and quantity Q_2. The impact of the subsidy is distributed between a fall in the market price and an increase in the quantity traded, with the balance between these depending on the elasticities of demand and supply involved.

Consumers have unambiguously gained from this change. The gain in consumer surplus is shown by areas $a + d + e$ on the graph. The welfare position for producers is less clear cut. The producer surplus before the change is area $a + b$, and after the change it is area $b + c$. Therefore the net gain or loss of producer surplus is given by $(b + c) - (a + b) = c - a$. Whether area c is bigger than area a, and therefore whether producers experience a net welfare gain, depends on the elasticity of demand (taking the supply curves as given). The geometry of the situation shown in Figure 3.6 is such that if demand is inelastic over the relevant range, area a is greater than area c, and producers experience a net welfare loss.

Figure 3.6 demonstrates that the distributional effects of policies can be complex even in simple cases. In the situation of inelastic demand just described the surprising result of a farm input subsidy is for consumers to gain and farmers to lose. Since this result is not intuitively obvious, it demonstrates the potential usefulness of attempts to measure the welfare effects of policies in this way.

This situation also reveals in a more concrete manner the significance of the compensation criterion defined earlier. There is a social welfare gain in this example because the consumers could *potentially* compensate the producers for their loss, and still remain better off than they were before (the consumer surplus gain given by area $a + d + e$ is unambiguously bigger than the producer surplus loss represented by area a minus area c). In other words, the input policy creates the potential for a Pareto improvement, and according to the compensation principle this is all that is required for the policy to be considered to have a net beneficial impact on social welfare.

World prices and opportunity cost

Readers will be familiar with the proposition that world prices represent the opportunity cost to a country of the commodities it produces or consumes. At a trivial level it can be seen that if a country can only produce a given commodity (say, tin cans) at a cost above the world market price, then the consumers of that commodity (in this case food canning factories) would be better off if cans were imported. Conversely, if a country can produce a commodity at a cost that permits its profitable sale in world markets at world prices, then it is said to have a *comparative advantage* in the production of that commodity.

The concepts of producer and consumer surplus are usefully consolidated by extending their application in a world price context, and this also helps to clarify the ideas of opportunity cost and comparative advantage. Initially, at least, we ignore various potential problems in defining the appropriate level of world prices, due to price or exchange rate instability, and we assume that a country is a price taker in world markets and that the world price is stable.

Consider, first, a situation in which a country lifts a previous import ban on a commodity, like maize, that is also important in the domestic market (Figure 3.7). The immediate impact of the policy change is to lower the price of maize from P_1, the previous market clearing domestic price, to P_w, the world price. Imports of maize are now freely allowed, and after supply and demand have adjusted to this situation a total quantity of imports equal to Q_d minus Q_s are purchased from the world market.

Figure 3.7. Welfare impact of imports at world prices.

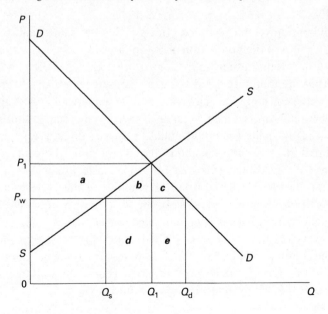

The economic impact of this change can be measured in two ways, both giving the same net results:

    (a) Using the concepts of producer and consumer surplus, there are the welfare effects of the change, measured as money transfers associated with the income position of producers and consumers.

    (b) There are the resource and commodity flows associated with the change, also measured in money terms.

These two aspects are always present in a policy analysis context of this kind. They are two sides to the same coin. For the example given in Figure 3.7, we have:

– *Welfare effects:*	Consumer surplus gain	$= a + b + c$	(gain)
	Producer surplus loss	$= a$	(loss)
	Net gain or loss	$= b + c$	(gain)
– *Resource transfers:*	Domestic resources saved	$= b + d$	(gain)
	Consumer outlay avoided	$= c$	(gain)
	New consumer expenditure	$= e$	(gain)
	Foreign exchange cost	$= d + e$	(loss)
	Net gain or loss	$= b + c$	(gain)

Taking the welfare effects first, consumers gain and producers lose, but the consumers could compensate the producers and still realise a net gain equal to areas $b + c$ in Figure 3.7. The compensation criterion applies. This is the social welfare gain of the move to free trade. It can also be described as the *gains from trade* realised by moving to free trade in this commodity.

A consideration of the resource effects yields the same result. Resources taken out of the production of maize (areas $b + d$) are presumed available to move into other, more competitive, branches of economic activity. They are therefore listed as a gain. Consumers are able to enjoy the new level of consumption at a saving compared to the old price, given by triangle c, and this is a gain to them. New consumer expenditure on maize as a result of its price fall, equal to area e, directly represents increased material consumption and is therefore a gain. These gains are offset by the foreign exchange cost of importing maize, equal to area $d + e$. When this cost is subtracted from the combined gains, it gives a net resource gain of $b + c$, the same as in the welfare measurement. The resource gain is the *efficiency gain* of moving to free trade.

The converse of the situation described so far is the loss that would result if the country were to move back from the free trade to an import prohibition. In this case, there would be a loss of consumer welfare equal to area $a + b + c$. The producer surplus would increase by area a, but producers would not be able to compensate the consumers by more than *a*, and thus area *b* + *c* would represent a net welfare loss.

Furthermore, since additional resources are required for domestic production equal to area *b* + *d*, consumers have lost their price advantage given by area *c* and their additional expenditure given by area *e*, and only *d* + *e* has been saved in foreign exchange, there is a net resource cost equal to area *b* + *c*. This net resource cost is called the *deadweight efficiency loss* caused by the import ban.

Examples of policy intervention effects

The foregoing example shows that some useful insights may be gained by looking at producer and consumer surplus in the presence of world prices for tradeable outputs or inputs. First, there is the notion of *gains from trade* and its opposite, the notion of *deadweight efficiency losses*. Second, there is the dual aspect of the measurement of policy intervention effects: the welfare effects as measured by changes in producer and consumer surplus, and the resource/commodity expenditure effects as measured by changes in commodity or resource flows involving producers, consumers, imports, exports and foreign exchange.

In order to consolidate these ideas, we examine four different types of policy intervention involving the prices of tradeable commodities. These are (a) an import tax on a food crop, (b) an export tax on a non-food export crop, (c) a consumer subsidy for a food crop, and (d) an input subsidy on a variable cash input.

Import tax

An import tax is a policy instrument commonly used to increase the domestic price of a food crop above world market price levels. There are many different types of import tax: for example, a percentage tax on the cif (cost, insurance and freight) import price (otherwise known as an *ad valorem* tax); a fixed or flat rate money tax per physical unit imported (e.g. $80 per ton); or a variable levy that collects the difference between an agreed minimum import price and the fluctuating world price. The graphical representation is similar for all these alternatives, but they would differ in actual measurement according to the way the tax operated on the domestic price compared to the world price.

Figure 3.8 illustrates the welfare impact of a flat rate import tax. Its main effect is to raise the domestic market price, P_d, above the world market price, P_w. Following the procedure set out above, the welfare and resource effects of the tax are traced as follows:

– *Welfare effects*:   Consumer surplus loss $= a + b + c + d$
                        Producer surplus gain $= a$
                        Tax revenue gain $= d$
                        Net welfare loss $= b + c$
– *Resource transfers*: Extra resources used $= b + e$
                        Consumption loss $= c + f$
                        Foreign exchange gain $= e + f$
                        Deadweight efficiency loss $= b + c$

Thus, the welfare impact of an import tax is that producers gain, the government gains, and consumers lose. There is a net welfare loss born by consumers. The new element in this picture compared to the previous example is the tax revenue accruing to government. It is possible that area *d*, the tax revenue gain, is the same or larger than areas *b* + *c*, so that the government could compensate the consumers for their loss. Thus although an import tax clearly involves a deadweight efficiency loss in terms of resource allocation, according to the compensation criterion the consumer welfare losses caused by the tax might be more than offset by government income.

Note that an import quota – i.e. a fixed limit on the level of imports, which causes the domestic price to rise above the world market level – can

Figure 3.8. Policy effects of an import tax.

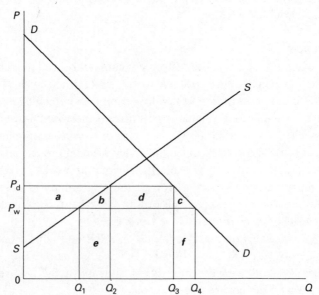

be analysed using the same diagram, but in that instance government tax income would not arise on the welfare side (Timmer, 1986a: 50–4).

Export tax

An export tax is a policy instrument commonly used to generate government revenue, especially in countries where the capacity to obtain government income by income or profit taxes is limited. Export taxes can take several different forms, such as a fixed tax per unit exported, a percentage tax on the fob (free on board) export price, or a graduated percentage tax that rises as the fob price rises. The last type is sometimes justified as aiming to reduce price instability for domestic producers. In all cases export taxes have the impact of reducing the producer price below the level that would have prevailed in the absence of the tax.

As an example of an export tax we take a non-food export crop. This allows us to dispense with the domestic demand curve, since we assume that domestic consumption is a minor element of the overall picture (Figure 3.9). The policy intervention effects of an export tax are as follows:

– *Welfare effects*:	Producer surplus loss	$= a + b$
	Tax revenue gain	$= a$
	Net welfare loss	$= b$

Figure 3.9. Policy effects of an export tax.

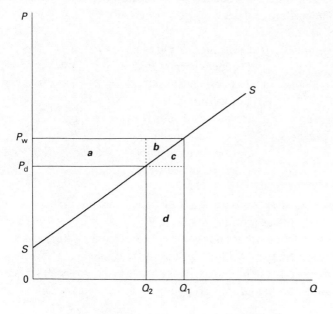

       – *Resource transfers*:   Resources saved $= c + d$
                              Foreign exchange lost $= c + d + b$
                              Deadweight efficiency loss $= b$

In the case of the export tax, the gain in government income, area a, is not sufficient to compensate for the loss in producer income, area $a + b$, and there is an unambiguous decline in social welfare. The major distributional impact is to transfer resources from producers to the state.

Food subsidy

Food subsidies are again a common type of policy instrument in developing countries and can take a variety of forms. Across-the-board consumer subsidies tend to be enormously expensive to implement, so efforts are usually made to target subsidies either by restricting them to urban consumers or to special target groups. However, in these instances practical difficulties arise concerning marketing margins and the insulation of low consumer prices from higher producer prices.

One way that governments can reduce market prices to the benefit of consumers is by subsidising the price of imported supplies. This is superficially attractive because only imports get the subsidy, but the subsidised import price becomes the ruling price for the entire domestic market. Figure 3.10 displays this case, in which the price for producers as well as for consumers is reduced by a subsidy per unit of imported supplies. The welfare and resource effects of a subsidy on imported food are as follows:

    – *Welfare effects*: Consumer surplus gain $= a + b + c + d + e$
                          Producer surplus loss $= a + b$
                          Tax costs of subsidy $= b + c + d + e + f$
                          Net welfare loss $= b + f$
    – *Resource*   Resources saved $= c + g$
       transfers: Consumption gain $= e + h$
                          Foreign exchange loss $= b + c + g + f + e + h$
                          Deadweight efficiency
                            loss $= b + f$

This type of subsidy is observed to be disadvantageous in several ways. The net welfare losses are real deadweight losses – it is not possible for consumers to compensate producers or the government for the losses and costs resulting from the subsidy. The subsidy is a drain on the government budget and is a drain on foreign exchange too. Even if producers could be insulated from the favourable price impact to consumers (administratively costly to ensure) so that the producer surplus loss does not occur, there is still a net welfare loss described as area *f* in Figure 3.10 which cannot be avoided for this type of policy intervention.

Input subsidy

Subsidies on variable cash inputs to production are very popular in developing countries and we shall be examining such subsidies in greater detail in Chapter 6 of this book. As a final illustration here of producer and consumer surplus in a world price context, Figure 3.11 displays the impacts in the output market of an input subsidy for a tradeable commodity in the world market. We assume again that the country is a price taker. Welfare and resource effects are summarised as follows:

– *Welfare effects*:	Producer surplus gain	= *a* + *b*
	Tax costs of subsidy	= *a* + *b* + *c*
	Net welfare loss	= *c*
– *Resource transfers*:	Extra resources used	= *c* + *b* + *d*
	Foreign exchange saving	= *b* + *d*
	Deadweight efficiency loss	= *c*

Figure 3.10. Policy effects of a subsidy on food imports.

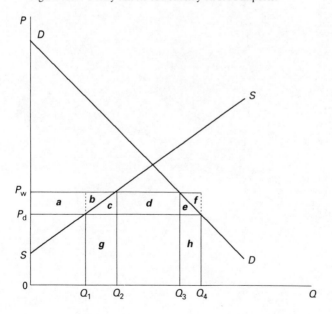

Thus an input subsidy involves an income transfer from government to producers. The cost of making this transfer is higher than the producer surplus gain so that there is a net welfare loss. This has its counterpart also on the resource side. Note especially in this example that the overall gains in output achieved as a result of the policy are beside the point as far as welfare and resource use efficiency are concerned. Extra output requires extra resources, diverted from an alternative activity that may in its own right be making a more effective contribution to social welfare.

A summary point on welfare losses

In each of the above cases, policy interventions that seek to make domestic prices depart from world market prices result in deadweight efficiency losses to the national economy. They also result in net welfare losses, though in one case – the import tax – the possibility was identified that the government revenue generated by the tax might more than offset the welfare losses incurred by consumers as a result of higher prices.

In terms of practical measurement, these deadweight efficiency losses or net welfare losses may often turn out to be trivial by comparison with the overall changes in expenditure involved. An inspection of the graphs

Figure 3.11. Policy effects of an input subsidy.

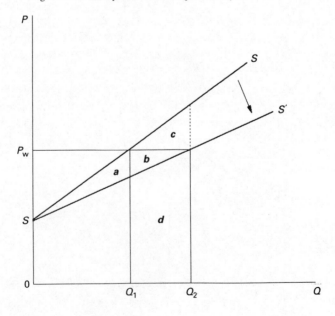

reveals that they are always the small triangles under or above demand and supply curves. However, triviality in measurement does not imply that such losses can be safely ignored. Policies that affect resource use in these ways have cumulative effects over time that go beyond what can be shown by comparative static policy analysis (Timmer, 1986a: 45–7).

Private, economic and social prices

The presentation of partial equilibrium analysis in this chapter has made use of various terms in applied welfare economics such as efficiency, equity, opportunity cost, social welfare, and so on. These terms can be usefully supplemented by a more precise definition of the different types of *prices* that are used in policy analysis, and by considering the purpose of looking at problems in terms of different prices.

One alternative is to measure the effects of a policy change in terms of the actual prices confronted by farm households and by consumers before and after the change. This is the way most of the partial equilibrium analysis of this chapter has been posed so far. An input subsidy, for example, reduces the price of a variable input to farm households and this increases their producer surplus. The actual prices paid or received by consumers and producers are called *private* prices, and policy analysis that solely measures welfare impacts in terms of such prices is *policy analysis in private prices*.

It was also shown above, however, that many policies create a divergence between domestic and world prices for commodity outputs or inputs, and that this divergence results in deadweight efficiency losses borne by society as a whole. These losses result because the private prices confronted by producers or consumers do not reflect *social opportunity costs*. This suggests that the gains and losses of a proposed policy change might also be measured in opportunity cost prices: world prices for tradeable inputs or outputs, and output foregone in their next best use for non-tradeable domestic factors of production (like land or labour). This would give a more accurate picture of the net social welfare impacts of a policy change than private prices.

Social opportunity cost prices are usually referred to as *shadow prices* or *economic prices*. Policy analysis that measures welfare effects in terms of such prices is *policy analysis in economic prices*.

The usefulness of such an exercise is revealed if one considers a simple case such as the impact on, say, millet producing households of a subsidy on phosphate fertilizer. While analysis in private prices might show that the policy was beneficial to farmers and yielded a net welfare gain to them (increased producer surplus), analysis in economic prices might show that the policy was not socially beneficial and involved a net social welfare loss. One reason that could cause such a difference would be if the extra return to using more phosphate fertilizer were lower than the cost – at world prices – of the additional fertilizer used. In other words, the productivity of the additional phosphate might not have been that big anyway, and certainly not big enough to justify the increase in phosphate imports involved.

It can be seen from this example that private evaluation of a policy on its own may serve to make an unjustified and costly intervention seem worthwhile. There are many possible resource adjustments in a farm system that might result in small increases in output, but if the real cost to society is larger than the increases in output obtained then a decision to go ahead with the policy requires very careful justification. There is thus a strong case for presenting the gains, losses, and net welfare effects of policies in both private and economic prices, so that the two can be compared and an informed decision may be made upon consideration of both of them.

It can be noted at this point that in the field of social cost–benefit analysis yet a third class of prices has been proposed in order to take into account the equity as well as efficiency goals of agricultural projects (see e.g. Squire & van der Tak, 1975: 6 and *passim*). These prices are called *social prices*, and they differ from economic prices in that they involve further adjustments to take into account income distribution objectives as well as output objectives. For example, if a specific aim of a policy or project is to create more rural employment, the wage level used in calculating the social cost of production might be lowered by some amount (known as an income distribution 'weight') below its opportunity cost level. This would have the effect of making that policy or project appear more socially profitable than in the absence of such an adjustment.

To summarise, the welfare impacts of policy changes can be valued in private or economic prices. Valuation in private prices yields a statement of private changes in the welfare of producers and consumers. For competitive markets and in the absence of trade policies this would coincide with social welfare changes. Otherwise, policy changes should be valued in economic as well as private prices. Economic prices are defined as social opportunity costs, i.e. world prices for tradeable commodities and output foregone for non-tradeables. It is also possible, but not universally agreed, that policies and projects could be valued at social prices representing income distribution as well as efficiency objectives.

Summary measures of price policy effects

Economists have developed a number of summary measures to describe the welfare impacts of policies that act on domestic input or output prices. These measures are sometimes referred to in the literature as 'measures of policy distortions'. This places emphasis on domestic price policies as departures from world prices, treated as the efficiency prices for social welfare.

The main summary measures that are encountered in the policy literature are listed first and then discussed in more detail below. They make extensive use of the distinctions between (i) tradeable inputs (inputs that can be valued at world prices) and non-tradeable inputs (typically called domestic resources or domestic factors), (ii) private and economic prices, and (iii) value added in private prices and value added in social prices. Value added is defined as the difference between the gross value of output (quantity × price) and the total cost of intermediate inputs. It represents the net amount available to distribute to the primary factors of production (land, labour and capital). This is a general definition of value added in economics, not one that is specific just to the measure listed here:

– *Summary Measures*

  Private cost ratio (PCR)

  Domestic resource cost (DRC)

  Nominal protection coefficient (NPC)

  (a) NPC output

  (b) NPC inputs

  Effective rate of protection (ERP)

  Profitability coefficient (PC)

  Subsidy ratio to producers (SRP)

Private cost ratio: The private cost ratio is the ratio of domestic factor costs (i.e. land, labour and capital) to value added in private prices. It therefore summarises the viability of the activity from a purely private viewpoint. PCR = 1 describes an exact break-even situation with normal profits. PCR < 1 describes a situation of excess profits. PCR > 1 describes a situation of private losses.

Domestic resource cost: The domestic resource cost ratio is the ratio of primary domestic factors at economic prices (i.e. land, labour and capital valued at economic opportunity cost) to value added in economic prices (value added calculated using world price for inputs and output). In other words it is a ratio measure of *economic efficiency* according to the previous distinction between private and economic efficiency. DRC = 1 describes an exact break-even position of economic efficiency (or comparative advantage). DRC < 1 describes economic profitability (comparative advantage exists). DRC > 1 describes economic losses (comparative disadvantage in that branch of activity).

Nominal protection coefficients: There are two of these, one for the output and one for the tradeable inputs (taken together). NPC is the simplest possible measure of the degree of protection afforded an output or an input. The NPC for output is simply the domestic market price over the world price. If NPC = 1 then domestic market price equals world price and there is no protection. If NPC > 1 then there is positive protection of output. For example an output NPC of 1.30 means that trade policy protects the domestic price at a level 30 per cent above the world price. If NPC < 1 then there is negative protection on output. This could only occur if an imported commodity were subsidised for the domestic market. The same ratio applies to traded inputs, only in this case one is looking to see how input costs are being subsidised or taxed. For example, an input NPC of 0.50 means that variable inputs in the domestic market are only costing producers 50 per cent of their world market value.

Effective rate of protection: This is defined as the ratio of value added in private prices to value added in world prices. Bearing in mind the definition of value added, the ERP is the private domestic price *minus* variable inputs in private prices divided by the border commodity price *minus* variable inputs in border prices. When none of these prices are distorted the ERP = 1. Policies such as import quotas or import tariffs on the output side, and input subsidies on the input side, cause private value added to be above economic value added, giving ERP > 1. Policies that depress producer prices or increase the price of inputs above world levels cause private value added to be below economic value added, giving ERP < 1. The effective rate of protection may be much higher than the nominal rate of protection on output if inputs are also being subsidised.

Profitability coefficient: This extends the ERP by taking into account distortions in domestic factor markets (land, labour and capital). It is defined as the ratio of net profits in private prices to net profits in economic prices. Alternatively, it is gross private revenue minus private costs (domestic factors plus tradeable inputs) divided by gross economic revenue minus economic costs (domestic opportunity costs plus tradeable inputs valued at world prices). Again, when PC = 1 there are no distortions, or perhaps distortions in one direction are offset by ones in the other direction. The PC is ambiguous when either private or social profits are negative, since the signs of both entries must then be known to permit a valid interpretation of the ratio.

Subsidy ratio to producers: This is calculated as the divergence between private and social profits (private profits minus social profits) as a proportion of gross economic revenue. It therefore describes the share of gross revenue measured in world prices that would be required if the entire set of commodity, factor and macroeconomic policies were to be replaced by a single tax or subsidy. This is most useful for comparing the effects of state interventions between different commodities, because it provides a single measure – comparable across commodities – of the degree to which each commodity benefits or disbenefits from state actions.

Some notes of caution are required regarding the validity and usefulness of these summary measures. *First*, the data demands for calculating some of the measures are considerable, and the data used are sometimes too fragmentary and inaccurate to support the final ratio that is calculated. *Second*, when cross-country comparisons of these ratios are made, rather dubious short-cuts are sometimes taken regarding the reference point (e.g. farm-gate, ex-mill, retail) of domestic prices (Westlake, 1987). *Third*, these single ratios are no substitute for trying to attain a better in-depth understanding of the complex economic processes that underlie them. Notwithstanding their popularity with visiting economic experts, they can easily result in misleading interpretations of policy effects and outcomes.

Summary

1. This chapter introduces the basic concepts and methods used in the partial equilibrium analysis of agricultural policies. The scope of agricultural policy analysis is discussed and seven types of policy effect are identified as relevant for consideration in a typical policy analysis: price effects, production effects, consumption effects, trade effects, budget effects, income distribution effects, and welfare effects.

2. The concept of elasticity is defined as the percentage change in one variable associated with a one per cent change in another

variable. Some alternative expressions for calculating elasticities are described with examples. The main elasticities encountered in agricultural policy analysis are identified as the price and income elasticities of demand, the price elasticity of supply, the input elasticity of yield, and the demand elasticity for a variable input.

3. The concepts of producer surplus and consumer surplus are introduced. On the graph of market supply, producer surplus is defined as the area above the supply curve and below the price line. In more concrete terms it is the gross margin obtained by subtracting total variable costs from gross farm income. It therefore represents the returns to the fixed factors of production of land, capital, or family labour; and is sometimes referred to as rent, or quasi-rent in this context.

4. On the graph of market demand, consumer surplus is defined as the area below the demand curve and above the price line. In more concrete terms it is the amount that consumers would be willing to pay for successive extra quantities of a commodity as its price falls *minus* what they actually pay for the total quantity purchased at the ruling market price. While there are some logical ambiguities associated with consumer surplus, these are of minor importance provided a commodity does not loom too large in consumer expenditure.

5. Producer surplus and consumer surplus are applied in the context of policy-induced divergences between world market prices and domestic prices. This allows the concepts of social opportunity costs, gains from trade, and deadweight efficiency losses to be defined and examined. It is shown that the evaluation of policy effects has a dual character – social welfare effects versus resource use effects – the net impact of each being the same. Policy instruments used to illustrate the partial equilibrium method in this chapter include an import tax, an export tax, a food subsidy and an input subsidy.

6. The evaluation of policy changes in private prices is contrasted with their evaluation in economic prices, and it is shown that both sets of prices are required in order to obtain an accurate picture of the costs and benefits of alternative policies. The possibility raised in the cost–benefit literature of using distributional weights to construct a third set of prices – social prices – is also briefly mentioned.

7. A number of summary measures used by economists to describe the efficiency impacts of price policies are defined and described. These are the private cost ratio (PCR), domestic resource cost (DRC), nominal protection coefficient (NPC), effective rate of protection (ERP), profitability coefficient (PC), and subsidy ratio to producers (SRP). A word of caution regarding the accuracy and usefulness of these summary measures is given, since they try to capture in single ratios typically rather complicated economic processes.

Further reading

An excellent source for applied welfare economics, including a comprehensive account of producer and consumer surplus is Just *et al.* (1982). The level of this may be too difficult for the non-economist reader, but it should be accessible to postgraduate students in agricultural economics. An alternative and clear description of producer and consumer surplus can be found in Mishan (1988: Chs. 7 and 10). Use of the concepts of producer and consumer surplus in the context of world prices, and associated discussion of gains from trade and deadweight efficiency losses, is set out with admirable clarity in Timmer (1986a), and, more comprehensively, in Tsakok (1990). Many aspects of the partial equilibrium approach to agricultural policies are discussed in McCalla & Josling (1985) and Colman & Young (1989: Ch. 12). For some practical examples of elasticity estimation and welfare analysis see Tweeten (1989: Chs. 5 and 6). Lastly, Monke & Pearson (1989) set out in detail a practical accounting method, called the Policy Analysis Matrix (PAM), for calculating the efficiency effects of policies. This method is based on a commodity-by-commodity approach to policy analysis, and it has the advantage in terms of contemporary computer technology of being orientated towards spreadsheet methods of organising policy data and analysis.

Reading list
Colman, D. & Young, T. (1989). *Principles of Agricultural Economics*. Cambridge University Press.

Just, R.E., Hueth, D.L. & Schmitz, A. (1982). *Applied Welfare Economics and Public Policy*. Englewood Cliffs, New Jersey: Prentice Hall.

McCalla, A.F. & Josling, T.E. (1985). *Agricultural Policies and World Markets*. London: Macmillan.

Mishan, E.J. (1988). *Cost–Benefit Analysis* 4th edn. London: Unwin Hyman.

Monke, E.A. & Pearson, S.R. (1989). *The Policy Analysis Matrix for Agricultural Development*. Ithaca: Cornell University Press.

Timmer, C. P. (1986a). *Getting Prices Right: The Scope and Limits of Agricultural Price Policy*. New York: Cornell University Press.

Tsakok, I. (1990). *Agricultural Price Policy: A Practitioner's Guide to Partial Equilibrium Analysis*. New York: Cornell University Press.

Tweeten, L. (ed.) (1989). *Agricultural Policy Analysis Tools for Economic Development*. London: Intermediate Technology Publications.

PART II

Agricultural policies

Introduction

This part of the book is composed of a set of eight chapters covering individual agricultural policies. The organising principle behind these eight chapters was described in Chapter 1, but is worth reiterating here. Policy topics are identified according to the influence they are designed to exert upon the small-farm system. Policies are related to farm outputs and farm inputs according to the following scheme:

    (a) *output policies*, including output price policy (Chapter 4) and output marketing policy (Chapter 5);

    (b) *input policies*, including variable input price policy and variable input delivery systems (Chapter 6);

    (c) *credit policy*, being concerned with working capital for the purchase of farm variable inputs (Chapter 7);

    (d) *mechanisation policy*, which is about farm fixed capital in the form of machines and implements (Chapter 8);

    (e) *land reform policy*, which is about the redistribution and legal status of land as a farm resource (Chapter 9);

    (f) *research policy*, including farming systems research (FSR) and farmer first research (FFR), which is concerned with the generation and diffusion of new farm technology (Chapter 10);

    (g) *irrigation policy*, which is about the provision of water as a variable farm input (Chapter 11).

These eight chapters follow a similar format, which is based in part on the objectives–constraints–instruments framework for policy analysis described in Chapter 2. Each chapter contains a statement of the policy area, definitions of special terms where relevant, policy objectives, policy instruments, examples of economic policy analysis, and lessons from past experience. All chapters also contain themes related to peasants and policy, and to women and policy. These are usually but not always discussed in sections towards the end of each chapter.

The use of this common format for the discussion of each policy is not applied inflexibly in an attempt to force all policies into a single mould. Each chapter has its particular emphasis according to the features of the policies under discussion, as well as taking into account the structure of the book as a whole.

Thus Chapter 4, on price policy, does not contain examples of the partial equilibrium analysis of price policy instruments, since these are already contained in Chapter 3. Chapter 8, on mechanisation policy, does not follow the objectives–instruments routine since most developing countries have not had clear aims with respect to farm mechanisation. Chapter 9, on land reform policy, places special emphasis on the political nature of land redistribution. Chapter 11, on irrigation policy, gives particular attention to the public good and common property resource aspects of the economic analysis of irrigation.

More generally, the treatment of each policy aims to provide a flavour of the special features of that policy to which economists and other writers have drawn attention. This has been done while trying to avoid undue reliance on policy emphases that are the results of swings in fashion, although this is inevitably not always successful. In particular, these chapters try to avoid taking an inflexible or dogmatic stance with respect to the state versus market debate which permeates the discussion of all policies. While the prevailing orthodoxy at the time of writing favours free market solutions for a wide class of problems, not all policies, or policy instruments, are either susceptible to that approach or necessitate it in order for solutions to problems to be found.

4

Price policy

Farm output price policy

This chapter is concerned with government policies that influence the level of prices received by farmers and paid by consumers for *farm outputs*. This is a narrower definition of price policy than is common in the literature, which sometimes also includes policies that affect the prices of farm inputs, farm machinery, land and labour, and farm credit. However, these other price policies are examined separately in subsequent chapters of this book, and this chapter focuses only on output prices.

Farm output prices are generally recognised as having three main functions in the economic system. These are (i) to allocate farm resources, (ii) to distribute incomes, and (iii) to encourage or retard investment and capital formation in agriculture (Mellor, 1968). These functions have also been described as the *signals*, *incentives*, and *instruments* for the allocation of resources and incomes (Streeten, 1987: 11).

The resource allocation function of farm prices follows from the optimising behaviour of producers in a market system as described by neoclassical production economics (Ellis, 1988a: Ch. 2). An increase in the general level of output prices, *ceteris paribus*, increases returns to all inputs in production, encouraging higher use of variable inputs, as well as providing higher returns to the fixed inputs of land, capital and family labour. A change in the relative price level of one output against another results in substitution between outputs as farm households adjust to the changing relative profitability of different outputs. For peasant households that consume a proportion of their own output, these adjustments may be modified by food security and other household goals.

The income distribution function of output prices has many dimensions. There is the fairly direct implication, for staple foods, that high farm prices raise producer incomes and lower the real incomes of consumers. This conflict is often encountered in the context of a rural–urban, country–city, or agriculture–industry type of policy debate. However, the income distribution effects of high food prices are never in reality as simple as that. High food prices have adverse effects for the rural landless (a growing proportion of rural households in many developing countries), and for small peasants who are net food purchasers, as well as for urban consumers.

The investment and capital accumulation role of farm output prices relates to their longer-run cumulative effects. High farm prices relative to those in other sectors increase the rate of return to capital in agriculture and encourage investment in various ways. At the household level, higher farm incomes may permit saving across seasons which in turn permits increased use of purchased cash inputs. Higher incomes also encourage the flow of credit into agricultural activities by improving the risk status of households. At an intersectoral level, higher food prices lower the relative rate of return to capital in the non-farm economy – via their impact on non-farm wage levels – and raise the relative rate of return in agriculture.

Some of the price policy instruments discussed in this chapter have already been examined analytically in terms of producer and consumer surplus in Chapter 3. Therefore, this chapter is more on the descriptive attributes of policy than on its welfare analysis, and the reader is referred to Chapter 3 for complementary material. The chapter proceeds as follows:

(a) to distinguish some main *objectives* of farm output price policy, as well as subsidiary objectives often cited as important reasons for price policy interventions;

(b) to consider different types of policy *instrument* employed in pursuit of price level objectives, as well as to identify the most popular instruments in common use in developing countries;

(c) to examine appropriate *criteria* for deciding price levels in a system of price interventions;

(d) to discuss the *effects* of price policies in three different areas, these being output and supply effects, price stabilisation effects, and income distribution effects;

(e) to summarise some of the *lessons* which have been learned from the successes and failures of output price policy in developing countries;

(f) to make some points concerning the status of *women* with respect to price policies.

Objectives of output price policy

There are three primary objectives of farm output price policy, which correspond to the three roles or functions of output prices already identified. These are *first*, to influence agricultural output; *second*, to achieve desired changes in income distribution; and *third*, to influence the role and contribution of the agricultural sector to the overall process of economic development.

There are many potential conflicts between these objectives. The achievement of desirable changes in income distribution (e.g. improving the incomes of the urban poor via low food prices) may be at odds with increasing farm output. Also, the third major objective needs to be specified with respect to its strategic direction. A policy to subordinate agriculture to the needs of industrial growth is different from one that treats the agricultural sector as a source of growth and employment in its own right.

There are many different secondary objectives of output price intervention which at one time or another feature strongly in the justification for price policy interventions advanced by developing country governments. These are always related to one of the above primary objectives, and the links are identified where appropriate in the following list:

(a) to increase aggregate agricultural output, across all crops and enterprises;

(b) to increase the output of individual crops or outputs, for example export versus food crops, perennial crops versus annual crops, drought-prone grains versus drought-resistant grains, grains versus root crops and so on;

(c) to stabilise agricultural prices, both in order to reduce uncertainty for farmers (and thus to raise output), and to ensure stable food prices for consumers and stability in the macroeconomic price environment;

(d) to stabilise farm incomes, as distinct from price stability, since stable prices may or may not stabilise incomes depending on the cause of price fluctuations and the degree of market engagement of different types of farm household;

(e) to achieve food self-sufficiency, this being an aggregate food security objective with links to both (a) and (b) above;

(f) to generate government tax revenue either from export taxes or import taxes, with short-term and cumulative effects cutting across all other objectives;

(g) to generate or save foreign exchange, and thus to contribute to the balance of payments;

(h) to ensure that the manufacturing sector is supplied with cheap food and cheap raw materials in order to accelerate the pace of industrial growth, this being a most important 'classical' objective of price policy;

(i) to maximise the investible surplus that can be extracted from agriculture for investment in the manufacturing sector of the economy, this 'surplus' being mobilised either through commodity taxation or through changes in the terms of trade.

Amongst these objectives, the final two have fallen into disrepute and will not be examined further here except where it is relevant to mention them in other contexts. A substantial body of knowledge now rejects the subordination model of agriculture in economic development as conceptually incorrect as well as observably harmful to the economic fortunes of countries that have pursued such a model. Therefore, the use of price policy to favour industrial growth over agricultural growth is no longer widely advocated. This does not mean that the subordination approach has totally disappeared: no doubt it still continues to influence the thinking of some bureaucrats and politicians in developing countries.

The other objectives can be divided broadly into three groups – those related to output, those related to stabilisation, and those related to income distribution – and they are discussed under those headings in the section on the impact of price policies below.

A final point on objectives concerns the difference between stated objectives and actual objectives, *explicit* objectives and *implicit* objectives. Without being unduly cynical it must be accepted that government leaders everywhere sometimes find it convenient to display a commitment, in words, to a particular path of action without necessarily matching it with concrete deeds. Conversely, they also sometimes find it convenient not to make too much noise about courses of action that they are actually pursuing. Therefore, the declared goals of farm price policy may not be accurately representative of price interventions actually implemented. This distinction is useful when investigating price policies.

Instruments of price policy

Farm output prices can be altered by government intervention in many different ways. Instruments are grouped here according to their type of impact on the level and stability of farm prices. The description of price policy instruments is followed by some observations concerning the interaction between instruments, and the relationship of instruments to objectives:

Trade policy instruments

These affect domestic agricultural prices by operating on the prices or quantities of either imports or exports. They include:
  (a) import taxes or subsidies, which increase or decrease domestic prices by raising or lowering the cost of imports in domestic currency;
  (b) quantitative restrictions on imports, which raise the domestic price above the import price;
  (c) export taxes, which are taken out of the fob export price and which lower the domestic price passed back to producers.

Exchange rate policy

The official conversion rates between the national currency and foreign currencies have a major impact on the domestic prices of tradeable agricultural commodities, and this impact is the same in direction for both import substituting and export commodities. A higher exchange rate (i.e. *less* domestic currency can be purchased for a given amount of foreign currency) results in a lower domestic currency equivalent of the world market price for both food and export crops. Conversely, a lower exchange rate (i.e. *more* domestic currency for a unit of foreign currency) results in a higher domestic currency equivalent of world market prices.

Taxes and subsidies

In addition to import or export taxes, already mentioned, farm output price levels can be affected by many types of domestic tax or subsidy imposed at differing points in the marketing chain. Some examples are:
  (a) local government levy on producers when they sell through specified marketing agents, this levy being deducted from the farm-gate price;
  (b) tax on the unprocessed commodity at the point of entry into processing;
  (c) consumption tax levied on the commodity in wholesale markets or at retail outlets;
  (d) consumption subsidy applied to the commodity at retail outlets, either generally or for specific retail outlets selling food to target groups of consumers;

(e) deficiency payment to producers in which they are paid a variable subsidy to cover the difference between a target farm-gate price and the actual farm-gate price obtained, where these differ.

Direct interventions

In addition to fiscal or exchange rate policies, governments frequently seek to influence prices by direct controls on the price formation, marketing, and storage of agricultural commodities. These controls require the creation of public marketing agencies in order to secure control over part or all of the marketed supply of designated commodities (see Chapter 5). Some common direct controls are as follows:

(a) marketed output confined to sale through state channels at fixed prices, these often being uniform fixed farm-gate prices announced in advance of the crop season;

(b) a variant of the same idea involves the enforced procurement by the state of all or part of the farm output at a fixed price;

(c) fixed or maximum retail prices for staple foods, with supplies being confined mainly to state outlets and penalties for illegal pricing by private retailers;

(d) fixed minimum prices to producers (floor prices) linked to state procurement from the market of all supplies offered at the floor price;

(e) fixed floor prices to producers and ceiling prices at wholesale or retail, linked to the operations of a buffer stock authority which buys at the floor during the harvest season and sells at the ceiling price at times of seasonal shortage.

Although these categories and lists of instruments cover many different types of intervention influencing farm price levels, they are by no means exhaustive since variations on them can be found at work in one country or another. For example, some countries have used multiple exchange rates in order to convert prices of farm commodities at an exchange rate different to that applying to other imports and exports in the economy. A higher exchange rate for agricultural crops means that domestic prices are lower for them than for other tradeable commodities, a policy clearly favouring industrial investment above agricultural investment. In other countries, price policies can be found that discriminate between different types of farm production unit, for example the output from the peasant sector is subject to a lower price than the output from the commercial farm sector.

It is unusual to discover a situation where only one or even just a few of these instruments are in operation at any one time. Much more common is to find that farm prices are being manipulated by a whole array of policy instruments, some of which may be pulling in different directions. This occurs for two main reasons: (a) new instruments are implemented without removing previous instruments in existence, and (b) different government departments are responsible for legislating different instruments, and coordination between them may be rather less than perfect. Thus trade and tax policies are usually determined by the Central Bank or the Ministry of Finance, while direct farm price interventions are devised and implemented by the Ministry of Agriculture. Whether these two sets of institutions coordinate adequately in setting the levels and direction of policy instruments is an open question.

Some types of policy instrument have proved more popular in certain regions of the world than others. Floor and ceiling price arrangements are common in Asia and South-East Asia. Fixed prices and state control over procurement have been popular in Sub-Saharan African countries. Multiple exchange rates have been used in some Latin American countries. Overvaluation of the exchange rate has occurred widely across developing countries in all three continents.

The links between objectives and instruments may be more, or less, direct depending on the tendency for instruments to multiply beyond their original intentions. The direction of the price effects of trade, tax and subsidy policies should say something about the objectives that brought such instruments into being, but not necessarily so. Many instruments have price or income stabilisation as an explicit goal (this applies especially to fixed price and floor price regimes), but the act of fixing prices can have much wider implications depending on the criteria used to determine price levels, and the way these criteria are applied over time. Alternative criteria for price fixing are the aspect of price policy to which we now turn.

Criteria for determining price levels

Having decided to intervene in the level and trend of farm prices, certain rules or guidelines are needed in order to determine minimum, maximum, fixed prices or acceptable price ranges. Even if the only instrument applied is a per cent tax on imports or exports, some sort of guideline is still required to determine the appropriate level of such a tax.

The literature on price policy recognises five different economic criteria or groups of criteria that can be brought to bear on price policy decisions. There is obviously a close relationship between objectives and criteria chosen: in some cases the objectives may on their own restrict choice between criteria for price level determination. The following paragraphs list the main criteria together with notes concerning their scope, validity and popularity in price policy analysis:

Cost of production criterion

Cost of production has in the past been one of the most popular criteria for price level determination. Its use has been widespread where fixed prices or floor prices are used as instruments of price policy. Cost of production seems especially applicable for deciding the floor price of staple food crops in locations or countries that are to some degree insulated from world prices by high transport costs or other barriers.

Expressed in simple terms, the cost of production criterion states that the level of the farm-gate price for a crop should be related to its average cost of production. However, a number of refinements are required in order to turn this basic idea into a workable criterion (Krishna, 1967: 518–19):

(a) the cost of production must be for a 'normal' year or for a moving average of three to five years;

(b) it must be the average total cost of production including valuation of land and labour at going market prices, not just the average variable costs of production;

(c) the average cost should be calculated from sample cost data for the main bulk of peasants using improved technology, not for low technology peasants nor for high technology commercial farmers.

A floor price fixed at the average total cost of production for improved technology peasants will ensure for them a market rate of return to their family labour and land. For higher cost low technology peasants it will provide an incentive to adopt new technology, and for commercial farmers it should provide an adequate surplus or profit as an incentive to increase marketed supply.

The cost of production criterion focuses on private rather than social returns to farm production (Ahmed, 1988a: 62). Its merits are that it is grounded in the real economic conditions of the majority of peasants, and that it provides a definite link between farm incomes and farm prices.

Its main defects are: *first*, it is sometimes difficult in reality to identify a majority group of representative farmers; *second*, costs of production can vary so greatly across farmers and locations that a simple average may be meaningless; *third*, some costs like cash rents for land vary with farm-gate price and therefore may cause a circular upward spiral in cost and price levels; and, *fourth*, prices fixed according to this criterion may cumulatively diverge from world prices at official rates of exchange.

Border price criterion

The border price criterion stems directly from the notion – already discussed in Chapter 3 – that world prices represent a country's short run opportunity costs (see also Timmer, 1986a and Ahmed, 1988a: 56–62). It focuses on social welfare and on economic efficiency, rather than on the private returns and private efficiency of the cost of production criterion.

Some definitions are useful. The term *border price* means exactly what it says: it is the world price at fob (free on board) for exports, or at cif (cost, insurance and freight) for imports, converted into domestic currency at the official exchange rate. This border price typically needs to be adjusted in order to bring it into comparison with domestic prices like retail prices, wholesale prices or farm-gate prices. When adjusted to the farm gate by subtracting marketing and processing costs, the resulting world prices are called *export parity* and *import parity* prices for export commodities and import commodities respectively. A useful description of the calculation of export or import parity prices from world prices is given in Gittinger (1982: 78–83).

Provided that a commodity is definitively either in excess supply (an export commodity) or in deficit (an import commodity), then export parity or import parity prices provide an unambiguous – though not entirely unproblematic – guide to world price opportunity costs. A problem of definition arises, however, for commodities that are broadly in self-sufficient supply, and for which there may be exports in good years and imports in bad years. The gap between export parity and import parity prices for such commodities may be very large, meaning that world prices provide no precise guide to appropriate domestic price levels.

An example of this feature is provided by staple grain prices in southern African countries. Here, the distance from main grain markets, coupled with inadequate shipping facilities and high cost land transport systems, means that import parity prices may routinely be some three or four times the level of export parity prices (Koester, 1986). For example, maize imported from the USA might have an import parity value of $300 in the centre of Zambia, while maize from the centre of Zambia destined for the USA (assuming such trade were to take place) would have an export parity value of $80. While these countries may represent an extreme in this regard, the same problem always exists in varying degrees for a staple grain in roughly self-sufficient supply. Another factor that is relevant here is that quality differences between domestic and world traded grain reduce the effective world price for domestic exports, and thus widen the export parity/import parity gap.

Although this would appear to pose problems for the border price criterion, in practice other factors to do with the history and strategic role of the crop in question are likely to help resolve the ambiguity either in one direction or the other. For example, the promotion of self-sufficiency in domestic staple grains is typically associated with goals of food security and foreign exchange saving. Excess supplies occur irregularly in years of especially good crops, and neither the quality of grain produced nor the distance from potential markets suggests that the country should become a permanent exporter. In this kind of situation the import parity price is evidently the correct guide to domestic price policy. In cases which remain ambiguous, a simple average of import and export parity prices would retain the spirit of the border price criterion.

A final point in this area of import and export parity prices is that the gap between these two sets of prices can be altered by changes in trade patterns. For example, in the case of the southern African countries referred to above, the gap is much wider if one is referring to grain trade with the industrial countries than it would be by reference to grain trade between countries within the same region.

Use of the border price criterion does not mean slavish adherence to the short-run level of world market prices, and there are few economists that would prescribe such a course of action. World prices for many agricultural commodities are notoriously volatile, and for staple food crops in particular such price instability would be unacceptable for producers and consumers, and destabilising for the macro economy and society at large. The rate of inflation in poor countries tends to be especially sensitive to upward price movements in basic foods, and is not that easily reduced when food prices fall.

Thus the world price used for the border price criterion should be a moving average world price for a type and quality of the commodity comparable to domestic production. The aim is to avoid cumulative divergence from long run opportunity costs, rather than to treat the immediate world price as a sacred totem. Even then there remain some difficulties with this criterion and these are considered briefly as follows (Ahmed, 1988a: 58–62):

(a) The domestic equivalent price of a given world price depends on the exchange rate. Since the aim of price policy based on border prices is to represent opportunity cost and comparative advantage, it may be necessary to use a shadow exchange rate in order to convert world prices to domestic equivalents. Shadow exchange rates are usually obtained by adjusting the official exchange rate for the difference between domestic inflation and international inflation when the former is higher than the latter (Tsakok, 1990; Ch.2).

(b) Internal marketing and processing costs that are deducted from the border price to derive import parity or export parity farm-gate prices may vary significantly for different locations, types of producer, and processing technology. The border price criterion in reality yields an array of farm-gate prices, with high variability around the average. The only way around this problem is to adopt a commonsense approach similar to that advocated for the cost of production criterion. The average parity price should be chosen for the majority type of farmer for which it is intended to guarantee a floor or fixed price.

(c) Finally, from the viewpoint of forward planning, medium- and long-term price projections have proved to be extremely inaccurate predictors of future world prices. The projections most commonly used by price policy units around the world are those provided on a regular basis by the World Bank under the title *Price Prospects for Major Primary Commodities*. For four or five years ahead these projections may be 100 per cent or more off the mark, and even near-term predictions for two years ahead have been found to be adrift, on average, by 30 to 40 per cent (Ahmed, 1988a: 61).

These points demonstrate that the border price principle is more elegant in theory than in its application to concrete price policy problems. In practice it is found that border prices, like other criteria, provide a *point of reference* for work on appropriate price levels rather than a definitive guide to such price levels. Of course, if government controls are abandoned altogether, including taxes, subsidies, floor and fixed prices, then border prices become the arbiter of domestic price levels as a consequence of moving to the free trade position. However, then also, the destabilising effects of world price fluctuations would be continuously felt through the domestic economy.

Terms of trade criterion

The terms of trade criterion refers to the trend of farm output prices relative to the prices of inputs and consumer goods that farmers purchase from the industrial sector. The terms of trade refers to agricultural output as a whole, not to individual crops, and therefore this criterion refers to the general level of farm-gate prices, not to relative price levels between outputs. The terms of trade is calculated by dividing an index of prices received by farmers by an index of prices paid by farmers for inputs and consumer goods.

The aim of the terms of trade criterion is to monitor the comparative level of prices between agriculture and industry. As with border prices, the intention is not necessarily to adhere closely to annual changes in these relative prices, rather to ensure that a cumulative divergence does not occur between farm and non-farm price trends as a result of price policy interventions. There may also be a deliberate policy intention either to reduce farm prices relative to industrial prices (as in the subordination model) or to raise farm prices relative to industrial prices (in order perhaps to redress a past disadvantage experienced by agriculture).

The terms of trade under consideration here is what is called the price terms of trade or the net barter terms of trade (because it compares price trends). It is also often called the 'rural–urban terms of trade' or the 'intersectoral terms of trade'. In the 'classical' literature on agriculture in economic development, the rural–urban terms of trade was considered a most important factor influencing the rate of capital accumulation and growth in each sector. For example, in the Soviet Union in the 1920s a mechanism called the 'scissors' was devised by which enforced procurement of grain from farmers at low prices was accompanied by high prices for the goods that farmers purchased from the industrial sector.

An example of a terms of trade analysis in a price policy context is given in Table 4.1. This refers to the evolution of farm-gate prices and incomes for crops sold through official marketing channels in Tanzania during the 1970s and 1980s. The example is used to illustrate some points about the use of the terms of trade criterion in price policy work as follows:

(a) Construction of a weighted index of farm-gate prices is not that easy.Farm-gate price data are not always available or accurate, and the weights, which should equal the share of each commodity in the total marketed value of all commodities may be difficult to obtain due to data unreliability. The best bet is to focus on a few crops of major strategic importance.

(b) A reliable index of prices paid by farmers for inputs and consumer goods is rarely available. The general consumer price index (CPI) must often be used instead, and this is likely to be based on urban rather than rural prices. It is also not likely to contain the prices of farm inputs like fertilizers and pesticides.

(c) A common error is to take food prices out of the CPI on the grounds that food itself should not enter the prices facing food-producing farmers. This is wrong because the retail price for food in rural areas represents the opportunity cost to farmers of deciding to market rather than retain food output. The retail price for food is also in a very real sense what farmers have to pay for food when they are in seasonal or permanent food deficit.

Table 4.1. *Tanzania: Terms of trade by crop categories 1970–1985[a]*

Year	Weighted real price indices, 1970 = 100.0[c]					Consumer price index (NCPI)
	Staple grains (3)[b]	Drought crops (3)[b]	Oilseeds (4)[b]	Export crops (7)[b]	All crops (17)[b]	
1970	100.0	100.0	100.0	100.0	100.0	100.0
1971	96.4	113.3	98.2	91.0	92.1	104.7
1972	83.3	109.8	89.4	89.3	88.8	112.7
1973	80.0	113.5	94.0	83.4	83.5	124.5
1974	74.8	129.8	80.0	72.0	73.1	148.4
1975	79.9	116.8	82.4	63.1	66.1	187.7
1976	112.2	131.5	97.8	95.3	97.7	200.6
1977	105.5	144.9	103.1	109.8	109.4	223.8
1978	103.9	151.5	124.9	82.1	86.5	249.3
1979	91.4	139.9	113.6	71.3	75.4	283.6
1980	82.8	107.4	89.2	64.4	67.6	369.5
1981	72.1	85.5	78.3	58.7	61.0	464.2
1982	78.4	69.5	70.2	56.9	59.9	598.6
1983	74.4	76.4	70.2	53.6	56.7	760.4
1984	69.7	73.0	66.6	50.9	53.8	1034.9

Notes: [a] Prices on which these series are based are official farm-gate prices for crop sales through state marketing channels. [b] Figures in brackets under the sub-headings are the number of crops in each group. Staple grains – maize, paddy, wheat; drought crops – sorghum, bulrush millet, cassava; oilseeds – groundnuts, sesame, sunflower, castor; export crops – cardamon, cashew, coffee, cotton, pyrethrum, tea, tobacco. This list is not exhaustive of producer prices fixed by government, but it contains almost all crops subject to price policy from the late 1960s to the mid 1980s. [c] Weighted price indices in money terms, deflated by the NCPI given in the last column. Weights are based on Fisher's ideal formula, and are the geometric mean of the share of each crop in the total value of all crops for the periods 1970–72 and 1980–82.
Source: Ellis (1988b: 74)

(d) Choice of base year for a terms of trade time-series can drastically alter the conclusions reached about the trend in the terms of trade. Selection of a year of unusually high farm prices (perhaps due to drought) would make it appear as if the terms of trade falls over time. A 'normal' year or an average of several years should be used as the base year of the series.

(e) The price terms of trade is arguably an inadequate measure of trends in relative profitability between agriculture and industry because it takes no account of output or productivity trends in the two sectors. A more accurate measure is the *income terms of trade* which compares gross income flows into agriculture (price × quantity) with the prices paid by farmers.

The net barter terms of trade is best seen as another *reference point* in a composite picture that is built up concerning appropriate levels of agricultural prices. The absence of such a reference point can be disastrous, as illustrated by the case-study given in Table 4.1. In Tanzania in the period 1970 to 1984 there was a failure to take domestic inflation into account in the fixing of producer prices for crop sales through state marketing channels. The consequence was that the price terms of trade fell by 46 per cent over this period (Ellis, 1988b).

Multiple parity criteria

The border price and the terms of trade are two types of *parity* criteria for deciding levels of floor or fixed prices. The word 'parity' simply means 'equal to' and so the border price criterion demands equality to world prices, and the terms of trade criterion demands trend equality to industrial prices. The cost of production criterion is not a parity criterion in this sense. It nevertheless embodies some notion of equality since the intention is to give farmers a price sufficient to cover the cash costs of production and to provide the same returns to land and to family labour as the market prices of those factors of production in the wider economy.

There are several other parities that can be brought into the price policy decision. For example, the Agricultural Prices Commission in India takes into account (i) intercrop price parity, (ii) input–output price parity, (iii) parity between raw material and finished product, and (iv) parity between prices received and prices paid by farmers, in addition to (v) cost of production, and (vi) intersectoral terms of trade (Kahlon & Tyagi, 1983: 162–246; Sarma, 1988: 157–61).

Intercrop parity refers to relative output prices between crops (for example, maize/paddy price ratio); input–output parity refers to output/ variable input price ratios (for example, the paddy/fertilizer price ratio in rice production); parity between raw material and finished product refers to the ratio of manufactured price to raw material price (for example, cotton textile/raw cotton price ratio); and parity between prices received and price paid by farmers refers to the farm-gate price divided by the price index for inputs and consumer goods purchased by farmers. This differs from the terms of trade only in that it is done on a single crop by crop basis instead of trying to describe relative price trends for the sector as a whole.

The likelihood that this array of considerations could be properly assimilated within a typical price policy unit in a developing country seems rather remote. There is too much information to digest, and no systematic way of prioritising certain parity criteria above other criteria. Even in India, which has extensive experience in these matters, it was found that 'the various criteria . . . were applied and emphasized in an uncoordinated way. . . . They were never integrated into an objective model to compute the price to be recommended' (Krishna & Raychaudhuri, 1980: 5).

Equality of income-earning opportunities within different types of farmers and between farm and non-farm households seems implicit in many of the parity criteria listed above. However, sometimes *income parity* enters the parity approach as a leading criterion in its own right. For example, the EEC Common Agricultural Policy (CAP) was founded largely on the idea that those obtaining their livelihood from the land should enjoy the same living standards as urban dwellers. In this instance, an income parity criterion dominates over other criteria, and prices are set so as to comply with income objectives.

The chief debate concerning criteria for fixing the floor price of staple grains has been between advocates of the cost of production criterion (Krishna, 1967; 1984) and advocates of the border price criterion (World Bank, 1986b; Timmer, 1986a). At the time of writing the tide of history is in favour of the latter rather than the former criterion.

Impact and effectiveness of price policy

In this section we consider briefly the impact and effectiveness of price policy instruments in three main areas: increasing farm output, stabilising prices and incomes, and influencing income distribution. Several examples of measuring the welfare gains and losses from price policy instruments like import or export taxes were given in Chapter 3, and these are not repeated here.

Whether price policy is the most effective instrument for achieving desired goals depends on comparisons with alternative instruments. For example, an output increase desired for a particular crop might be achieved by (i) an increase in its output price, (ii) a reduction in its input prices, (iii) research into higher yielding varieties, or (iv) investment in an irrigation scheme. Similarly, income stabilisation for farmers may perhaps be achieved by stabilising farm-gate prices, but might be achieved more efficiently by growing crops with more stable yields in the face of climatic variations.

Price policy and farm output

The critical features in considering the output impact of price policies is to distinguish aggregate farm output from individual crop output. In addition, for staple food crops, it is useful to think through the impact of higher prices on the proportion of total output that is sold in the market. The concern here then is *first* with aggregate farm output, *second*, with individual crop output, and *third*, with household decision-making in the semi-subsistence food producing peasant household.

Some preliminary definitions are necessary since terms like 'output', 'supply' and 'marketed surplus' are sometimes confused. Output always refers to the total production of the farm or farm sector. The proportion of the output that is sold in the market is sometimes referred to as the 'marketed surplus' (i.e. the surplus above the consumption requirement of the household) and sometimes as the 'market supply'. These two terms are equivalent. The quantity retained by the household for home consumption is called the 'subsistence' quantity.

The response of aggregate farm output to changes in the general level of farm prices is likely to be low in the short-term, rising only gradually in the longer term. Estimated short-run output elasticity values range between 0.1 and 0.3, rising to between 0.4 and 0.6 in the medium or longer term (say three to five years). In other words, a 10 per cent increase in real farm-gate prices can be expected to result at best in about a 2 per cent output increase in the short term and a 5 per cent rise in the long term.

The reason for this is that some farm resources (land and fixed capital) and technology are fixed in the short term, but can be increased or made more productive in the longer term. It means that price policy is rather a blunt instrument for effecting growth in total farm output. Other longer-term policies such as research policy and irrigation investment are likely to have a more powerful direct effect on growth. This does not mean that positive farm prices can be neglected for aggregate output growth – undoubtedly they are essential – rather that not too much can be expected from changing the general farm price level alone.

By contrast, changing relative prices between individual crops can have dramatic effects on the intercrop composition of total farm output, and on the marketed supply of individual crops. A substantial literature has established the price responsiveness of peasant farmers to changes in single crop prices (e.g. Helleiner, 1975; Askari & Cummings, 1976). The degree of this responsiveness depends on the type of crop and on the scope for intercrop substitutability at farm level in terms of climate, soils, and other resource constraints.

For perennial tree crops (e.g. coffee, cocoa, rubber, and so on) the price response of output is subject to lags of several years. However, for many annual crops, especially short-season grains and pulses, intercrop substitution can be rapid and large for small changes in market price, provided that some degree of confidence surrounds the new output price ratios. For example, in Tanzania, the marketed supply of drought crops (millets, sorghum and cassava) rose by over 600 per cent in three years when the state decided to provide a guaranteed outlet for such crops at fixed prices (Ellis, 1982: 271–2).

Major food staples represent complications when assessing the likely impact of output price changes, and it is here that factors specific to peasants are most evident. The impact of a staple food output price rise involves complex trade-offs between competing objectives in the peasant household. The price rise is an incentive to higher output, but it also increases income, which may lead to increased home consumption. In formal economic terms there is a positive substitution effect in production (the output response to a price increase is expected to be positive), but a negative substitution effect opposed to a positive income effect in consumption. This makes the market supply response of a semi-subsistence household indeterminate in theoretical terms (Nakajima, 1986: 197).

In practice, the market supply response of staple foods in peasant economies has been found to be almost always positive, although it may sometimes be low (Timmer *et al.*, 1983: 158). Many other factors than just the farm-gate price decide the proportion of the total output that is sold in the market, and food security is often one of the most important of these. In general, the more smoothly and predictably the markets for inputs and outputs work the more likely will peasant producers commit themselves to market transactions.

Where markets fail or disintegrate due to state ineptitude, economic collapse or civil war then peasants are observed to retreat into the safety of subsistence and to withdraw from market exchanges in inputs and outputs. In such situations it may be better to have no price policy at all than one the implementation of which aggravates, rather than alleviates, the market failures in the rural economy at large.

Price policy and stabilisation

Stabilisation is one of the oldest and most common reasons given for state intervention in agricultural markets, and it features strongly in the agricultural policies of the industrial countries as well as developing countries. Free markets in farm products are notoriously prone to volatile price changes. These occur due to variability in the nature conditions of farm production (rainfall, winds, floods, pests, diseases) and due to the lag between planting decisions and the harvesting of the output. An account of price instability in agricultural markets, including cobweb models, can be found in a number of sources (e.g. Tomek & Robinson, 1981: Ch.9).

Governments seek to stabilise prices for several reasons (Timmer, 1989). On the production side the aims are to reduce risk, increase marketed supply by reducing the necessity for peasants to rely on their own output, and stabilise farm incomes. On the consumption side the aims are to ensure stable wage costs for the non-farm economy, and to protect the urban poor from malnutrition or starvation. The price of a country's staple grain tends to receive special attention in these respects.

The simple analytics of price stabilisation can be examined using the partial equilibrium methods advanced in Chapter 3. Figure 4.1 displays the case where price instability is caused by supply variability. The intersection of the supply curve (not shown) with the demand curve oscillates between point A and point B. The price is stabilised at the mid-point of the two extremes by the operation of a buffer-stock authority. The figure may be interpreted in three steps as follows:

(a) If a deficit supply situation develops, and supply falls to Q_2 – i.e. the price would have risen to P_2 – sales are made from the buffer stock to keep the price at P_e.

Consumer surplus gain $= a + b$
Producer surplus loss $\ = a$

Buffer-stock income $= d + g$ (from sales)

(b) If a surplus supply situation develops, and supply rises to Q_1 – i.e. the price would have fallen to P_1 – purchases are made by the buffer stock to keep the price at P_e:

Consumer surplus loss $= c + d + e$
Producer surplus gain $= c + d + e + f$
Buffer-stock costs $= e + f + h$ (from purchases)

(c) The summary position of these welfare and resource changes is as follows:

Buffer stock cancels out: $d + g = e + f + h$
Consumer surplus loss: d (because $c + e = a + b$)
Producer surplus gain: $d + e + f$
Net welfare gain: $e + f$ (accrues to producers)

Thus the conclusion is that price stabilisation yields a net social welfare gain. Moreover, when price instability is caused (as in Figure 4.1) by supply shifts rather than demand shifts, producers gain and consumers lose, but producers would be able to compensate the consumers and still come out ahead.

Figure 4.1. Welfare effects of price stabilisation when supply shifts.

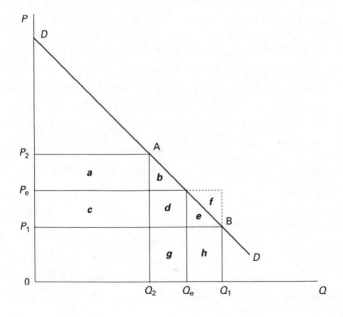

Some economists regard this as an oversimplified picture giving a spurious welfare gain. The purported gains can be reduced or made to vanish by altering the shape or slope of the demand and supply curves. Moreover, the model assumes costless storage. When the costs of operating a public buffer-stock authority are taken into account, including storage and administration, the purported social welfare gains soon disappear. A solution to this is to make flexible use of imports to assist with price stabilisation, thus reducing the scope and cost of buffer-stock operations.

One further point often raised in the context of price stabilisation is whether it stabilises or destabilises farm incomes. It can be shown for the supply instability case considered above, that if the elasticity of demand is above 0.5, producer incomes fluctuate more with stable prices than with unstable prices (Ahmed, 1988b: 1037; Schmitz, 1984: 18–20). At the level of the farm, rather than total supply, this depends on whether a farmer is a deficit or surplus food producer (Lipton, 1980: 9–13). Peasants who are food-deficit gain from price stabilisation, but those who are surplus food producers may experience more income instability, depending on their elasticity of demand for output.

Debates between economists about the costs and benefits of price stabilisation can become very intricate even for a single commodity market (Newbery & Stiglitz, 1981). The view here (and also argued in Timmer, 1989) is that a degree of price stabilisation almost certainly yields positive social benefits for commodities, such as main food staples, the prices of which can affect major macroeconomic and social variables. However, the most efficient choice needs to be made amongst the various alternative instruments of stabilisation, and for staple foods greater use of imports rather than domestic stocks to equilibriate the domestic market would in many cases reduce the long-run costs of stabilisation.

Finally, it is incorrect to think that stability, whether of prices or of incomes, is solely dependent on price policy instruments. Stabilisation of crop yields in the face of climatic variation is an important alternative, and this comes about through research and technology policy rather than from price policy.

Price policy and income distribution

Governments often invoke income distribution as a reason for price intervention. In the industrial countries, farm income considerations are paramount in determining the instruments of policy and the level of farm prices. In developing countries it is more likely for the incomes of urban consumers to feature strongly in farm price decisions. However, other objectives, such as narrowing regional income disparities or raising the incomes of poor farmers growing particular types of crop, are also sometimes encountered.

To discover the income distribution effects of particular types of price intervention it is necessary to go behind the gross income transfers that are measured in the partial equilibrium analysis of policies. The concepts of producer surplus and consumer surplus do not measure income distribution effects. Producers and consumers must be distinguished between more accurate social categories: landless labour from peasants, food surplus peasants from food deficit peasants, sharecroppers from leasehold farmers, rich consumers from middle-income and low-income consumers (Mellor, 1978).

To unravel the income distribution effects and side-effects of farm prices is beyond the scope of this chapter. The following is a selective list of main points, given space limitations, and relates only to the price of a staple food like rice or maize:

(a) peasants are not the only rural dwellers, and they vary greatly between each other as well as differing from other rural households;

(b) higher food prices directly benefit only food surplus farmers, and they reduce the real incomes of landless labourers and food-deficit farmers;

(c) amongst food surplus farmers, higher prices increase the incomes of those with a large marketed surplus more than those with a small marketed surplus, with the pure commercial farmer gaining most of all;

(d) these effects depend in part on whether high prices are imposed from outside (production staying the same) or are caused by a decline in production (due perhaps to drought);

(e) when the latter occurs the income effects depend on whether prices rise more than, the same as, or less than the fall in supply;

(f) if prices rise more than the fall in supply (implying inelastic demand) then farmers who have remained in surplus will gain, while all those who have become deficit producers will lose, the extent of the loss depending on how much grain they need to buy in;

(g) urban consumers are not homogeneous either, they are usually divided for purposes of investigation into at least three and often more income groups;

   (h) the effect of higher food prices is most severe on poor consumers who spend a large proportion of their income on food;

   (i) the proportion of income spent on food declines with rising incomes, and this means that higher food prices cause a lower proportional decline in real incomes for richer consumers.

These points show that food price changes have manifold effects on income distribution which are difficult to trace and to measure. This provides an argument for *not* using farm output prices for generalised and poorly specified income distribution goals, but rather having special programmes for special cases. Evidently, price stabilisation schemes must choose price levels or ranges that achieve some sort of balance concerning income effects on different major social groups, but beyond this price policy is an imprecise instrument for pursuing income distribution objectives.

Lessons of price policy experience

Agricultural price policies were a popular topic of research in the 1980s and a considerable amount of empirical work was undertaken to assess their working both on a global scale and with respect to individual countries. The World Bank conducted various cross-country comparisons of price intervention effects (Bale & Lutz, 1981; Lutz & Scandizzo, 1980; Scandizzo & Bruce, 1980) as well as doing research on individual countries (Tolley, Thomas, & Wong, 1982), and synthesising price policy evidence from diverse sources (World Bank, 1986b). In addition, evidence from many case studies became available in this period, for example, from Tanzania (Ellis, 1982; 1983a), India (Kahlon & Tyagi, 1983), Indonesia (Timmer, 1986b), Kenya (Jabara, 1985), Mozambique, Tanzania, Zambia and Zimbabwe (Harvey, 1988).

The cross-country comparisons of price policy undertaken by the World Bank used the same partial equilibrium analysis and summary ratios for measuring price intervention effects as set out in Chapter 3 above. Nominal and effective protection ratios were calculated for a large number of countries – though not always with an eye to great accuracy (Westlake, 1987) – and net social welfare losses were calculated using the concepts of producer and consumer surplus.

The results of the cross-country studies suggested that there was a tremendous bias against agriculture in the price policy practices of most developing countries. It was concluded from this that the poor agricultural output performance of some developing countries, especially in Africa, could be attributed to bad price policy. The result was widespread advocacy of the dismantling of price policy interventions, a process that has occurred in varying degrees in some countries, often under pressure from external aid donors.

Some lessons to be derived from past price policy experience in developing countries are set out in the following paragraphs. These take into account price policy successes as well as failures, and they are not predicated on the free market fundamentalism which has been prevalent in writing about this topic in contemporary times:

Proliferation of instruments

It is true that price policy instruments tend to be piled one upon another over time often with scant regard to their compatibility in contributing to specified goals. This may occur due to competing aims of different state agencies, for example the interest of the Ministry of Finance in tax revenues, or of the Ministry of Agriculture in higher output, or of a Marketing Board in a wide marketing margin. It follows that successful price policy requires a single unit, like the Agricultural Prices Commission in India or BULOG (for food crops) in Indonesia, which is recognised by all other agencies as having *the* dominant coordinating responsibility for price policy formulation.

Limited intervention

Price policy should be limited to a few commodities of strategic importance either as staple foods or export earners (Krishna, 1967: 517). This is partly because governments and state agencies are limited in their capacity to process, digest, and act on information received. It is also because the more commodities included in a price policy the more complex the effects and side-effects of the relationships between them, and this complexity multiplies for each additional commodity covered.

Exchange rate overvaluation

Exchange rate overvaluation has been proven to have major detrimental effects on farm price levels in a great number of countries.

Inflation

State agencies are observed to have great difficulty in taking systematic account of inflation in price policy decisions, and a widespread tendency is observed to discuss proposed price changes in nominal rather than real terms.

Producer prices as residual

Prices set according to the border price criteria can still result in distorted farm-gate pricing if producer prices are regarded as a residual by deducting the costs of an inefficient monopolistic state marketing agency from the border prices.

Floor prices versus fixed prices

Floor prices linked to minimal state involvement in the purchase and sale of commodities seem to work much better than fixed prices which maximise the purchase and sale of commodities by state agencies.

Lack of criteria

Many governments do not in fact apply any objective criteria to price policy decisions, which are instead made according to political expediency and half-baked personal whims. It follows that at least one or two criteria properly formulated and systematically applied are better than no criteria at all.

Inadequate data

Data flows on farm costs, farm-gate prices, and market prices are often inadequate for the proper monitoring of a price policy system, as well as for the proper working of private markets.

Price policy and women

Price policies seldom, if ever, take women into account. But the effectiveness of price policy in achieving stated goals may be influenced by gender considerations at the level of the household. Moreover, price policy may have impacts on the livelihoods of women that are ignored or unanticipated in their formulation. Several different possibilities can be distinguished:

(a) women's time allocation can be a constraint on the price responsiveness of output where there is limited substitutability of male and female labour time;

(b) low farm prices cause households to use less hired labour, thus reducing employment for women from landless households, and vice versa for high farm prices;

(c) price-induced switches in cropping patterns may change the balance of labour inputs, or land use, or incomes, between men and women;

(d) price policy is used to promote crops, for example export crops, for which men have greater control over resources and incomes than women, thereby reducing the economic independence and options of women.

The existence of gender-related impacts in the price policy arena does not necessarily mean that these can be taken into account in price policy. For one thing, price policies usually apply countrywide, and many different – perhaps even opposing – gender effects may occur for the same price policy in different peasant communities within a country. For another, there may be overriding economic criteria in the approach to farm prices (e.g. border pricing), which make gender an issue that it is not possible to address in price policy. Nevertheless, a heightened level of gender awareness in policy circles remains relevant for price policy, because examples can arise where the gender effects of a proposed change in relative prices are inescapable.

Summary

1. This chapter examines various facets of output price policy in developing countries within the objectives–constraints–policies framework. The chapter covers the objectives, instruments, criteria, effectiveness, and lessons of price policy.

2. Three primary objectives of price policy are identified, these being *first*, to increase agricultural output, *second*, to achieve desired changes in income distribution, and *third*, to influence the role of the farm sector in overall economic development.

3. There exist many different instruments that the state can use to influence the level and trend of farm prices. Most instruments can be assigned to the four categories of *first*, trade policy, *second*, exchange rate policy, *third*, tax and subsidy policy, and *fourth* direct interventions such as floor prices and fixed prices. It is pointed out that direct price interventions also require the advent of state marketing or buffer stock institutions in order to substitute the market in varying degrees.

4. The chapter discusses the main types of criterion that have been advocated for deciding price levels when floor or fixed prices are part of price policy. The four main criteria are *first*, cost of production criterion, based on the full average production cost for a designated majority type of farmer, *second*, border price criterion, *third*, terms of trade criterion, and *fourth*, multiple parity criteria involving comparisons between many different

types of prices and price ratios. The relationship between border prices and parity prices is discussed. Terms of trade concepts and problems are also covered in some detail.

5. The impact and effectiveness of price policy is discussed with respect to increasing farm output, stabilising farm prices and incomes, and pursuing income distribution objectives. For farm output and market supply responses the crucial distinction is made between the aggregate agricultural sector sensitivity to price changes and the price responsiveness for individual crops. The latter can be very high, even in the short term, and even when the aggregate response is quite low due to resource and institutional constraints.

6. Price stabilisation is examined and the points are made: *first*, that simple partial equilibrium analysis indicates welfare gains from price stabilisation; *second*, that whether farmer incomes are stabilised when prices are stabilised depends on the origin of price fluctuations and the elasticity of supply; and *third*, that the administrative costs of stabilisation may outweigh the simple calculation of social gains and losses such that stabilisation must be considered as a public goal that merits subsidy from government to achieve its purpose.

7. The impact of farm prices on income distribution is discussed, and the main point is made that producers and consumers cannot be regarded as homogeneous entities where interpersonal incomes are concerned. Prices affect the incomes of peasant households differently according to whether they are near landless, food deficit, or food surplus; and urban consumers differently according to their levels of income. Farm output prices are an imprecise and inefficient instrument for achieving general and widespread income distribution objectives. Their use is better restricted to alleviating the food purchase problems of designated groups at risk of malnutrition or starvation (see Chapter 13 below).

8. The chapter briefly summarises the experience and lessons of price policy interventions as they have been written about in numerous papers, reports and books. Lessons are identified concerning proliferation of price policy instruments, limiting the scope of price policy, exchange rate overvaluation, taking inflation into account in price fixing, avoiding the residual determi-

nation of producer prices, floor prices versus fixed prices, lack of criteria, and data inadequacies.

9. The position of women with respect to price policies is briefly considered, and the reader is referred to Chapter 12 for a comparative summary of the gender dimensions of agricultural policies.

Further reading

Amongst the policies covered in this book, price policy has one of the biggest recent literatures due to the interest displayed in the topic during the 1980s. With regard to earlier material, Krishna (1967) is a classic article covering the objectives, criteria, and supply response aspects of price policies; and Mellor (1968) is useful on the economic roles of farm prices. More recent works covering the goals, instruments, and criteria of price policies are Tolley *et al.* (1982: Ch. 1), Ahmed (1988a), Streeten (1987), and Timmer (1986a). The last is especially recommended for setting out the border price criterion with admirably clarity. Accessible papers for the non-economist on price stabilisation are Timmer (1989) and Knudsen & Nash (1990).

Useful country case-studies written during the past decade include, on Tanzania, Ellis (1982); on Korea, Bangladesh and Thailand, Tolley *et al.* (1982); on India, Kahlon & Tyagi (1983) and Sarma (1988); on Fiji, Ellis (1984); on Kenya, Jabara (1985); on Indonesia, Timmer (1986b) and Ellis (1990); on Mozambique, Tanzania, Zambia and Zimbabwe, Harvey (1988); on Malawi, Harrigan (1988); and on Malaysia, Pletcher (1989).

Reading list

Ahmed, R.U. (1988a). Pricing Principles and Public Intervention in Domestic Markets. In *Agricultural Price Policy for Developing Countries*. ed. J.W. Mellor and R.U. Ahmed, Ch. 4. Baltimore: Johns Hopkins.

Ellis, F. (1982). Agricultural Price Policy in Tanzania. *World Development*, **10**, No. 4.

Ellis, F. (1984). Relative Agricultural Prices and the Urban Bias Model: A Comparative Analysis of Tanzania and Fiji. *Journal of Development Studies*, **20**, No. 3.

Ellis, F. (1990). The Rice Market and its Management in Indonesia. *IDS Bulletin*, **21**, No. 3.

Harrigan, J. (1988). Malawi: The Impact of Pricing Policy on Smallholder Agriculture 1971–1988. *Development Policy Review*, **6**, 415–33.

Harvey, C. (ed.) (1988). *Agricultural Pricing Policy in Africa*. London: Macmillan.

Jabara, C.L. (1985). Agricultural Pricing Policy in Kenya. *World Development*, **13**, No. 5.

Kahlon, A.S. & Tyagi, D.S. (1983). *Agricultural Price Policy in India*. New Delhi: Allied Publishers.

Knudsen, O., & Nash, J. (1990). Domestic Price Stabilization Schemes in Developing Countries. *Economic Development and Cultural Change*, **38**, No. 3.

Krishna, R. (1967). Agricultural Price Policy and Economic Development. In *Agricultural Development and Economic Growth*, ed. H.M. Southworth and B.F. Johnston, Ch. 13. New York: Cornell.

Mellor, J.W. (1968). The Functions of Agricultural Prices in Economic Development. *Indian Journal of Agricultural Economics*, No. 1.

Mellor, J.W. & Ahmed, R.U. (1988). *Agricultural Price Policy for Developing Countries*. Baltimore: Johns Hopkins.

Pletcher, J. (1989). Rice and Padi Market Management in West Malaysia, 1957–1986. *The Journal of Developing Areas*, **23**, 363–84.

Sarma, J.S. (1988). Determination of Administered Prices of Foodgrains in India. In *Agricultural Price Policy for Developing Countries*, ed. J.W. Mellor and R.U. Ahmed, Ch. 9. Baltimore: Johns Hopkins.

Streeten, P. (1987). *What Price Food? Agricultural Price Policies in Developing Countries*. London: Macmillan.

Timmer, C.P. (1986a). *Getting Prices Right: The Scope and Limits of Agricultural Price Policy*. New York: Cornell University Press.

Timmer, C.P. (1986b). The Role of Price Policy in Rice Production in Indonesia 1968–1982. In *Research in Domestic and International Agribusiness Management*, ed. R.A. Goldberg, pp. 55–106. Greenwich, Conn: JAI Press.

Timmer, C.P. (1989). Food Price Policy: The Rationale for Government Intervention. *Food Policy*, **14**, February.

Tolley, G.S., Thomas, V. & Wong, C.M. (1982). *Agricultural Price Policies and the Developing Countries*. Baltimore: Johns Hopkins.

5

Marketing policy

Marketing policy

This chapter sets out the main components that are required in order to think systematically about agricultural marketing, and to assess the objectives, instruments and impact of policies by which states intervene in marketing systems. There are close links between this chapter and the preceding one, since certain types of price policy, for example fixed prices or floor and ceiling prices, require the intervention of state marketing agencies in order to be implemented.

The chapter begins by introducing various concepts and methods commonly encountered in the policy analysis of agricultural marketing. It then proceeds as follows:

(a) to set out some main *objectives* of state intervention in agricultural marketing systems, including links to price policy aims and instruments;

(b) to describe the different types of policy *instrument* commonly chosen by governments in order to achieve stated or unstated objectives with respect to the marketing of farm output;

(c) to examine selected topics in the *policy analysis* of marketing systems, including analysis of marketing margins, measuring market integration, and analysis of price versus state impacts of buffer-stock operations;

(d) to consider some of the main *lessons* from the experience of developing countries in marketing interventions, with special focus on the problems of parastatal agencies in crop marketing;

(e) to consider rather more broadly the status of *peasants* with respect to marketing systems, and factors which are overlooked in the interaction between peasant producers and private marketing agents;

(f) to make some observations concerning the role of *women* in agricultural marketing systems, and the impact of policies upon that role.

Concepts in the study of marketing

The marketing of farm output is typically thought to play a dual role. One dimension is the transmission of price signals between consumers and producers. For example, an increase in demand for pineapples causes prices to rise in an urban centre and this information is passed back to producers through the marketing system. The other dimension is the physical transmission of the commodity from points of production by farmers to points of purchase by consumers.

The physical movement of the commodity from farmer to consumer itself has three further dimensions, and it is recognition of these that is the cornerstone of many types of policy analysis of marketing. The marketing system transforms the commodity in *time, space,* and *form,* which means that the consumer is able to buy the commodity (i) at a different time from its harvest and sale by farmers, (ii) at a different place from its point of sale by farmers, and (iii) in a different form (e.g. maize flour) compared to its sale by farmers (e.g. maize grain).

Each of these dimensions has special attributes of its own, which distinguish one from the other, and which between them describe the range of activities that are involved in crop marketing.

The *time* dimension refers to all aspects of storage across seasons (interseasonal storage) and across years (inter-year storage). Storage has costs and risks. Storage costs consist mainly of the money tied up in the stocked commodity (interest charges), the quantity and quality losses of commodity in store that rise over time, and the accounting costs (depreciation, etc.) of capital invested in storage facilities. Storage is risky because future prices may not rise sufficiently to compensate for the costs involved. In many countries household storage by peasants is an important proportion of the total volume of interseasonal storage.

The *space* dimension refers to all aspects of the transport of commodities from location of sale to location of final purchase. Transport distances may be local (to nearby village markets), medium distance (to provincial centres), or long distance (to capital cities or ports of export). Distances and costs depend on the location of surpluses and deficits, and on the commodity (for example light versus bulky commodities, durable versus perishable commodities). Like storage, transport involves risks concerning price differences between origin and destination, and, for perishables, the condition of the commodity on arrival. These risks are much greater in situations of disintegrating infrastructure, shortages of fuel and spare parts, commodity movement restrictions, and related difficulties.

The *form* dimension refers to all changes in the physical attributes of the commodity between farmer and consumer. It includes not only direct processing (e.g. milling) but also cleaning, sorting, labelling, packaging, canning and so on. The form dimension varies greatly between commodities, and is also the one that changes most as development proceeds due to changing demand patterns as incomes rise. For fruit and vegetables, alterations of form can be minor (cleaning and grading perhaps), but for cereals, for example, the form can vary from minor processing e.g. brown rice) to refined and packaged supermarket products (pasta, cakes, biscuits). The costs, and therefore the margins, involved in changes of form can therefore vary over a wide range.

The overall difference between the purchase price of a commodity by consumers and its sale price by producers is called the *marketing margin*. The marketing margin covers all three dimensions of marketing and can therefore sometimes be usefully thought about as the sum of a seasonal margin, a spatial margin, and a form margin respectively. However, it is rare for these dimensions to be observable in such a simple threefold scheme, except when one particular dimension is being investigated in depth. For example, the spatial dimension may involve several movements – separated in time and form – from farm to village market, from village store to mill, from mill store to wholesale market, and from wholesale market to retail shop.

For this reason, marketing systems are more typically thought of as vertical commodity systems or marketing channels, in which the commodity passes through a sequence of stages or events. The main sequential stages in a marketing system commonly identified are:

(a) *primary procurement* (sometimes also called 'assembly'), in which the commodity is purchased from farmers and assembled at local village, or district level stores, or mills;

(b) *processing,* in which the commodity is milled or otherwise transformed prior to onward distribution;

(c) *wholesale,* in which the commodity changes hands in bulk at wholesale markets; and

(d) *retail,* in which the commodity is sold to its direct consumers;

(e) where a commodity is destined directly for export, the fob *export* stage replaces the wholesale stage.

A bewildering array of actual movements and changes of ownership are often involved in these vertical marketing stages. Figure 5.1 provides an illustration for the case of rice marketing in Indonesia. The government of Indonesia operates a floor price for paddy and a ceiling price policy for rice, and the state procures around 5 per cent of total output, equivalent to 1.5 million tons of rice, at the floor price. Farmers sell their paddy to small paddy traders or to contract harvesters (called *penebas*) who purchase the crop standing in the field. Paddy also enters the market system via the traditional harvesting arrangement whereby harvest labour receives a physical share of the total harvest (the *bawon* system). Small traders may be acting independently or may be procuring paddy on a commission basis for intermediaries or for millers.

If market prices are at or near the floor, rice from millers is delivered into the state procurement system. Quite a large proportion of this rice is 'laundered' through cooperative institutions, which on paper are the preferred agents for state procurement and which receive a small premium above the floor price for their deliveries. In periods when the market price is above the floor, rice is freely traded in the private system, and flows in diverse ways from millers, to rice traders, to wholesalers or urban markets, to retail, and to consumers. The farm-gate share of the retail price is typically in the range of 80–85 per cent.

The state disposes of rice held in public store in two ways. First, it sells rice on the open market in order to defend a rice ceiling price in the lean season. This is called 'market operations'. Second, the state supplies rice rations to the civil service, parastatal employees, and the military. This is called 'budget group' distribution.

An important more general point arising from this kind of complexity is the meaning that can be attached to market price data collected by government agencies and compiled as official price statistics. The reliability of such prices depends partly on the proportion of total trade volume that is exchanged at an open market price. This tends to be reasonably accurate for retail prices and wholesale prices where the commodity changes hands in market centres or in shops. However, the prices paid to producers or the prices into-mill are much less reliable because they often involve complicated transactions between parties who may be related by credit and other obligations, and which are not openly announced.

A particular problem in this respect attaches to so-called 'farm-gate' prices. Official 'farm-gate' price series are often not producer prices at all, they are instead prices for the small proportion of the unprocessed

Figure 5.1. Rice marketing channels in Indonesia. Source: Author's own fieldwork and Mears (1981: 106).

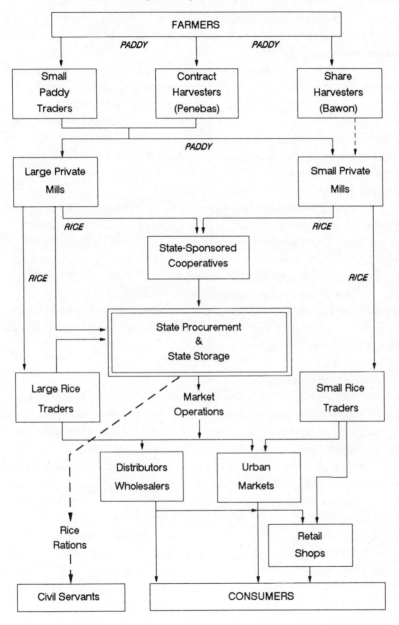

product (e.g. paddy or maize grain) that is transacted openly in local village markets where prices can be easily collected. These prices may be inaccurate as a measure of the average level or dispersion of prices received by farm households, even though trends in them may roughly follow farm-gate price trends.

A final set of ideas related to marketing channels are those concerning the analysis and measurement of the functioning of the system. For marketing channels to work efficiently in a neo-classical economics sense, there should be numerous traders operating at every different level of the system, and information should be freely available to all participants. The approach used by economists to try to capture how closely actual marketing systems approximate to this is called the *structure–conduct– performance* approach.

The threefold emphasis here is on *first* the structure of marketing channels, i.e. the number, size, and diversity of participants at different levels; *second,* the conduct of marketing enterprises, i.e. the reliability, timeliness, quality control, standardisation, and so on by which market- ing activities are undertaken; and *third,* the performance of the market- ing system as a whole, i.e. the speed and accuracy of price adjustments through the system, the stability of prices and margins, the technical and allocative efficiency of each stage, and the accuracy and adequacy of information flows throughout the system.

Objectives of marketing policy

The objectives of government intervention in agricultural mar- keting are closely related to perceptions about the structure, conduct and performance of private marketing channels. Also important are the links between marketing interventions and other objectives, especially those of price policies. The view that private traders are able to exploit farmers or consumers by the exercise of local monopoly power is widely prevalent as a reason or an excuse for marketing interventions. The objectives most commonly advanced for government marketing policies are as follows:

(a) *To protect farmers or consumers from parasitic traders.* This is the age-old reason for marketing interventions, based on the idea that middlemen are able to extract monopoly profits from their position between scattered and ill-informed producers, on the one hand, and captive consumers, on the other hand. According to this view, the marketing margin is wider under typical systems of private trade than would be possible either with a truly competitive marketing system or with a state-run marketing system. Most governments have opted for the latter rather than the former solution to the purported problem. This can be explained sometimes by the predominance of ethnic minorities in trading activities (e.g. Asians in East Africa, Chinese in Java, etc.), making exclusion of them an undeclared aim of state policy in this area.

(b) *To stabilise or increase farm-gate prices.* Output price policies designed to stabilise or increase producer prices may require state marketing interventions to achieve their aims. This certainly applies to fixed producer prices which can only be implemented if all marketed output is sold through the same channels. Even with lesser degrees of intervention there is often an implicit view that private traders have a destabilising effect on prices due to hoarding and speculation. The advent of state systems of floor and ceiling prices linked to buffer stocks is designed to place limits on instability caused by such reasons.

(c) *To reduce the marketing margin.* This links to the first objective stated above. The state may intervene specifically to narrow the gap between consumer and producer prices. There are various instruments available to this end as we shall see shortly. Reducing the size of the gross marketing margin may be part of trying to raise producer prices by increasing the producer share of a given retail or export price, or it may be related to trying to reduce urban food prices for consumers.

(d) *To improve quality and minimum standards.* A common objective of marketing interventions is to try to raise the quality of farm output, especially for export crops which confront rigorous quality norms in international markets. Quality control and minimum standards are often considered as regulatory rather than as direct intervention functions of governments, but this distinction may not always be apparent in the practical implementation of quality standards.

(e) *To increase food security.* Food security is often put forward as an important reason for marketing intervention. Originating in the first reason above is the idea that private traders take advantage of incipient food shortages to buy up and hoard grain for speculative purposes. The argument goes that this behaviour, while rational enough for the traders involved, exacerbates food shortages and increases price instability. Therefore, means must be implemented for avoiding these detrimental effects on national food security.

Instruments of marketing policy

Governments of developing countries have used many different instruments to influence the working of agricultural marketing channels. These range from attempts to replace private channels almost entirely by state institutions, through partial involvement of state bodies, licensing of approved traders and processors, and minor regulatory functions concerning quality standards, grading and hygiene. The following list describes various types of intervention without going into a lot of detail on the specific forms each type can take:

(a) *Monopoly parastatals.* This category includes all those government-owned institutions that represent some form of monopoly control over one or other stage of the marketing system. It includes marketing boards, which are widely prevalent throughout the developing countries, especially for traditional export crops such as coffee, tea, cocoa, rubber, tobacco, and so on. Organisations in this category vary in the number of stages of marketing in which they may be involved. At one end of a wide spectrum they may handle just the final sale to foreign buyers at fob export, while also regulating the way the export price is passed back down the marketing chain and policing of the relevant quality standards involved. At the other end they may handle all stages of marketing, processing and final sale from the producer to the consumer or to export. In some countries, crop parastatals have also been responsible for crop development functions including input subsidies, crop-specific research, credit provision, extension work, and so on.

(b) *Non-monopoly parastatals.* This category includes a wide range of different institutions that provide one particular channel, but not the exclusive channel, through which crop sales by peasants are transferred to consumers. The predominant form of non-monopoly parastatal is the state buffer-stock authority for staple food grains. The tasks of such an authority are to implement floor and ceiling prices for major food grains. This is done by buying in all grain offered by farmers or traders at a 'floor price' or 'delivery price', and by selling grain out of public store in order to prevent retail market prices from going above an agreed ceiling. There are many different ways this basic idea of keeping prices within a preset range can be implemented in practice.

(c) *Farmer cooperatives.* This may seem a strange category to include amongst 'state marketing interventions', but alas marketing cooperatives are rather rarely devised and run by farmers themselves; it is more common for them to be invented by the state and to be staffed by government appointees. Marketing cooperatives are usually found in conjunction with one or other of the parastatal systems already listed. Their typical task is to undertake the primary procurement (assembly) stage of marketing, for onward delivery to licensed processors or to designated parastatals. Sometimes it is compulsory for all farmers in a particular location, or growing a particular crop like coffee or cocoa, to belong to the designated cooperatives.

(d) *Trader licensing.* Where the state does not itself take direct responsibility for marketing, it sometimes tries to control the private trade by licensing designated enterprises. Licences are both a source of state income and a threat. The source of income is the licence fee, often supplemented by the bribes needed to secure the licence in competition with other traders. The threat is the loss of the licence if the trader is perceived not to be playing the game according to the way that state officials wish to see it played.

(e) *Instruments to improve market conduct and performance.* There are three distinct types of instrument within this category of intervention. The *first* is the provision of improved information to marketing system participants. This includes news services on market prices and other market information that can be readily summarised in newspapers, on the radio, or on television. The *second* is the regulatory function of setting and enforcing quality standards, weights and measures, and hygiene regulations. The *third* is provision of marketing facilities such as floor spaces in towns and villages for retail and wholesale markets, auction rooms, weighing equipment, and so on. To some degree this is a type of public infrastructure investment, but as such it needs to be distinguished in cost and scope from really big public investments such as roads, railways, electricity grids, and so on.

(f) *Instruments to improve market structure.* The various types of state marketing enterprise already listed above under (a) and (b) are often described by those who have decided on that type of intervention as improving market structure. However, a different sense in which improving market structure could be interpreted is to increase the amount of competition in the marketing system by encouraging new private entrants at each level of the system. This has not been the preferred method of increasing marketing efficiency in developing countries. However, it is becoming a more popular method under pressures for deregulation by external agencies like the World Bank or the IMF. The most effective means of increasing participation and reducing barriers to entry appears to be for the government to provide credit or seed money to enable new entrants to get started (Abbott, 1987: Ch.3).

To summarise the discussion above, most instruments are seen to fall into two main categories. The first category, and by far the most prevalent one until relatively recently in most developing countries, is the substitution of private trade by state marketing agencies. Of the various

different types of these, monopoly marketing boards have been especially prevalent in Sub-Saharan African countries, and buffer-stock type
authorities have been prevalent in Asia and South-East Asia. These
differences are clearly not accidental and reflect diverse historical back-
grounds in terms of trading traditions and marketing policies extending
back into the colonial period.

The second category is the support of improvements in the functioning
of private trade with only minimal state intervention. This was not the
preferred alternative of most governments until budgetary and other
constraints as well as severe marketing failures began to force a rethink of
previous policies from the mid-1980s onwards.

Policy analysis of marketing systems

The performance of marketing systems is subject to routine
monitoring and analysis in all developing countries, though the degree of
detail and the methods by which this is done vary enormously. Data on
the prices of staple foods in major urban areas are almost always
collected, and this may be supplemented by the routine collection of data
on other prices at different points of the marketing chain for food and
export crops. In matters of data collection and analysis there are close
links between the type of price policy being implemented and the scope of
state involvement in marketing channels. The implementation of a floor
and ceiling price policy, for example, requires timely and accurate data
on short-term trends in producer and consumer prices for representative
locations throughout the country.

Analysis of price and margin data follows the space, time, and form
dimensions of marketing systems. A considerable amount can be learned
about the functioning of a marketing system by examination of trends in
prices and marketing margins for different locations and for different
crops. Some typical types of analysis undertaken with price and margin
data are as follows:

(a) Examination of seasonal price trends and margins, this corresponding to the time dimension of marketing. For a single price, like the
wholesale price of a staple grain, variations in price level between surplus
and deficit seasons reflect the functioning of interseasonal storage operations either in the private sector or the state sector or both combined. If
these variations are significantly larger in one part of a country than
another, this may indicate problems that require further investigation. If
they are getting larger over the years, then either private storage is
becoming less competitive or public stabilisation efforts are becoming

less effective. In either case more research is indicated to discover the causes of observed trends.

(b) Examination of spatial price trends and margins, this corresponding to the space dimension of marketing. Differences in margins for places which vary in distance from markets should, at a given point in time, reflect transport cost differences. Typically, for a given wholesale or retail price in a major urban centre, producer prices will vary according to distance from the market. However, this variation may be dampened or even eliminated by the implementation of spatially uniform fixed or floor prices. Again, as with seasonal trends and margins, inspection of spatial price information for the same crop in different locations or different crops in the same location can reveal much about the working of the marketing system and the effectiveness of state marketing policies.

(c) Examination of the overall marketing margin. Many aspects of the functioning of marketing systems can be explored via the overall margin between the retail (or export) price and the farm-gate price. *First,* there is seasonal variation in this margin, a facet already discussed under paragraph (a) above. *Second,* there is variation in the viability of different types of institution operating within the same marketing margin. For example, public marketing agencies may be making losses where private ones make profits, or perhaps the private ones operate within a larger margin by buying and selling at unofficial prices (parallel markets). *Third,* there is variation over time, and this can be very revealing. For example, in a study of the gross marketing margin for six export crops in Tanzania, it was discovered that the producer share of the sale price had fallen from 70 per cent to 41 per cent over a ten-year period (Ellis, 1988b: 78). The figures are reproduced as Table 5.1. The main reason for the declining share was that state parastatal monopolies were absorbing an even larger share of the marketing margin in an attempt to cover a spiralling increase in the unit cost of their marketing operations.

Methods for analysing prices, margins, and trends are described in detail with many numerical examples in Goetz & Weber (1986), which also contains an excellent bibliography on methods of marketing analysis. It is proposed here to review briefly five topics in the policy analysis of crop marketing which reveal in different ways the kinds of policy problem that arise in this area and the method used to examine them. The five topics are:

(a) analysing the impact on farm-gate and retail price levels of changing the size of the marketing margin;

(b) examining the impact of an export tax on the retail price of an export commodity;

(c) measuring the degree of marketing integration, i.e. the efficiency of the marketing system in transmitting prices between consumers and producers in space and time;

(d) understanding what occurs to prices and margins when there are seasonal reversals of commodity flows between rural and urban areas; and

(e) analysing private versus public participation and costs of inter-seasonal storage when the state performs buffer-stock operations.

Impact on prices of changing the margin

The gross marketing margin between producer and consumer prices can be changed by the state in several different ways. One way is to impose, eliminate, or vary the level of a sales tax, for example a retail sales tax or a producer levy per kilogram sold. A second way is to reduce transport costs, say by opening a new trunk road or reducing the price of

Table 5.1. *Marketing margin for export crops 1970–1980[a]*

Year	Producer value		Marketing margin		Export value
	T.Shs m.	%	T.Shs m	%	T.Shs m
1970	620.2	70.5	259.1	29.5	879.3
1971	626.1	67.9	296.3	32.1	922.4
1972	676.9	65.5	357.0	34.5	1033.9
1973	720.2	63.1	421.8	36.9	1142.0
1974	680.0	47.4	755.3	52.6	1435.3
1975	851.3	51.9	788.6	48.1	1639.9
1976	1148.7	61.1	730.7	38.9	1879.4
1977	1585.7	46.4	1831.5	53.6	3417.2
1978	1264.1	44.5	1575.6	55.5	2839.7
1979	1214.4	45.0	1481.3	55.0	2695.8
1980	1403.6	41.2	2001.9	58.8	3405.5

Notes: [a] Crops covered are cardamon, cashew, coffee, cotton, pyrethrum, smallholder tea, tobacco. Producer value refers to volume marketed through official channels, multiplied by state fixed farm-gate prices. Export value is the same volume multiplied by fob export prices. The marketing margin is the difference between producer and sales value, and represents all income flows not returned to farmers. Currency is the Tanzanian shilling (T.Shs).
Source: Ellis (1988b: 78).

fuel. A third way might be to reduce storage costs by offering private storage agents credit terms at subsidised interest rates.

The gross marketing margin is represented on a supply and demand diagram (Figure 5.2(a)), by the price difference when supply and demand

Figure 5.2. (a) Marketing margin in terms of supply and demand. (b) Result of narrowing the margin.

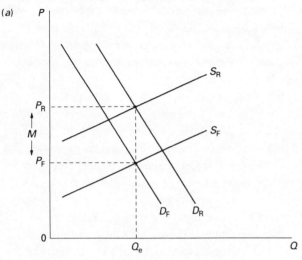

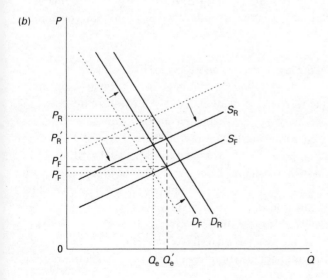

at the farm level (S_F and D_F) are equated at the same quantity as supply and demand at the retail level (S_R and D_R). In Figure 5.2(a) the equilibrium quantity is Q_e, and the gross marketing margin (M) is P_R minus P_F. This diagram assumes linear demand and supply curves, and margins that stay the same over every range of quantity. These assumptions may not be very realistic but this is not important for grasping the basic analysis involved.

The impact of a reduction in the margin can be represented by the retail supply curve (S_R) moving closer to the supply curve at farm level (S_F), and the farm level demand curve (D_F) moving closer to the retail demand curve (D_R). This is shown in Figure 5.2(b), where the change of position of those two curves is shown by the arrows. It is clear from this diagram that the producer price has fared differently from the retail price after this change. More specifically, there has been a relatively small increase in the producer price, from P_F to P'_F, and a much larger decline in the retail price, from P_R to P'_R. If we were to pursue the analysis by comparing producer and consumer surplus before and after the change (see Chapter 3) we would find that consumers had gained more than producers by narrowing the margin.

The reason for this result is that, as drawn on Figure 5.2, the supply curve is more elastic than the demand curve. This result can be generalised, and it turns out that (i) if the elasticity of demand is lower than the elasticity of supply, consumers gain more than producers from a change in the marketing margin, (ii) if both elasticities are approximately the same they share the gain equally, and (iii) if the elasticity of demand is higher than the elasticity of supply, producers gain more than consumers from the change.

Impact on the retail price of an export tax

In the preceding example, margins were drawn as if they remained constant irrespective of quantity levels or absolute levels of prices. In practice, margins do not behave in this way, and different components of the overall marketing margins are likely to behave in different ways. Margins can be fixed, as in a fixed per unit tariff of $0.10 for transporting a bag of maize from A to B; they can vary with throughput due to economies of scale, as might happen if a given milling capacity is more highly utilised; or they can take the form of a percentage mark-up as is typically observed for retail margins.

The way in which margins vary can have important implications for policies designed to alter the distribution of gains in vertical marketing systems. An example is provided by the case of an export tax policy on banana exports adopted jointly by the Central American banana exporting countries in the mid-1970s. The basic data are given in Table 5.2. At that time the export price of bananas was around 10¢ per kg and the retail price in the United States import market was around 35¢ per kg.

The exporting country governments decided to impose an export tax of 5.5¢ per kg, and part of the economic argument surrounding this decision was that the tax would be passed on to consumers as a fixed amount, thus raising the consumer price to 40.5¢, an increase of 16 per cent with supposedly negligible effects on banana demand. At the same time the exporting countries would achieve at a stroke a substantial increase in their proportional share of the retail price, from 28.5 per cent to 38.3 per cent.

As shown in Table 5.2, the governments of the banana exporting countries were incorrect in their supposition that the banana margin between export and retail was fixed in absolute terms.

When the dust had settled on this tax – a fascinating case-study of conflict between developing country states and multinational fruit companies – the overall margin between export and retail was proportionally the same as before the imposition of the tax. The marketing margin remained roughly proportional because its main components – the retail margin, the wholesale margin, and shipping – were either customarily in percentage terms or contained a percentage mark up within them. This story can be found partly in Ellis (1983b), and partly in FAO (1986: 8–11).

Measuring market integration

As already mentioned, market integration refers to the transmission of price signals across geographical space and over time. The performance of marketing systems in this respect is considered important because efficiency and competition depend on accurate, timely, and

Table 5.2. *Banana export tax in Central America 1974–77*

Prices/margins	Before tax	After tax	
		Intended result	Actual result
fob price (US¢/kg)	10.0	15.5	15.5
Share of retail price (%)	28.5	38.3	28.5
Retail price (US¢/kg)	35.0	40.5	54.0

available price information. The process by which prices tend to be equalised across space, allowing for transport cost differences, is called spatial arbitrage. The word 'arbitrage' refers to the continuous process of direction and redirection of commodities by traders in order to take advantage of price variations in different locations.

An integrated market is one in which spatial arbitrage works well. The opposite is a fragmented or segmented market, in which either barriers to commodity movement or failures of information result in price differences being greater than transport costs, or in prices moving in different directions at the same moment in time. Note that a market can be integrated without necessarily being connected by physical commodity flows at a particular point in time. Prices in different locations may for reasons of good information adjust rapidly in line with each other even in periods when there is little commodity flow between them because they are individually in supply–demand balance. Thus the term connection refers to the existence of physical commodity flows, and while this is usually thought of as being an important part of market integration, occasions can arise where markets that are integrated are nevertheless disconnected for short periods.

The conventional method way of measuring market integration is to see whether or not prices (e.g. wholesale prices) in two or more locations move closely in line with each other or not. The usual method is to undertake correlations between price time-series in pairs of markets. A correlation coefficient of 1.00 is taken to indicate perfect market integration, while correlations approaching zero would indicate increasing degrees of market segmentation. Several well-known past studies employed this method to test for the efficiency and competitiveness of marketing channels in India and West Africa (Lele, 1971; Jones, 1972).

This method suffers from several potential defects as argued in a critical paper by Harriss (1979). First, prices in different locations or districts may move in line with each other not due to spatial arbitrage but because similar patterns of events may be common to them, such as rainfall patterns or the incidence of drought. Second, prices in two segmented locations may move in line with each other not because they influence each other, but because they are both influenced by a third location, for example a major grain-deficit city. Heytens (1986) argues that this does not negate integration, it merely corresponds to the distinction between market integration and market connection that we made above. Third, price series may move in line with each other due to general economic trends such as the countrywide rate of inflation. Clearly correlation analysis, or any other method for measuring market integration, should use deflated prices corrected for inflation, not current money prices.

The study of price correlations remains the simplest method for finding out whether price information is transmitted between locations. However, an alternative method that overcomes its weaknesses has been proposed (Ravallion, 1986) and tested (Heytens, 1986; Timmer, 1987). This method involves using regression analysis applied to lagged price variables to test how quickly price changes in one market cause price changes in other markets, and thus the speed of transmission as well as its accuracy is captured by the measures proposed. The interested reader is referred especially to Timmer (1987) for an accessible account of this method.

Commodity flow reversals

One occurrence that could upset the attempt to measure market integration is when the flow of a staple food commodity reverses direction between urban and rural areas (Timmer, 1974). This can happen, for example, when an overall food-deficit country fixes a ceiling price for the food staple which it defends by the release of stocks or by imports sold in the main urban centre.

Figure 5.3(a) displays what would normally occur to the marketing margin in the absence of state intervention. The vertical axis measures the price levels of a staple food. The horizontal axis measures time, T, over an interval that begins with the main annual crop harvest, H_0, and ends with the next main harvest, H_1.

Rural and urban prices increase more or less in parallel as the country approaches its season of maximum grain deficit just before the next harvest. This is the trend shown between time H_0 and time t_1 along the horizontal axis. When the harvest begins to come in at time t_1 both prices begin to decline and they continue to decline until the next season of maximum supplies on the market at time H_1. In this case urban prices are always above rural prices and the flow of grain is always from the surplus rural to the deficit urban area.

Now assume that the state intervenes to set a ceiling price for the food staple, and that it defends this ceiling price mainly with imports (food aid shipments, for example) sold in urban areas (Figure 5.3(b)). The urban price can now only rise until it hits the urban ceiling price (at time t_1). Since rural prices continue to rise, reflecting the cost of storage in rural areas, the marketing margin for moving the grain from country to city is squeezed, and it is no longer viable to move the commodity from country to town. At this point the state must take full responsibility for supplying the urban area. The rural price continues to rise until a large enough margin above the urban ceiling price is opened up to encourage a reverse

Figure 5.3. (*a*) Seasonal rural and urban prices without intervention.
(*b*) Impact of an urban ceiling price.

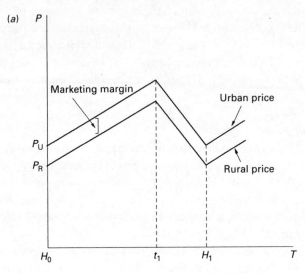

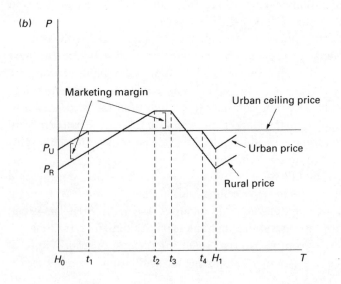

flow of grain from city to country (at time t_2). When the new harvest begins to come in (at time t_3), rural prices decline, taking away the reverse margin, and resulting in re-establishment of the normal margin (at time t_4).

Note that in this model, there are two periods during the crop cycle – given by sub-periods t_1 to t_2 and t_3 to t_4 in Figure 5.3(b) – in which there are no physical flows of the commodity between rural and urban areas because no margin exists that would make such flows viable for private traders. In these sub-periods the markets are temporarily not connected, but they are still integrated in the sense that traders are acting on price information which is freely and quickly available through the system.

This is one example that illustrates the impact of a policy instrument such as a ceiling price on the extent of state involvement in the market for a staple grain, and on the direction of commodity flows in space and time. In this case, the ceiling price causes the state to become entirely responsible for provisioning the urban population during a significant part of the annual crop cycle. Another example follows.

State versus market in interseasonal storage

The other major consideration in state implementation of a floor and ceiling price regime is its impact on the balance between private and public interseasonal storage (Timmer, 1986a: 63–6). Three components of this impact are worth examining. These are: (i) the effect on the motivation for private storage, (ii) the extent of state involvement in the physical purchase, storage and sale of the commodity, and (iii) the cost of public storage.

Figure 5.4(a) displays in a simplified way what occurs when there is no price intervention and all storage is undertaken by private traders. The vertical axis measures prices and margins. Thus P_L (lowest price) is the price at which traders buy from farmers at the peak of harvest, P_H is the highest price of sale to consumers up to the next harvest, and $(P_H - P_L)$ is the maximum storage margin. The horizontal axis combines both quantity and time information in a single measurement, i.e. it represents the total quantity sold by farmers from harvest H_0 which then flows through the marketing system over the time period, T, up to the next harvest H_1.

Given these definitions, the gross revenue earned by farmers is the harvest price, P_L, multiplied by the total quantity harvested, $H (= T)$, and this equals the rectangular area, f, in Figure 5.4(a). The price to consumers rises in order to cover storage costs which cumulatively increase over time-period, T. The total cost of private storage (including

Figure 5.4. (*a*) Storage margin and private marketing. (*b*) Impact of state policy on state costs.

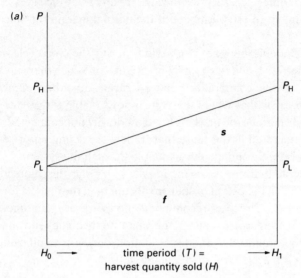

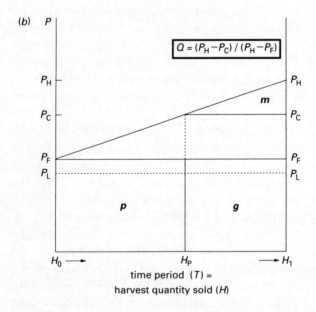

the competitive profits of storage agents) is given by the triangular area, *s*, in Figure 5.4(*a*). In other words it is given by $\frac{1}{2}H$ (half the total harvest quantity involved $\times (P_H - P_L)$ (the full seasonal price rise needed to store grain up to the next harvest).

$$s = \tfrac{1}{2}H \times (P_H - P_L)$$

Now suppose that the state intervenes in this staple food market by setting a floor price above the previous lowest price level obtained by farmers, at P_F (Figure 5.4(*b*)). Farmers receive an addition to their total revenue equal to area $(P_F - P_L) \times H$, assuming the same quantity sold at the higher price. The state also sets a ceiling price, P_C, which is lower than the previous maximum seasonal price to consumers. In other words, the state reduces seasonal price instability by narrowing the margin for interseasonal storage. The full seasonal unit cost of storage remains $(P_H - P_F)$, but a proportion, *Q*, of this is above the ceiling price and cannot be recouped by traders from market sales.

$$Q = (P_H - P_C)/(P_H - P_F)$$

Several consequences for private participation and government costs arise from this scenario. Private traders are now only prepared to procure the staple up to a volume that they know they can sell while still covering storage costs. The volume is given as $(H_P - H_0)$ in Figure 5.4(*b*), implying that private procurement has a farm-gate value equal to area *p*. The remainder of the harvest $(H_1 - H_P)$ must be procured by the buffer-stock authority at floor price P_F, thus requiring procurement finance equal to area *g*.

In addition, the state must re-imburse the buffer-stock authority a subsidy for the storage costs incurred above the level that is recouped by the ceiling price. This subsidy is equal to triangular area *m* in Figure 5.4(*b*):

$$m = \tfrac{1}{2}(H_1 - H_P) \times Q(P_H - P_F)$$

This expression can be reformulated with some interesting results. The geometrical properties of a right-angle triangle like $P_F P_H P_F$ in Figure 5.4(*b*) mean that the ratio $(P_H - P_C)/(P_H - P_F)$ – defined above as Q – must be the same as the ratio $(H_1 - H_P)/H$ which is the proportion of total volume (*H*) that now passes through state channels. Hence $(H_1 - H_P)$ equals $Q \times H$. Substituting this result into the above expression of *m* gives:

$$m = \tfrac{1}{2}(Q \times H) \times Q(P_H - P_F)$$

Therefore $m = s \times Q^2$

by substitution of the earlier definition of *s*.

Two important results flow from this analysis. The first is that if the ceiling–floor price margin ($P_C - P_F$) fixed by government is less than the competitive (efficient) market cost of interseasonal grain storage, then the state will experience an extent of participation in the crop market that will vary directly with the size of Q, the share of storage costs not covered by the margin. At the extremes when $Q = 0$, the private sector does all the marketing, when $Q = 1$, the state must do it all. Governments may sometimes unwittingly find themselves handling a much larger proportion of grain sales than had been intended, when pursuing a different objective, namely, the squeezing of the marketing margin in order to benefit producers or consumers.

The other result is that the subsidy costs of buffer stock operations varies with the square of the squeeze on the storage margin, Q. The relationship between margin squeeze and subsidy cost is not, as might be expected, a linear one, it is instead a power relationship. This means that subsidy costs spiral upwards, as the state margin between floor and ceiling prices for a staple grain becomes further adrift from real storage costs.

Lessons of marketing policy experience

There exist many studies of marketing systems in developing countries, including cross-country comparisons (World Bank, 1986b: 85–93; Ahmed & Rustagi, 1985), detailed investigations in particular regions (Lele, 1971; Jones, 1972), and country case-studies, for example, on Indonesia (Mears, 1981; Timmer, 1974), on Ghana (Southworth *et al.* 1979), on Tanzania (Ellis, 1983a; 1988b), on Bangladesh (Crow, 1989). There also exist several edited collections on marketing boards and parastatals (Arhin *et al.*, 1985; Hoos, 1979), and some articles on privatisation of marketing systems (in Christiansen, 1989).

It is useful to distinguish problems that are specific to parastatal marketing agencies from other lessons that can be derived from the experience of marketing interventions in developing countries. Marketing parastatals exist, in one guise or another, in almost all developing countries. They tend to exhibit certain features in common, and therefore tend to be prone to similar types of weakness, in most countries. Some common features and defects of marketing parastatals are as follows:

(a) They are set up as semi-autonomous bodies with supposedly independent decision-making capability in the domain of the tasks they have been set, for example the procurement and storage of a food staple, or the processing and sale of an export crop like coffee. However, they are rarely in practice permitted independent decisions: senior managers are usually political appointees and internal decisions are dominated by political expediency.

(b) They often operate within constraints determined by wider government policies, for example, farm-gate prices and retail prices which determine the margin within which they must operate, or exchange rate policies which determine the domestic currency equivalent of world market prices. These constraints may on their own ensure non-viability of the enterprise, especially if enforced losses or subsidies are inadequately recouped by central government.

(c) They must also follow state regulations in other respects, such as government conditions of service and salary scales, and these rarely promote a spirit of dynamism. They are more likely to invoke a spirit of income supplementation by misuse of the powers of office. Marketing parastatals have proved themselves to be prone to overstaffing, misappropriation of funds, dubious accounting practices and numerous similar defects.

(d) They are often prone to much higher overhead costs than would be incurred by private traders undertaking the same marketing functions. This may occur due to a legal obligation to provide the same service in many different locations irrespective of the costs involved. For example, in Tanzania in the 1970s separate monopoly marketing parastatals were created for six different export crops. Each parastatal had to create a countrywide infrastructure of procurement and transport facilities, all staffed permanently through the year, even though the harvest of an individual crop in a particular location might only last for two or three weeks. The absurdity of this situation was demonstrated by one local branch of the Tobacco Authority of Tanzania which had 15 permanent salaried employees and a truck in order to purchase 13 tons of tobacco leaf during two weeks each year (Ellis, 1983a: 234).

(e) Marketing parastatals are sometimes required to take on additional public-sector functions which they are not necessarily well adapted to undertake organisationally, and for which they are not adequately reimbursed by central government, thus reinforcing their financial overheads, and accounting weaknesses. Examples are preparation and implementation of externally-funded crop development projects, provision of subsidised crop inputs, credit provision, extension work, and crop-specific research.

(f) Marketing parastatals have been known to treat the farmers from whom they purchase as the residual recipients of whatever money is left when their unit costs are deducted from the unit crop sales value. This was true for the export crop parastatals in Tanzania in the 1970s and early 1980s, with the consequence that farmers received a lower and lower share of export prices (see Table 5.1 above). Since these unit costs were forever being inflated by non-marketing functions (as in (e) above), high overheads (as in (d) above), and misappropriated funds (as in (c) above), this was not exactly a desirable outcome of the way the border price criterion was applied in this case.

Marketing parastatals, especially monopoly marketing agents, have proved susceptible to major weaknesses and it is peasant crop producers (rather than consumers) who are typically placed at greatest disadvantage by these weaknesses. There have been, of course, exceptions to the typical experience. The Kenya Tea Development Authority, a parastatal with crop development functions, used to be cited as one (Lamb and Muller, 1982), and the Fiji Sugar Corporation in the early 1980s was another (Ellis, 1988c).

An examination of these, and other exceptions, shows that the basis of their success required some combinations of (i) genuine autonomy from government, (ii) management appointments on the basis of merit rather than political patronage, (iii) salary and reward structures different from civil service conditions, and linked to performance, (iv) capacity to dispense with the services of ineffective or corrupt personnel, (v) formal mechanisms for participation and feedback from farmers, (vi) an overseeing framework (e.g. a commodity council) independent of government, and containing balanced representation between growers, marketing agency, and government. Such attributes are rarely found united in a single state organisation, and it is doubtful whether an appeal to them can provide justification for parastatal forms of crop marketing, given the more general failures of this type of intervention.

The experience of developing countries in crop marketing intervention has other lessons than those associated with marketing boards or crop parastatals. One we have already noted is that attempts to squeeze the marketing margin below the true cost of carrying out marketing functions results in potentially large budgetary costs for the state, and a much larger degree of state intervention than may be strictly necessary in order to achieve certain objectives, like a realistic degree of price stability. A second is that misapplied marketing policies with respect to producer prices and marketing margins result in parallel markets, which defeat whatever was the intention of state control in the first instance. A third is that trader licensing causes an artificial barrier to entry into marketing, reduces competition, and is invariably associated with corruption, which causes the cost of licences to traders being much higher than the official fee.

The outcome of these considerations is that there are possibly quite a few cases where dismantling of state marketing systems would result in an improvement in marketing services – both for farmers and consumers – compared to state intervention. Certain case-studies have shown that the state can ensure floor prices to producers and relatively stable prices to consumers with fairly minimal direct intervention in the marketing system. For example, Indonesia achieved this for many years by state procurement of 5 per cent or less of production and by using imports to help balance the domestic market. Finally, state assistance to help develop the infrastructure of the private marketing system, i.e. the creation and encouragement of widespread wholesale and retail markets and trading facilities, is likely to prove a less costly means of improving marketing systems than the creation of state marketing monopolies.

Peasants and marketing

It is common to make quite a sharp distinction between the activities of production and those of marketing. Households and individuals engaged in production are referred to as 'peasants' or 'farmers', while people engaged in marketing are 'traders' or 'middlemen'. As we have seen these terms are sometimes given ethical connotations as well as descriptive meanings. Peasants and farmers are the good guys while traders and middlemen are the bad guys. The former are routinely thought to be at the mercy of the latter, and the latter are considered exploitative and parasitic. These superficial characterisations are sometimes aggravated due to ethnic or caste differences between farmers and traders.

The reality is of course a great deal more diverse and complicated than these stereotypes. Peasants are not uniform in the scope and success of their farming activities, and they are most certainly not uniformly disengaged from marketing activities. Very poor peasants in staple food producing areas (e.g. in Asia and South-East Asia) often engage in petty trade in order to supplement farm incomes that are insufficient on their own for family survival. Richer peasants and emerging commercial farmers engage in trade as part of the process of becoming richer. Some of them use trade as a means of generating resources to expand farm operations; others use trade as an eventual escape route out of farming.

Then there are the cases, prevalent in West African history for example, in which a gender basis underlies different patterns of engagement in marketing between men and women in peasant households. The tradition was for men to specialise in cultivation and women to specialise in trade and marketing. There are clearly many exceptions to the notion that peasants and traders can be neatly set apart.

Besides sometimes being traders themselves, peasants are also sometimes tied to traders by market or non-market contractual obligations (Crow, 1989). For example, traders may make cash advances to peasants the repayment of which at harvest time precludes an open market sale at the market price. Similarly, peasants may be sharecroppers with multiple obligations to landlords involving interlocked factor and output markets (Ellis, 1988a: Ch.8). Small traders, in turn, may be locked by credit obligations and patronage to larger traders at points further along the marketing chain. Where state agencies are heavily involved in crop marketing, it is not unusual to observe that various types of obligation, payoff and patronage have transferred themselves from private traders to state officials.

To summarise, several cautionary points about peasants, markets, and marketing policy arise from these considerations. *First*, peasants interact with marketing agents in a multiplicity of ways, and it is a mistake to make generalisations about the nature and effect of such relationships without careful observation. *Second*, whether peasants, or particular subsets of peasants, are exploited by middlemen is an empirical issue that cannot be determined by abstract deductive logic, and which is in practice very complicated to research (see Crow, 1989). *Third*, if exploitation is proven to exist then it is not at all clear that the total replacement of private by state trading channels is the best long-run method for solving the problem. *Fourth*, the real key to whether peasants are disadvantaged by the way marketing systems work is whether the individual producer has any range of effective choice concerning the buyer, timing, and location of commodity sale.

Marketing policy and women

Agricultural marketing in developing countries is a branch of activity in which women often have high levels of participation, and there are many instances where marketing has traditionally been considered

more of a female than a male activity. Women can engage in marketing in
several different ways, for example, (i) as private traders whose chief
source of income is trading, (ii) as stallholders in village and town
markets, (iii) as the person in the farm household chiefly responsible for
selling selected or all outputs, (iv) as the processor of farm output prior to
their consumption or sale in markets.

Marketing policies typically neglect gender despite the importance of
women in marketing roles. A few examples will suffice:

(a) monopoly state marketing boards by-pass and substitute for
private forms of marketing altogether, and by doing this they
may exclude women from diverse levels of marketing activity in
which they were formerly engaged;

(b) other state-sponsored marketing agencies, like cooperatives,
tend to be dominated by male officials and bureaucrats, even
when operating in places where women have a tradition of
marketing;

(c) men rather than women may be favoured for the issue of trading
licences in those cases where private marketing activity is regulated by a state licensing system.

Women's role in marketing is not only affected by gender-oblivious
marketing policies, it is also affected by state policies towards new
processing technology. In many societies women have chief responsibility
for the post-harvest processing of food whether for home consumption or
sale, and this can be regarded as a marketing activity when the output is
for sale. A well-documented case is the very large fall in employment for
women in the hand-pounding of rice due to the spread of small rice mills
in Asia in the 1970s.

Unlike with price policy, the role of women in marketing is readily
perceived, and is not conceptually difficult to take into account in policy
formulation. This does not mean, of course, that women's needs have
been taken into account in conventional marketing policies any more
than they have in conventional price policies.

Summary

1. This chapter is concerned with marketing policy, its origins,
objectives, instruments, and success or failure. A central issue is
the respective roles of private traders and state agencies in
commodity marketing. Marketing interventions are closely related to output price policies.

2. The chapter introduces and defines various concepts that are central to the policy analysis of marketing systems. These include the idea of the marketing margin, and its different dimensions as a space margin (to cover transport costs), time margin (to cover storage costs), and form margin (to cover processing). Marketing functions are often usefully analysed as vertical commodity systems comprising a number of sequential stages such as primary procurement, processing, wholesale, and retail. A further approach is to think of marketing in terms of its structure (number, size, and diversity of firms), conduct (reliability, timeliness, quality, and so on), and performance (speed and accuracy of price transmission and information, technical and allocative efficiency of operations).

3. Some typical objectives of marketing policy are (i) to protect farmers or consumers from supposedly exploitative traders, (ii) to stabilise or increase farm prices, (iii) to reduce the size of the marketing margin, (iv) to improve quality and minimum standards, and (v) to increase food security. These objectives may be broadly compatible with each other, although there is always tension between price levels for producers and those for consumers as in the case of price policy.

4. Some typical instruments used by governments in order to try to achieve these objectives are (i) creation of monopoly parastatals to replace private traders in one or more stages of the marketing system, (ii) creation of non-monopoly parastatals, such as buffer-stock authorities, aimed at regulating prices and margins via state purchase and sale operations, (iii) creation of farmer cooperatives to substitute for private traders at the level of primary procurements, (iv) control of private traders via licensing systems, (v) improvement of market conduct and performance via information provision, regulating quality and hygiene standards, and providing infrastructural facilities for wholesale and retail markets, and (vi) improving market structure by facilitating new entrants into private trade. Note that the last of these is the opposite to the first two in approach, even though the same aims may be involved.

5. The chapter provides a brief overview of the policy analysis of marketing systems centred on the analysis of marketing margins and their trends. Five topics are considered in a little more depth, these being (i) the impact on producer and retail prices of

changes in the marketing margin, (ii) the impact on the retail price of changing the export price of an export commodity, (iii) measuring market integration, (iv) commodity flow reversals, and (v) impact for government stock operations of squeezing the storage margin. These topics provide a diverse set of insights into the impact of state interventions on prices and margins.

6. Some lessons from developing country experience in marketing policy are considered. Special attention is given to the defects of marketing parastatals, which include problems of motivation, overstaffing, duplication of infrastructural facilities across different crops, high administrative and capital overheads, unsuitable tasks and functions, residual determination of producer prices and many others.

7. The chapter concludes that government efforts to improve and regulate the working of the private trade may have rather better long-run prospects than the mainly failed experiments in parastatal marketing. However, this conclusion is not stated as an ideological panacea for all types of marketing problem. An important role for the state is always likely to exist in matters as sensitive as the purchase and sale prices of staple foods. It is right that this should be so, and debate must often centre on improved methods of intervention rather than on no intervention at all.

8. The position of women with respect to marketing policies is briefly considered, and the reader is referred to Chapter 12 for a comparative summary of the gender dimensions of agricultural policies.

Further reading

Some useful introductory material on marketing issues can be found in several sources, the main concerns of which are price policy or food policy. Examples are Timmer *et al.* (1983: Ch. 4), Timmer (1986a: Ch. 3), and Mellor and Ahmed (1988: Chs. 4 and 5). An excellent overview of methods of marketing analysis, including numerical examples as well as useful additional references, is Goetz & Weber (1986). This is a publication in the Michigan State University series on agricultural marketing and another useful one in the same series is Holtzman (1986). Also useful is the standard earlier textbook on agricultural price formation by Tomek & Robinson (1981). The critique of the use of price correlations to measure market integration is given in an important paper by Harriss (1979). For newer methods to measure

124   *Marketing policy*

market integration, not for the quantitatively faint hearted, see Ravallion (1986), Heytens (1986) and Timmer (1987). Two accessible case-studies on marketing margin effects of government policies are Timmer (1974) and Timmer (1986a: 61–6). For an edited collection on marketing boards see Arhin *et al.* (1985), and for privatisation of marketing institutions, see the papers on this topic in Christiansen (1989). The paper by Crow (1989) is recommended both for its insights into the true complexity of peasant–trader exchange relationships, and as a reminder that the reduction of marketing systems to simple economic models carries dangers of over-simplification and inaccuracy.

Reading list

Arhin, K., Hesp, P. & van der Laan, L. (eds) (1985). *Marketing Boards in Tropical Africa*. London: Kegan Paul International.

Christiansen, R.E. (ed.) (1989). Privatization. Special Issue of *World Development,* **17,** No.5.

Crow, B. (1989). Plain Tales from the Rice Trade: Indications of Vertical Integration in Foodgrain Markets in Bangladesh. *Journal of Peasant Studies,* **16,** No. 2.

Goetz, S. & Weber, M.T. (1986). Fundamentals of Price Analysis in Developing Countries' Food Systems. *MSU International Development Papers,* Working Paper No. 29.

Harriss, B. (1979). There is Method in My Madness: or is it Vice Versa? Measuring Agricultural Market Performance. *Food Research Institute Studies,* **XVII,** No. 2.

Heytens, P.J. (1986). Testing Market Integration. *Food Research Institute Studies,* **20,** No. 1.

Holtzman, J.S. (1986). *Rapid Reconnaissance Guidelines For Agricultural Marketing and Food System Research in Developing Countries*. Michigan State University, International Development Working Paper No. 30.

Mellor, J.W. & Ahmed, R.U. (1988). *Agricultural Price Policy for Developing Countries*. Baltimore: Johns Hopkins.

Ravallion, M. (1986). Testing Market Integration. *American Journal of Agricultural Economics,* February.

Timmer, C.P. (1974). A Model of Rice Marketing Margins in Indonesia. *Food Research Institute Studies,* **13,** No. 2.

Timmer, C.P. (1986a). *Getting Prices Right: The Scope and Limits of Agricultural Price Policy*. New York: Cornell University Press.

Timmer, C.P. (1987). Corn Marketing, In *The Corn Economy of Indonesia,* ed. C.P. Timmer, Ch. 8, pp. 201–234. Ithaca, New York: Cornell University Press.

Timmer, C.P., Falcon, W.P. & Pearson S.R. (1983). *Food Policy Analysis*. Baltimore: Johns Hopkins.

Tomek, W.G. & Robinson, K.L. (1981). *Agricultural Product Prices*. Ithaca and London: Cornell University Press.

6

Input policy

Variable input policies

This chapter concerns the ways governments try to influence the quantities and combinations of purchased variable inputs used by small farmers in developing countries. Purchased variable inputs include chemical fertilizers (nitrogen, phosphate, potassium, sulphate, etc.), pesticides, weedicides, seeds of improved and high yielding varieties, fuel, animal feeds, and others. Water is also an important variable input under irrigated conditions where water control by the farmer is possible. However, irrigation water raises special issues, which are examined separately in Chapter 11.

Variable input policies have three main dimensions. The *first* is the *price level* of variable inputs, and concerns state actions to influence the prices paid by farmers for inputs like fertilizer or pesticides. The *second* is the *delivery system* for variable inputs, and concerns state actions to improve the physical flow of inputs to farmers. The *third* is the *information* available to farmers concerning the type, quantity, and combination of inputs appropriate for their farm systems.

In some cases it is also useful to include *credit* for the purchase of variable inputs as a *fourth* dimension of input policies. However, in the way this book is organised, the topic of credit is handled on its own in Chapter 7.

New seeds, fertilizers and irrigation water are *complementary* inputs. This means that the highest levels of yield are only achieved by the simultaneous increase of all three types of variable input in the correct proportions. If one input (say, fertilizer) is missing then the productivity gains of the new technology may be limited, and the farmer may do better to stay with traditional varieties that are less sensitive to levels of chemical inputs.

The complementarity between new crop varieties, water control, and chemical inputs, leads to the idea of delivering an input *package* to farmers in order to achieve desired rapid increases in agricultural output. An earlier literature called this the 'Green Revolution package'. The 'package' approach envisages a major role for the state: investment in public irrigation schemes, delivery to farmers of certified seeds together with the appropriate quantities of fertilizers and other farm chemicals, provision of credit, and advice concerning the proper agronomic practices to put into effect.

The package approach to inputs has become less prevalent in recent times, although elements of it are still to be found in agricultural development projects. Past problems with the approach were its high overhead cost per farmer, the relatively small numbers of farmers that could be included in each scheme, insensitivity to local variations in soil and climate, insensitivity to pre-existing farming systems (see Chapter 10), failures of credit repayment (see Chapter 7), and failures of input delivery (see below).

In summary, the key elements in input policy discussion concern input prices, input delivery, complementarity between inputs, input packages, and advice to farmers. This chapter examines these aspects within the framework of the following aims:

(a) to set out the main *objectives* of input policies;
(b) to describe and define the most common *instruments* of input policies;
(c) to summarise some main *problems* and *debates* that arise in discussions about the efficacy of input policies;
(d) to set out the logic behind the *dynamic disequilibrium* argument in favour of fertilizer subsidies;
(e) to provide an example *partial equilibrium analysis* comparing a fertilizer subsidy policy and a price support policy to achieve a given output objective;
(f) to show the different ways in which the financial and economic *gains or losses* from fertilizer subsidies may be distributed between farmers and fertilizer manufacturers;
(g) to summarise the *lessons* of input policy interventions;
(h) to consider the implications for *women* of the working of variable input markets and state input policies.

Objectives of input policy

The objectives of state intervention in the markets for farm variable inputs are mainly to do with accelerating the adoption of new farm technology. In other words, they are concerned with increasing agricultural output, rather than with income distribution or other types of social objective. Sometimes, however, income distribution is built into input policy via the target constituency of an input delivery program (e.g. 'small poor farmers'). Sometimes also, input policies are used to compensate for the adverse impact of other policies operating on farm households (e.g. low food prices).

Various reasons suggest that the successful adoption of new technology by farmers may be slow and uneven if left entirely to 'market forces'. Information flows are a critical factor in rapid technological change, and information scarcity is prevalent in peasant communities (Stiglitz, 1986b). Some new inputs – such as the new seeds themselves – require a change from non-market behaviour (saving own seed for future sowing) to market relations (buying approved seeds). Markets may not be developed for such inputs, and controls on the quality and consistency of supply are required (e.g. to ensure the genetic purity of new seeds). The state may also intervene in order to avoid errors in the input combinations chosen by farmers.

Expanding on these considerations, the objectives of state intervention in input markets can be distinguished between the general and the specific, and between farmer, input market, and input supply dimensions as shown in the following list:

General
(a) In general, to accelerate and to make more uniform the successful adoption of new technology by farmers, in situations where (i) farmers are thought to underestimate the gains to be made by adopting new input combinations, and (ii) markets are considered unable to deliver the new inputs with sufficient competitiveness, timeliness, quality, accuracy of information, and geographical coverage.

Farmers
(b) To overcome risk-averse behaviour by farmers, which causes them to underestimate (to 'over-discount') the returns to using new inputs.
(c) To avoid mistakes in input use by farmers, which might happen on a trial-and-error basis, because a high occurrence of such mistakes will tend to accentuate risk aversion and slow down the uptake of new inputs by farmers.

(d) To avoid the adoption of plainly wrong or even dangerous inputs by farmers, sometimes caused by over-zealous sales behaviour by private input supply companies in poorly regulated markets.

Input markets

(e) To provide a delivery system for inputs under conditions where private markets in farm inputs are non-existent, unevenly developed, or uncompetitive.

(f) To combine input delivery with credit provision in order to alleviate the working capital constraint on the adoption of new inputs.

(g) To regulate and control the market for improved seeds, in order to ensure the genetic quality of named varieties in seed replication and seed delivery to farmers.

(h) To regulate and control the market for pesticides or disease-control chemicals in the context of measures designed to contain the spread of pests or diseases in crops grown under monoculture or near-monoculture conditions.

Input supply

(i) To maximise the use of domestic rather than imported supplies of farm inputs, either across the board, or in specific product lines.

(j) To provide a sales outlet, perhaps at subsidised prices, for a high cost domestic industry that is protected from import competition by import taxes or an import ban.

This list is not exhaustive. It merely serves to pinpoint some of the more prevalent reasons for state interventions to be found in government policy documents or international agency reports. As is true for all the types of intervention discussed in this book, there are often as many hidden agendas behind input policies – political, bureaucratic, or income supplementing – as there are 'above-board' objectives.

Instruments of input policy

Instruments used by governments in order to implement input policies may be grouped according to the three dimensions of input policy already identified. The first of these is to influence the *prices* that farmers pay for variable inputs, especially the critical inputs like seed and chemical fertilizers. The second group consists of interventions in the *delivery* of farm inputs, whereby the state may wholly or partially replace private agents in the distribution system for inputs. The third group concerns the provision of *information* on inputs to farmers, which in most developing countries is the task of the state agricultural extension service.

These categories of instrument are clearly not mutually exclusive. State delivery of inputs also involves state decisions on input prices, and extension services are sometimes, but not always, integrated with state delivery agencies. In the following discussion each group of instruments is examined in turn, with emphasis placed on the relationship between instruments and objectives.

Input price policy

Intervention in the level of prices paid by farmers for variable inputs is widespread throughout the developing countries. Prices may be fixed ex-factory when delivery takes place through private channels, or may be fixed at the farm-gate when delivery is by state agencies. Price fixing may apply only to major strategic inputs such as fertilizer, or may be implemented across a range of purchased variable inputs.

Provided that delivery systems are working, price fixing can serve the purposes of removing one of the risk elements of input purchase (price instability), and of ensuring that all farmers pay the same price, irrespective of location, social status, or season.

In addition to fixing prices, most governments have also in the past subsidised them for inputs such as fertilizer. Rates of input subsidy can vary over a wide range from quite low levels to over 50 per cent. The subsidy may be paid at importation (for imported inputs), to the domestic manufacturing industry (in order to ensure an agreed level of ex-factory price), or to the state input distribution agency in those cases where a state agency has exclusive rights of input delivery to farmers.

Some interesting arguments surround input subsidies, especially for fertilizer, and the economic logic of them is considered later in the chapter. In relation to objectives, input subsidies are designed to provide an incentive for the more rapid adoption of modern inputs than would occur in their absence. They do this by raising the net income gains from a given level of input use, and by moving outwards the profit maximising level of input use. Input subsidies may also be used as a method for maintaining adequate levels of return in farm production in the face of low output prices intended to benefit urban consumers.

Input price fixing may occur even if delivery is in private hands. For example, fixed ex-factory prices are often imposed on fertilizer manufacturers. However, it is more common for fixed prices to be associated with state control over the delivery of inputs to farmers.

Input delivery systems

State delivery agencies for farm inputs can take many different forms, between as well as within countries. At one end of the spectrum there may be an Agricultural Development Corporation with wide ranging responsibilities for input delivery, credit provision, and extension services to farmers. In other cases these functions may belong to separate institutions, or input delivery may be fragmented between a number of project agencies for particular crops or particular regions. In some cases, input delivery is combined with crop marketing, research and extension in crop-specific parastatals; in others, input delivery is handled by branches of the state credit agency, while extension is run from the central Ministry of Agriculture; in still others the cooperative system has a role to play as exclusive final distributor of inputs to farmers.

In spite of this multiplicity of potential institutional arrangements, the basic concepts of state input delivery remain the same. These are to replace, either partially or wholly, a private delivery system that is considered inadequate to the task of supplying farmers with timely inputs at stable and competitive prices. The perceived inadequacy may be lack of geographical spread of outlets, unwillingness to supply small quantities of inputs to small-scale clients, poor information feedback between farmers and urban traders, local trading monopolies, and a host of other reasons.

Information on inputs

Lack of practical and relevant information has long been recognised as an important barrier to rapid and widespread adoption of innovations by farmers. This applies not only to variable inputs, but also to the cultivation practices and farming systems appropriate to new seeds.

The traditional method of conveying new information to farmers relies on the government extension service. An extension system is composed of a body of trained extension officers, each of whom is allocated a district or area within which to provide advice and to carry out training for individual farmers or groups of farmers. The number of farm households allocated to each extension officer varies widely in different countries, from a lowest level of around 50, to upper levels of 500 or 600, and no doubt even higher in some instances.

Ideas about extension have evolved over the years, and many different models can be found within and across developing countries. In earlier times, extension tended to be a one-way, top-down, information process, and extension officers worked mainly with market-orientated and innovative farmers (the 'progressive farmer' approach). A popular, more recent, model has been the 'training and visit' (T & V) system with features such as the improved integration of extension with research, several levels and types of information officer, and regularity of events, for example a weekly training program and fortnightly farm visits. Current emphasis is on two-way information flows, interactive training methods, and farming systems research (see Chapter 10).

The relative success of extension systems in assisting farmers to adjust to new technology is inevitably variable. There are some examples of a high degree of complementarity between training and other components of delivery systems to farmers. However, extension services can also be ineffective for many different reasons: lack of communication and conflicts between different state agencies involved in agricultural development programs; lack of logistical support from base; lack of means of transport for getting around villages and farms; lack of motivation due to poor remuneration and inadequately defined or confusing goals.

Aside from extension services, information on inputs can be conveyed to farmers in several other ways: field days run by research stations, widely distributed information leaflets, radio programmes for farmers, and so on. It is accepted that the state should play a role in these channels of farmer education. For farming communities making the transition from non-purchased inputs to purchased inputs, reliance solely on commercial information provided by competing private sector agents could be misleading or confusing. Thus the twofold role of the state with respect to input information is (i) to ensure consistency in the advice being given across different avenues of communication to farmers, and (ii) to ensure compatibility between input advice and the agronomic requirements of specific crops and varieties such that inputs are deployed to most productive effect by farmers.

Input policy problems and debates

This section summarises the main conceptual defects and practical difficulties that have been encountered with respect to input subsidies and state delivery systems. It then goes on to summarise briefly some of the debates in the policy literature that compare input policies with alternative methods for achieving the same objectives.

Input subsidy problems

A range of problems and side-effects associated with subsidies on the prices of variable inputs are now recognised. In part this recognition follows the more general trend of scepticism about the efficacy of state controls. In part it results from the inability of many developing countries to continue to bear the financial burden of open-ended input subsidies. The net effect, including the result of pressure from donors like the World Bank, is that input subsidies are tending to be lowered or eliminated in many countries. Some main problems with input subsidies are as follows:

(a) The border pricing argument: the divergence between a low domestic price to farmers and a high import price is socially inefficient. This results in a misallocation of resources because farmers are not making their production decisions according to the opportunity cost to society of the resources employed.

(b) The cost control problem: the long term budgetary cost of input subsidies grows over time and is difficult to predict. It grows over time precisely because the subsidised price induces a rapidly growing volume of sales, but the rate of this growth (the accelerated uptake by farmers) is not known in advance. A subsidy which begins as a minor budgetary item at low levels of sales can quickly become a drain on state resources, reaching as high as 20 or 30 per cent of the government budget in a poor country.

(c) The cost recoupment problem: except when fertilizers are delivered free under aid agreements, the costs of input subsidies must be recouped from some source of tax revenues. These might be general tax revenues, for example from import taxes, or from urban taxpayers, or even from farmers via land or export taxes.

(d) Farm resource misallocation problems including:
   (i)   excessive use of an input (e.g. too much urea so that the crop falls over);
   (ii) inefficient substitution of scarce for abundant factors of production (e.g. substitution of a subsidised weedicide for weeding labour, or substitution of chemical-intensive for labour-intensive disease control methods);
   (iii) inefficient substitution of crops that make more use of the subsidised input for crops that make less use of the input, even though market demand patterns for the crops are in the opposite direction;
   (iv) diversion of subsidised inputs from the target crop of government subsidy policy (e.g. an export crop like cotton) to other crops favoured by the farmers (usually staple food crops).

(e) Problems of delivery failure or diversion, including:

(i) failure of supply to meet demand at the subsidised price, causing formal or informal rationing of the input;

(ii) illegal marketing of the input at unofficial prices, usually reflecting supply failures either locally or nationally;

(iii) smuggling of the input across the border with an adjacent country, reflecting the price gap between the countries created by the subsidy.

(f) Equity problems: an input subsidy is regressive in its effect on income distribution since it benefits most those farmers who use more of the input and these will tend to be the wealthier farmers. The larger the proportion of variable input costs relative to other costs, like family labour or land rent, the greater are the gains in net income from a low price for such inputs.

For these various reasons some leading authorities on agricultural development have never been in favour of price subsidies on inputs (see e.g. Mellor, 1966: 293). Others have become converted to an anti-subsidy view due to the resource misallocation and financial problems of subsidies (World Bank, 1986b: 94–7). Still others continue to think that subsidies have an important temporary role in encouraging farmers to raise input use levels (e.g. Tarrant, 1982; Timmer, 1986b).

State delivery problems

The delivery of variable inputs to farmers by state agencies is prone to many of the same difficulties as apply to state marketing agencies (Chapter 5). Indeed, sometimes input delivery and crop marketing functions are located within the same parastatal agency. These problems are well recognised and do not need to be spelt out in great detail. They include:

(a) biases of rationing when the input is in short supply, typically favouring wealthy clients who are in a position to pay the 'under-the-table' costs of acquiring input supplies;

(b) biases against small and poor farmers even when supply is unconstrained, usually due to the linkage between state credit provision and input delivery;

(c) cumbersome and sometimes unworkable bureaucratic procedures for the release and delivery of inputs to farmers or cooperatives, which tend to favour those who can afford to persist with the paperwork or can pay others to do so;

(d) underpaid and poorly motivated officials who have no incentive to conduct transactions with speed and efficiency;

(e) failures of delivery to remote and outlying depots, causing erratic availability even when overall supply is unconstrained;

(f) more general logistical defects in the geographical allocation and movement of inputs, resulting in timeliness failures for seasonal inputs like fertilizer;

(g) failures to transmit information on changing farmer input needs back to supply depots and manufacturers.

Some people argue that these problems are susceptible to correction by devising more effective and responsive state agencies. However, there are deeper problems with public delivery systems. State delivery differs from the price mechanism in an important respect which is easy to overlook. The market is indifferent to who buys the product provided he or she can pay the going price; not so state agencies, which must always have rules and regulations governing target farmers, quantity allocations, lending guidelines, deposit requirements, repayment schedules, and so on.

A key concept that sometimes arises in discussion of input delivery is that of *access*. Access means the ability of people, especially the mass of low-income people with a multitude of different circumstances, to acquire the commodities and services provided by state agencies. They are often prohibited from doing so because they do not quite fit the categories for which a particular agency was designed. And the more that agencies are differentiated in order to cater for multiple products and services for many different target groups, the more likely it is that an individual applicant will not fit the eligibility rules of the particular agency he or she approaches for a commodity or service.

The process by which state agencies multiply according to differences of function, product or service has been described as *itemisation* (Harvey *et al.*, 1979: 29–70). The opposite process, in which a number of different products and services – such as input delivery, credit and extension – are combined in one agency, is described by the same authors as *packaging*. Both itemisation and packaging can create problems of access, the former for reasons already described, the latter because the target group of an expensive 'package' is often narrowly defined in order to constrain the total cost of the package, or because clients must subscribe to the entire 'package' or nothing at all.

The substitution of state for private agencies is seen to involve more complicated considerations than the superficial market versus non-market ideologies that often inform discussion. This comes back to the 'market failure' versus 'state failure' distinction made in Chapter 1. The observation that the market is not working well does not of necessity imply that the state can do better. It must be borne in mind that state agencies almost always imply bureaucracy. Bureaucracy in turn involves eligibility rules, which can cause unpredictable access problems for its clients.

Some policy debates

The wisdom of using input subsidies rather than other methods in order to accelerate the adoption of new technology by farmers has long provoked disagreement amongst economists and other development specialists. Specifically, arguments have centred on (i) output price support, (ii) credit subsidies, and (iii) improved delivery at full-cost prices, as potentially superior methods for achieving the same aims as input subsidies. The arguments put forward in these three contexts are described in the following paragraphs:

(a)   *Input subsidy versus price support*

Two types of argument are encountered here: the first concerns farm-level resource allocation effects; the second concerns the social welfare and government budgetary costs of one type of policy instrument against another.

With respect to resource allocation, it has been argued that supporting the level of the farm output price has a less distorting effect on resource use than an input subsidy. This is because a rise in farm output price increases by equal proportions the returns to all factors of production, leaving the farmer free to make input substitution choices according to market prices. This is said to avoid the adoption by farmers of the socially inefficient input combinations caused by reducing prices of selected inputs.

The counter argument is that input subsidies can usefully be used as a *temporary* incentive to boost input use (see the section below entitled 'Fertilizer policy and dynamic disequilibrium').

With respect to social welfare, it has been argued that for a given level of net social cost, a fertilizer subsidy policy may have a greater output effect than an output price policy, and is therefore a more efficient instrument for achieving a desired target increase in a crop output.

(b)   *Input subsidy versus credit subsidy*

Again, this debate is about avoiding the farm-level resource allocation distortions that may be caused by changing relative prices between inputs. Subsidised credit enhances the ability of farmers to increase the use of all cash inputs, without interfering with relative opportunity costs between inputs. Thus socially inefficient input substitution is avoided by credit subsidies (see, however, Chapter 7 for the problems that beset subsidised credit).

(c)   *Input subsidy versus delivery systems*

This debate is between those who consider that allocative decisions by farmers can be left to take care of themselves provided that the appropriate technical and information conditions are met (e.g. Mellor, 1966; Desai, 1988); and those who consider that price incentives can provide a powerful, even if temporary, spur to the rate of adoption of new technology (e.g. Timmer, 1986b; Parikh, 1990). Another way this is expressed is to contrast *long-term* technology policies with *short-term* price policies. It is argued by those in favour of subsidies that short-term price incentives are needed in order to ensure that farmers take advantage of the potential rises in productivity that became available to them. This is the 'dynamic disequilibrium' argument, to which we now turn in the specific context of fertilizer policy.

Fertilizer policy

The various propositions concerning input subsidies and delivery systems can be taken further by reference specifically to fertilizers. Chemical fertilizers are by far the most important purchased variable input in terms of their yield impact in conjunction with new seeds, and in terms of the volume and gross value of their consumption compared to other inputs. Fertilizer use has experienced remarkably high rates of growth in some developing countries. For example, in India fertilizer use increased from 0.8 million tons in 1965 to 7.7 million tons in 1983 (Desai, 1988: 206). In Indonesia, fertilizer use increased from 0.2 million tons in 1970 to 4.5 million tons in 1986 (Indonesia, 1987: 56).

The foregoing review of debates about input policy raised certain issues that are worth pursuing further in terms of the formal economic analysis that underlies them. Therefore, in this section, we examine three such issues further: the concept of 'dynamic disequilibrium' as an argument for subsidising fertilizer; the comparison between a fertilizer subsidy and a price support policy for achieving a stated output goal; and the incidence of fertilizer subsidy distinguished between farm sector and manufacturing sector beneficiaries of such a subsidy under differing conditions.

Fertilizer response and dynamic disequilibrium

The purpose here is to describe the economic logic of the 'dynamic disequilibrium' argument for implementing price subsidies on a variable input, like fertilizer. Figure 6.1 displays two contrasting yield response curves for rice. The lower curve represents the low initial yield and relatively small yield gain for a traditional rice variety at different levels of urea use by the farmer. The upper curve shows the higher initial yield and much greater response to urea of a high yielding rice variety, assuming that all other requirements to achieve the highest possible yield are met (water, labour use, disease-control, etc.).

Both curves embody *diminishing returns* to fertilizer use: as the quantity of urea increases, yields increase, but at a diminishing rate along the curve. This feature also ensures that a biological maximum yield is defined (point G on the lower curve and point E on the upper curve), and that yields fall if excessive quantities of urea are applied.

Figure 6.2 shows the same two curves, only this time the *economic optimum* level of urea use is shown on each curve for given prices of rice and fertilizer. The profit maximising levels of urea use are at point F on

Figure 6.1. Fertilizer response curves for rice.

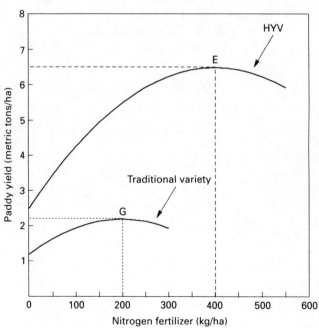

the lower curve, and point C on the upper curve, and the tangent line at each of these points represents the fertilizer/paddy price ratio. At these points the profit maximising condition holds that the marginal value product of urea (MVP) equals its marginal factor cost (MFC). The reader who has difficulties with this construction should refer to Ellis (1988a: Ch. 2).

The problem is how are the majority of farmers to be persuaded to move from F to C, or even, in some cases, to move to C from zero previous fertilizer use.

The answer to this varies. Some economists would say that the problem centres on ensuring that the production function – i.e. the technological potential to realise yield level C – shifts upwards from the lower curve to the upper curve. This means focusing attention on the technical and physical requirements of that upward shift: yield improvements from research, diffusion of research results to farmers, distribution of new seeds, and physical availability of variable inputs. According to this line of reasoning, if the technological conditions are met, farmers will automatically tend to combine inputs in the correct proportions relative to their market prices.

Figure 6.2. Optimum levels of fertilizer use.

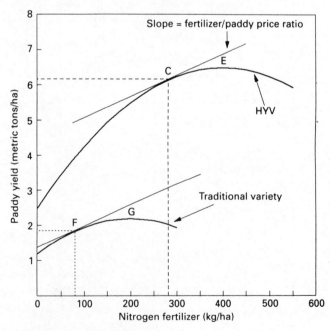

The opposing line of reasoning is that technological developments – especially major breakthroughs like the advent of new seeds – move far in advance of the changes in farm household decision-making necessary in order to realise their benefits. Farmers tend to adhere to cultivation practices, input types, and input levels that they already know. In order to encourage them to use new methods, it is necessary to demonstrate the gains of making the change, and the only way to do this is to provide a special incentive in the form of lower prices for those inputs that farmers must use in large quantities.

This argument is called the *dynamic disequilibrium* reason for implementing input subsidies, and it is taken further in Figure 6.3. Despite an improving technological environment, as already shown by the upward shift in the fertilizer response function, farmers either continue to use no fertilizer at all (point A), or stick to the level of fertilizer use to that they are already accustomed for the previous technology (point B). This causes a divergence between the yield levels that could be achieved as technology changes, and the yield levels that are actually obtained by

Figure 6.3. Incentive effect of lower fertilizer price.

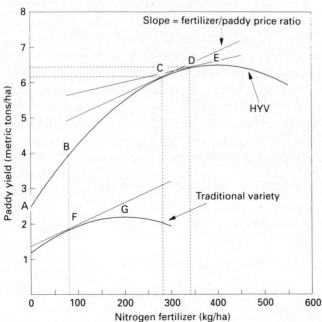

staying on the same level of fertilizer use. There is a *dynamic disequilib-rium* between the economic optimum level of yield (point C) and actual levels of yield (points A or B).

Lowering the price of fertilizer causes the fertilizer/paddy price ratio to fall; this lowers the slope of the price ratio line, and the equilibrium level of fertilizer use is increased, such as from C to D in Figure 6.3. The intention is not that farmers on average should reach fertilizer use D, but rather that they are given an incentive to make the jump from negligible fertilizer use to a level closer to the optimum requirements of the new technology. If farmers were actually to move to D their level of fertilizer use would be excessive in terms of the social opportunity cost of fertilizer, even if making sense from the private profitability viewpoint.

It is in this important sense that a fertilizer subsidy (or any other kind of input subsidy) should be strictly a *temporary* policy instrument, because if farmers are given time to adjust fully to the low price then socially inefficient resource use occurs. The difficulty is that once farmers become accustomed to low fertilizer prices – even if only for a few seasons – a political pressure is created to maintain low prices in the long term.

The fertilizer/paddy price ratio, which determines the optimum rate of input use on the response curve, plays a critical role in this model. A comparison of this price ratio in 13 Asian countries for the period 1979–81 revealed a range between 0.4 and 5.2 (Barker *et al.*, 1985: 238). In Indonesia, the ratio was reduced, using subsidies, from 1.3 in the early 1970s to between 0.5 and 0.6 in the late 1980s (Ellis, 1989: 71).

To the extent that a graph like Figure 6.3 can be regarded as an accurate representation of the nitrogen response of paddy yields, it is worth noting that the nearer the peak level of yield is to the economic equilibrium position, the smaller the gain to be obtained from further price adjustments, and the lower the likely responsiveness of farmers to changes in prices. This can be expressed in a set of inter-related elastici-ties associated with fertilizer use and fertilizer demand:

(a) σ = yield elasticity with respect to urea use = $\dfrac{\text{\% rise in yield}}{\text{\% rise in urea use}}$

(b) β = demand elasticity for urea = $\dfrac{\text{\% rise in urea use}}{\text{\% fall in urea price}}$

(c) ε = yield elasticity with respect to urea price = $\dfrac{\text{\% rise in yield}}{\text{\% fall in urea price}}$

These elasticities can be calculated for changing price ratios, if the equation of the response curve has been estimated statistically from field observations. For the illustrative equations used to construct these graphs, it is the case that for the top curve in Figure 6.3 the above elasticities would have values of 0.084, −0.11, and −0.009, respectively, over the range in which the fertilizer/paddy price ratio is reduced from two to one. In other words a 10 per cent rise in fertilizer price in this area of the response function would cause only a 1.1 per cent fall in fertilizer demand and a 0.09 per cent fall in yield. This illustrates a further aspect of prolonged use of fertilizer subsidies: once farmers have adjusted to optimum levels of fertilizer use, the subsidy can almost certainly be phased out without causing a severe fall in fertilizer use or yields. Indonesia in the late 1980s provides a good example of this situation (Hedley & Tabor, 1989; Ellis, 1990).

Input subsidy versus price support: An example

This example provides an opportunity to make use of the concepts and methods of policy analysis set out in Chapter 3. The method of the example is adapted from a case-study given in Barker & Hayami (1976).

Suppose that the government of a food-deficit country decides to pursue a goal of self-sufficiency, but is not prepared to wait for this to occur by the gradual adoption of new technology by farmers. The staple food is maize, which has hitherto been imported and sold to consumers at the world price. The government wishes to keep the consumer price at the import parity level. Two alternative instruments are available for raising domestic output: *either* (i) to raise the producer price above the world price level, *or* (ii) to lower the price of fertilizer. Policy analysis is used to determine which of these instruments can attain the goal at lower cost to the government and with minimum losses in social welfare.

The example is depicted in the demand–supply diagram of Figure 6.4. Domestic demand for maize is shown by the curve DD, and domestic supply by curve SS. The world price of maize is P_w, and with free importation this means that domestic production is Q_p and domestic consumption is Q_c. The level of imports is $(Q_c - Q_p)$. The quantity of domestic production that is consumed as subsistence by farm households is Q_h, and this is held constant for the purposes of the analysis, hence the origin of the graph is at Q_h rather than at zero.

In order to achieve self-sufficiency, domestic production must rise to the same level as consumption at level Q_c. This can be done *either* by raising the producer price to P_s, for example by providing price support on marketed sales equal to P_s minus P_w, *or* by lowering the fertilizer price, causing a supply shift to $S'S'$, such that output increases to Q_c even at the world price. The basic data and assumptions of the example are set out in Table 6.1.

Given these conditions and assumptions, the two alternative policies can be analysed as in Boxes 6.1 and 6.2. Percentage increases and new levels refer to what is required in order to achieve the self-sufficiency objective.

In order to trace through the implications of the alternative policy, the fertilizer subsidy, it is helpful to make use of a separate graph for the fertilizer market, and this is given in Figure 6.5. This graph shows the domestic demand curve for fertilizer together with prices before (P_{fw}) and after (P_{fs}) the subsidy, and the quantities of fertilizer consumed before (F_1) and after (F_2) the subsidy. The calculations in Box 6.2 may be traced partly in Figure 6.4 and partly in Figure 6.5.

Note that a net welfare gain (rather than a loss) occurs for the fertilizer subsidy policy due to the simplifying assumptions of the model. Specifically, the calculations for both alternative policies neglect the increase in

Figure 6.4. Price rise versus input subsidy – output market.

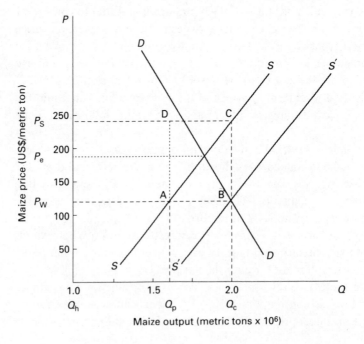

Maize output (metric tons x 10⁶)

Table 6.1.

Quantities		Million metric tons
Domestic consumption	(Q_c)	2.0
Domestic production	(Q_p)	1.6
Farm household consumption (held constant)	(Q_h)	1.0
Domestic marketed supply	$(Q_p - Q_h)$	0.6
Market deficit (imports)	$(Q_c - Q_p)$	0.4
Fertilizer consumption	(F_1)	0.05
Prices		US$ per metric ton
World maize price	(P_w)	120
World fertilizer price	(P_{fw})	150
Elasticities		Elasticity
Price elasticity of supply, maize	(α)	0.25
Price elasticity of demand, fertilizer	(β)	0.50
Elasticity of response, maize yield	(σ)	0.10

BOX 6.1.
Policy alternative I: Output price support

Percentage output increase $100 \times (Q_c - Q_p)/Q_p =$ 25%
Percentage increase in output price $25/\alpha = 100\%$

Producer price with support $(P_s) =$ US$240 per metric ton
Unit level of support $(P_s - P_w) =$ US$120 per metric ton

Producer surplus gain   = area P_wACP_s (Figure 6.4)
   = $(P_s - P_w) \times (Q_p - Q_h) + \frac{1}{2}(P_s - P_w) \times (Q_c - Q_p)$
   = $120 \times 0.6 + 0.5 \times 120 \times 0.4$
   = US$96 million

State support cost   = area P_wBCP_s (Figure 6.4)
   = $(P_s - P_w) \times (Q_c - Q_h)$
   = 120×1.0
   = US$120 million

Net welfare loss   = area ABC   (Figure 6.4)
   = $(P_s - P_w) \times \frac{1}{2}(Q_c - Q_p)$
   = US$24 million

In summary, the producer support scheme entails a gain to producers of US$96 million, a cost to the government of US$120 million, and therefore a net loss in social welfare equal to US$24 million.

resource costs other than fertilizer required to achieve the self-sufficiency level of output. Since the fertilizer subsidy involves a departure from opportunity cost pricing, it would undoubtedly display a net welfare loss in a full social accounting exercise. However, because these extra costs

---

BOX 6.2.
Policy alternative II: Input subsidy to fertilizer

Percentage output increase $100 \times (Q_c - Q_p)/Q_p = $ 25%
Percentage fertilizer increase $25/\sigma = 250\%$

New level of fertilizer $(F_2) = 175\,000$ metric tons
Change in fertilizer demand $(F_2 - F_1) = 125\,000$ metric tons

Old fertilizer price $(P_{fw}) = $ US\$150 per metric ton
Percentage decrease in fertilizer price $250/\beta = -500\%$

New fertilizer price $100 \times (P_{fs} - P_{fw})/P_{fs} = -500$
                          $P_{fs} = P_{fw}/4$
                          $P_{fs} = $ US\$37.50

Producer surplus gain   = area $P_{fs}CDP_{fw}$ (Figure 6.5)
                    (cost saving on old fertilizer use)
      plus   area ABQ_cQ_p (Figure 6.4)
                    (value of increased output)
    minus   area F_1CBF_2 (Figure 6.5)
                    (cost of extra fertilizer use)
           $= (P_{fw} - P_{fs}) \times F_1 + (Q_c - Q_p) \times P_w - P_{fs} \times (F_2 - F_1)$
           $= 6 + 48 - 5$
           $= $ US\$49 million

Government subsidy
   cost $= $ area $P_{fs}BAP_{fw}$ (Figure 6.5)
           $= (P_{fw} - P_{fs}) \times F_2$
           $= 112.5 \times 175\,000$
           $= $ US\$20 million

Net welfare gain $= $ US\$29 million

In summary, the fertilizer subsidy policy yields a gain to producers equal to US\$49 million, a subsidy cost to government of US\$20 million, and a net social gain of US\$29 million. It is therefore revealed to be a superior policy to producer price support. This superiority is measured by the difference between the net social welfare effects of the two policies, which is US\$29 million plus US\$24 million, an advantage on the side of fertilizer policies totalling US\$53 million.

are neglected equally for both alternative policies, the measured superiority of the fertilizer subsidy remains unaffected by their omission.

Fertilizer subsidies: Gainers and losers

A final aspect of fertilizer subsidies examined here concerns quantifying the amount of subsidy, and identifying its beneficiaries. It is often assumed that farmers are the sole beneficiaries of fertilizer subsidies, but this assumption is seldom entirely accurate, and may be completely wrong. The impact of subsidies on the domestic fertilizer industry as well as on farmers needs to be examined.

Fertilizer subsidies involve both financial and economic costs. The financial costs are the actual expenditure incurred by government in order to maintain a low fixed price to farmers; economic costs measure the loss in social welfare resulting from the divergence between the subsidised price and the social opportunity cost (border price or opportunity cost) of fertilizer.

Figure 6.5. Price rise versus input subsidy – input market.

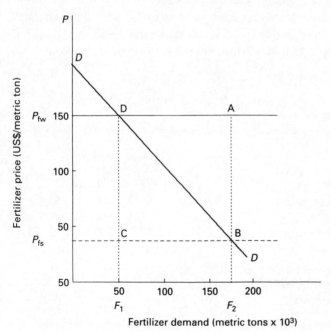

Table 6.2 illustrates three cases. In the first case (Case 1) the ex-factory cost of fertilizer (US$140) is higher than the border price (US$100). The financial subsidy incurred by government (US$75) represents an economic subsidy to farmers (US$35) that is less than the economic subsidy to domestic fertilizer manufacture (US$40). Thus, in this case, if the farm price were raised by US$35 per metric ton, the whole of the remaining subsidy would be to industry, not to farmers.

In the second case (Case 2) the ex-factory price and the border price are the same. The financial subsidy is still US$75. The entire subsidy accrues to the farm sector, since the domestic fertilizer industry is competitive at world prices.

In the third case (Case 3), the border price is above the ex-factory price. The financial subsidy is lower than the economic subsidy to farmers, because the gap between the farm price and the border price is bigger than the gap between the farm price and the industry price. The whole economic subsidy accrues to farmers, while industry is in economic terms taxed because it would be better off exporting the commodity than selling into the domestic market at cost.

Lessons of input policy

Various advantages and disadvantages of state interventions in input markets have already been set out in an earlier part of this chapter. There remain three summary points about the historical experience of input policy implementation which are put forward here as follows:

Table 6.2. *Example data for fertilizer subsidy calculations (Prices in US$/ton)*

			Case 1	Case 2	Case 3
1A	Ex-factory price		140	120	100
1B	Border price		100	120	130
2	Distribution cost		55	55	55
3A	Financial delivered cost	(1A + 2)	195	175	155
3B	Economic delivered cost	(1B + 2)	155	175	185
4	Farm price		120	100	120
5A	Financial subsidy	(3A − 4)	75	75	35
5B	Economic subsidy				
	to industry	(1A − 1B)	40	zero	−30
	to farmers	(3B − 4)	35	75	65

(a) Although unfashionable at the time of writing, input subsidy policies have worked well in some countries over particular periods of their history. An example is Indonesia, where under a highly favourable price regime, fertilizer use on rice grew from 0.5 million metric tons in the mid-1970s to 3 million tons in the mid-1980s, a rise in the use per hectare from 70 kg to over 300 kg. Average rice yields increased by about 60 per cent over the same period (Ellis, 1990: 44–6).

A fundamental condition for subsidies to have the desired impact is for there to be unlimited supplies of the input available at the subsidised price. Otherwise, formal and informal rationing occurs and the consequent market disruption is likely to negate the potential benefits of the policy. Even if successful, input subsidies should be implemented for limited duration only. Many of the problems associated with input subsidies may be traced to their remaining in place long after any reasonable argument can be put forward for their continuation.

(b) Problems with state input delivery systems are widespread and endemic, matching the same types of problem that occur with state marketing organisations. In some cases, these defects have been so severe that even the most inadequately functioning private market might have done better than the state agencies concerned.

(c) Despite these difficulties in organising delivery in some kinds of economy, the current emphasis in the input policy literature is on delivery and information rather than on price policy (Desai, 1988). This reflects the more general disenchantment with price policies in developing countries. However, there remain many unresolved problems in the area of input delivery (Shepherd, 1989), and a concensus is yet to emerge on the appropriate roles and functions of the private sector *vis à vis* the state sector in this branch of agricultural policy.

Input policy and women

Input policies seldom take women into account. This is perhaps understandable where input prices are concerned, for much the same reasons as those encountered in output price policy. However, the type, delivery, advice, and crop specific aspects of inputs have evident gender dimensions, and a sample of these is cited as follows:

  (a) intensive input application requires more labour time, and this may or may not be feasible within the constraints of time allocation procedures within the household;

  (b) one particular input, herbicides, saves time in weeding, and this may be women's time saved when women do the weeding;

(c) information and safety precautions concerning the use of chemical inputs may be communicated to men, rather than women, with obvious implications for women's health and safety;

(d) more generally, women may not be taught how to use fertilizers and other chemical inputs properly, resulting in waste, incorrect use, use on the wrong crops, and so on;

As we have seen, input policy covers a diverse bundle of policy issues in the prices, access, and information on purchased variable inputs, and it is difficult therefore to generalise about gender impacts. An obvious requirement is for extension workers to advise women rather than men, when it is women undertaking the tasks where new technology is involved.

Summary

1. This chapter examines the policies pursued by governments with respect to off-farm variable inputs required by farmers in order to realise the gains of new technology. Variable inputs, like new seeds, fertilizers, and water are *complementary*, and they permit the biggest output gains only when used in optimum proportions. This chapter does not discuss water as a variable input, since this topic is covered in a later chapter (Chapter 11).

2. Three dimensions of state intervention in input markets are identified. These are *first*, the price level of variable inputs, *second*, the delivery system for variable inputs, and *third*, the information made available to farmers concerning the appropriate type, quantity, and combination of purchased inputs.

3. The general objective of variable input policies is identified as the more rapid and widespread adoption of new technology by farmers than would occur by market forces alone. This objective includes the subsidiary aims (a) to overcome risk-averse and conservative behaviour by farmers; (b) to provide input delivery in situations where private markets in farm inputs are non-existent, unevenly developed, or uncompetitive; and (c) to fulfil certain specialised functions such as seed multiplication or disease-control programs.

4. Instruments of input policy may be grouped according to the three dimensions already cited. The most popular input price policy is to provide subsidies on key inputs, like fertilizer, and to fix the farm delivery price of such inputs. The most popular delivery policy is to create state input delivery agents, and these

may or may not be combined with other interventions such as marketing policy or credit policy. The chief method of conveying information to farmers is via the extension service, although other methods like research station open days, leaflet distribution, farmer radio shows, and interactive research methods also play an important role.

5. Input subsidies possess certain economic disadvantages: they involve departures from social opportunity cost, and unpredictable budgetary burdens. They can also cause resource inefficiency at farm level, including excessive input use, inefficient substitution of scarce for abundant inputs, inefficient substitution of crops that use much of the subsidised input for crops that use little, and diversion of inputs from targeted crops to other crops.

6. State delivery systems are likewise prone to various problems, including failure to meet demand at subsidised prices, biases of rationing when supply is insufficient, unworkable bureaucratic routines for the release and delivery of inputs from store, various logistical defects, and information failures. Many of these problems can be summed up by the concept of *access failures* to the goods and services state agencies are supposed to provide.

7. Three of the key debates about the comparative merits of input subsidies are briefly outlined, these being (a) input subsidy versus output price support; (b) input subsidy versus credit subsidy; and (c) input subsidy versus delivery system improvement.

8. Three aspects of fertilizer policy are selected and examined in more economic depth. These are (a) the concept of *dynamic disequilibrium* as an economic argument for the use of fertilizer subsidy as a temporary policy instrument, (b) the calculation of the costs and benefits of a fertilizer subsidy versus a price support scheme, illustrated with an example; and (c) an examination of the gainers and losers from a fertilizer subsidy under alternative assumptions about border prices and domestic fertilizer production costs.

9. Some main lessons in the historical experience of input interventions are, *first*, input subsidies have been successful in some countries over certain historical periods, but a fundamental requirement of success is that sufficient supplies are available at the subsidised price levels, *second*, state delivery systems often

fail to deliver the goods, and *third*, at the time of writing price interventions are unfashionable, and seem likely to remain so for the foreseeable future, thus the interesting area for debate is on the appropriate mixture of state and private roles in delivery and information to farmers.

10. The position of women with respect to input policies is briefly considered, and the reader is referred to Chapter 12 for a comparative summary of the gender dimensions of agricultural policies.

Further reading

Input policies are described briefly but to the point in Streeten (1987: Ch. 6) and World Bank (1986b: 94–7). An earlier more detailed coverage is given in Mellor (1966: Ch. 16). Several articles on input policies are recommended. They include Desai (1988) which is vigorously against price intervention and in favour of delivery improvement; von Braun & Puetz (1987) which is a case-study in input delivery failure; Hedley & Tabor (1989) on input subsidies in Indonesia; Shepherd (1989) on privatisation of fertilizer marketing in Africa; and Ahmed (1987) which examines the gainers and losers from fertilizer subsidies in Bangladesh. More difficult for the non-economist reader are Barker & Hayami (1976); Tolley *et al.* (1982: Ch. 7); and Timmer (1986b), which examine in different ways input subsidies compared to price support as policy alternatives.

Reading list

Ahmed, R.U. (1987). Structure and Dynamics of Fertilizer Subsidy: The Case of Bangladesh. *Food Policy*, February.

Barker, R. & Hayami, Y. (1976). Price Support Versus Input Subsidy for Food Self-Sufficiency in Developing Countries. *American Journal of Agricultural Economics*, November.

Desai, G. (1988). Policy for Rapid Growth in Use of Modern Agricultural Inputs. In *Agricultural Price Policy for Developing Countries*, eds J.W. Mellor and R.U. Ahmed, Ch. 12. Baltimore: Johns Hopkins.

Hedley, D.D. & Tabor, S.R. (1989). Fertilizer in Indonesian Agriculture: the Subsidy Issue. *Agricultural Economics*, 3, 49–68.

Mellor, J.W. (1966). *The Economics of Agricultural Development*. New York: Cornell University Press.

Shepherd, A. (1989). Approaches to the Privatization of Fertilizer Marketing in Africa. *Food Policy*, May.

Streeten, P. (1987). *What Price Food? Agricultural Price Policies in Developing Countries*. London: Macmillan.

Timmer, C.P. (1986b). The Role of Price Policy in Rice Production in
  Indonesia 1968–1982. In *Research in Domestic and International
  Agribusiness Management,* ed. R.A. Goldberg, pp. 55–106. Greenwich,
  Conn: JAI Press.
Tolley, G.S., Thomas, V. & Wong, C.M. (1982). *Agricultural Price Policies
  and the Developing Countries.* Baltimore: Johns Hopkins.
von Braun, J. & Puetz, D. (1987). An African Fertilizer Crisis: Origin and
  Economic Effects in the Gambia. *Food Policy,* November.
World Bank (1986b). *World Development Report 1986.* Oxford University
  Press.

7

Credit policy

Credit and rural financial markets

The topic of this chapter is the provision of credit to farm families in developing countries. Credit provision has been one of the most popular types of state intervention in the agricultural sector, as well as being the largest agricultural sector recipient of aid funds from external aid donors.

Ideas about credit policy changed considerably during the 1980s. This chapter makes a distinction between the concepts, objectives, and instruments of 'old credit policy' – meaning the previously dominant and conventional ideas about credit provision to farmers – and the features of 'new credit policy' emerging in the 1990s.

The topic of credit has its own concepts and definitions, which it is useful to make clear at the outset. Credit is a sum of money in favour of the person to whom control over it is transferred. The provision of credit involves two parties: a lender and a borrower. It also involves a price for the transfer of control over money, which is the interest rate charged by the lender to the borrower. At a simple level, neoclassical economics treats the market for credit like any other market: it contains a demand schedule, a supply schedule, and a price – the interest rate – that adjusts to bring demand and supply into balance.

The *lender* in a credit transaction is the individual or institution, called a financial intermediary, that provides a supply of credit to potential borrowers. Once the loan has been made, the borrower has control over its use, but incurs a debt obligation to repay the money to the lender as well as to pay the interest on the loan. The *borrower* in a credit transaction is the person or enterprise who has a demand for credit in order to (i) achieve intertemporal transfers of consumption, (ii) even out fluctuations in availability of cash to buy recurrent farm inputs, or (iii) make an investment in order to realise future increases in income.

Credit is sometimes confused with capital, and it is also occasionally confused with farm inputs. Credit is not capital, but it can be used, amongst other things, to make an investment such as buying an irrigation pump, which is capital. Credit is not an input into farm production like seeds, fertilizer, pesticides, or labour hours. However, it can be used, amongst other things, to improve the ability of farmers at critical times of the year to buy these inputs. When used for this purpose it is often called 'working capital'. Credit can be used to buy today what would otherwise not be possible to buy until tomorrow. This purchase might be for consumption, or for production.

These aspects of credit point to one of its most significant characteristics, its *fungibility*. The term fungibility refers to the interchangeability of the uses to which credit can be put. Fungibility makes it easy for the borrower to divert credit from one use to another (funds are diverted from seeds to shoes). The borrower can also substitute borrowed funds for other money (the funds are used for seed, but this releases other money to buy the shoes). *Diversion* and *substitution* can occur even if the credit is delivered in physical form. Credit given in the form of a bag of seeds can still be sold in order to buy a pair of shoes.

In addition to lenders and borrowers, the other main actors in a rural financial system are savers. The *saver* is the person, or household, or institution that is prepared to supply funds to be held by a financial institution in return for an income flow in the shape of interest payments. The saver *deposits* money with the institution, and in so doing transfers control over the money to the institution. The latter can in turn use the money in order to make loans to borrowers. At the same time the institution incurs a debt obligation to the saver.

This process of saving, lending and borrowing is called financial intermediation. It is a process in which debt claims by savers over lenders are converted into debt claims by lenders over borrowers. The institutions that enable this to take place by bringing together savers and borrowers with differing needs in space and time are called *financial intermediaries*.

Credit may be informal or formal, private or state in origin. Informal credit channels refer to the financial services provided by moneylenders (rich farmers, traders, and others in the rural economy who lend money on the basis of personal knowledge of each transaction). Formal credit channels are those bound by the legal regulations of a country, and they include private banks, state banks, registered cooperatives, and a host of others. The entire system of institutions and the way they work is called the *rural financial system*.

Credit transactions are not costless, and there is no single rate of interest that covers the costs of and returns to the three principal actors – borrowers, lenders, and savers – in the system. Instead, each type of participant faces what are called *transaction costs*, and rates of interest diverge in order to allow for the recoupment of these costs by the intermediary. For example, the interest rate to borrowers needs to be higher than the interest rate to savers by at least enough to cover the lender's costs per unit of money, for otherwise the lending operation is not viable. Indeed, the lender must typically charge a risk premium over and above deposit interest rate plus unit cost, in order to provide some cover against loan defaults by borrowers.

A typical device for selecting borrowers is to demand that the borrower provide some *collateral* for the whole or a proportion of a loan. Collateral might be a plot of land (if owned freehold by the borrower), a piece of equipment, a draft animal (e.g. a bullock), or a proportion of the crop (called a 'crop lien'). The inability of tenants and poor farmers to provide collateral in the private or informal financial systems is one of the main reasons for creating institutional credit schemes. Even when collateral exists it does not entirely remove the risk element of making a loan, because realising the money value of collateral is seldom straightforward or costless.

This chapter has the following purposes:

(a) to set out the *objectives* of what we have called the 'old credit policy', elements of which remain very important in the motivation of governments and aid donors to institute and support credit schemes;

(b) to describe the *institutions* of old credit policy, and the *instruments* used in order to achieve credit policy objectives;

(c) to examine the *defects* of traditional approaches to credit, which arise in the critical literature on credit policy;

(d) to outline emerging changes of emphasis, new objectives, and new instruments, which are the hallmarks of what might be called *new credit policy*;

(e) to discuss the importance of *institutional innovation* for the establishment of viable and self-sustaining rural financial systems with small farmers as their main clients;

(f) to make some connections between credit policy and *peasants*, especially with respect to the savings behaviour of peasants and the role of moneylenders as opposed to formal credit agencies;

(g) to consider briefly the status of *women* with respect to credit policies.

Objectives of old credit policy

Credit has always had a special place in mainstream thinking on agricultural development. For several decades, indeed, donor assistance towards credit provision was the largest single category of aid to the agricultural sector in developing countries (World Bank, 1975). In the 1950s and early 1960s, credit provision was considered a key instrument for breaking the 'vicious circle' of low incomes, low savings, and low productivity. However, in that period emphasis was far more on market-orientated farmers and commercial agriculture (plantations and estates) than on peasants.

From the mid-1960s, and up to the present time, small farmers and the rural poor have increasingly become the chief target of credit interventions. There are many reasons for this, including emerging ideas about the efficiency of small farmers, their output potential with new technology, their lack of cash at critical periods in the crop or livestock season, their lack of collateral for loans, and the exploitative or monopolistic behaviour of private moneylenders. In addition, since the early-1970s, a strong equity dimension emerged in the aims of credit schemes and small farm projects.

The objectives of credit policies, and the reasons for their popularity with governments and aid donors alike, are summarised as follows:

(a) to alleviate a critical constraint hampering growth in agricultural output, this constraint being lack of cash to make needed farm investments (irrigation, drainage, pumps, tractors, buildings) and to purchase 'modern' variable inputs (fertilizer, pesticides, fuel, feeds, etc.);

(b) to replace the fragmented and incomplete rural financial market represented by private moneylenders, these credit sources supposedly having the effect of impoverishing their clients rather than assisting them to improve their productivity;

(c) to accelerate the adoption of new technology by peasant farmers, by providing working capital for the seasonal purchase of variable inputs, and thence optimising the complementarity between inputs essential for the success of Green Revolution technology;

(d) to assist small farmers to overcome their inability to borrow from commercial or informal credit sources, due to lack of collateral and lack of information;

(e) to provide short-term credit in order to bridge seasonal and temporary cash shortfalls of small farmers, compared to the medium- and long-term lending preferences of commercial financial institutions;

(f) to achieve equity goals, whether these are related to intra-rural, inter-regional, or rural–urban income distribution;

(g) to offset the disincentive effects for small farmers of policies unfavourable to them including low output prices, over-valued exchange rates, and inefficient market interventions by the state;

(h) to gain favour with farmers for political purposes, including forthcoming elections, and so on;

(i) to take advantage of the sometimes overwhelming generosity of foreign aid donors, who seem to be prepared to pump large amounts of money endlessly into rural credit projects.

Note that the first two of these goals are general and apply across the agricultural sector. The next five are specific to small farmers, and imply targeting of loans, and criteria for borrower selection. Some of these are output orientated, and some are equity orientated. The last two are not serious points in policy analysis, but nor are they irrelevant to government decision making with respect to credit projects.

Institutions of old credit policy

The traditional approach to credit policy is for funds for lending to farmers to be predominantly supply-led. This means that they originate from the central bank or from external donors, rather than from local saving in the rural economy. Many different institutions may be involved in the channelling of central or external funds to farmers, even within a single country. Across the developing countries, some of the most popular institutional ways of organising credit are as follows:

(a)   *State agricultural banks*

These are probably the dominant type of agency that are specialised in delivering loans to farmers, and they tend to undertake few, if any, other financial services (von Pischke *et al.*, 1981). They have names like Agricultural Development Bank, Agricultural Finance Corporation, Rural Development Bank, and so on. This type of credit agency has major branches outside the capital city, but these are rarely to be found in truly rural locations. Sometimes they are linked to cooperatives as the ultimate lenders to farmers (see below).

(b)   *Multi-purpose development agencies*
This category covers development institutions such as integrated rural development agencies, regional development authorities, river basin authorities, and so on. These institutions are typically area-based. They carry out a wide range of development functions within a specified location, and credit delivery is likely to be combined with other components of a development 'package' including new seeds, variable inputs, and advice, perhaps covering several crops or types of farm enterprise.

(c)   *Crop and project authorities*
These differ from the preceding category in that they narrowly focus either on a single crop, or on a much more restricted geographical area, like a settlement scheme. This category includes crop parastatals such as coffee boards, cocoa boards, tea authorities, and so on; and crop projects such as coconut development schemes, smallholder sugar schemes, maize improvement projects, and so on. This type of organisation used to be favoured by the World Bank (1975: 15) for credit delivery, because loan repayment could be built into the crop marketing arrangements of the authority.

(d)   *Commercial banks*
The involvement of private banks in rural financial systems varies widely. However, there are few examples of the spontaneous expansion into rural areas of the mainly urban-based commercial banking systems. Nevertheless, some governments have actively used the private formal banking system to pursue credit policy goals, and this is usually done by implementing banking regulations in such a way as to try to force private banks to participate in farm credit schemes and to open rural bank branches.

(e)   *Cooperatives and farmer groups*
This category covers a multitude of different types of organisations from nationwide state-sponsored farmer cooperatives to local initiatives in cooperation by farmers themselves. Cooperatives are quantitatively significant in credit policy, because they are often used as the

ultimate lenders to farmers within top-down structures of credit delivery. Occasionally they are also viable local credit organisations in their own right.

Instruments of old credit policy

The institutions created or regulated by the state in order to deliver credit to farmers represent by themselves a type of instrument for implementing credit objectives. The way these institutions operate, and the constraints imposed on them by government policy, also involve more specific instruments for achieving goals such as output growth, equity, small farm coverage, and short-term credit. Some main instruments of state credit policy in developing countries are:

(a)   *Low interest rates*

One of the most popular instruments of credit policy in developing countries has been to subsidise the rate of interest on loans to farmers. The reason for this is the belief that the demand for credit by small farmers is highly sensitive to the interest rate, i.e. demand for credit is very elastic. This belief is probably wrong (see below), but if it is considered true, then the only way to get farmers to make more use of credit – for example in order to buy new types of cash input – is to lower interest rates. Interest rates in agricultural credit schemes have regularly been half, or even less than half, the opportunity cost of funds for the financial institutions involved.

A common way of operating an interest rate subsidy is for the lending institutions to be able to 'rediscount' agricultural loans at the central bank. This means that a lender making loans to farmers at eight per cent interest can replenish its funds from the Central Bank at, say, five per cent interest. This allows the lender a margin of three per cent to cover transactions costs. The size of the subsidy depends on the opportunity cost of funds to the central bank. For example, if interest rates in international financial markets are 15 per cent, then the central bank incurs a loss equivalent to 10 per cent on funds that are rediscounted to credit agencies at five per cent. However, it is common for a proportion of credit funds, especially in poor countries, to involve concessional loans from external donors at below market interest rates. Therefore, actual financial losses incurred by the Central Bank may be lower than is indicated by market interest rates.

(b) *Credit targeting*

The orientation of credit policy towards small farmers involves extensive use of targeting devices. Evaluations of earlier subsidised credit schemes commonly showed that larger farmers were their chief beneficiaries, for a variety of reasons which are examined in the next section.

New borrowers can be identified in a number of different ways. For crop and project-type lending, the project design may already determine the target group for credit delivery (smallholder tree crop projects, etc.). In more general credit schemes, the target group may be defined according to various criteria such as farm area or family income, for example, all farmers with under 2 ha in crop production. Some examples of target group criteria are given in Padmanabhan (1988: 21–2).

(c) *Loan portfolio regulations*

Various devices may be used by governments to restrict the decision-making flexibility of financial institutions, or to try to enforce compliance with state objectives. These types of device are usually associated with state regulation of the private banking system, but some of them may be applicable also to state credit agencies.

One device is to set a minimum to the proportion of agricultural sector loans out of total loans. For instance, financial institutions may be obliged to maintain at least 50 per cent of their loans in agricultural lending. Another device is to stipulate maximum permissible loan sizes, in order to avoid too large a share of total loans going to large borrowers. A third device is to place restrictions on the term structure of the loan portfolio, such that the major proportion of total loans are short-term loans. The reason for this is the view that small farmers mainly require short-term loans, i.e. as working capital for input purchase, while large farmers require medium and long-term loans for capital investment.

(d) *Miscellaneous instruments*

Many other instruments can be used by governments in order to try to fulfil specified goals related to the provision of credit to farmers. Sometimes credit is provided in kind. For example, a bag of fertilizer is delivered to the farmer rather than the money to buy a bag of fertilizer. This is in order to overcome the problem of fungibility, but it is unlikely to be successful, because if the farmer really wants to realise money for other purposes, the physical credit will be sold for cash.

Another common instrument is for credit provision to be linked to crop marketing, especially for export crops which are sold through a marketing board. The repayment of the credit can then take the form of a deduction from the price received by the farmer, thus avoiding problems of loan recovery.

Defects of old credit policy

Since the mid-1970s, a considerable volume of critical literature has appeared concerning credit policies in developing countries (Shaw, 1973; McKinnon, 1973; Donald, 1976; Fry, 1982; von Pischke *et al.*, 1983; Adams *et al.*, 1984). Interestingly, this literature pre-dates by almost a decade the more general tide of anti-state writings in development economics, and it is very specific in its focus on credit. The central components of the critique are set out in the following paragraphs.

(a)   *Fungibility*

The fungibility attribute of credit, and of loanable funds more generally, invalidates most state targets and regulations for credit delivery (von Pischke & Adams, 1980). Fungibility exists in all tiers of the credit system, from the farmer, to the financial intermediary, and to the central bank.

At farmer level, fungibility means that loans targeted for specific purposes (e.g. fertilizer use in cotton cultivation) may be used by the household for quite different ends (e.g. purchase of a sewing machine to make garments). Funds can be substituted or diverted (see von Pischke & Adams, *loc cit*, for some examples). Delivery of credit in physical form is an ineffective solution. Ultimately, farm households will deploy borrowed funds in the uses that give them the highest marginal return in consumption or production.

At the lender level, fungibility means that cheap funds can be substituted for own funds in the preferred loan portfolio, usually biased towards low-risk established clients. Loan portfolio regulations can easily be evaded. Non-farm loans can be classified as farm loans by simple tricks of form filling. Loan size limits can be evaded by making multiple small loans under different names to the same borrower.

At the central bank level, donor funds for rural credit schemes mean more foreign exchange. While the credit itself may be channelled towards small farmers, thus satisfying donor wishes, the extra foreign exchange may be used to buy missiles or tanks, heavy industrial equipment, or swimming pool pumps for the rich.

Fungibility also helps to explain why credit projects may appear to have been successful in ex-post project evaluations, even when rural financial markets and institutions are plainly in a mess (Adams, 1988). Evaluations of credit projects often assume that the entire change in the output of project farmers is attributable to credit provision, an assumption known as 100 per cent *additionality*. Due to substitution and diversion – aspects of fungibility – 100 per cent additionality is a most implausible outcome of credit provision. Moreover, it is impossible in practice to identify changes that would have occurred in the absence of formal credit from those that occurred as a result of formal credit.

(b)   *Low interest rates*
Subsidised interest rates create several negative effects for the long-run viability of rural financial institutions, as well as for borrowers and savers. *First*, there are many recorded instances, especially in the 1970s, when the real rate of interest in credit schemes was negative. The real rate of interest refers to the actual interest rate deflated by the annual rate of inflation. For example, if the actual rate of interest (r) is eight per cent, and the rate of inflation (c) is 20 per cent, then the real rate of interest (i) is -10 per cent. This is derived from the formula:

$$i = (1 + r)/(1 + c) - 1$$

A negative real rate of interest virtually makes the loan a gift from the lender to the borrower (the latter pays back less in real terms than was borrowed). More formally, it causes a transfer of real resources from lending institutions to borrowing farmers, thus undermining – possibly decisively – the viability of lenders.

Second, low interest rates to borrowers make it impossible to offer attractive interest rates to savers. The rate offered to savers must be below the borrowers' rate by an amount reflecting transaction costs. This could mean that the rate on savings deposits is negative in real terms, or so low that almost any alternative use of the funds would make more sense to the potential saver.

Third, low interest rates may mean that it is impossible for the lending institution to cover the transaction costs of making loans within the margin between the borrower interest rate and the rate the lender must pay for securing funds from the central bank, or from its own savers. This further damages lender viability, and may result in transaction costs being transferred, as non-interest costs, to borrowers (e.g. paperwork fees, etc.). In addition, it may result in diversion of loans to big borrowers since unit transaction costs are always much lower for big loans than for small loans (Gonzalez-Vega, 1977).

Fourth, low interest rates cause an excess of demand over supply of credit, resulting in formal or informal credit rationing. Rationing tends to favour the big and rich borrower over the small and poor borrower due to personal contacts, ability to make gifts to officials, favours granted and returned, and so on.

(c)   *Transaction costs*

The goals and regulations of many subsidised, target-orientated, credit schemes cause a big rise in the transaction costs of lenders, whether these are private or state institutions. Lending to large numbers of small borrowers costs more per unit of money than lending to small numbers of big borrowers (Ahmed, 1989; Sarap, 1990). The paperwork and reporting requirements of externally funded credit schemes tend to be much larger than those associated with normal commercial lending. High transaction costs threaten the viability of lending institutions, cause transfer of costs to borrowers (see above) or savers, and result in lender preference for few big loans rather than many small ones.

Some studies have shown transaction costs of financial intermediaries like rural development banks to range up to 25 per cent (and sometimes over) the value of loans disbursed. If the margin within which this cost is to be met is only two or three per cent, the lending institution will find it impossible to sustain this kind of financial operation in the long term.

(d)   *Loan recovery*

Formal credit schemes have an abysmal record concerning loan recovery from farmers. Studies published in the early 1980s indicated average loan failure rates across samples of credit schemes at around 25 per cent, rising to 80 per cent in some cases (see e.g. Padmanabhan, 1988: 66).

Loan default is typically considered to be caused by two main factors: (i) inability to repay (e.g. due to crop failure), or (ii) unwillingness to repay (e.g. due to viewing the loan as a grant, or as political patronage). It may also be a function of the borrower's perception about the penalties of not paying, especially in terms of getting future loans. Where borrowers have no stake in the lending institution (they are not savers), and where they can see that credit availability is of limited duration (as in many fixed period donor-funded projects), the incentive to default is high.

The entire working of certain types of credit scheme or project may not be conducive to high proportions of debt recovery: collateral is not required as a loan condition; the cost of pursuing defaulters is high relative to the size of loans; lending officials are indifferent to default in the face of their own problems (low salaries, backlog of paperwork); the institution is not too concerned provided donor funds keep arriving; and so on.

(e)   *Savings failure*
Saving was some time ago dubbed 'the forgotten half of rural finance' (Vogel, 1984). The argument is that since rural credit agencies fail to encourage rural saving, they also fail to possess funds that can make them independent of central or external funding. Thus they are also incapable of surviving as self-sustaining financial institutions in the long term.

There are many strands in the savings argument, some of which have already been covered above. *First*, some credit schemes are entirely supply driven and envisage no role for savings from the outset; *second*, even those credit institutions that are permitted savings deposits do not encourage them because they are heavily orientated to external funds ('addicted to outside funds for their sustenance' – Adams, 1988: 355); *third*, some formal credit institutions deliberately discourage saving by imposing high transaction costs upon savers (inconvenient hours, standing in line, red tape – Adams & Nehmann, 1979); *fourth*, some credit agencies may try to encourage savings deposits but are unsuccessful due to the unrealistic levels of interest they can offer.

The central conclusion to emerge from this critique of conventional credit policies is their self-defeating nature. They are self-defeating because few of their components are sustainable in the long run. The institutions are not sustainable due to reliance on external funding, failure to cover transaction costs, high levels of loan default, and lack of savings. The low interest rates are not sustainable due to their adverse effects on savings and on the ability of lenders to cover costs. The small-farm orientation is not sustainable when it is forced upon credit agencies by regulation and is operated in a manner that is detrimental to their viability.

New objectives and new instruments
The outcome of identifying these problems of traditional credit schemes is that, in most countries, credit systems need rethinking as to

their methods of operation, viability, and sustainability. Some countries already possess examples of rural credit schemes that have worked quite well, and others are beginning to experiment with new ideas. The redefinition of the objectives, instruments, and institutions of credit policy means *neither* that the small-farm or rural-poor orientation of policy needs to be abandoned, *nor* that the state has no role in the fostering and regulation of new initiatives.

Perhaps the most important attribute of a successful credit system is that it should be self-sustaining in the long run, not reliant on ever increasing subsidies to cover losses, and not dependent forever on injections of external funds from foreign aid donors. A credit institution that comes into being just to provide money for the start up of a tree crop project, then winds up when the money runs out, is not development – of the rural financial system – in any meaningful sense. Likewise, an agricultural development bank that spends most of its management energy trying to ensure the continuing flow of subsidised funds from the central bank or from foreign aid donors possesses doubtful merit as a development institution.

The critical new *objective* of credit policy is therefore the creation of a self-sustaining rural financial system. As already stated, this does not exclude the continued pursuit of various older objectives, especially those related to small farmers and poor rural people. It does, however, mean a major rethink of the instruments of credit policy and the institutions created to implement them. Here we consider first the directions of change in instruments that are required, before moving to the important issue of viable institutional innovations.

Savings mobilisation
The generation of funds from savers is considered a key feature of self-sustaining credit institutions. First, a strong savings base reduces the reliance on external funding. Second, savers and borrowers are often the same people at different points in time in the community, reducing the information costs of transactions. Third, people tied to an institution for both saving and borrowing are less likely to default on loans. Fourth, farmers with savings can often self-finance small outlays so that loans become orientated to bigger outlays with lower transaction costs per unit of money.

A traditional view that small farmers and poor rural people are unable to save has been shown to be wrong in several experiments (see e.g. the description of the Grameen Bank in Bangladesh given in Hossain, 1988).

The main features of the rural poor in this context are: their income is uneven, their potential to save often involves very small amounts, they cannot afford 'costs' associated with saving (including time and distance costs), and they are naturally concerned with the security of saving.

For peasants who are not-so-poor, lack of saving is much more to do with lack of opportunity, or distrust of the alternatives available, than to do with low savings capacity. Households keep their assets in goats or cattle rather than in the bank, especially when the bank discourages savings, or appears to be run by untrustworthy officials.

Interest rate level

A self-sustaining financial system requires an interest rate on loans sufficient to cover the three components of (i) the interest rate paid to savers, (ii) the average cost of making transactions, and (iii) a risk margin to cover the probability of default.

The level of the first component should correspond roughly to the opportunity costs of funds in the wider economy, and must be high enough to ensure that savers face a positive real rate of return on their deposits. The second component is impossible to cover if administrative costs are inflated by high overheads, over employment, poor motivation, and similar ills. An efficient margin between the borrowing and lending rate of interest is in the region of 4–6 per cent or lower, for example, savers receive 10 per cent, borrowers pay 15 per cent. The size of the third component, the risk margin, falls as the loan recovery rate improves (see below).

The main challenge facing an interest rate policy designed to improve the credit system is to reduce transaction costs. A realistic rate of interest can be set in terms of wider market rates, but credit agencies will remain non-viable if their costs are greater than the interest margin permitted between borrowing and lending. A buoyant financial institution that is expanding its operations autonomously over time will experience falling unit transaction costs due to the larger volume of money handled relative to administrative overheads.

The traditional view that market interest rates discourage farmers from making use of credit is wrong in most cases. It rests on the mistaken assumption that credit demand by farmers is highly elastic with respect to the price of credit, whereas for small farmers requiring short-term loans to overcome cash flow problems, demand is in reality inelastic. This is demonstrated in part by the continued high proportion of total credit that is supplied by private moneylenders, usually involving interest rates of 50 per cent or higher on short-term loans.

Loan recovery

It is now widely acknowledged that poor loan recovery performance is an unacceptable feature of any credit scheme. Poor loan recovery amounts to giving borrowers a gift, it encourages the use of credit for non-productive purposes, and it promotes the idea that rural development is more about cash hand-outs than about improved productivity and output. Some big small-farm credit schemes in certain countries have had default rates as high as 80 per cent in the past. It is possible that such credit schemes had an overall negative effect on the capacity of farmers to sustain their livelihoods in the long term, which is certainly not what development efforts should be about.

There are many reasons for low rates of loan recovery (see above and Padmanabhan, 1988: 66–70). There is therefore no single solution to the problem, though tougher recovery discipline (e.g. no new loans until old loans are repaid), more realistic interest rates (which ensure that loans cannot be mistaken for gifts), more joint saving and borrowing operations (which give borrowers a long-term stake in the lending agency), all have a role to play.

Nevertheless, there remain various reasons for default that are unavoidable, or that require more care at the inception of a credit scheme. Natural calamities such as floods or drought can make repayment impossible in the locations and seasons where they occur, though this is a time and location specific reason, and not an excuse for persistent defaults. When credit is earmarked for crops or enterprises that turn out to be non-viable either due to mistakes (e.g. inaccurate rainfall predictions, or failure to conduct soil tests), or due to other state policies (e.g. low output prices), then responsibility for credit failure lies less with the borrower and more with the lending agencies.

The changes of emphasis with respect to these instruments lead to changes in the criteria by which the success or failure of a credit scheme may be measured. Adams (1988: 365) suggests that instead of target group achievements (number of target borrowers reached by a given scheme), the criteria for success should include (i) the number of clients reached as both savers and borrowers, with the normal expectation for a viable institution being many small savers and fewer, larger, borrowers, (ii) declining transaction costs over time, reflecting expansion of services and success in attracting new clients, (iii) improved loan recovery, and

(iv) total volume of savings achieved, and significance of savings in sources of funds for onward lending.

Institutional innovations

The successful reorientation of credit away from the mainly supply-led, state agricultural bank, type of scheme requires imagination and experimentation in devising new credit institutions (Braverman & Guasch, 1986: 1263). Credit provision needs to be located in a context of diverse institutions providing several different services, not a single bureaucracy providing just one kind of service.

The required elements of more appropriate and efficient institutions reside partly in the changed agenda of credit policy (saving, loan recovery, self-sustainability), and partly in the experience of credit institutions that have proved successful in such terms. Key elements are viability, self-sufficiency, access, and efficiency (Padmanabhan, 1988: Ch. 13).

There are several case-studies that provide useful indications of how these elements may be created and combined (von Pischke & Rouse, 1983; Padmanabhan, 1988: *passim*). One interesting case-study is the Syndicate Bank in India (Bhatt, 1988: 286–90), another one is the Grameen Bank in Bangladesh (Biggs, 1984: 66–9; Egger, 1986: 449–51; Hossain, 1988). The latter has become a celebrated example of how very poor and landless rural people can save, borrow credit, and repay loans by participating in a credit agency adapted to suit their needs. The Grameen Bank was experiencing an average loan recovery rate of 99.5 per cent in 1988. Some general conclusions arising from these case-studies are listed below:

(a) Small farmers and poor people can save. However, the saving needs to be organised in special ways. Regular, once a week, saving of a fixed amount (with extra saving optional) is one possibility, facilitated by door-to-door collection with a minimum of paperwork. Linking of saving with capacity to borrow works well, for example, automatic loan access up to twice the value of savings in case of emergency (like crop failure); automatic loan access for investment (like a water pump) up to some multiple of savings; regular saving as part of the way loan repayment is organised, and so on.

(b) Group lending, and group responsibility for repayment, seem promising ways of organising loans. Groups are formed according to predetermined criteria reflecting homogeneity of interests (e.g. land ownership under 0.5 acres as in the Grameen Bank case); they are small so that everyone knows what the others are doing (e.g. five members in the Grameen Bank case); and they take on collective responsibility for ensuring that loans are properly utilized and repayments are made. The penalty for default is that the entire group loses its capacity to lend or to save with the institution, thus powerful social pressures ensure compliance with group responsibilities.

(c) Lending agencies need to reduce administrative costs, reduce bureaucracy and paperwork to minimum reporting standards, create incentive and promotion structures according to the performance of officers (in attracting savers, making loans, recovering overdue repayments), decentralise decision-making and initiative to branch offices, and so on.

Obviously there is no single solution, or blueprint, to the institutional organisation of agricultural credit in developing countries. Each country must experiment with its own models, and more than one model may be applicable according to the scope and functions intended.

Whatever the institutional models adopted for credit agencies – even when these are based on market principles governing the supply and demand for loanable funds – the state is required to continue to play a regulatory role in rural financial markets. The reason for this is that the success of financial institutions is always dependent on the trust of their clients. In the absence of trust people do not save, and financial institutions are liable to experience unstable cycles of confidence with many failures and bankruptcies. Thus even minimum regulation requires enforceable rules regarding the loan ratio of credit institutions, and the security of the deposits of savers.

A note on the pace of change

By referring to the historically most common forms of credit policy as 'old credit policy' and counterposing this to 'new credit policy', the false impression may have been given that credit delivery to farmers in developing countries has undergone a radical restructuring in recent times. This is not an accurate picture. Existing credit institutions in developing countries are part of the post-Independence (or post-Second World War) *status quo*, built up over a period of two or three decades. The *status quo* by definition changes little or slowly, especially with respect to state institutions, and so it is with agricultural credit institutions.

Even though the critique of credit policy became widespread well in advance of the more general critique of government interventions in the 1980s, it is possible that credit policies will in the end change more slowly than other branches of state policy towards agriculture. Price controls can often be lifted at the stroke of a pen, state institutions can rarely be disposed of in this manner. Case-studies of viable and self-sustaining credit agencies like the Grameen Bank in Bangladesh remain exceptions rather than the rule.

Peasants, moneylenders, and credit policy

The traditional or 'old' ideas about rural credit in developing countries are predicated on various assumptions about peasant household behaviour and the working of markets in the peasant economy.

One set of assumptions concerns the saving and borrowing behaviour of the household, irrespective of the type of financial market the household faces. These tend to be pessimistic: the peasant has no resources (= cash) to save, and is unwilling to borrow except at giveaway interest rates. The discussion of this chapter shows that both these assumptions are questionable. For the peasant household, saving is a matter of the form in which it is safest and most convenient to hold assets. Peasants keep resources not used for consumption in many different forms: gold coins under the bed, a piece of land in another village, cattle, goats, and so on. An appropriate rural financial institution can tap these savings by causing 'asset-switching' into interest bearing deposit accounts.

Likewise, peasants do not have 'a high price elasticity of demand for credit'. On the contrary, the use they make of private moneylenders shows that for essential seasonal cash borrowing for inputs they will borrow money even when the interest rate is as high as 10 per cent per month.

The second set of assumptions concerns the working of informal credit (moneylenders). These assumptions tend to be correct – moneylenders do not by themselves bring into existence a rural financial market because every transaction is unique, non-replicable, and involves a different interest rate – but the inferences drawn from them are sometimes wide of the mark. It is true that the informal market for credit is incomplete and involves interlinked transactions (Ellis, 1988a: Ch. 8). However, some of the merits of this defective market from the peasants' viewpoint need to be recognised, especially in contrast to state credit schemes.

Credit from moneylenders is based on personal knowledge of the borrower (who may or may not be tied to the moneylender through land tenancy, etc.). This credit is timely (it does not require queueing or form filling), it is local (it does not require travel by bus or train), it is often explicitly fungible (the moneylender will lend for the emergency transport of a relative to hospital, as well as for nitrogen fertilizer), and it is not always extortionately expensive when the costs and risks of the money-lender are fully taken into account (although sometimes it is). An interesting point about moneylenders is that in a country like India they tend to be regarded with far more suspicion by academics and policy makers than by the peasant farmers who make use of their services (Padmanabhan, 1988: Ch. 12).

As stated in Chapter 1 of this book, state policy towards peasants is often about integrating peasants into the market, and making those markets work better over time. In the case of credit policy it is uncertain whether either of these aims has been achieved, even though many billions of dollars have flowed into rural societies through credit schemes. A rural credit system that relies on *ad hoc* donor or central bank support in order to provide credit at non-market interest rates is no more a complete market than the moneylenders it purports to replace.

Credit policy and women

Formal credit schemes do not typically take gender into account. In practice, they tend to be gender-biased towards men. It is the male head of household who is usually approached and registered for the provision of institutional credit. However, it is becoming more widely recognised that women can make good use of credit in their own right for activities that improve their own livelihoods and the income security of their families. Some negative aspects of male-biased credit provision are as follows:

(a) it reinforces other trends whereby women become excluded from activities in which they formerly had economic control, this control being passed to men (food processing and produce marketing are relevant examples);

(b) credit for labour-saving equipment and machines may displace more women than men in farm and non-farm operations;

(c) credit for cash crop production in which men are engaged may result in increasing conflicts of land and labour use between men and women;

(d) in some cases formal credit schemes directed to men may replace informal credit systems controlled by women.

There is no defensible reason for credit policies to be biased towards men. Women have great potential for the productive use of credit, as demonstrated by experiments such as the Grameen Bank in Bangladesh, and by numerous non-government credit programmes. It is possible that women are more reliable than men at using credit for the purposes for which it was designated, and at repaying loans.

Summary

1. This chapter is about the provision of credit to small farmers and the working of rural financial markets in developing countries. Credit policy tends to consist of government efforts to make more loanable funds available to farmers. In many cases this takes the form of specialised farm credit institutions concerned with the one-way supply of funds to farmers from external aid donors or from the central bank.

2. The chapter begins by defining terms. *Credit* is defined as a sum of money in favour of the person to whom control over it is transferred, and who undertakes to pay it back. Credit is distinguished from farm *capital* and from farm *inputs*. *Lenders*, *borrowers*, and *savers* are defined. The key characteristic of credit is its *fungibility*. This includes diversion and substitution of funds across various uses. *Informal* credit (from moneylenders) is distinguished from *formal* credit (from the private or state banking system). The entire system of credit institutions and the way they work is called the *rural financial system*.

3. Reflecting a long-standing debate about credit policy, the chapter makes a distinction between 'old credit policy' which follows established lines of credit delivery to farmers; and 'new credit policy' based on revised ideas about savings, interest rates, and the roles of credit. It is emphasised that 'old credit policy' remains the dominant approach to credit provision in developing countries.

4. The objectives of the 'old credit policy' are orientated to the delivery of credit to farmers – especially small farmers – in order to overcome the monopoly power of private moneylenders, the lack of collateral of small farmers, and the absence of a proper market in loanable funds. Objectives include alleviating constraints on the purchase of modern variable inputs; accelerating the adoption of new technology; providing short-term credit; achieving equity goals related to intra-rural or rural–urban income distribution; and offsetting the disincentive effects of other state policies such as price policy.

5. Instruments deployed in order to achieve these objectives include subsidised interest rates, credit targeting, loan portfolio regulations, and others. Institutions of credit delivery include state agricultural banks, multi-purpose development agencies, crop and project authorities, commercial banks, and co-operatives. Cooperatives are often used as the ultimate lenders to farmers within top-down structures of credit delivery.

6. The problems and flaws of traditional credit policies are examined. These include (i) the ease of evasion of targets and regulations due to *fungibility*; (ii) low interest rates with adverse effects on savings, transaction costs, and viability of lending institutions; (iii) high transaction costs causing non-viability of lending institutions; (iv) low rates of loan recovery; and (v) widespread failure to encourage savings, thus neglecting half of the demand and supply equation for loanable funds, ensuring continued dependence of financial institutions on external finance, and ensuring non-sustainability of those institutions in the long term.

7. New objectives, instruments, and institutions arise from the defects of the old. The principal new aim should be to develop self-sustainable rural financial institutions. This means charging a realistic interest rate on loans, encouraging saving as the main source of funds, and ensuring much higher rates of loan recovery. It also means abandoning the exclusively supply-orientated credit systems that prevail in most developing countries, but it does not of necessity mean that the small-farm bias or the state-led character of credit policy should disappear. The state is always going to play a major role in the regulation of financial markets, as it does in the industrial countries, even if its institutional presence becomes lower than hitherto.

8. The successful reorientation of credit policy in the future requires an imaginative and experimental approach to institutional innovation. Rural credit provision needs to be located in a context of diverse institutions providing lots of different services, not a single bureaucracy providing just one kind of service. The few case-studies of successful credit institutions show that devices like regular small savings collected on the doorstep, group lending and group accountability for loan repayment, and improved incentive and performance methods within financial institutions, provide potential ways forward.

9. Past credit policies have tended to make wrong assumptions about peasants, viz. that they are unable to save, and that their demand for credit is highly sensitive to the level of the interest rate. Although they have made correct assumptions about moneylenders, viz. that they do not represent a 'market' in credit, they have wrongly concluded that moneylenders have no role to play in the system. The crunch point, however, is that in creating non-viable, loan-orientated, institutions, entirely dependent on external subsidies, they have established no more of a proper market for loanable funds than the informal credit they purport to replace.

10. The position of women with respect to credit policies is briefly considered, and the reader is referred to Chapter 12 for a comparative summary of the gender dimensions of agricultural policies.

Further reading

A text that provides a readable and comprehensive review of credit policy issues is Padmanabhan (1988). Several earlier books and collections are important in the critique of traditional credit policies (Donald, 1976; Howell, 1980; von Pischke *et al.*, 1983; Adams *et al.*, 1984). Papers and reports in the same vein are von Pischke *et al.* (1981); Adams & Graham (1981); Adams & Vogel (1986); Schaefer-Kehnert & von Pischke (1986); and Adams (1988). On institutional innovations and successful components of credit schemes see von Pischke & Rouse (1983); Biggs (1984: 66–9); Braverman & Guasch (1986: 1257–8); Egger (1986); and Bhatt (1988). For those interested in a case-study of a non-farm credit scheme orientated to the rural poor, with many potential lessons for farm credit schemes, the study of the Grameen Bank in Bangladesh by Hossain (1988) is highly recommended.

Reading list

Adams, D.W. (1988). The Conundrum of Successful Credit Projects in Floundering Rural Financial Markets. *Economic Development and Cultural Change*, **36**, No. 2.

Adams, D.W. & Graham D.H. (1981). A Critique of Traditional Agricultural Credit Projects and Policies. *Journal of Development Economics*, **8**.

Adams, D.W., Graham, D.H. & von Pischke, J.D. (eds) (1984). *Undermining Rural Development with Cheap Credit*. Boulder, Colorado: Westview Press.

Adams, D.W. & Vogel, R.C. (1986). Rural Financial Markets in Low-Income Countries: Recent Controversies and Lessons. *World Development*, **14**, No. 4.

Bhatt, V.V. (1988). On Financial Innovations and Credit Market Evolution. *World Development*, **16**, No. 2.

Biggs, S.D. (1984). Awkward but Common Themes in Agricultural Policy. In *Room for Manoeuvre: An Exploration of Public Policy in Agriculture and Rural Development*, eds. E.J. Clay and B.B. Schaffer, Ch. 5. London: Heinemann.

Braverman, A. & Guasch, J.L. (1986). Rural Credit Markets and Institutions in Developing Countries: Lessons for Policy Analysis from Practice and Modern Theory. *World Development*, **14**, No. 10/11.

Donald, G. (ed.) (1976). *Credit for Small Farmers in Developing Countries*. Boulder, Colorado: Westview Press.

Egger, P. (1986). Banking for the Rural Poor: Lessons from some Innovative Savings and Credit Schemes. *ILO Review*, **125**, No. 4.

Hossain, M. (1988). *Credit for Alleviation of Rural Poverty: The Grameen Bank in Bangladesh*. International Food Policy Research Institute, Research Report 65, February.

Howell, J. (ed.) (1980). *Borrowers and Lenders: Rural Financial Markets and Institutions in Developing Countries*. London: ODI.

Padmanabhan, K.P. (1988). *Rural Credit: Lessons for Rural Bankers and Policy Makers*. London: Intermediate Technology Publications.

Schaefer-Kehnert, W. & von Pischke, J.D. (1986). Agricultural Credit Policy in Developing Countries. *Savings and Development*, **10**, No. 1.

von Pischke, J.D., Adams, D.W. & Donald, G. (eds) (1983). *Rural Financial Markets in Developing Countries*. Baltimore: Johns Hopkins.

von Pischke, J.D., Heffernan, P.J. & Adams, D.W. (1981). *The Political Economy of Specialized Farm Credit Institutions in Low-Income Countries*. World Bank Staff Working Paper No. 446. Washington D.C.: World Bank.

von Pischke, J.D. & Rouse, J. (1983). Selected Successful Experiences in Agricultural Credit and Rural Finance in Africa. *Savings and Development*, **7**, No. 1.

8

Mechanisation policy

Farm mechanisation: Definition and concerns

This chapter is about the role of the state in influencing the pace and direction of mechanisation in small-farm agriculture in developing countries. A definition of mechanisation is that it comprises non-human sources of power for undertaking agricultural tasks and activities. There are three main types of technology that fit this definition. *First*, there are hand-tools or implements that increase the effectiveness of human power or energy. *Second*, there is animal-draught power, in which machines or equipment are driven by animals such as buffalo, oxen, horses, mules, donkeys, or camels. *Third*, there is mechanical-power, in which engines or motors, powered by petrol, diesel or electricity, are used to drive a great diversity of farm machines.

Mechanical-power can be further distinguished between *stationary* machines and *mobile* machines. Stationary machines have a fixed location and require the task to be brought to them (for example a water pump or a threshing machine). Mobile machines are able to carry out moving tasks; this type includes the important categories of four-wheel tractors, and two-wheel power tillers.

Mechanisation policy is concerned with the appropriate pace of the transition between the three main types of mechanical technology, given the resources and constraints of both the farm sector and the economy at large. State actions can retard or accelerate the rate of mechanisation, and in several cases they have been shown to promote a rate of tractorisation – the adoption of four-wheel tractors – in excess of what is indicated by economic efficiency criteria. Mechanisation policy is also about the comparative impact of different types of mechanical innovation on output, employment, income distribution, and farm size.

The format of this chapter differs from the norm for the other policy chapters in the book. This is due to the absence of a coherent set of policies in developing countries that can be designated as 'mechanisation policy'. Most developing countries have followed fragmented and partial policies towards farm implements and machines.

Thus the objectives–instruments–problems sequence of preceding chapters is not applicable here. Instead, the chapter moves towards trying to establish some basic criteria for a consistent state approach to farm mechanisation. This is done in the following steps:

(a) some key *economic concepts* related to mechanisation are introduced, for application later in the chapter;

(b) the propositions and empirical evidence concerning *farm tractors* in developing countries are reviewed;

(c) commonplace *policy failures* concerning mechanisation are examined, taking into account empirical evidence as to their impact;

(d) some alternative *sequences* of mechanisation are considered, taking into account the *diversity* of available mechanical technologies;

(e) some main criteria underlying a *consistent mechanisation policy* are put forward; and, finally,

(f) the impact of mechanisation policy on *peasants* and *women* is briefly considered.

Economic concepts of mechanisation

Implements and machines possess certain economic properties that distinguish them from other inputs into farm production. In addition, the economist is concerned with the changing relationship of output to resource use that occurs when a mechanical innovation takes place.

A *first* distinguishing feature of machines is that they represent a flow of services from an initial investment in *fixed capital*. Variable inputs, by contrast, are used up in a single cycle of production. Machines require servicing and maintenance to prolong their productive life, and, with the exception of tools and implements, they require fuel to run (a variable input), and they require spare parts in the event of breakdown.

The output contribution of mechanisation is compromised from the outset if the economy is unable to deliver servicing, fuel, or spare parts for imported or domestically produced machines. This happens when the markets for such items are fragmented or unevenly developed, when transport infrastructures break down, when the foreign exchange runs out, or when non-replicated brands of machines are imported under aid schemes or barter trade deals.

A *second* distinguishing feature of machines is their *indivisibility*. A particular type of machine comes in single units, or in discrete sizes. A given size of machine has a technical *operating capacity* in terms, for example, of kilograms of maize that can be husked per hour, or hectares of land that can be ploughed in a working day. The fixed cost of owning a machine (given mainly by its annual depreciation rate), per unit of task performed, declines as capacity utilisation increases. Variable operating costs, per unit of task performed, stay more or less the same, but begin to rise as the maximum operating capacity is approached due to rising breakdown and supervision costs.

Taken together, these cost factors ensure that there is a minimum unit cost of machine operation, associated with a given level of capacity utilisation that is likely to be quite close to the rated capacity. Failure to use a machine up to the minimum unit cost level incurs a cost penalty to the operator that can rise rapidly as the rate of utilisation falls.

These attributes of indivisibility, operating capacity, and minimum cost mean that, for machines like tractors, there is a close relationship between machine capacity and *optimum farm size*, which is the area size of farm that minimises average unit production costs (Ellis, 1988a: 193– 6). The farm size aspects of tractor purchase by farmers are one of the critical issues of mechanisation policy in developing countries. In short, certain types of machine – principally four-wheel tractors but also in some places two-wheel power tillers – are uneconomic for their owners in the absence of farm size increases. Thus mechanisation can create an impetus to consolidate and expand farm holdings, with potentially adverse equity effects with respect to agrarian structure, employment and income distribution.

A *third* distinguishing feature of some, but not all, types of mechanisation is that it is labour-saving. Machines replace people, and in history, this was the prime motivation for farm mechanisation in labour-scarce regions like North America. Mechanisation is often posed as being the opposite to the seed–fertilizer–water technology in this regard. The former saves labour by making it more productive, the latter saves land by making it more productive.

It is necessary, however, to be cautious about the types of machines and circumstances to which this labour-saving feature applies. It applies most powerfully when machines such as four-wheel tractors or combine harvesters replace human labour power or animal-draught power. It applies much less forcefully, and may not apply at all, for items of mechanical equipment that permit more intensive crop cultivation, thence requiring more labour to handle the increased output. For example, the innovation of the plough in place of shifting cultivation is labour-using rather than labour-saving. The same is also true for irrigation pumps, which permit more multiple cropping to take place.

The bottom line in economic terms for assessing the merits of mechanisation is whether it increases output for a given total resource cost. In other words, whether it makes a *net contribution* to farm output (Binswanger, 1978: 3–6). Another way of stating the same effect is for resource costs to have decreased for a given level of output.

The net contribution of mechanisation corresponds to the neoclassical economic concept of technical change (Ellis, 1988a: Ch. 11). On an isoquant diagram, such as Figure 8.1, it corresponds to a movement inwards towards the origin of an iso-product curve (I_1) representing a fixed level of output. Given fixed relative prices between labour and capital represented by the parallel isocost lines, P_1, technical change involves a movement in the cost-minimising operating position for the farm from point A to point C.

Figure 8.1. Factor substitution versus technical change in farm mechanisation.

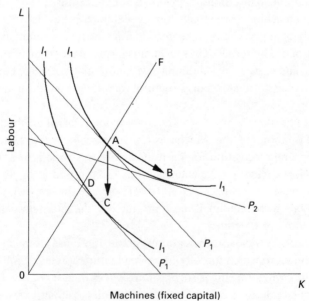

Machines (fixed capital)

Figure 8.1 displays several other features. An entirely different type of change is involved if there is no reduction in total production cost (iso-product line I_1 stays in the same place), and the same level of output is produced with a different combination of labour and capital. The move from point A to point B represents such a shift. At point B less labour and more capital equipment is used than at A, but the level of output stays the same.

The move from point A to point B is called *factor substitution*, and it can only occur in the sense shown in Figure 8.1 if relative prices change – the price of capital falls relative to the price of labour – making B the new optimum point on the old isoquant, as shown by the isocost line P_2. If mechanisation fails to increase total output for a given total resource cost, but results in significant displacement of labour by machines, then factor substitution is considered to have taken place. The hypothesis that this is what happens when four-wheel tractors are introduced into peasant farming systems is called the *substitution view* of farm mechanisation (Binswanger, 1978: 3).

A further consideration of potential relevance shown in Figure 8.1 is the lack of symmetry in the inward movement of isoquant I_1 towards the origin. Labour-saving occurs between points A and C, even though factor prices have not changed. When this happens technical change is said to be *biased*, and in this instance the bias is a labour-saving one. Bias in technical change is defined by reference to unbiased or 'neutral' technical change, in which factor proportions – i.e. the ratio of labour to capital – stay constant (e.g. all points along line ODF have constant factor proportions). Ellis (1988a: 214–17) explains this in more detail than space allows here. A feature of labour-saving technical change is that the share of labour in the total value of output falls relative to the share of capital, even when the relative prices between the two factors stay the same.

An important final point for the economic approach to mechanisation concerns the distinction between private prices and economic prices of machines. Substitution of labour by machines of the type displayed in the move from A to B in Figure 8.1 may occur because the private price ratio confronted by farmers changes in favour of capital, even though the social opportunity costs of resources have not changed (Griffin, 1979). The private costs of mechanisation can be artificially lowered due to sub-sidised credit, subsidised machines, overvalued exchange rates, low fuel costs, and similar distortions.

In summary, some useful economic concepts surrounding mechanisation include fixed capital versus working capital, indivisible resources versus divisible resources, and labour-saving technology versus land-saving technology. Mechanisation tends to be associated in general with fixed capital, indivisibility, and labour-saving. Seed–fertilizer–water technology, by contrast, is associated with working capital, divisible resources, and land-saving. Mechanisation can involve a change in factor proportions (less labour, more capital), *either* because machines substitute for labour with no increase in net output (substitution view), *or* because technical change occurs (net contribution view), but has a labour-saving bias.

Farm tractors: Propositions and evidence

Much of the controversy surrounding farm mechanisation in developing countries relates to four-wheel tractors. This is not surprising since four-wheel tractors most obviously represent the substitution of machine power for animal power or labour power in operations like ploughing, harrowing, sowing, weeding, and spraying crops. Two-wheel tractors (power tillers) also represent similar substitutions, but for fewer farm operations, and with better adaptation to farm sizes in developing countries. They do not therefore generate quite the same intensity of debate as four-wheel tractors.

Those in favour of tractors argue that lack of power is a real constraint on increased agricultural output in developing countries. This is the *net contribution view* already discussed, and some of its main propositions as far as tractors are concerned are as follows:

(a) Tractors increase crop yields per hectare. They do this due to deeper tillage of the soil, more consistent soil preparation, more accurate delivery to the soil of seeds and fertilizers, and generally more timely and uniform cultivation operations.

(b) Tractors speed up land preparation between crop cycles, allowing an increase in multiple cropping compared to animal-draught or manual land preparation.

(c) Tractors permit a higher value crop mix to be grown, by releasing labour from routine operations, which can then be used for additional, higher marginal return, tasks.

(d) Tractors permit additional land to be placed under cultivation by freeing up the grazing land previously required for draught animals.

(e) Tractors are able to place under cultivation land that would otherwise remain idle, for example by reclaiming swamp land, by ploughing heavy soils, or by carrying out heavy works in difficult terrain.

(f) Tractors represent a power source for multiple tasks on the farm, not just cultivation. These include driving stationary machines like pumps or threshers, and on-farm or off-farm transport.

These are the proposed output benefits of tractors. Some advocates also point to the consumption benefits of tractors, including the reduction in the drudgery of farm work that they represent, and their use for transport and travel aside from farm tasks.

A major comparative study carried out at the end of the 1970s on the impact of tractors in South Asia found little evidence in support of the above propositions (Binswanger, 1978). Its author concluded:

> The tractor surveys fail to provide evidence that tractors are responsible for substantial increases in intensity, yields, timeliness, and gross returns on farms in India, Pakistan, and Nepal. (*Ibid*: 73)

Moreover:

> ... loss of employment may relieve landless labourers of drudgery but it clearly increases rather than reduces their suffering. They have accepted to perform the arduous tasks only because they were forced into them by lack of better alternatives. (*Ibid*: 75)

Other findings have also supported this *substitution view* of tractors in India (Agarwal, 1981), in Bangladesh (Gill, 1983), and in Indonesia (Lingard & Sri Bagyo, 1983). Several important points about the impact of tractors, and about measurement of their effects, emerge from these and other studies:

(a) Evidence purporting to show that tractors increase yields almost always wrongly attributes to tractors yield gains from other causes, for example new seeds, increased fertilizer use, or improved water supply. When the separate sources of yield gains are properly identified, tractors are found to have no significant impact on yields per hectare.

(b) Tractors do not necessarily result in the expansion of cultivated area to incorporate previous grazing land. The reason is that tractors are less reliable than draught animals, and peasants tend to keep their animals even when tractor power is available. This applies especially when there are problems with the quality and supply of oils and fuels, lack of spare parts, and uncertainty about the ability to repair a tractor if it breaks down.

(c) Tractors do not result in a quicker turnaround between crops, because other factors, such as seasonal climatic variations, allocation of water in canal irrigation systems, ground water availability, and disease or pest control regimes are more important than machine power in deciding the rhythm of multiple cropping across the seasons.

(d) Tractors can dramatically accelerate increases in farm size, and their adoption inevitably involves 'the pervasive factor of farm size and the nature of the causal relationship between farm size and mechanisation' (Lingard & Sri Bagyo, 1983: 66). In a sample survey undertaken to examine the impact of tractorisation in Pakistan in the early 1970s, average farm size before and after the acquisition of tractors increased from 18 to 44 hectares (McInerney & Donaldson, 1975: 32).

(f) Tractors also have a dramatic effect on labour use per hectare, with the number of full time jobs lost per four-wheel tractor ranging between five and fifteen according to different estimates.

In summary, the notion that machine power is an absolute constraint on higher output, and its corollary, that the output gains of tractors are sufficient to outweigh their disadvantages for farm size and employment, are not sustained by the bulk of evidence where tractors are concerned.

It should be noted that most of the detailed work on this topic has been done in South or South-East Asia, and much of it is rather dated (being based on research of the 1960s and early 1970s). The conclusions are unlikely to apply with such force in regions with lower population density, and with seasonal labour constraints. An earlier comparative study on tractors in Latin America was critical of the pace of tractorisation there, for similar reasons to those cited for Asia (Abercrombie, 1972). In contemporary Africa, other constraints such as lack of foreign exchange, lack of spare parts, inadequate servicing facilities, high fuel costs, and so on may be more relevant for taking a cautious approach to mechanisation than the lack of output gains applicable in the Asian case.

Policy failures and effects

It is widely thought that the past lack of a consistent approach to mechanisation in many developing countries led to a pace and direction of machine purchase by farmers that was inappropriate given resource availabilities and social opportunity costs. The often inadequate and piecemeal nature of government approaches to farm machinery is captured in the following quotations:

> Past government policies [in Latin America] concerning agricultural mechanisation have thus been somewhat haphazard and inconsistent . . . Moreover, in most countries government assist-

ance has been indiscriminate in that there has been little control over the types of machinery for which, for example, credit has been extended. (Abercrombie, 1972: 36)

And again:

> It would be wrong to say that the Government of India has followed a policy of promoting mechanisation to the maximum. It would be more correct to say that it has had no policy whatsoever. [The government] has let manufacturers produce and sell whatever farm machinery they wanted to and let farmers introduce whatever mechanisation that caught their fancy. The result has been disastrous. (Rudra, 1987: 489)

Thus in some countries economically inefficient types of farm mechanisation are observed to have occurred not due to a deliberate or co-ordinated policy, but as a result of what amounts to a permissive muddle on the part of the state. Some common features of this muddle that have been noted in several different settings are as follows:

(a) Delivery of highly subsidised credit to farmers (see Chapter 7) *either* specifically for tractor purchase, *or* for general input use, but easily spent on machines due to the fungibility of credit.

(b) Credit offered to farmers at interest rates that turn out to be negative in real terms due to high rates of inflation. Farmers end up repaying less in real terms than was borrowed. The effect of this is to cheapen greatly the real capital cost of machines purchased with the credit.

(c) Encouragement and protection of a domestic tractor industry under import substituting industrialisation (ISI) policies, without regard to agricultural sector impact. Special tax concessions to ISI tractor industries, enabling them to sell tractors cheaply in the domestic market.

(d) Imports of tractors duty-free, or under concessionary purchase agreements with aid donors ('tractor dumping'), or under bilateral trade deals with centrally planned economies. Tractor imports duty-free sometimes paradoxically coincide with high tariffs on spare parts. Non-replicated trade or aid deals with bilateral donors can mean a batch of tractors with no spare parts or support services.

(e) Overvalued exchange rates, with a pervasive effect in lowering the relative cost of imported machinery, equipment, and spare parts.

(f) Cheap fuel and oil policies. Many of the larger developing countries have tended to price fuel and oil at levels well below those prevailing in most industrialised countries, even when they are oil importers, and even when oil purchases are an immense drain on scarce foreign exchange.

(g) Tractor promotion linked to mistaken ideas about the output benefits of large-scale agriculture in countries that have opted for state farms, or village collective farming, as components of their agricultural development strategy.

Several points may be noted about this list. *First*, policies are incomplete and partial, and many of them reflect a preoccupation with tractors to the exclusion of other types of farm mechanisation. *Second*, a number of these partial policies work by reducing the real cost of tractors to farmers, thus causing a divergence between the private prices and social opportunity costs of tractors. Tractors are made privately profitable but remain socially inefficient.

Third, lack of policy coherence can result in non-sustainable mechanisation even for those farmers or enterprises fortunate enough to acquire machines at low prices. There is no point in importing 20 000 tractors from Spain or Hungary, say, if the only country from which you license imports of spare parts is Canada.

Fourth, growth of machinery use in some countries is linked with the advocacy of state farms as a type of agricultural enterprise, and in this case the area size of farm is designed for capacity utilisation of large machines. Unfortunately, rather a lot of empirical evidence suggests that this formula is a guarantee of success neither in raising agricultural output, nor in lowering the unit cost of farm production compared to the peasant sector.

Sequences and diversity of mechanisation

Debates about farm mechanisation in developing countries are less to do with either its outright rejection or its unqualified approval, than to do with the appropriate rate and direction of mechanisation given trends in resource use and relative prices. In the absence of any state intervention, but armed with an encyclopaedic knowledge of the entire range of machines available worldwide under current technology, a farmer would be expected to select only items that lead to a rise in net income. Given the small farm size and low wage rates faced by the typical developing country farmer, it is unlikely that the four-wheel tractor would be chosen from this hypothetical range of available equipment and machines.

Of course, neither farmers nor policymakers in developing countries have in practice an encyclopaedic view of available mechanical technologies. Policymakers have tended in the past to be mesmerised by tractors, and so too have been those farmers with a wider view of the world outside the village. This is because tractors are the most visible symbol of 'modern' farming in the industrialised countries. It is also to some extent because tractors and other farm machines are produced and marketed by global corporations (e.g. International Harvester) which compete vigorously for a worldwide market share.

A comparative examination of mechanisation trends in the history of developed and developing countries (Binswanger, 1984) emphasises the potential diversity of mechanical devices, the need to identify specific operations rather than take a whole-farm approach to mechanisation, and the sequence of mechanisation that tends to occur as relative prices change. In this light, tractors are seen to represent rather an extreme example of labour-saving technology, becoming economically viable only when a genuine scarcity of labour in agriculture begins to force up the cost of labour relative to the cost of machines. It is notable that widespread tractorisation in Western Europe (excluding the United Kingdom) did not occur until the mid-1950s.

Binswanger (1984: 17) makes a distinction between *power-intensive* farm operations and *control-intensive* farm operations. The former rely predominantly on additional energy, while the latter depend on human control as well as more energy. According to Binswanger, stationary power-intensive operations like milling, threshing, chopping, crushing sugarcane, or pumping water are the least sensitive to relative wage levels, the first to be mechanised, and the mechanisation of some of them result in higher labour use (e.g. water pumps).

Sequentially, the next category of operations to be mechanised is mobile power-intensive operations, the main one of which is ploughing. These are sensitive to relative wage levels, and become justifiable to mechanise only once a significant rise in real wages begins to occur.

The final category of operations to be mechanised are those that require skill as well as energy, and these can include (depending on the crop) sowing (or transplanting), fertilizer application, weeding, and harvesting. These are even more sensitive to relative wage levels, often continue to be performed by hand when other operations have been mechanised, and only become entirely mechanised when labour shortages and high real wages occur.

These are very broad brush strokes by which to characterise the sequence of mechanisation, and they are bound to be inaccurate at the level of practical detail. They nevertheless provide some useful ideas for mechanisation policy. *First*, there is the idea of a graduated *sequence* of mechanisation, the pace of which depends on changing relative factor prices and the resource situation in different locations. *Second*, there is the idea of separating farm *operations* according to their differing power needs, rather than taking the farm as a whole. *Third*, there is the idea of *selective* mechanisation by farm operation, rather than the indiscriminate mechanisation of the entire farm.

Towards consistent mechanisation policies

A consistent approach to farm mechanisation in developing countries should comprise at least two essential components. The *first* concerns price policy towards machines and equipment; the *second* concerns technology policy and institutions. In the following paragraphs these two components are discussed in turn:

Prices and mechanisation

Given past experiences of the rapid uptake of tractors due to artificially low costs of machine purchase, the main criterion for price policy towards mechanical technologies is that the cost of machines to farmers should be no less than their opportunity cost to society. Unlike the case of variable inputs (Chapter 6), no substantive arguments have been advanced for subsidising the prices of most types of farm machines either on efficiency or equity grounds.

This criterion implies that both explicit and hidden subsidies to machines should be removed. These include the use of cheap credit to buy machines, subsidies to domestic machinery manufacturers, and tariff exemptions on imports. Ideally, where imports are artificially cheapened due to overvalued exchange rates, a compensating tax would be applied so as not to over-stimulate the pace of machinery purchases by farmers and the tendency towards a large machine bias.

The opportunity cost criterion provides a first approximation to an appropriate price policy for agricultural machines and equipment. Machinery prices are typically relatively easy for the state to influence without resort to direct intervention, by varying the levels of import taxes or sales taxes levied on machinery supplies. This means that different types of mechanisation – for example, labour-saving versus labour-using mechanisation – can be encouraged or discouraged by fine-tuning relative prices, while still using opportunity cost as the baseline position from which to proceed. This allows for the principal of *selectivity*, already

mentioned earlier, to enter the mechanisation strategy adopted by
government.

Technology policy and mechanisation

A vast literature exists on the topic of 'appropriate technology',
much of which is concerned with the development of types of machines
and equipment that are more appropriate to the needs of developing
country farmers in terms of low cost, ease of purchase of component
materials, availability of spare parts, low running costs, labour intensity
of operation, and so on. Most developing countries possess appropriate
technology projects and programs, though these are not always well
integrated into the wider policy environment, and in many cases are
relegated to the fringe of state policy preoccupations.

Much of the earlier discussion suggests that the problem of farm
mechanisation is largely one of the range of choice available. It is not that
tractors are everywhere and always the wrong machines to buy, it is that
sometimes they are the only machines to buy. Appropriate technology is
one important potential means of widening the range of choice. Appropriate technology ideas are broadly consistent with the economic concept
of social opportunity cost, though for specific machines and projects
incompatibilities can arise (Stewart, 1987: 2–3).

An interesting contrast can be observed between the fragmentary and
low status of appropriate technology policy, and the integrated and
relatively high status of seed technology policy in agricultural research
stations. Much can be learned from developments in agricultural research
policy (see Chapter 10) for the design of an appropriate technology policy
for farm machines, and indeed the same institutions might be used for
both purposes. Relevant ideas include farming systems research (especially to identify constraints that might be eased by mechanical devices),
feedback between farmers and design teams, and on-farm trials leading
to modifications and improvements of trial machines.

An additional requirement of successful machinery or equipment
development is for links to be forged between design teams and local
manufacturers. A continuous process of interaction is required during the
design and development phase of a new machine, especially concerning
feasible components and materials. Many good ideas in appropriate
technology have come to nothing due to (i) failure to involve manufacturers in design, (ii) lack of feasibility of volume production, and (iii)
neglect of the problems of sales and marketing of mechanical innovations.

Bringing these various considerations together, a technology policy towards farm mechanisation might contain the following objectives and components:

(a) the provision of a wider range of choice to farmers, by improved screening of machines available in the world market, by the adaptation of imported designs to local conditions, and by maintaining a national design capacity, perhaps linked to existing support for appropriate technology work;

(b) integration of these screening and design tasks into a viable institutional framework, the most obvious one that suggests itself being the existing agricultural research system, that could be modified to take on mechanisation-related activities (this already occurs to some degree in some countries and at the level of the international research institutions, see, for example, IRRI, 1983; 1986);

(c) identification of local machinery manufacturers, preferably located near to research stations, prepared to participate in machinery design and development, but at low R & D cost to themselves up to the stage when a production go-ahead is intended. Many different methods of achieving this kind of link could be devised.

In summary, a consistent mechanisation policy in a developing country should ensure that the farming sector follows a path of mechanical change that is economically efficient in terms of farm size, labour availability, wage levels, and the social opportunity cost of machines. The two main elements of such a policy are an approach to prices that emphasises opportunity cost criteria, and an approach to technology that emphasises increasing the range of machinery options especially at the low-cost, labour-using, end of the scale of alternatives.

Neither of these elements need involve substantial state interventions or high state costs. If left to themselves, prices will tend to reflect opportunity costs, and adjustments at the margin are only required within the context of strengthening the operation of opportunity cost criteria. The technology component can best be achieved by integration with the agricultural research system, thus widening the use of existing facilities and incurring relatively small additional costs (in some countries, there may even be savings from rationalisation by doing this).

Mechanisation and peasants

Peasant production is generally characterised by a high reliance on family labour, the use of simple hand tools for cultivation and other tasks, and the use of animal-draught power in some agrarian societies.

Peasants have been shown to be adept at modifying simple mechanical technologies to suit their own farming system requirements, and are also quick to adopt low-cost new mechanical technologies when these are complementary to existing farm sizes and resource availabilities.

Most power-driven equipment is beyond the reach of peasants, though processes of social differentiation in agriculture always mean that some farmers are able to purchase power equipment, especially if attractive incentives such as subsidised interest rates are available. Even two-wheel power tillers are typically too high in price and too large in operating capacity for small farmers to purchase them just for individual use in those regions that are suited to their capabilities. The IRRI studies on mechanisation in rice farming have shown that in countries such as Indonesia, two-wheel power tillers were no less prone to result in a net substitution of labour for capital than four-wheel tractors elsewhere (Lingard & Sri Bagyo, 1983). Peasants in those societies sometimes use power tillers on an hourly or daily hire basis from the richer farmers who can afford to purchase them.

Large machines such as four-wheel tractors or combine harvesters tend to accelerate the elimination of peasant farmers and their replacement by large-scale commercial family farmers or capitalist enterprises exclusively dependent on hired wage labour. This process can mean consolidation of land holdings and a rapid rise in the proportion of rural dwellers who become landless agricultural labourers.

Mechanisation policy and women

In recent agrarian history, women appear to have been more strongly affected by mechanised post-harvest technologies in the threshing and milling of grain than by farm mechanisation. This has already been mentioned briefly in the chapter on marketing policy above. Mechanisation of paddy threshing and rice milling causes a substantial fall in the employment opportunities of women in the labour-abundant societies of South and South-East Asia.

Other gender consequences of mechanisation are more diverse and mixed. It is sometimes argued for Sub-Saharan Africa that seasonal labour is a binding constraint on increased output, and that selective mechanisation could help to remove this constraint. Since a high proportion of farm labour is contributed by women, it is often the time allocation of women that is the operative constraint in this argument. The difficulty is that power-tillers and related types of equipment that are suitable to small-scale farms are often unsuitable for the soil and climatic conditions that prevail in much of Sub-Saharan Africa.

Mechanisation is a policy issue that obviously permits examination of the differential impact on men and women of proposed farm or post-harvest technologies. Mechanisation is sometimes advocated for its reduction in the drudgery of women's lives, but this needs to be set within a context of existing patterns of activity between households of different types, and employment alternatives for women who may otherwise have few options for family survival.

Summary
1. This chapter is concerned with the role of the state in influencing the pace and direction of mechanisation in small-scale farming in developing countries. Mechanisation is defined as the use of non-human sources of power for undertaking agricultural tasks.
2. Three basic types of mechanical technology are identified as (a) hand-tools or implements that increase the effectiveness of human power, (b) animal-draught machines or equipment which make use of animal power, and (c) engine or motor driven machines, which make use of mechanical-power. Mechanical power is further subdivided into *mobile* machines and *stationary* machines.
3. The basic absence in most developing countries of a coherent set of policies that can be designated 'mechanisation policy' means that this chapter deviates from the objectives–instruments–problems sequence followed elsewhere in this book. Instead, various aspects of farm mechanisation are explored prior to arriving at some ideas concerning the components of a consistent mechanisation policy.
4. Various economic concepts of mechanisation are reviewed. Machines are fixed inputs, they are indivisible, their unit cost of operation decreases as capacity utilisation increases, and this means that small farm size may be inappropriate for their efficient use. The central debate concerning farm tractors is whether they increase output for a given resource cost (*net contribution view*) or whether they substitute capital for labour for the same resource cost (*substitution view*). The economic concepts of technical change and factor substitution underlying this distinction are discussed with reference to a diagram.

5. The tractor debate is summarised. Supposed advantages of tractors are higher yields, timely land preparation leading to more multiple cropping, release of labour to higher value activities, cultivation of previous grazing land, and extension of arable land by reclaiming swamps, etc. The bulk of research finds little support for these propositions, except the last. Tractors do not attain higher yields than intensive manual cultivation. Their presence or absence is not the key determinant of multiple cropping practices. They do not necessarily result in the rapid release of land from animal grazing. They may, however, alleviate seasonal labour bottlenecks in countries that do not have a class of landless agricultural workers.

6. Previous rapid trends of tractorisation in some developing countries were due to the inadequacy and piecemeal nature of state policies, leading to a permissive atmosphere of tractor growth. This included credit for tractor purchase, negative real interest rates on tractor loans, tax concessions to ISI tractor industries, duty free tractor imports, bilateral trade deals, over-valued exchange rates, and others. The main effect of such policies was to reduce the private price of tractors below social opportunity cost, thus encouraging the economically inefficient substitution of people by machines.

7. One of the factors causing lack of coherent policy initiatives on farm mechanisation in the past has been the focus on tractors. An examination of historical sequences of mechanisation, and identification of the differing power needs of different farm operations, emphasises the diversity of farm machines, and the merits of selective mechanisation of farm tasks as factor prices change over time. The location specificity of selective mechanisation is also important.

8. A consistent mechanisation policy in a developing country should ensure that the farming sector follows a path of mechanical change that is economically efficient in terms of farm size, labour availability, wage levels, and the social opportunity cost of machines. The two main elements of such a policy are an approach to prices that emphasises opportunity cost criteria, and an approach to technology that emphasises increasing the range of machinery options especially at the low-cost, labour-using, end of the scale.

9. Peasant production is typically associated with a high reliance on family labour, hand tools, and animal-drawn implements. Peasants are adept at modifying simple mechanical technologies to suit their own farm requirements. Most power driven equipment is beyond the reach of most peasants, except in the comparatively rare cases where a competitive market in machine hire exists. Large machines such as four-wheel tractors or combine harvesters accelerate the elimination of peasant farmers and their replacement by large-scale commercial family farmers or capitalist agricultural enterprises exclusively dependent on hired labour.

10. The position of women with respect to mechanisation policies is briefly considered, and the reader is referred to Chapter 12 for a comparative summary of the gender dimensions of agricultural policies.

Further reading

The literature on mechanisation policy in developing countries is uneven in geographic coverage and thin on recent research. South and South-East Asia predominate amongst easily obtainable published works. The two comparative studies on mechanisation by Binswanger, one on tractors in South Asia (1978), and one on comparative historical aspects (1984) are recommended. So too is an earlier paper by Abercrombie (1972) on mechanisation in Latin America. For a more Africa orientated perspective see Clayton (1983: Ch. 8). Empirical studies that tend to support the substitution view of tractors include Agarwal (1981), Gill (1983), Lingard (1984), and McInerney & Donaldson (1975). Two useful collections of papers on mechanisation, mainly but not entirely orientated to Asia, are IRRI (1983) and IRRI (1986). A stimulating review of technology policies in India, including mechanisation, is provided by Rudra (1987). For a classic economics paper that sets out clearly the producer and consumer surplus analysis of a labour-saving mechanical innovation see Schmitz & Seckler (1970).

Reading list

Abercrombie, K.C. (1972). Agricultural Mechanisation and Employment in Latin America. *International Labour Review*, **106**, No. 1.

Agarwal, B. (1981). Agricultural Mechanisation and Labour Use: A Disaggregated Approach. *International Labour Review*, **120**, No. 1, January.

Binswanger, H.P. (1978). *The Economics of Tractors in South Asia*. New York: Agricultural Development Council.

Binswanger, H.P. (1984). *Agricultural Mechanization: A Comparative Historical Perspective*. World Bank Staff Working Paper No. 673. Washington D.C.: World Bank.

Clayton, E.S. (1983). *Agriculture, Poverty and Freedom in Developing Countries*. London: Macmillan.

Gill, G.J. (1983). Mechanised Land Preparation, Productivity and Employment in Bangladesh. *Journal of Development Studies*, **19**, No. 3.

International Rice Research Institute (IRRI) (1983). *Consequences of Small-Farm Mechanisation*. Los Banos, Philippines: IRRI.

International Rice Research Institute (IRRI) (1986). *Small Farm Equipment for Developing Countries*. Los Banos, Philippines: IRRI.

Lingard, J. (1984). Mechanisation of Small Rice Farms in the Philippines: Some Income Distribution Aspects. *Journal of Agricultural Economics*, **XXXV**, No. 3.

McInerney, J.P. & Donaldson, G.F. (1975). *The Consequences of Farm Tractors in Pakistan*. World Bank Staff Working Paper No. 210. Washington D.C.: World Bank.

Rudra, A. (1987). Technology Choice in Agriculture in India over the Past Three Decades. In *Macro-Policies for Appropriate Technology in Developing Countries*, ed. F. Stewart, Ch. 2. Boulder, Colorado: Westview Press.

Schmitz, A., & Seckler, D. (1970). Mechanized Agriculture and Social Welfare: The Case of the Tomato Harvester. *American Journal of Agricultural Economics*, **52**, 569–77.

9

Land reform policy

Introduction

Land reform policy covers a wide range of social changes involving the access of people to land, the ownership structure of land, the size structure of land holdings, and legal or contractual forms of land tenure.

In the hierarchy of state interventions affecting farm inputs and outputs, land reform is a special case. This is due to a number of considerations which are explored as this chapter proceeds, but include the considerations that (i) land is more than just 'another resource' in farm production, (ii) land ownership structures are inseparable from structures of social status and power in the agrarian economy, and (iii) land reform is often associated with social upheaval and dramatic change, rather than the relatively stable political and social conditions upon which the implementation of other policies is typically predicated.

Thus land reform differs from the price policies and technology policies of the other chapters in this book due to its often politically controversial nature. This becomes apparent when we go through the same exercise in defining the nature, intent, scope, and problems of land reform policy as we have done for other policies in the book. The approach and coverage of this chapter is summarised briefly as follows:

(a) to describe the scope and nature of land reform, and to provide some relevant *definitions*;

(b) to set out the *objectives* that provide the reasons and logic of a variety of different types of land reform;

(c) to consider alternative *paths of change* in land tenure which might be planned, or occur as a result of land reform;

(d) to examine some major *instruments* by which different types of land reform policy have been put into effect;

(e) to identify and to discuss the major defects and *problems* that are associated with the failure of land reform policies or with their only partial success;

(f) to suggest some *lessons* that can be derived from experiences of land reform in the post-war era;

(g) to discuss the current and future *relevance* of land reform as a policy topic, given that less enthusiasm seems to prevail for radical changes in land tenure systems worldwide in the 1990s than was true in the era from the 1950s to 1970s;

(h) to consider briefly the standing of *peasants* in relation to different types of land reform policy.

Nature, scope and definitions

The fundamentally political nature of land reform must be recognised at the outset. Land reform seldom involves making only a minor adjustment in the socio-economic environment. Historically, many land reforms have attempted to change social relationships of property ownership, wealth, social status, and political power. As such they tend to be contested, in the political sphere, between those forces seeking to put land reform into effect, and those often powerful members of society expecting to lose from it. The following quotations from Herring (1983) illustrate this point:

> Agrarian reforms worthy of the name transform rural society through alterations in the property structure and production relations, redistributing power and privilege. (Ibid: 11)

> Land reforms that genuinely overturn the rural society and economy are frequently the product of cataclysmic historical events, often revolutions, which are neither policy options nor common occurrences. (Ibid: 268)

At the heart of this politically charged nature of land reform policies are differences between *land* as a resource, and other farm inputs and outputs examined elsewhere in this book. Some essential attributes of land are as follows:

(a) Land is a *resource* in agricultural production, but is ultimately fixed in supply within a nation state (and indeed globally). While land can be transferred between uses, meaning that supply for a particular use is seldom completely inelastic, the potential to increase its availability at the extensive margin is either non-existent or involves high costs (draining swamps, building sea walls, etc.). The fixed nature of land supply makes it different from labour power, fertilizers, ploughs, or camels, all of which in varying ways are reproducible resources.

(b) Land is a stock of *capital*, a fixed asset or investment, and a measure of wealth. Land plays multiple roles in these regards. The value of land – the price per hectare – seldom merely reflects the expected rate of return to land as a capital investment in agricultural production. Land is also held as a livelihood security, as a financial security (e.g. as a hedge against inflation), as a transfer of wealth across the generations, and as a resource for consumption purposes (e.g. country estates held by urban elites for leisure purposes). The price of land reflects all these demands, services and uses.

(c) Land is often *private property*, and as such is inalienable in law. Land ownership is formalised in legal documents (title deeds, etc.) and inscribed in land registration lists. Exceptions are communally owned lands in peasant societies, where rights of land access may be by custom or use (called 'usufruct' rights), and state owned lands. Private property in land is usually heritable in law, meaning that an additional motivation for ownership is the transfer of land across generations.

(d) Agricultural land ownership involves *social relations* between, for example, feudal lord and serf, landlord and share tenant, landowner and cash tenant, owner-occupier and wage labour, plantation owner and wage labour. Freehold owner occupiers – especially small-scale owner-occupiers – are comparatively recent in the social history of most countries, and are usually the result of land reform. Peasants have historically derived their access to land by tenancy or by customary tenure rather than by ownership.

The nature of rights of access to land, for example freehold, leasehold, sharecropping, village or customary use rights, is called the *land tenure system*. Land tenure systems are 'old, and thickly interwoven in the social and economic fabric' (Warriner, 1969: xvii), and are therefore only changed with difficulty. Land tenure may be inscribed and defended by law, or may depend on unwritten custom and patronage between land owners and those who till the land under a wide variety of different arrangements.

The definition of land reform used in this chapter is the *redistribution of property ownership in land or other rights of access to the use of land*. The outcome of this redistribution must be left open because many alternatives are possible. For comparison with other definitions of land reform see Warriner (1969: xiv), Lipton (1974: 270), or World Bank (1974: 3).

This definition excludes certain types of state intervention that some writers include in land reform. Land reform is not tax reform. The instigation of property taxes, estate duties, or taxes on idle land are not land reform, even though in the long term they may have a minor impact on land ownership and its uses. Nor are the other policies treated in this book land reform:

> The redistribution of property in land is a very difficult change to carry through, far more difficult and controversial than these other institutional improvements, and it cannot be put on the same level. (Warriner, 1969: xv)

Sometimes a distinction is made between 'land reform' and 'agrarian reform'. The former is used to describe only the transfer of ownership or rights over land, the latter to describe the whole host of legal, institutional, and social changes that accompany, result, or 'ought to occur' from land reform. This distinction can be confusing and is not followed here. Land reform and agrarian reform are treated as synonymous in this chapter.

Finally, there is disagreement about whether 'land settlement' should be included in land reform. Land settlement usually involves creating new farms – either owner operated or leased – on new lands (frontier settlement), on previously unutilised state lands, or in sparsely populated regions (for example, the transmigration program of the Indonesian state, designed to relieve land pressure on Java by establishing farm settlements in islands of low population density).

Since land settlement does not involve the redistribution of property rights in land under existing cultivation, it is often excluded from the rubric of land reform. However, the counter argument can be made that land settlement does alter a country's overall ownership distribution of land. Moreover, there are cases, for example the resettlement of previous European settler farms in Africa, that cross definitional boundaries. The preference here is to keep settlement in view under the topic of land reform, even though recognising that it does not represent the same order of social change as mainstream land reform. After all, settlement is about the access of farm families to land, which is the subject of this chapter.

Objectives of land reform

The structure of land ownership in a country is rooted in centuries old events and social changes. Once established and consolidated, the land ownership structure tends to remain fixed, with little if any change, unless dramatic changes like wars or revolutions sweep away the existing titles of landowners to their property. In many regions of the world, these historical land ownership structures were extraordinarily unequal, deriving from conditions in which populations were sparsely scattered across the landscape, and enormous tracts of land were routinely granted to individuals by rulers or confiscated in wars between rival princedoms.

Pressures for land reform arise due to the growing disparity between this highly unequal, but fixed, structure of land ownership, and the rapid changes otherwise taking place in society. Such changes include population growth, increased mobility, development of the market, income growth, and changing forms of economic exchange or social interaction. Eventually, the disparity between rigid land ownership and accelerating social change becomes so wide that explosive social forces are set in motion.

Bearing in mind this background, land reform always has a mixture of political, social and economic objectives. While these are often inextricably linked, it is helpful to separate them for purposes of discussion:

Political objectives

The political objectives of land reform depend on the forces and pressures that have created the opportunity for a land reform to be considered, and on whether a revolutionary change in political power is involved. Several different possibilities present themselves:

(a) land reform occurring as the outcome of revolutionary political change, its main objective being to strengthen and consolidate the basis of the new state;

(b) land reform as a platform for liberal ('market-orientated') political groups, its main objective being to undermine the power of a land-based elite;

(c) land reform as a platform for socialist political groups, its main objective being to institute cooperative, collective, or state forms of agricultural production;

(d) land reform as a defensive measure by conservative political groups, determined to prevent social change by making an appearance of change in land tenure systems, or by making the minimum change considered necessary to maintain the social *status quo* (this has been called 'defensive land reform').

Needless to say, these are not distinctly separate alternatives. Land reform sometimes occurs as the result of unlikely coalitions between political groupings with different ultimate aims in view.

Social objectives

The main social objective of land reform is usually some concept of 'social justice'. This is allied to both political and economic reasons and motivations. On the political side, in different ways and for different reasons, increased social equality may feature as an argument of both liberal and socialist advocates of land reform. On the economic side, social justice is linked to questions of employment, income distribution, efficiency, and the size of the domestic market.

Social justice also has a force of its own. Ideas about what is unacceptable in terms of the power that some members of society have over other members evolve and change over time. Some features of feudal and semi-feudal land tenancy – bonded labour, labour service tenancy, peonage and so on – are generally regarded as offensive and unacceptable in late twentieth century societies. So too are the extreme juxtapositions of wealth with poverty, power with servitude, associated with such land tenancy practices.

Economic objectives

The two main economic objectives of land reform are to reduce absolute poverty and to increase agricultural output. These are the equity and efficiency goals of land reform.

Land reform can be an important potential instrument of poverty reduction because it eliminates the near-slavery nature of certain types of land tenancy (see above), and because a reduction in the inequality of land ownership should increase the real incomes of farm families, and may increase the number of farm families able to obtain an acceptable livelihood from the land.

The output and efficiency goals of land reform rest on several propositions about the lack of efficiency of pre-reform types of tenure, and on two opposing views about the optimum post-reform farm size structure. The pre-reform ownership structure may be inefficient due to idle lands, extensive land use methods with low output per unit area, absentee ownership, and microeconomic inefficiency of share tenancy (Ellis, 1988a: 143–6).

Opinion about the optimum post-reform farm size structure is divided between two groups: those who advocate large size of unit on the grounds of economies of scale, and those who advocate small size of unit on the grounds of family efficiency (Dorner & Kanel, 1971; Berry & Cline, 1979). The former view leads to advocacy of cooperative, communal or state farms as the means for raising agricultural output after the land reform. The latter rests on the farm size-efficiency argument in which the relative factor prices confronted by small farmers is thought to result in more intensive cultivation and higher output per unit area than occurs on large farms (Ellis, 1988a: 201–6).

Another economic argument for land reform is the need to enlarge the size of the domestic market as economic development proceeds. A mass of very poor tenant farm families paying landlords in kind in order to till land for bare survival does not provide a market for the outputs of domestic industry.

Paths of change in land tenure

Land reform can have many different starting points in terms of the pre-reform agrarian structure, and many different end points in terms of the post-reform land ownership structure. Some major categories of starting point and end-point are listed in Table 9.1. The discussion here centres on the history and logic of movements between them.

Many land reforms in history are associated with the dismantling of feudal land ownership structures and tenancy systems. Feudal land tenure systems prevailed in Europe prior to the rise of capitalism, and were carried to Central and South America by the Spanish conquest. Different variants of the same type of land ownership system have existed, or continue to exist, in China, Japan, and South and South-East Asia.

Feudal land distribution is characterised by the original granting of land by rulers or warlords to powerful individuals (princes, lords, chiefs, army officers) in return for services rendered (assistance in military campaigns, provision of soldiers or supplies, etc.). In Latin America, for example, the King of Spain made grants of vast tracts of land to the individuals who led the Spanish conquest of the continent, who organised the shipment of gold and silver back to Spain, or who assisted the crown in its rule over the colonies.

As a long-term result of these land grants, Latin America entered the twentieth century with a highly unequal distribution of land ownership. As late as 1960 it was estimated that the upper 20 per cent by size of farm holdings in Latin America (comprising holdings in excess of 50 ha) accounted for 90 per cent of the total agricultural land area (World Bank,

1974: 56). In extreme cases (Guatemala, Ecuador, Peru) the largest 10 per cent of farm holdings owned 85 per cent of total agricultural land (Barraclough & Domike, 1970: 48).

Feudal land distribution is distinguished not only by inequality of land ownership, but also by archaic forms of farm tenancy. Labour service types of tenancy, in which the peasant family is permitted to till a small piece of land for household needs in exchange for unpaid labour on the landowner's estate, remained widely prevalent in Latin America until the second half of the twentieth century. It remains in existence, although often in disguised forms, in parts of Latin America, and in South and South-East Asia. Sharecropping tenancy (sometimes referred to as 'semi-feudal' land tenure) remains prevalent worldwide, especially in Asia.

Table 9.1. *Pre-reform and post-reform land tenure forms*

Pre-reform	Post-reform
Feudal estates	*Private ownership*
Share cropper	Small owner-occupier
Labour service	Large owner-occupier
Wage labour	Cooperative enterprise
'Semi-feudal' tenancy	*Tenancy access*
Share cropper	Share cropper
Labour service	Cash-rent tenancy
Village/communal	*State ownership*
Traditional access	State/leasehold
'Minifundia'	State/communal
	State/operated
Corporate ownership	*Corporate ownership*
Plantations	Plantations
Estates	Estates
	Outgrower schemes
Land frontier	*Settlement schemes*
Not used	Frontier settlement
	River basin settlement
	State land settlement
	Resettlement

Note: The two sides of this table are just lists of alternative tenure arrangements; they do not imply one-to-one changes reading across horizontally. For example, feudal estates with labour service tenants may become state-owned communal farms; village land may become small owner-occupier or state leasehold.

Sharecropping customs and arrangements can vary widely in terms of the division of output between landowner and tenant, and in other obligations that the tenant has to observe in order to remain secure in the tenancy.

The break-down of feudalism usually involves social tension and violence, and historically it has often been the case that nothing short of revolution ensures that it happens. This is because the landowning class under feudalism *is* the ruling class in feudal societies. It is only if another powerful class emerges to challenge the existing order (e.g. an urban capitalist class) that violent upheaval may be averted. This is what occurred in some Western European countries in the eighteenth and nineteenth centuries, and in some Latin American countries in the 1960s and 1970s. Elsewhere, either socialist revolutions (e.g. Russia – 1917, China – 1949, Cuba – 1959, Ethiopia – 1974) or liberal–capitalist revolutions (e.g. France – 1789, Mexico – 1917, Bolivia – 1952) were instrumental in creating the conditions for land reform to take place.

There are many possible paths away from feudal land tenure systems, and some of the main ones are exemplified by previous historical experiences:

(a) Land previously tilled by tenants may be sold to them as freehold owners. This may also involve a change in the size distribution of holdings as well as its ownership (e.g. Japan – 1890 and 1947, South Korea – 1950, Taiwan – 1951, Bolivia – 1952). This is the preferred alternative of the small farm size for efficiency school of thought, which favours the creation of a small-farm freehold peasantry.

(b) Land expropriated from large landowners by the state may be leased to small farmers either on an individual or a cooperative basis (e.g. the *ejido* system created in Mexico – 1917). Various types of cooperative may be legislated by the state as transition either towards corporate farms (Peru – 1964) or towards communal farms (Chile – 1973).

(c) Land expropriated from large landowners by the state may be kept under state ownership and operated as state farms or communal farms. This is the *collective agriculture* alternative favoured in history by several countries that have undergone socialist revolutions.

(d) The most limited type of land reform is to change legislatively the rules of tenancy, for example by prohibiting labour service contracts, lowering the landowner's share in share cropping tenancy, or converting share tenancy to cash tenancy. This type of land reform tends to be the kind of minimalist gesture favoured by conservative forces undertaking land reform as a defensive measure. It has occurred in the post-war period in countries with 'semi-feudal' land tenure systems (e.g. India, Pakistan, Philippines).

Although the transition from feudalism is by far the most important – and not yet completed – type of land reform worldwide, other types of land reform are relevant to the complete picture and should not be neglected:

(a) Village/communal types of usufruct rights to land may be altered by introducing freehold ownership, and initiating a process of land title registration. This may be combined with a goal to consolidate previous fragments of land considered too small for family cultivation. Land consolidation may take place subsequently anyway due to transactions in freehold land by the richer members of rural society. For critical views and case-studies of this type of reform see Bromley (1989) and Cramb & Wills (1990).

(b) Village/communal types of land rights may be converted to state ownership, with a view to introducing cooperative or communal farms in order to realise economies of scale in agriculture. This type of strategy was implemented by Tanzania (from 1967) under its *ujamaa* village program.

(c) Plantations – typically operated by private companies rather than by families – may be nationalised, or may be converted into outgrower schemes, with small farms around a central processing facility. This occurred, for example, to the Fiji sugar industry in the 1920s (Ellis, 1988b: 47–8), and to many sugar, banana, rubber, tea, and oil palm plantations during the 1960s and 1970s when nationalisation of foreign plantation enterprises was a popular development objective.

(d) Large owner-operator farms – previously owned by foreign nationals – may be nationalised by the state, converted into cooperatives, or divided into freehold parcels for small-farm development. This occurred in many African countries after the achievement of independence from former colonial powers in the 1960s and 1970s. This process is sometimes referred to as 'resettlement' to distinguish it from 'new settlement' or 'frontier settlement'.

(e) The state may open up new areas to settlement, or make unused state lands available for settlement, usually involving the provision of a basic infrastructure prior to allocating the land to small or medium farmers. Land may be sold to settlers freehold, or may be retained in state ownership with leasehold land tenure for farm families. The biggest settlement program in recent history has been the transmigration program in Indonesia in which farm families from the overcrowded island of

Java are moved to sparsely populated locations in the much larger islands of Sumatra, Kalimantan (Borneo), Sulawesi (Celebes), and Irian Jaya (West New Guinea).

There are several distinctions and debates that feature in all these land access transitions. The *first* is distribution versus collectivisation. Some land reforms distribute former landowner holdings to tenants, agricultural workers, and others with a claim to access. Others prefer to keep large holdings intact, or even to amalgamate holdings, in order to operate them as state or communal farms. This is a consequence, *second*, of the conflicting arguments about farm output growth: the small family farm for efficiency *versus* the realisation of economies of scale in large-scale agriculture.

A *third* distinction is between the maintenance of various types of tenancy (including leasehold from the state), and private ownership with freehold land title. The slogan 'land-to-the-tiller', which is popular in connection with the politics of land reform, is predominantly about the creation of freehold farms for former tenants and landless workers.

The *fourth* distinction is between changing the ownership distribution of land and changing the farm size distribution. These are not necessarily synonymous. Land ownership can be changed – including distributing to tenants the land that they formerly tilled on the landowners' property – without changing the boundaries or sizes of cultivation units. A change in farm size distribution means actually redrawing the map of agricultural cultivations, by dividing larger ownership units into smaller ones, reducing or increasing the size of tenant farms, or amalgamating micro-plots into family farms.

Instruments of land reform

The topic of instruments of land reform is already covered in part by the discussion of paths of change in land ownership, tenancy, and farm size. The choices made with respect to the end results of the land reform are in an important sense instruments of the land reform process. In addition, however, land reform instruments include such issues as the payment of compensation, the setting of exemptions or ceilings, and the rules of distribution to land reform beneficiaries.

Three main groups of land reform instruments can be identified. These are (i) instruments of *tenancy reform*, (ii) instruments of *land redistribution*, and (iii) instruments of *land settlement*.

The first and third of these groups can be dealt with quite quickly. *Tenancy reform* does not involve the redistribution of existing private titles to land, it merely means changing the rules concerning legal and illegal types of contract between landowner and tenant. Tenancy reform typically means the prohibition of certain feudalistic types of tenancy – mainly tied labour of various kinds – and the modification of others – e.g. by imposing a ceiling on the landowner's share in share tenancy contracts. The effectiveness of these instruments is compromised in practice by the diversity and unwritten nature of the relations between landowners and tenants in many rural situations (see below). Further instruments of tenancy reform are to convert feudal or semi-feudal tenancy arrangements to a cash rent basis, and to impose rules on landowners regarding the security of tenure of their tenants.

Land settlement likewise does not involve enforced redistribution of previous private titles to land. It usually involves the release of state land for settlement, the opening up of new lands for settlement, or the resettlement of land abandoned by former owners. Land settlement requires a set of criteria and rules for deciding the categories of rural dweller who should be eligible to apply for a farm; the size of holding that is appropriate given the soils, climate, and crop choices of the settlement area; the amount of capital required by each settler in the form of loans to get started on cultivation; the repayment rules for those loans; whether to lease or sell the land to its new occupiers; and the price and method of recoupment in the case of transfer of freehold title.

Land redistribution does mean reallocating the ownership of land between people, and the rules for this are a great deal more difficult to formulate and to implement than in either of the other more modest types of land reform. Warriner (1969: 17–22) identifies four main components: *expropriation, compensation, exemption*, and *distribution*. In the following paragraphs we examine each of these briefly in turn:

Expropriation
The first step in a redistributive type of land reform is to expropriate the land that it is intended to reallocate. This is politically the most difficult action amongst all instruments of land reform. Where land reform comes about as a consequence of a socialist revolution, expropriation may be automatic and widespread with few exemptions. In all other cases, expropriation is the outcome of a political process involving many trade-offs and compromises.

The most common instrument is to set a *ceiling* for the amount of land that landowners can retain for their own continued use, and to expropriate all land above that area. The size of this ceiling has varied widely in different land reforms, from 500 ha in Iran, to 150 ha in some Latin American land reforms, and between two and four hectares in post-war Japanese land reform. These ceilings tend to reflect the pre-existing farm size structure, the intensity of cultivation, and the nature of the pressure for land reform by peasant political groupings. In some cases, expropriation has only applied to land registered in particular types of holding, for example the colonial *zamindari* types of land grant in India were expropriated in the post-Independence period.

Compensation

The amount of compensation for land reallocated in land reform legislation is another difficult and highly charged matter. It is rare for there to be no compensation at all, but also equally rare for the full market price of land to be paid. It has usually been beyond the financial capacity of land-reforming states to pay the full market price for land confiscated. It is even doubtful whether a meaningful market price could be defined in the political atmosphere that typically accompanies land reform.

One method of paying compensation is to take the value of land as registered for land tax purposes. This undervalues the land by market price criteria, but is at least consistent for all landowners. Compensation is often split into two components: an immediate cash payment, and an allocation of government bonds redeemable at some future date. Depending on the way this is set up, it is possible for the level of compensation to be eroded by inflation so that the real cost to the state is much lower than the nominal cost when compensation is agreed.

Exemptions

Many land reforms in practice contain exemptions to the criteria that are established in law for expropriation. These exemptions represent political compromises in the drafting of legislation, and they can be fatal for the realisation of the goals of the reform. A common exemption in Latin American land reforms was to exempt land that could be shown to be already under 'efficient' farm production. Apart from opening the door to interminable legal proceedings as to the meaning of efficient agricultural use, this type of exemption means that the beneficiaries of the land reform end up with the least fertile land.

Other exemptions relate to institutional land owners (charitable bodies, mission stations, Church lands, etc.), corporate land owners (land farmed by registered capitalist companies), or foreign land owners (land operated by foreign companies).

Distribution

Land reform legislation must also set down the criteria and instruments for post-reform land allocation. In part, this involves decisions we have already discussed, such as whether to distribute or to collectivise, whether to go for tenancies or owner-occupier farms, whether to retain land under state ownership or permit freehold registrations, and so on.

The allocation of land distributed after a land reform also involves criteria concerning maximum and minimum sizes of holdings, unless land is reassigned to former tenants with no planned changes in holdings size. A failure to set minimum farm sizes could mean the advent of a large number of holdings that are below family subsistence in output, and with fragmentation in later years these might become uneconomic to operate. A failure to set maximum farm size has the reverse effect of reducing the total number of holdings available, and permitting fewer, larger, farmers a relatively high standard of living while other rural dwellers may remain landless and extremely poor. Both minimum and maximum criteria are in practice rather insensitive instruments given the variability in soils, climate, topography, crop choices, and other features of agricultural zones.

Problems of implementation

Land reform, like all public policy, is in part a shadow play involving the manipulation of symbols; the actual policy demonstrably reflects considerations more pressing and mundane than abstract ideals of social justice or economic rationality. (Herring, 1983: 3)

There are many reasons why the actual outcomes of land reforms do not live up to the promises of the rhetoric that surrounds their legislation. Some of these reasons are associated with compromises made during the legislative process. Others are related to the practical problems of implementation in an environment where the losers will do their best to evade or thwart the intentions of the legislators. Some common reasons for land reform to turn out very different in practice from its theoretical intent are as follows:

(a) Foot dragging at the legislative stage. Opposition politicians ensure that the legislation takes months, even years, to become law. This delay gives landowners more time to rearrange their property in order to evade expropriation (see below).

(b) Modifications and exemptions. In order to get land reform into law, its promoters are forced to make numerous compromises in its scope and coverage, such that the final legislation may no longer serve the original goals intended. A good example is the agrarian reform law passed in the Philippines in 1988 (Putzel & Cunnington, 1989: 63–74).

(c) Evasions by landowners. Landlords have many ways of evading land reform legislation, especially if given time to make the necessary arrangements (Feder, 1970). Retention ceilings can be evaded by re-registering land in countless different names. Land titles and registration documents can be altered by making bribes to low-paid government officials in land registration offices. Tenancy regulations can be circumvented by reaching side-agreements with tenants, or by intimidating them into signing false documents.

(d) Timidity of tenants. Some types of land reform impose the onus for making land tenancy or land title claims on tenants. Tenants may not understand their rights and obligations under the new legislation, the paperwork may be too complex, they may have been intimidated by landowners into 'voluntarily' ceding their rights, they may fear that the land reform is short-lived and be therefore unprepared to confront their landlords.

(e) Role of the courts. Many countries have a legal system that is, to some degree, independent of the legislature, and that tends to be a conservative force in society at large. Landowners may forestall compliance with land reform legislation by referring every case to the courts. Landowners may bring litigation to the courts that tests the interpretation of every clause in the legislation. The courts may find loopholes and rule in favour of landowners, thus further undermining the credibility and intention of the legislation.

(f) Legal title problems. Even in highly organised industrial societies, land registration and transfer of titles can be time consuming and subject to lengthy delays. Delays in issuing title deeds for land confiscated under a land reform can result in many types of intimidation and abuse. Landlords may repossess land that has been distributed on the grounds that the new owners do not have legal title. Some peasants may grab land off other peasants in order to enlarge the size of holdings that they intend to register.

(g) Failures of institutional adaptation. It has been common to observe in the wake of land reform that rural institutions and state bodies like banks, credit agencies, input delivery outlets, and local planning agencies fail to adjust fast enough to the change in their clientele. Where these institutions have become used to dealing almost exclusively with landowners in rural areas, they adapt inadequately to serving the needs of the small producers, and their regulations may prohibit proper access by the new farmers to the services they are supposed to provide (a classic 'access' problem – see Chapter 6).

Lessons from the historical experience

The relative success or failure of past land reforms helps to identify some of the ingredients that are required for land reform to succeed in achieving its economic goals of improved equity and efficiency. However, even more so than with other policies, it must be emphasised that the historical, political and social context of land reform is unique to each setting in which it arises. There is no blueprint approach to land reform that can avoid the political confrontations and compromises that are inherent in its formulation and implementation.

To give one example of this problem, consider the ambiguities confronting a socialist party that gains control of a provincial or national parliament with support largely from farm tenants and peasant organisations in a semi-feudal rural society. The ideology of the party, although strong in its sympathy for the underdog, may also involve firm leanings towards collective agriculture. The small-farm tenants who voted for the party wish to become independent owner-occupier peasants, not collective farmers. The party has to make an alliance with a centre party to make any headway in its reform proposals. And so on. An excellent case-study of these conflicts and paradoxes, for Kerala State in India, is given in Herring (1983: Chs. 6 and 7).

Past land reforms may be an imperfect guide to the political manoeuvring required to bring them into being, but they do provide some guidance on instruments that are likely to fail in their implementation; post-reform land tenures that are more successful than others; supporting policies required for success; and problems in the interpretation of impact. These lessons of past reforms are summarised briefly here as follows:

(a) Tenancy reforms that do not involve change of land titles or land redistribution are observed to have negligible impact on tenant status, tenant incomes, farm efficiency, or technical innovation. They can be evaded or twisted too readily and cannot be policed.

(b) Land redistribution with ceiling area retentions by landowners has also been found to have severe flaws, even though it is the predominant non-revolutionary type of redistributive land reform. The problem is the ease with which land can be registered under new names, or assigned between numerous family members. Some authors on land reform have argued for zero retention of tenant land by landowners as a solution to this problem (Prosterman & Riedinger, 1987: 182–3).

(c) Many land reforms have failed to achieve expectations due to ambivalence and experimentation in the operation of post-reform farms. The direct transfer of freehold ownership to peasant farm families (South Korea, Taiwan, Japan) has worked much better – in terms of stability, incomes, efficiency, and technical innovation – than the host of experiments in cooperative, semi-collective, semi-state, communal, or state farms attempted in Latin America, parts of Africa, and parts of South-East Asia. Sometimes the failures result from government ambivalence (the ownership-type implemented was an unsatisfactory political compromise), sometimes from lack of supporting resources (see below), sometimes from lack of motivation, and sometimes from bureaucratic inefficiency.

(d) Many writers consider that the absence of supporting policies – price policy, credit policy, input policies and so on – have contributed to the lack of success of land reform in many cases (Lipton, 1974; Nguyen & Martinez-Salvidar, 1979; Prosterman & Riedinger, 1987: Ch. 8). They may be right, but the advocacy of more generalised state assistance to land reform beneficiaries must take into account the potential defects of state institutions, and the wider context of state versus market roles which is a recurring theme in this book.

(e) Evaluating the impact of land reform, especially the impact on the ownership structure and size distribution of holdings, is extremely difficult. The outcome of land reform is partly an illusion (Herring, 1983: 269). The pre-reform structure is unlikely to be known with any degree of accuracy, and the post-reform structure reflects landowner evasions of the reform as well as genuine redistribution. Land registration records must be treated with suspicion, since it is easy enough to get them altered in some developing countries. Finally, output growth is impossible to attribute to land reform unless all other social, economic, and agronomic factors can be accounted for. In practice, it is probably easier to distinguish the failures of land reform than its successes.

Current and future relevance

As the twentieth century comes to an end, land reform seems to be a much lower priority for state action in developing countries than was the case in the three decades following the Second World War (Lehmann, 1978; de Janvry, 1981b; Atkins, 1988).

A number of explanations can be provided for this waning interest in land reform, although it may be premature to conclude that land tenure systems are no longer an issue in development policy. It is not uncommon for economic policies to experience swings of fashion, and land reform happens not to be a fashionable policy at the time of writing.

Some good reasons for extreme swings in the popularity of land reform are apparent in the preceding treatment of land reform policies. Land reform is a politically exhausting issue. Its close association with social strife and revolutions means that it tends to take the form of large discrete jumps, followed by a period of retrenchment, rather than a continuous and even process of change.

In terms of market economics, the more radical types of land reform possess several paradoxes (Atkins, 1988). They involve violating the sanctity of private property which is a cornerstone of the market economy. Their economic justification in terms of improving the working of the land market could readily, by extension, be applied to other imperfect markets (input markets, output markets, capital markets) with no end to the amount of state intervention thus legitimated. No wonder that neoclassical economists have an ambivalent and contradictory attitude to land reform, both desiring the outcome of an independent freehold peasantry and, simultaneously, being deeply suspicious of the political steps that are necessary to achieve that goal.

There are other reasons why land reform should be a less urgent priority in those developing countries that underwent land redistributions in the 1950s to 1970s. Some of these are as follows:

(a) high rates of urbanisation and industrialisation have taken the social pressure off land access, and, in some cases, transferred it to the urban 'informal' sector;

(b) feudal tenure relations have just about disappeared as a result of the past reforms, even if the resulting land ownership distribution leaves much to be desired – it is much more difficult in a market economy to launch an attack on a landed capitalist class, including richer peasants, than on a landed feudal class (de Janvry, 1981b);

(c) disappointment with the outcome of previous reforms, especially in relation to the high social and political cost of their execution;

(d) a shift in priorities and pressures away from land access, including the productivity gains of the seed–fertilizer–water revolution, and the plight of the growing rural landless who could not numerically be accommodated with land rights even in the event of further land reform.

Having made these points, it is nevertheless concluded that land reform is not a dead issue for the future. Some countries are at the time of writing struggling with contemporary land reforms (e.g. the Philippines). Other countries have land reform legislation on the books that has never been properly implemented, but which a future change in political line-ups could reinvigorate. Finally, it would seem that some interesting shifts and reversals in land tenure systems could emerge with the social change occurring in Eastern Europe and the Soviet Union. State and collective farm systems may be dismantled, and their land sub-divided into family farms. The peasant farm family could re-emerge as a social and economic force of some importance after disappearing for half a century or more.

Peasants and land reform

Peasants are often the driving force of land reforms, even if they are not the only or even the main beneficiaries of the reforms as they are finally implemented. Peasant revolt against the oppressions and constrictions of feudal land tenure systems can provide a powerful social force and political lever for land reform. Exceptions are pre-emptive land reforms undertaken by reformist states from above.

Reference has already been made to the ambivalence of socialist political groups towards peasant demands for improved, more equitable, and more stable access to land. On the one hand, socialist parties or coalitions typically require peasant pressure and support in order to gain the political power required to implement land reform. On the other hand, following Lenin, socialists are suspicious of peasants due to their conservatism, individualism, and designation as petty capitalist producers.

The outcome of this ambivalence is that many land reforms have resulted in the institution of cooperative, collective, or state organisations of production rather than the freehold or leasehold tenure of small family farms. These experimental types of farm organisation have not in general worked well (but see Meyer, 1989, for an intermediate case). There is no shortage of reasons that can be invoked to explain their failure: the ignorance of the peasants, poor leadership, bureaucratic inefficiency, insufficient supporting policies, lack of financial support, and so on.

Most of these excuses for failure miss the point. Peasant production is *par excellence* an individual farm household type of production, in which the efficient management of resources results from family cooperation, and the motivation to succeed is based on household survival and income security. These factors are stripped away when the peasant is turned into a reluctant labourer in a joint enterprise, the rules for which are devised in a capital city far away.

Without doubt, empirically, the most successful land reforms for poor peasants and tenants have been land-to-the-tiller programs, such as those implemented in Japan, Taiwan, and South Korea after the Second World War. This may be an unpalatable conclusion for those who consider that social cooperation holds the key to improving the living standards of poor farm people in developing countries. However, the experience in a great many developing countries during the last half century seems to show that freehold or leasehold peasant family farms provide better prospects for efficient and innovative farm production than state imposed larger-scale types of production organisation.

Land reform policy and women

The independent rights of women to land have tended to receive little, if any, attention in land reforms. Land reform tends to be either insensitive to gender or is male biased, the latter especially with respect to the registration of ownership title to land following the reform.

If the definition of land reform is momentarily widened to include all policies governing the re-registration of land titles, the privatisation of common or community land, and the distribution of public lands, then women are often deprived of long-established rights of land access in the process of reform. This also at a stroke can remove women from independence of resource allocation decisions, control over the product of the land, and bargaining strength against men concerning women's labour time. In short, male-biased land registration decisions can sharply and irreversibly worsen the social subordination of women to men. Some examples are as follows:

(a) redistributive land reform registers new holdings in the name of men, even though women used to have independent access to a plot on the landowner's land;

(b) tenancy reform results in lease contracts being drawn up in the names of male tenants, when previously women as well as men possessed sharecropping rights and obligations;

(c) traditional rights of female land inheritance are ignored in the design of laws for the registration of communal or village lands in private ownership, and the land becomes the freehold property of male household heads, thus also sometimes switching from female to male inheritance;

(d) land re-registration laws designed to remove anomalies and ambiguities from existing ownership records ignore customary female land use rights, and pass ownership of female lands to male household heads;

(e) land improvement projects – including irrigation schemes, area-based agricultural development projects, and resettlement schemes – deliver ownership of improved plots to men, even though previous land access in that area involved extensive customary use rights by women.

A comparative review of 13 Latin American agrarian reforms (Deere, 1985) concluded that they overwhelmingly benefited men, even when cooperative or communal post-reform land use was instituted. The chief reason for this was that male household heads were almost always treated as the beneficiaries of reform, and therefore all supporting measures (inputs, credit, extension information, and so on) were also channelled to male household heads. Even in post-reform cooperatives, women became excluded and alienated from subsequent organisation and decision-making on reform lands.

The tendency to register land in male names reflects deep-seated male-dominance in all societies. Since bureaucracies and legal systems tend to be dominated by men, pleas for women are regarded as minority views or are ignored by decision-making bodies. Yet on the face of it, land reform policies perhaps more so than some other policies in this book, lend themselves to taking account of women's land rights in policy implementation.

Summary

1. This chapter is about land reform policies in developing countries. It begins by emphasising the unique character of land reform compared to other price and technology policies. This uniqueness resides in the multiple social and economic roles of land as a resource, and in the often highly charged political nature of land reform. Land reform involves dispossessing land-owners of their private property in law, and redistributing this land for improved social equality and higher agricultural production.

2. The need for land reform derives from the rigidity of land ownership structures established over the length of previous history, compared to the rapidity of social changes otherwise

taking place in society. Such changes include population growth, spread of the market economy, income growth, and changing norms of social interaction. Eventually, the disparity between rigid land ownership and accelerating social change becomes so wide that explosive social forces are set in motion.

3. Land reform has political, social, and economic objectives. *Political objectives* include (i) the consolidation of the new state after revolutionary political change, (ii) undermining the power of a land-based elite by liberal or socialist political groups in power, or (iii) defensive land tenure change by conservative political forces wishing to maintain the *status quo*. *Social objectives* are to do with social equality, emancipation of social groups living in conditions of servitude, and sweeping away non-market barriers to social change. *Economic objectives* include income distribution, employment, and productivity goals. With respect to output and efficiency, there is a divide between advocates of large farms for economies of scale – including state and collective farms – and advocates of small family farms for efficiency.

4. There are many paths of change between pre-reform land tenure systems and post-reform land ownership and farm size structures. In the history of land reform over the past century, the dismantling of feudal and semi-feudal land tenure has been the most prevalent starting point. Post-reform land tenure systems have included changes in tenancy contracts and freehold title for small farmers (distributional reforms), as well as cooperative, collective, and state farms (collectivist reforms). Other types of land reform have included the institution of freehold tenure on previous village or community lands, collectivisation of community lands, division of plantations into smallholdings, and state nationalisation of plantations or estates.

5. Several opposing arguments feature in all land access transitions. The *first* is distribution versus collectivisation. Some land reforms distribute former landowner holdings to tenants, agricultural workers, and others with a claim to access. Others prefer to keep large holdings intact, or even to amalgamate holdings, in order to operate them as state or communal farms. This is a consequence, *second*, of the small family farm for efficiency argument versus the realisation of economies of scale in large-scale agriculture. *Third* is the continuation or creation of farm tenancy versus private ownership with freehold land title. *Fourth*

is changing the ownership distribution of land versus changing the farm size distribution.

6. Three main groups of land reform instruments can be identified. These are (i) instruments of *tenancy reform*, (ii) instruments of *land redistribution*, and (iii) instruments of *land settlement*. The first and third of these do not involve redistribution of pre-reform lands. The second involves land redistribution and requires rules regarding *expropriation, compensation, exemption*, and *distribution*. For example, a land reform involving feudal pre-reform ownership, may expropriate all lands above a ceiling retention area permitted per landowner, compensate the landowner with state bonds redeemable at a future date, exempt charities and religious institutions, and distribute the land as freehold title to former tenants.

7. A land reform faces many practical problems of formulation and implementation, and it may turn out quite different in shape and impact to the original intention of its promoters. Difficulties include legislative delays, modifications and exemptions, landowner evasions, litigation in law courts, title registration problems, and failures of supporting institutions and policies. Due to these problems, tenancy reform without redistribution is virtually doomed to failure, and redistributive reforms tend to have a less favourable impact on the land access and incomes of poor people than was intended.

8. Land reforms are less prevalent in the 1990s than they were in the period from the 1950s to the 1970s, but they have certainly not vanished from the agenda of agricultural development strategy. Reasons for less interest in them now than in the past include (i) the disappearance of true feudal tenure systems as the result of past land reforms, and the rise of market relations, (ii) the increased urbanisation of many developing countries so that urban poverty and access have become more important than rural poverty and access, (iii) the political complexity and eventual flaws of past land reforms, and (iv) the impact of HYV technology on the incomes of small farmers, possibly diffusing the pressure for improved land access, at least for the time being.

9. Some final points are made concerning the role and status of peasants in land reforms. Peasants are often the instigators and prime movers of land reforms, but not always their prime beneficiaries. Many governments have made the error of build-

ing land reform on the basis of peasant political pressure, only to create post-reform farm production institutions unsuited to peasant aspirations. The most successful land reforms have been those that created a freehold peasantry as beneficiaries of the reform. With few exceptions, cooperative, collective, and state farming has been a disappointing failure.

10. The position of women with respect to land reform policies is briefly considered, and the reader is referred to Chapter 12 for a comparative summary of the gender dimensions of agricultural policies.

Further reading

There exists a rich and varied literature on land reform, reflecting its earlier priority status in strategies of agricultural development. The classic textbook is Warriner (1969) which contains general principles as well as several case-studies. More recent in the same tradition are King (1977) and Prosterman & Riedinger (1987), the latter having a strong ideological bias towards the freehold small family farm. Useful collections of papers, including case studies of land reforms in many different countries, are Stavenhagen (1970), Dorner (1971), Lehmann (1974), and Ghai *et al.* (1979). See also Hakimian (1990: Chs. 4 and 5) on land reforms in Iran. Three World Bank publications – World Bank (1974), Walinsky (1977) and Eckstein *et al.* (1978) – provide useful comparative material. A typology of land reforms is provided by de Janvry (1981a or 1981b). An account of the impact on women of land reforms in Latin America is given in Deere (1985). A recommended and stimulating book on the politics of land reform in South Asia is Herring (1983). Finally, several recent papers provide readable accounts of facets of land reform not discussed in much detail in this chapter, including Atkins (1988) on the paradoxes for neoclassical economics of land reform policies; Meyer (1989) on a Latin American case-study which combines individual and collective dimensions; Bromley (1989) and Cramb & Wills (1990) on problems of privatising community usufruct lands; and Oldenburg (1990) on land consolidation policies in India.

Reading list

Atkins, F. (1988). Land Reform: A Failure of Neoclassical Theorization? *World Development*, **16**, No. 8.

Bromley, D.W. (1989). Property Relations and Economic Development: The Other Land Reform. *World Development*, **17**, No. 6.

218   *Land reform policy*

Cramb, R.A. & Wills, I.R. (1990). The Role of Traditional Institutions in Rural Development: Community-Based Land Tenure and Government Land Policy in Sarawak, Malaysia. *World Development*, **18**, No. 3.

Deere, C.D. (1985). Rural Women and State Policy: The Latin American Agrarian Reform Experience. *World Development*, **13**, No. 9.

de Janvry, A. (1975). The Political Economy of Rural Development in Latin America: An Interpretation. *American Journal of Agricultural Economics*, **57**, No. 3.

de Janvry, A. (1981a). *The Agrarian Question and Reformism in Latin America*. London: Johns Hopkins.

de Janvry, A. (1981b). The Role of Land Reform in Economic Development: Policies and Politics. *American Journal of Agricultural Economics*, **63**, No. 2.

Dorner, P. (ed.) (1971). *Land Reform in Latin America: Issues and Cases*. Madison: University of Wisconsin.

Eckstein, S., Donald, G., Horton, D. & Carroll, T. (1978). *Land Reform in Latin America: Bolivia, Chile, Mexico, Peru and Venezuela*. World Bank Staff Working Paper No. 275. Washington D.C.: World Bank.

Ghai, D., Khan, A.R., Lee, E. & Radwan, S. (1979). *Agrarian Systems and Rural Development*. London: Macmillan.

Hakimian, H. (1990). *Labour Transfer and Economic Development: Theoretical Perspectives and Case-Studies from Iran*. Hemel Hempstead: Harvester Wheatsheaf.

Herring, R.J. (1983). *Land to the Tiller: The Political Economy of Agrarian Reform in South Asia*. New Haven: Yale University Press.

King, R. (1977). *Land Reform: A World Survey*. London: Bell & Sons.

Lehmann, D. (ed.) (1974). *Agrarian Reform and Agrarian Reformism: Studies of Peru, Chile, China and India*. London: Faber and Faber.

Meyer, C.A. (1989). Agrarian Reform in the Dominican Republic: An Associative Solution to the Collective/Individual Dilemma. *World Development*, **17**, No. 8.

Oldenburg, P. (1990). Land Consolidation as Land Reform, in India. *World Development*, **18**, No. 2.

Prosterman, R.L. & Riedinger, J.M. (1987). *Land Reform and Democratic Development*. Baltimore: Johns Hopkins.

Stavenhagen, R. (ed.) (1970). *Agrarian Problems and Peasant Movements in Latin America*. New York: Doubleday.

Walinsky, L.J. (ed.) (1977). *Agrarian Reform as Unfinished Business: The Selected Papers of Wolf Ladejinsky*. Oxford University Press.

Warriner, D. (1969). *Land Reform in Principle and Practice*. Oxford: Clarendon Press.

World Bank (1974). *Land Reform*. Washington D.C.: World Bank, Rural Development Series Paper.

10

Research policy

Research policy

Research policy is about the role of the state in, and about alternative approaches to, the generation and diffusion of new agricultural technology for farm households.

There are several dimensions covered by this description of research policy. The *generation* of new agricultural technology refers to the factors underlying the supply of innovations. It includes the forces determining the topics selected for research, the institutional organisation of research, the resources allocated to research, the management of research, and the outcomes of research.

The *diffusion* of new agricultural technology refers to the factors underlying the adoption of innovations by farmers. It includes farm-level and economy-wide constraints affecting technology adoption, the adaptation of research findings to local conditions, off-farm and on-farm trials of new crop varieties, interactive adaptive research involving farmers in the research process, and the provision of extension services or other dissemination methods for spreading information between farmers.

The *role of the state* is somewhat less contentious with respect to research policy than it is with respect to many of the other policies examined so far in this book. There is a broad consensus amongst economists that a significant proportion of agricultural research must be regarded as a *public good*, requiring funding by the state even in countries pursuing free market philosophies. The reasons for this are as follows (Schultz, 1990: 376–7):

(a) most types of agricultural innovation once released are in the public domain, and cannot be protected by patent or copyright laws, for example seed varieties, changes in cultivation practices, adaptations to implements or buildings using local materials, new cropping systems;

(b) private enterprise restricts itself to applied research of a kind that lends itself to copyright protection, such as branded inputs or machinery, and this is a small fraction of the agricultural research required to achieve output, equity, and food security goals;

(c) the farm families who are one main category of beneficiary from research could not individually organise and finance the scale of research required for widespread advances in farm technology (note that this is not the same as saying that farmers have no role in the research process, on the contrary they are envisaged nowadays to play a major role);

(d) the consumers who are the other main category of research beneficiary would not of their own volition organise and finance agricultural research.

An important distinction is between *formal* and *informal* research. Formal research refers to research activities undertaken within national or international research institutions, or by large private corporations. Informal research refers to experimentation and innovation undertaken by farmers themselves, a capacity that is strongly emphasised in the recent literature (Richards, 1985; Chambers *et al.*, 1989). Informal research includes adaptation by farmers of innovations emanating from the formal research system, the unplanned spread of varieties not released by research stations, and farmers' own inventions with respect to variety selection, cultivation practices, conservation methods, or design of farm implements.

An important attribute of informal research is what is called *indigenous technical knowledge*. Farmers possess an accumulated, and mostly unwritten, fund of knowledge concerning plants, soils, climate, seasons, pests, diseases, agronomic practices, and so on. Individual farmers experiment and learn over a lifetime of wresting a livelihood from the land. This knowledge remains largely untapped and ignored by formal research systems and conventional approaches to research. While the validity of this knowledge should not be falsely romanticised – some of it will be folklore of no proven benefit – it is also true that it has been ignored in the past to the detriment of more rapid progress in solving the problems of resource-poor farmers in difficult environments.

Formal agricultural research involves *basic* research as well as *applied* research. Basic research is scientific investigation that advances the knowledge of feasible biological processes in agriculture, but which may not have immediate application in farming practice. Applied research is orientated towards achieving a practical objective, such as resistance to a disease in a variety of wheat that already possesses agronomically desirable characteristics. Applied research often requires the prior success of basic research – e.g. new methods of modifying the genetic characteristics of plant varieties – in order to make advances in solving specific problems.

Adaptive research refers to the adjustment of technology to a particular set of farming conditions. This may take the form of further selection of variety attributes of a different kind to those emphasised in the original applied research. National adaptations of crop varieties released by international agricultural research centres are of this form. Adaptive research also includes the interactive process of on-farm trials and feedback to research stations that is a feature of farming systems research (FSR).

Research policy is *par excellence* a technology policy, in the context of the distinction between price policies and technology policies made elsewhere in this book. Price policies establish a context for farm-level technical change that may inhibit or accelerate the rate of adoption of innovations. They are normally considered as having only short- and medium-term effects on farm output, whereas technology policy holds the key to sustained long-term growth in farm productivity. The weight of evidence suggests high returns to agricultural research in most parts of the world (Evenson, 1981). The inference is also drawn that most governments under-resource agricultural research relative to other budgetary allocations yielding much lower returns to investment.

This chapter proceeds according to the following format:

(a) the *organisation* of the formal research system is described, with special attention to the role of the international agricultural research centres (IARCs);

(b) alternative approaches to the *supply* and *demand for innovations* are examined, under the sub-headings of transfer of technology, adaptive technology transfer, multiple sources of innovation, farming systems research, and farmer first research;

(c) the approach to agricultural research known as *farming systems research* (FSR) is set out in greater detail with respect to its principles, methods, and limitations;

(d) the approach to research policy designated as *farmer first research* (FFR) is set out with respect to its concepts, methods and limitations;

(e) the *goals and priorities* of state-funded types of research are summarised in the light of the preceding examination of alternative approaches and types of agricultural research;

(f) the use of the concepts of consumer and producer surplus for measuring the *economic impact* of research investment is set out, including a discussion of alternative methods and the limitations of research impact studies;

(g) finally, some observations are made on the status of *women* in the context of alternative approaches to research policy.

Organisation of formal research

Formal agricultural research is divided between public research institutions and private research institutions. This chapter is mainly concerned with public or state-funded research, not with private research. This is because research policy mainly involves approaches, priorities, and decisions concerning the former rather than the latter type of research. Nevertheless, the nature and coverage of private research needs to be taken into account in the overall picture of technological change in agriculture.

There are three main tiers in public or state-funded agricultural research. These are the international research, national research, and national extension levels of research organisation. The international level is composed of a network of international agricultural research centres (IARCs) which are funded by bilateral and multilateral aid donors. The national research level is composed of state-funded agricultural research or experimental stations, sometimes financed with aid-donor support. The extension level refers to the national agricultural extension service, which is typically regarded as the main channel for the diffusion of innovations to farmers.

There are many different dimensions of scope and function determining the way this system works at the international level, the national level, and the interaction between them. The core of the international system for food commodities is a set of 13 centres, which are grouped together in an organisation called the Consultative Group on International Agricultural Research (CGIAR). The CGIAR centres are listed together with relevant information on their focus and coverage in Table 10.1.

The CGIAR is a relatively recent creation, taken against the background of the century or so during which systematic agricultural research on tropical commodities has been undertaken. The CGIAR was founded in 1971 in order to consolidate and extend a model for international agricultural research represented by the pre-existing centres of IRRI and CIMMYT (see Table 10.1), and in order to place the financing, priorities, and coordination of such centres on a sound long-term footing. The

Table 10.1. *Research centres affiliated to the CGIAR, 1986*

Initials (year started)	Name of research centre	Location	Main topic	1986 budget US$ m
IRRI (1960)	International Rice Research Institute	Philippines	Rice	21.6
CIMMYT (1966)	Centro Internacional de Mejoramiento Maiz y Trigo	Mexico	Maize, wheat	21.9
IITA (1967)	International Institute of Tropical Agriculture	Nigeria	Food crops	22.0
CIAT (1968)	Centro Internacional de Agricultura Tropical	Colombia	Food crops	21.4
CIP (1971)	Centro Internacional de la Papa	Peru	Potatoes	10.9
WARDA (1971)	West African Rice Development Association	Liberia	Rice	2.1
ICRISAT (1972)	Int. Crop Research Inst. for the Semi-Arid Tropics	India	Food crops	21.2
ILRAD (1973)	Int. Laboratory for Research on Animal Diseases	Kenya	Animal diseases	10.4
IBPGR (1974)	Int. Board for Plant Genetic Resources	Italy	Genetic centre	4.5
ILCA (1974)	Int. Livestock Centre for Africa	Ethiopia	Livestock, Africa	14.4
IFPRI (1975)	Int. Food Policy Research Institute	USA	Food policy	4.3
ICARDA (1976)	Int. Centre for Agricultural Research in Dry Areas	Syria	Food crops	18.1
ISNAR (1980)	Int. Service for National Agricultural Research	Netherlands	National research	3.8

Abbreviations: Int. = International; Inst. = Institute.
Source: Judd *et al.* (1987: 40–1)

CGIAR secretariat is located at the World Bank in Washington, with an associated Technical Advisory Committee (TAC), responsible for setting priorities and guidelines, located at FAO in Rome. There are a dozen or so international research centres created since the mid-1970s that are not yet affiliated to the CGIAR (Ruttan, 1987: 70–3).

The CGIAR centres work on food commodities and they are individually specialised partly by commodity (e.g. rice, maize, wheat) and partly according to major agro-economic zones (e.g. the semi-arid tropics). The centres are conceived as fulfilling various roles, including the invention of new varieties, their transfer for adaptation to national research centres, the training of national research scientists, the more general coordination and diffusion of research information between centres and between countries, and the orderly conservation of genetic materials.

The CGIAR centres have received much attention worldwide since the mid-1970s, and there is a tendency to overlook other categories of international agricultural research (Biggs, 1990). Export commodities like coffee, cocoa, rubber and cashewnuts have their own international research networks, which are much older than the CGIAR system, but which tend to be less systematic in the generation, storage, retrieval and transmission of research materials and information. In addition, many of the previous colonial powers – England, France, Holland – have tropical research institutes with diverse expertises in tropical agriculture.

In terms of the division of tasks between international and national research levels, the international centres tend to focus on basic and applied research, while national research stations focus on applied research and adaptive research. Basic research requires expensive laboratories, equipment, and scientists, which only a few of the larger developing countries would be able to afford. Nevertheless, the international research centres represent only a small fraction – about five per cent – of worldwide recurrent expenditures on developing country agricultural research.

The scope and function of national research stations is diverse and variable across and between countries. Some research stations are location or ecological-zone specific, others are multi-purpose, others are commodity specific. Research on food crops tends to take place in location specific, multi-crop, experimental stations. Research on export crops tends to be located in commodity-specific research stations, for example coffee research station, tea research institute, sugar research institute, and so on. Links between national and international research centres are maintained via the transmission of genetic materials, workshops and seminars, short courses, and individual contacts. These links inevitably work unevenly in space and time.

Turning now to formal private research, this also has international and national levels. The international level consists of the research and development (R & D) departments of agribusiness corporations. These may be machinery suppliers (e.g. General Motors, International Harvester), chemical input suppliers (e.g. ICI, Bayer), or plantation companies (e.g. Unilever, Del Monte, United Brands). These companies have overseas subsidiaries operating in developing countries, and the bigger subsidiaries may undertake their own R & D work adapting technologies for local markets. Plantation companies commonly undertake on-farm research within their own estates or plantations or at particular sites within their geographical spread of operations.

The scope and functions of private research agencies differ from those of the public research agencies. Private research tends to focus on *product innovation* (the invention of new branded products) rather than *process innovation* (the invention of superior methods for producing the same product). This is because it is much easier to capture privately the returns to product innovation than to do so for process innovation. This explains why private research tends to be concentrated in input supply industries rather than crop or livestock productivity improvements. The exception to this rule is the vertically-integrated plantation enterprise, where cost reductions achieved in production add to the profitability of the integrated operation as a whole, and are therefore worthwhile for the company to try to achieve.

Supply and demand for innovations: Alternative models

The major preoccupation of writing on research policy is identifying the determinants of the supply and demand for innovations, i.e. the factors causing a stream of useful innovations to arise from the research process, and those enabling the adaptation and adoption of new crops and methods by farmers. Some propositions in this area are *descriptive*, i.e. they try to pinpoint the critical factors on both sides of the research equation from the analysis of past experience. Others are *prescriptive*, i.e. they put forward new ideas for improving the generation and diffusion of new agricultural technology by the research system.

The following discussion identifies five alternative models or 'approaches' that are concerned with the supply and demand for agricultural innovations in developing countries. These are not models in the formal sense of the term. Nor are they mutually exclusive, indeed elements of all of them can be found operating in the agricultural research system at any given moment of time. All of them contain elements of both descriptive and prescriptive argument. Their relationship to each other is partly sequential in historical time, since they represent changing ideas about the way research systems should operate. The five models are:

1. Transfer of technology
2. Adaptive technology transfer
3. Farming systems research
4. Farmer first research
5. Multiple sources of innovation

Transfer of technology

The pure transfer of technology model was the dominant approach to agricultural research in the 1950s and 1960s. In this, the generation and diffusion of innovations is a linear process from rich-country research institutes to poor-country research stations, and from them to extension officers and to farmers.

There is of course a whole world view bound up in this perception, albeit one that has become discredited with the passage of time. This view includes ideas such as (i) the most modern is the best, (ii) there is a single frontier of world scientific knowledge, (iii) agricultural technology has global transferability irrespective of local ecological conditions, and (iv) poor-country farmers are traditional and they must undergo a quantum transformation to become modern farmers. The transfer of four-wheel tractors to developing countries in the 1960s (Chapter 7) exemplifies this model.

The transfer of technology model sees the farmer as a passive recipient of new technology. If the farmer adopts the technology, then he or she is progressive. Failure of adoption is attributed mainly to psychological factors: irrationality, conservatism, traditionalism, and so on. The model could be dismissed as absurd if remnants of it did not still persist in the thinking of some politicians, bureaucrats, scientists, and academics.

Adaptive technology transfer

This model differs from the previous one in that the location-specific requirements of technology are recognised, and farmer behaviour is no longer seriously regarded as a barrier to adoption. Attention shifts to adapting new technology to local conditions, and on removing socio-economic constraints to adoption by farmers, such as the availability of complementary inputs or credit.

The adaptive technology transfer model was the prevalent model of the 1970s and early 1980s. The creation and expansion of the CGIAR system represents an important outcome of its preoccupations. In this model the generation and diffusion of innovations remains a predominantly linear process. However, the site of innovation generation is moved to developing country locations, and adaptation of innovations by national research systems to suit local conditions is envisaged. Extension still plays a major role in transmitting new technologies to farmers, and indeed the training and visit (T & V) system originating in this period envisages an enhanced role for extension (Benor and Harrison, 1977).

Limited feedback occurs in the adaptive model: feedback from farmers to country research stations occurs via extension agents in the T & V system; and feedback from national research stations to international research centres occurs via the professional interaction of scientists in the two levels of the system.

A major preoccupation of the adaptive model was identifying and alleviating the causes of weak adoption (as identified by a yield-gap between farmers and research stations) or non-adoption by farmers. These causes were regarded as 'constraints' to the successful adoption of high yielding varieties by farmers. They included lack of credit, lack of inputs, and lack of information on the correct balance of complementary inputs. The solution was input 'packaging' (Chapter 6), a widespread policy tool of the 1970s.

The adaptive transfer model worked fairly well for the 'green revolution' crops (rice and wheat) cultivated under relatively homogeneous ecological conditions, with (relatively) simple cropping systems, available complementary inputs, and low risk climatic conditions. The model proved a disappointing failure, however, for resource-poor farmers operating under diverse ecological conditions, with complex cropping systems, poor or absent input markets, and high risk climatic conditions (Chambers & Jiggins, 1987).

Farming systems research (FSR)

Farming systems research emerged in the mid-1970s and became prevalent in the 1980s, as a response in part to the failure of green-revolution-type innovations to reach resource-poor farmers growing crops other than wetland rice or wheat. FSR greatly changes the status of the farm household and the farm system in the generation and diffusion of new technology. It does this by such devices as placing emphasis on discovering from farmers themselves their goals and constraints, routinely including on-farm trials and farmer participation in the testing of new varieties or methods, and instituting iterative and interactive feedback mechanisms between farmers and researchers.

Farming systems research is an important development in the implementation of research policy and its main features are set out in more detail below. At this stage it can be noted that it entails a departure from the mainly linear transfer mechanism implied by the two preceding models. In FSR, the priorities of research are at least in part determined by farmer circumstances, rather than by scientists' preferences or the research manager's prior decisions. Moreover, the progress of research, and the directions of its adaptive component, are in theory quite strongly influenced by information feedbacks from farmers.

FSR is complementary to the existing formal agricultural research system, and does not seek to substitute or replace it. It adds several procedures that would not otherwise be present to sequences of research decision-making and design. It represents another step forward in recognising the rationality of peasant decision-making, and unlike the adaptive transfer model it encourages the adaptation of research to fit the farmer's circumstances rather than the adaptation of farmer's circumstances to fit a predetermined research output. Under an FSR philosophy, the constraints faced by resource-poor farmers are taken seriously, and the likelihood that such constraints can be removed is treated with caution. The technology must be adapted to the constraints, not *vice versa*.

Farmer first research (FFR)

For some observers, the FSR solution to the problem of matching research priorities to farmer needs does not go far enough in drawing on the knowledge and experimental skills of farmers. The expert staff of the research station – scientists, social scientists, and their assistants – remain firmly in control of the data elicited from farmers, the design of on-farm trials, and the nature of the technology eventually recommended for widespread adoption. From this viewpoint, FSR does not make for a true break with the linear path of technology transfer, it modifies that path by introducing some major feedback loops between points along the linear route.

The farmer first model (so-called due to Chambers *et al.*, 1989, but originating in the 'farmer-back-to-farmer' model of Rhoades & Booth, 1982) envisages the supply and demand for innovations as a circular process beginning and ending with farmers, rather than a linear process beginning with scientists and ending with farmers. This circle has no particular point of departure since it involves a continuous interaction, on a basis of partnership, between scientists and farmers, and the components of the process need not take place in any particular order. In many cases, diagnosis will prove to be the most commonsense departure point in FFR (as is the case with FSR). However, alternative starting points are to elicit from farmers information or methods that they have found useful (scientist learning from farmer), or to begin on-farm experiments under farmer control (farmer and scientist learning together).

The farmer first model constitutes an even more radical departure from orthodox research practice than does FSR. It is set out in more detail later in this chapter, including a comparative summary of its major features against those of FSR.

Multiple sources of innovation

This model is concerned with the factors affecting the supply of innovations, and the criteria used to select between alternative technologies that become available. Its main emphasis is on showing how different political, economic and institutional contexts determine what is considered good or bad, relevant or irrelevant, and cost effective or inefficient in research. In other respects it is compatible with the FFR view of research policy.

The multiple sources of innovation model (Biggs & Clay, 1981; Biggs, 1990) proposes that ideas and genetic resources for new technology spring from multiple sources, not just from a narrow sequence of basic and applied research carried out by scientists within the formal research system. It is pointed out that the genetic material that later became the foundation for green revolution wheat varieties in India came first from farmers' own informal selection procedures in Japan, was later worked on in United States, then in Mexican research institutes, and was finally transferred to India in the 1960s. This was not a neat linear process, nor did it begin, as often described, with the scientists working on wheat in CIMYTT in Mexico in the late 1950s.

More generally, most improvements in crop varieties originate at some point from varieties grown on farmers' fields. Many other ideas and methods concerning tillage, weed control, pest control, farm implements, crop storage, and so on originate from farmers and take multiple routes before being worked on in research stations. Moreover, many innovations by-pass the formal research system altogether, or involve them only accidentally at a particular stage of diffusion. There are many contemporary examples of adaptive work by farmers on seed varieties rejected by research stations, including some notable cases of their rapid spread in farmers' fields (Maurya, 1989).

The policy lesson of the multiple sources of innovation model is that the linear world view and method of formal science may be a slow and inefficient means of achieving widespread improvements in the productivity of farm systems. Research policy worldwide and nationally should encourage far more cross-transfer of genetic materials and ideas: from farmers to farmers, from farmers to scientists, between research stations, across countries, and between national and international research centres. Moreover, the scientific method should be more attuned to going out and looking for ideas and materials rather than spending most resources and time on laboratory activity.

The multiple sources of innovation model is complementary to the farmer first model. It emphasises the non-linearity of the process by which new farm technology is generated, and the many different sources in space and time of genetic materials and farming methods.

Summary

A comparative summary of these five models of the supply and demand for innovations is provided in Table 10.2. This focuses on a limited number of broad features, not on detailed points of theory or method. The four features that are compared are (i) the overall process by which technology is transmitted from point of origin to destination, (ii) the basic sources of agricultural innovations, (iii) the reasons for non-adoption of innovations by farmers, and (iv) the policy emphasis on the diffusion side of research that follows from those reasons.

These models represent in part a historical progression in ideas about research policy. However, it would be wrong to see them as mutually exclusive advances in research policy or practice with each model being superseded in time by the next model in line. In practice, elements of all models are present in the research system at any one time (as suggested, indeed, by the multiple sources model), but the dominant focus and allocation of resources have changed unevenly in different places over time.

Nor is it correct that adherence to one particular line of research policy reasoning means the wholesale rejection of other models. For example, the farmer first approach sees itself as complementary to formal research and to farming systems research. Likewise, the multiple sources of

Table 10.2. *Alternative models of agricultural innovation*

Name of model	Path of transmission	Sources of innovation	Reasons for non-adoption	Research policy emphasis
Transfer of technology	Linear: – DCs–LDCs–extension–farmer	DC Research: – scientists – basic/applied research	Farmer psychology: – irrational – traditional – conservative	Transfer: – progressive farmers – education
Adaptive technology transfer	Linear: – IARCs–NARCs–extension – farmer	IARCS: – scientists – local adaptation by NARCs	Constraints: – markets, prices – credit – inputs – information	Remove constraints: – markets – credit – inputs
Farming systems research	Linear: – farmer feedback – interaction	Researchers: – multi-disciplinary – improved adaptation	Constraints: – farm resources – farming system – H/H goals	FSR sequence: – diagnosis – OFT – recommend
Farmer first research	Circular: – farmer-back-to-farmer	Farmers: – ITK – experiments – adaptation	Inappropriate: – wrong technology	Role reversals: – farmer equal partner – farmer OFT
Multiple sources innovation	Diverse: – many sources – many paths	Multiple: – farmers – researchers – national/global	Same as for FFR	Diversity: – locations – sources – ideas

Abbreviations: IARCS = International Agricultural Research Centres; NARCS = National Agricultural Research Centres; ITK = Indigenous Technical Knowledge; H/H = Household; OFT = on-farm trials.

innovation model is consistent with the farmer first approach but emphasises different aspects of the process of technology transmission.

At the time of wrinting, considerable resources have been devoted in
international research centres and in many national research systems to
farming systems research. Some international centres and some national
research agencies have also conducted programmes along farmer first
lines. In view of the contemporary importance of these proposed
methods, a more detailed account of their logic and method is given in the
next two sections.

Farming systems research

In spite of considerable variability of methods that have been
described as farming systems research, there exists a basic consensus on
the main principles that distinguish this approach from other ways of
achieving technological improvements for small farmers. These principles and concepts are listed as follows (adapted from Merrill-Sands,
1986: 89–90):

(a) *FSR is farmer-orientated*. FSR views small farmers as the clients of
agricultural research. Its main goal, therefore, is to generate technology
relevant to their constraints, needs and priorities. Several mechanisms
are employed to attain this objective: (i) farmers are integrated into the
research process, (ii) the existing farming system is studied before
proposing technological solutions to problems, and (iii) technologies are
adapted to the circumstances of a specific, relatively homogeneous,
group of farmers.

(b) *FSR is systems-orientated*. FSR views the farm in a holistic manner
and focuses on interactions between components. In practice, the *whole
farm system* serves as the framework for analysis, but specific components
(e.g. crop production), sub-systems (e.g. consumption preferences), or
interactions (e.g. time allocation and tasks) may be targeted for intervention.

(c) *FSR is problem-solving*. FSR first identifies technical and socio-
economic constraints to improved production, then endeavours to develop solutions that are appropriate for the management conditions of
the system, and that are consistent with household goals.

(d) *FSR is multi-disciplinary*. Biological and social scientists collaborate in order to understand the conditions under which small farmers
operate, to diagnose constraints accurately and to develop appropriate,
improved, technologies.

(e) *FSR involves on-farm research.* On-farm research provides the context for collaboration between farmers and researchers. On-farm research also permits technology to be evaluated under the environmental and management conditions in which it will be used.

(f) *FSR provides feedback from farmers.* FSR channels feedback on farmers' goals, needs, priorities and criteria for evaluating technologies to station-based agricultural scientists and national policy-makers.

(g) *FSR is complementary to mainstream research; it does not replace it.* FSR draws on commodity and laboratory research, and adapts its results for the specific environment and socio-economic circumstances of a target group of relatively homogeneous farmers. Sometimes 'off-the-shelf' research output can be utilised, sometimes problems are returned to research stations for further applied research.

(h) *FSR is iterative and dynamic.* Adjustments are made in technology design as understanding and communication with farm families develop.

It is rare for all these principles to be adhered to in a single FSR project or program (Merrill-Sands, 1986: 90–1). However, if the absence of particular items results in redefinition of the method, a proliferation of terms for closely allied ideas results (*Ibid.*: 93). It is not only the set of principles that defines FSR, but also the sequence of events by which these principles are implemented. Here again there is variation in how many of the full set of activities is likely to be conducted in any one program. However, the following sequential stages in the conduct of FSR are common to many FSR manuals and projects:

(a) *Classification.* This step identifies homogeneous groups of farmers with similar natural and socio-economic characteristics. It provides the basis for the targeting of research and extension to particular farm types or 'recommendation domains'.

(b) *Diagnosis.* This involves the study of current farm systems in order to identify the constraints, needs and priorities of the target group of farmers. Diagnosis is multi-disciplinary. The biological scientist identifies agronomic potential and constraints, while the social scientist identifies socio-economic constraints and farm household objectives. Diagnosis may be done in two stages, the first using rapid rural appraisal type techniques to obtain a quick and low-cost assessment of major features, and the second requiring a more formal survey to substantiate or refine the conclusions of the first.

(c) *Experiment.* This is the *on-farm research* step of FSR. It concerns the design, monitoring, and evaluation of on-farm trials with the participation of selected farmers from the target group. The on-farm trials provide the adaptive research dimension of FSR. Experimentation at research stations may also occur as a complement to on-farm trials.

(d) *Recommendations*. The results of on-farm trials are analysed in order to formulate recommendations for the adoption of new varieties or techniques by farmers. In the iterative approach of FSR, recommendations are tested before being accepted for wide diffusion in the recommendation domain.

(e) *Implementation*. The recommended changes in farm systems or methods are implemented across the zone of target farmers. In many FSR programs, extension officers have an important role to play in implementing technical recommendations. Implementation may also involve support services such as the multiplication of seeds, or the supply of essential supporting inputs to farmers.

(f) *Evaluation*. The success of the research recommendations is monitored and evaluated in terms of such criteria as rate of adoption by farmers, problems encountered, modifications required, and output gains or input savings achieved. This is again an iterative and feedback process requiring continuous involvement by research station staff.

These six stages of FSR, and their links and feedbacks to the formal research system are depicted in Figure 10.1. The concerns and focus of the diagnosis phase are shown in Figure 10.2. These two diagrams are adapted from an early manual on farming systems research (Byerlee & Collinson, 1980). A useful additional representation of the procedures and interactions involved is given in Maxwell (1986: 68).

It should be emphasised that this procedure is not regarded as a rigid blueprint for the conduct of FSR. The heterogeneity of farm communities, and the many different types of research program in operation, mean that there are endless permutations in the emphasis that should be placed on some activities rather than others. Nevertheless, mainstream FSR is fundamentally considered as a logical *sequence* of events, and this makes for an important conceptual difference from the farmer first approach.

Several limitations and problems of FSR have been identified in the literature, though the relevance of some of these is likely to vary across different types of FSR program in space and time (Heinemann & Biggs, 1985; Collinson, 1988). Some points that may be relevant to the FSR method in general are:

(a) FSR grew up around the well-endowed international agricultural research centres. National FSR programs tend to be heavily reliant on aid-donor financial support. This calls into question the *sustainability* of FSR when donor enthusiasm wanes.

(b) FSR became overblown in the 1980s due to the almost reckless enthusiasm of aid donors for the concept. Its productivity gains in relation to the resources committed are unproven, and its outcome in terms of increased understanding of farming systems is disappointing. While enormous energy has been expended in preparing FSR manuals, methodologies, guidelines, and newsletters remarkably little material has been produced on FSR results, insights, impacts, or lessons.

(c) FSR contains an inherent contradiction between its aim to carry out quick and cost-effective diagnosis of farmers' problems (Collinson, 1981), and the dynamic adjustment of farming systems to changes in the environment such as price trends, switches in relative prices between crops, unstable prices or input supplies, and changing market opportunities (Maxwell, 1986). The contradiction can be overcome by viewing FSR as a continuous interactive process over a timescale of 10 to 12 years, but this jeopardises the cost-effectiveness of the method.

Figure 10.1. Farming systems research: sequence. Source: Adapted from CIMMYT (1984: 366).

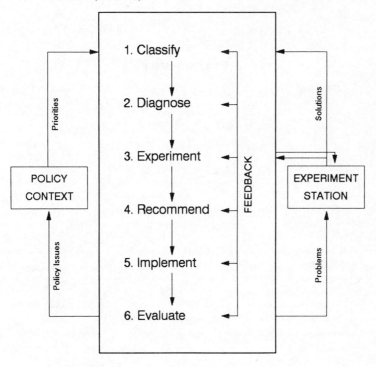

(d) FSR generates a voluminous quantity of empirical information on farming systems and household goals, but most of these data are shelved once the requirements of the FSR research sequence have been satisfied. Few mechanisms exist in FSR programmes for the further elaboration of these data in a form that would be useful for more general agricultural policy such as price policy, marketing policy, credit policy, and so on. In

Figure 10.2. Farming systems research: diagnostic survey. Source: Adapted from CIMMYT (1984: 370).

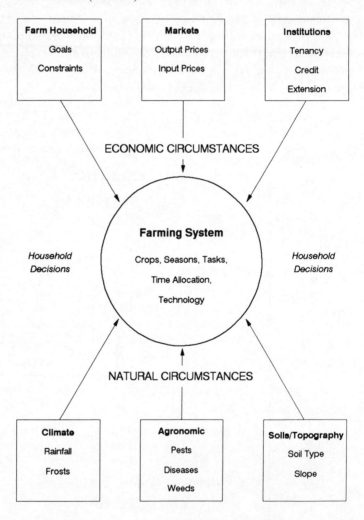

other words, FSR lacks links to the larger agricultural policy environment, and for this reason much of its data gathering is wasted.

These points do not deny the merits of FSR as a conceptual breakthrough in the management of agricultural research for small farmers, but they do place question marks on the degree to which FSR creates a sustainable local capability in the methods it advocates, and on the cost efficiency of large externally funded FSR programs.

Farmer first research

A first point to make about farmer first research is that it is not necessarily a substitute for FSR, nor is it composed of a logical sequence of steps that taken together define a set of research rules to follow. It is possible to interpret FFR as no more than a modification of the ideas already present in the FSR methodology. On the other hand, when all the elements that have been proposed for FFR are collected together, the makings of a distinctive model for farmer-orientated research seem to be present.

Several alternative terms have been used in the early genesis of an FFR approach. These have included *farmer-back-to-farmer* (Rhoades & Booth, 1982), *farmer-first-and-last* (Chambers & Ghildyal, 1985), and *farmer participatory research* (Farrington & Martin, 1988). The term *farmer first research* used here is based on the collection of ideas contained in Chambers *et al.* (1989). The main principles of FFR are set out as follows:

(a) *FFR is resource-poor farmer orientated.* FFR is not a general methodology applicable to any developing country farmer, nor even to all small farmers. It is orientated specifically to resource-poor farmers, characterised by the relative *complexity, diversity,* and *risk-proneness* of their farming systems and livelihoods (Chambers *et al.,* 1989: xiii). In particular, FFR makes a distinction between the types of farm system for which 'green revolution' technology proved a major breakthrough, and resource-poor farmers whose conditions have seen little change.

(b) *FFR emphasises the indigenous technical knowledge of resource-poor farmers.* FFR takes it as axiomatic that the proven survival capability of resource-poor farmers contains many lessons that scientists can learn from farmers, rather than the other way round.

(c) *FFR emphasises the experimental and innovative capability of resource-poor farmers.* Resource-poor farmers experiment and innovate all the time in the struggle to obtain their livelihoods under changing circumstances (Richards, 1985). This capacity for experimentation should be harnessed by the research system via the collaborative design of on-farm trials under farmer control.

(d) *FFR has multiple points of entry and exit.* FFR does not require a stepwise approach to small-farm innovation. The point of entry may be farm systems-wide diagnosis (as in FSR), or may be single-problem orientated, joint experimentation with farmers, or learning from farmers' methods that may be useful for transfer to other farmers.

(e) *FFR puts farmers in control.* Under FFR it is farmers who decide research priorities, farmers who conduct experiments, and farmers who evaluate the success or failure of a research initiative.

(f) *FFR involves role reversals.* FFR requires scientists to reverse their conventional status and role in their relationship to farmers (Chambers *et al.*, 1989: 181–6). Scientists learn from, consult, supply ideas to, support, and collaborate with farmers. Farmers analyse problems, decide priorities, make choices, and undertake experiments.

The book by Chambers *et al.* (1989) contains a great many examples and a wealth of detail concerning the pursuit of a farmer first approach to research. Several useful tabulations comparing definitions of resource-poor farmers versus 'resource-rich farmers', transfer of technology versus farmer first models, and methodological differences between farmer-orientated approaches are contained in Chambers & Jiggins (1987: 42–3), Chambers & Ghildyal (1985: 21), and Farrington & Martin (1988: 10–11).

An evident difficulty, when contrasting this approach to FSR, is that in the absence of any structure in the method it remains heavily reliant on individual initiative by scientists and researchers. Other potential problems with FFR are the same as, or similar to, ones encountered with FSR. They include reliance on external funding, lack of incentive on the part of researchers, lack of transport, insufficient budgetary allocations for field work, and lack of professional recognition for this kind of work for scientists.

Goals and priorities of research

The different models of research policy for developing-country agriculture have differing implications for the way research priorities are determined. This section considers the goals of research policy, and the way these goals are converted into research priorities within international and national agricultural research systems.

The general goals of research policy are essentially the same as those of other agricultural policies: *growth*, *equity*, and *food security*. However, the nature of the contribution of research to these objectives differs from other policies.

Research contributes to growth by increasing the productivity of farm resources, especially those resources that are more limited in availability. For example, HYV research aims to raise yields per scarce hectare of land. Research contributes to equity goals by, for example, lowering the real cost of foods consumed by poor people, increasing the output of crops grown by poor farmers, or focusing on the problems of resource-poor farmers. Research contributes to food security by, for example, enabling national self-sufficiency to be achieved in a country's staple food, breeding disease or drought resistance into a staple food, or improving the durability of food stocks after harvest.

It is sometimes considered helpful in research policy discussion to distinguish an intermediate set of goals, not quite as general as growth, equity, and food security, nor so precise as to preclude room for choice in research topics. Some intermediate level goals might be to: increase staple food yields, increase yield stability, improve output quality, save imported inputs, increase employment, ensure environmental sustainability, and so on. A list of such intermediate goals advanced by Chambers (1982) with respect to research goals for resource-poor farmers is: ecological *stability*, higher *productivity* of scarce resources, higher *livelihood intensity* (a combination of more employment and more stable or higher incomes), *continuity* of incomes and food supplies, and greater *equity* in resources and income flows in the rural community.

At quite the other end of the scale, a research programme can involve very precise goals with respect to some broader objective. Thus a plant breeder working on improvements in the genetic characteristics of a high yielding variety of grain may have aims such as (Anderson *et al.*, 1987: 203):

(a) *adaptability* – greater tolerance to locational variations in soils, climate, day length, and so on;
(b) *hardiness* – ability to withstand unexpected variations in heat or cold, water availability (e.g. flooding or drought), and so on;
(c) *less vulnerability* – reduced vulnerability to pests and diseases;
(d) *responsiveness* – higher yield response to cash inputs like fertilizer;
(e) *competitiveness* – ability to outcompete weeds in field growth, especially in marginal environments.

The research policy problem is how to decide between these myriad general, intermediate, or specific research goals. In other words, it is how to convert goals into research priorities so that scarce resources can be allocated between research stations, between broad topic areas, and between budgets for research on specified topics.

The answer to this problem varies between station and laboratory type research compared to farmer-orientated types of research. Orthodox formal research envisages research priorities as being an essentially top-down administrative matter. Policy-makers determine the overall research budget and the broad objectives to be followed; research managers decide the narrower objectives and the allocations of budgets between projects. Several methods for improving the ordering of priorities in this context have been suggested by economists:

(a) *Commodity congruity index*. This is based on the idea that funds allocated to commodity research should be roughly proportional to (i.e. congruent with) the importance of each commodity in total agricultural output (Boyce & Evenson, 1975: 15). The congruity index (I) is calculated as follows:

$$I = 1 - \Sigma(C_i - R_i)^2$$

In this, C_i is the share of commodity i in agricultural GDP, and R_i is the share of commodity i in the total budget allocated to commodity research. If these proportions are roughly equal for most commodities – especially the big commodities with a large share of agricultural GDP – the expression $\Sigma(C_i - R_i)^2$ will tend to zero, and I will then be close to one. If, on the other hand, the research budget allocations to commodities are wildly different from the relative importance of commodities in agricultural GDP, the right hand expression will be high and I will be low.

Investigation during the 1970s showed that many developing countries had commodity congruity index values less than 0.5, revealing a major discrepancy between research budget allocations and economic importance of commodities. A typical problem in the past was excessive allocation of research funds to export commodities, even in large poor countries where staple foods were much more important in agricultural GDP. The commodity congruity index enables this imbalance to be identified and suitable adjustments in the balance of research funding to be made.

(b) *Scoring models*. This method is based on asking experts to order research priorities, then aggregating the results according to the 'scores' attained by alternative topics in a list. The experts consulted may be scientists within the research system itself, disciplinary specialists in universities, policy advisors to decision-makers, and so on.

There are many different ways of implementing the basic idea of scoring (see for example Schuh & Tollini, 1979: 38–43). The chief advantage of this method is that priorities can be based on in-depth knowledge of the scientific feasibility of achieving certain goals. Its disadvantage in a developing country setting is that it is somewhat detached from the clients of research, the small or resource-poor farmers.

(c) *Ex-ante cost–benefit analysis*. Not surprisingly, economists would like to see research resources allocated to those topics that yield the highest net social return to the outlays involved. Cost–benefit analysis provides a logical framework within which to compare research budget allocations on this basis. However, there are numerous problems with trying to measure the benefit stream of research activity in advance of the research being undertaken. It is rare for scientists to be able to predict with any degree of accuracy the relative success of research along particular lines, let alone quantify the impact of successful research on agricultural output and resource use.

Perhaps the main point about *ex-ante* cost–benefit analysis is that some attempt to gauge in advance the cost-effectiveness of alternative research projects may be better than no attempt at all in situations where other methods for ordering priorities are unavailable or doubtful. At best, this type of analysis would provide some orders of magnitude that the research decision-maker could take into account alongside other relevant information in choosing priorities.

Farmer-orientated approaches to research policy create an entirely different perspective on the setting of research priorities and the allocation of research budgets. In both farming systems research and farmer first research the farmers determine, in varying degrees, the priorities of research. In FSR, this happens as part of the sequential process in which a diagnosis of the problems and constraints is an early stage. In FFR, resources must be allocated to farmer interaction types of activity, within which farmers decide their own goals and priorities of research.

Since farmer-orientated research is complementary to, rather than a substitute for, commodity and disciplinary research, the major research policy decision is to allocate resources between these two types of research activity. Once this decision is made, much of the research activity both on- and off-research station is determined by the feedback interactions with farmers. Within a mixed research system involving some laboratory lines of enquiry as well as farmer-orientated research, there is scope for the use of several different methods for prioritising research allocations:

(a) an aggregate resource allocation decision must be made between laboratory- and farmer-orientated activities, but there is no widely accepted methodology for dividing resources between these two types of research;

(b) for laboratory and on-station types of research, priorities can be determined according to methods like the congruity index or priority scoring; the former of these is the simplest and most direct way of providing some quantitative basis for research allocations between commodities;

(c) instead of scoring, it might be decided to adopt some intermediate-level criteria as an aid to research planning, such as those proposed by Chambers (1982) and listed above;

(d) farmer-orientated research largely determines its own research priorities once budgetary allocations to this type of activity have been made, and the work is underway;

(e) for farmer-orientated research to be successful it is essential to avoid undue constraints on the mobility of research teams, and on the scope of their activities; this is a key aspect of research management at the local level;

(f) a final point concerns the danger of over-specifying priority research topics, and over-constraining research flexibility. This applies to all types of agricultural research. Positive research outcomes depend in part on personal and team qualities of creativity, curiosity, and 'serendipity' (the happy accident). These qualities can be extinguished by over-zealous direction of research activity by non-researchers.

Economic evaluation of research impact

While the topic of goals and priorities is to some extent about the *ex-ante* evaluation of the outcome of alternative research directions, this section is concerned with the *ex-post* evaluation of the outcome of agricultural research that is already completed.

Ex-post evaluations are concerned with examining the cost-effectiveness of investment in agricultural research with respect to the achievement of goals like output growth, resource use efficiency, employment, and so on. An objective of many economic studies is to construct an *ex-post* cost–benefit analysis of research investment. This involves quantifying a stream of net social benefits deriving from the research, and comparing the present value of this benefit stream to the investment cost of the research program. Several different methods have been used to identify and to measure the size of this stream of benefits resulting from research, using time series data.

(a) *Input saving*. Estimating the real resources saved over time for a given level of farm output provides one measure of the efficiency gains from research investment.

(b) *Production function*. If research expenditures, or some other proxy for research activity, are entered as a variable in an aggregate agricultural production function, an indirect estimate is obtained of the importance of research in explaining the level of agricultural output over time.

(c) *Consumer and producer surplus*. In theory this permits the most complete picture of the social welfare gains of research investment to be constructed, including the relative level of net benefits accruing to producers and consumers over time. Since this method corresponds to our previous treatment of the social welfare gains and losses of agricultural policies (Chapter 3), and because it also provides a direct measure of the net benefits of research required for cost–benefit analysis, it is examined in more detail in the following paragraphs.

The basic approach is to assume that research causes a shift in the supply curve (for a particular crop or for agricultural output as a whole) to the right. The marginal cost of producing successively greater quantities of output is reduced, and therefore farmers are collectively prepared to supply more at each market price level than before. The social welfare gains and losses from research are depicted in Figure 10.3. This contains a single demand curve, *DD*, and two supply curves representing the position before research (*SS*) and after research (*S'S'*). The social welfare changes associated with this construction are as follows:

$$\text{Consumer surplus gain } = a + d + e$$
$$\text{Producer surplus gain } = (b + c) - (a + b)$$
$$= c - a$$
$$\text{Total social welfare gain } = d + e + c$$

To measure these changes, either information must be obtained or assumptions must be made about the shape of the demand and supply curves, and the price elasticities of demand and supply. It is typically assumed that elasticities can be held constant over the interval that is being examined, i.e. that they are arc elasticities or that the curves have constant elasticity over that range. The supply shift can be measured *either* horizontally (i.e. as an output increase for a given cost level) *or* vertically (i.e. as a cost decrease for a given level of output). For examples and discussion see Norton *et al.* (1987), Evenson & Flores (1978), or Schuh & Tollini (1979: 26–33).

The farm sector can either gain or lose from technical change that shifts agricultural supply to the right, depending on the elasticity of demand. This can be seen by taking the two extreme examples of (i) a perfectly elastic demand curve (Figure 10.4(a)), and (ii) a perfectly inelastic demand curve (Figure 10.4(b)). In the former case, there is no consumer surplus (consumers continue to pay the same price), and producers gain the entire area c. In the latter case, consumers gain area ($a + d$) due to the fall in price from P_1 to P_2. Producers lose area a but gain area c. Thus their net position depends on whether area a is greater than, equal to, or less than area c. This is a matter for empirical investigation, and could go either way for producers.

The real world situations to which these alternatives correspond are those of export crop production, and a protected domestic staple food production, respectively. The farm sector producing crops for export faces an elastic demand curve given by the world price for the commodity. The farm sector producing a domestic staple food for which there are barriers to imports faces a relatively inelastic demand curve, and domestic consumers gain from technical change due to the fall in price that occurs as domestic supply increases.

Figure 10.3 Welfare impact of investment in research.

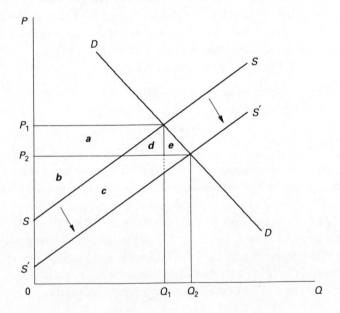

Studies that have used this type of construction in order to measure the returns to investment in research have routinely discovered high internal rates of return, in the range of 40 to over 100 per cent per year (Evenson, 1981). The conclusion is that most governments could invest

Figure 10.4. (*a*) Research impact with elastic demand. (*b*) Research impact with inelastic demand.

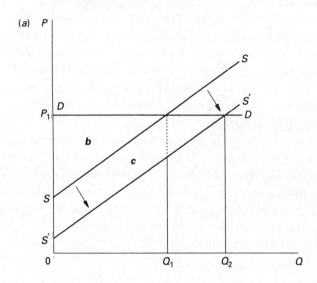

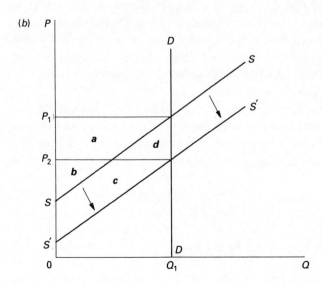

more money in agricultural research and obtain social returns higher than those obtained in other uses of scarce public funds.

Various problems, limitations, and doubts have nevertheless been identified concerning these types of impact study of agricultural research. Some of these are summarised as follows:

(a) The definition of research investment (the cost side of the cost–benefit calculation) is problematic. Should this include only the investment in the research projects that are known to have achieved gains in efficiency, or all national agricultural research, or national research plus those components of international research without which national gains in output may not have been realised? How many years of research investment should be aggregated in the investment cost of the research? The net gains from research can be made to vary over a wide range by altering the definition of research costs.

(b) The definition of output gains, or resources saved, involves similar ambiguities. Many research impact studies assume that the whole rise in output over time, compared to some base level, is attributed to research. This neglects the many other factors that may be contributing to rising output over time, including improved functioning of markets for inputs and outputs, investment in infrastructure and communications, output and input price effects, farmer-own advances in resource use efficiency, and so on.

(c) Some authors would question the usefulness of measuring the impact of research in such narrow economistic terms. Typical economic impact studies neglect the differential rates of adoption of innovations by different types of farmer, the income distribution effects within the farm sector, and the viability of the research institutions created (Horton, 1986). Concern with the equity and access aspects of innovations may result in the identification of disadvantages that largely offset the pure efficiency gains of research investment.

(d) These types of impact study tend to neglect long term environment and sustainability effects of research station innovations, and in some cases gains in productivity experienced over a 5- or 10-year time horizon may be negated by later declines in productivity due to adverse environmental impacts.

(e) Impact studies tend to be solidly located within the linear, research station to farmer, interpretation of the way research policy works to increase agricultural productivity. This means that they often wrongly attribute output gains occurring from other sources or for other reasons (see (b) above) to research investments that are narrowly defined for a particular set of formal research institutions. There are particular conflicts of interpretation surrounding the respective contributions of international and national research centres to advances in productivity, and there are wider issues of overstating the case for formal research in general, compared to informal research, indigenous technical knowledge, and multiple sources of innovation.

Research policy and women

The conventional model of research policy – variations on the theme of technology transfer – is usually insensitive to gender. Research priorities are determined mainly by the criterion of raising output, irrespective of women's role in farming systems. The same is not true, or should not be true, for the research policy models denominated above as farming systems research (FSR) and farmer first research (FFR). Research that involves close observation of farming systems, interaction with farmers, on-farm trials, feedback between farmers and research stations, and so on should automatically incorporate the role, needs, and objectives of women into its method.

The orthodox approach to research policy has flaws where gender is concerned. Some relevant issues are as follows:

(a) The historical bias in some parts of the world towards research on export crops or major food staples often resulted in the neglect of subsistence crops cultivated by women;

(b) New crops or cropping systems are imposed on farmers without taking into account the gender division of labour in the farm household, and the allocation of women's time, thus resulting in innovation failures;

(c) Extension officers have a well-known and documented bias towards communicating with male household heads, even concerning crops or practices that are within the domain of women.

The need to take gender into account in research policy has been recognised and discussed in the literature on FSR and FFR (Moock & Okigbo, 1986; Chambers *et al.*, 1989). There have also been research initiatives on the role of women in farming systems by CGIAR centres (e.g. IRRI, 1985). Of course there is always a big gap between the theory and the reality of these efforts to integrate the gender dimension into the practice of agricultural research. Research systems have a long way to go in this regard.

Summary

1. This chapter is concerned with research policy, which is defined as the role of the state in, and alternative approaches to, the generation and diffusion of new agricultural technology for farm households. The *generation* of new technology refers to the factors underlying the supply of innovations. The *diffusion* of new technology refers to the factors underlying the adoption of innovations by farmers.

2. A distinction is made between *formal* and *informal* research. The former refers to research activities undertaken within national or international research institutions, or by large private corporations. The latter refers to experimentation and innovation undertaken by farmers themselves.

3. The organisation of formal research is described. There are three main tiers in *public formal research*: the international agricultural research centres, national agricultural research stations, and national extension systems. The core of the international system is a network of 13 centres, which are grouped together in an organisation called the Consultative Group on International Agricultural Research (CGIAR). *Private formal research* takes place within the integrated structure of global agribusiness corporations in machinery supply, variable input supply, and plantation agriculture. Private research tends to focus on *product innovation* (the invention of new branded products), while public research focuses on *process innovation* (the invention of superior methods for producing the same product). This is because it is easier to capture privately the returns to product innovation than to do so for process innovation.

4. Five main approaches to the supply and demand for innovations are identified, although it is emphasised that these are not mutually exclusive in space or time. The five approaches are:

   (a) *Transfer of technology*. The dominant model of the 1950s and 1960s. Envisages a linear transfer of modern technology from centres of research excellence (mainly in the industrial countries) to developing country farmers via extension services. Failure of adoption mainly attributed to psychological barriers.

   (b) *Adaptive technology transfer*. The dominant model of the 1970s and early 1980s. Recognises the necessity to adapt new technology to local conditions. The CGIAR system created to facilitate this. Linear transfer modified and runs from CGIAR centre, to national research station (for location-specific adaptation), to extension services, and to farmers. Failure of adoption mainly attributed to exogenous (prices etc.) and farm level constraints. Cure is to eliminate the constraints.

(c) *Farming systems research*. A popular model of the 1980s complementary to adaptive technology transfer. Recognises that technology generation requires knowledge of on-farm constraints and priorities, with feedback and interaction between client farmers and research stations. Linear transfer modified to include a sequence of farmer-orientated steps including (i) selection of target homogeneous group of farmers, (ii) diagnosis of farm system and farm household constraints and objectives, (iii) on-farm trials of new technology with feedback to research stations, (iv) recommendations for wider diffusion within the target group, and (v) evaluation of adoption with feedback for modifications required. Failure of adoption attributed to farm level constraints and failure to understand household needs and priorities. Solution is to discover properly these reasons and to produce or adapt technology suitable for farmer conditions.

(d) *Farmer first research*. A rising model in the late 1980s and early 1990s. Rejects the linear transfer approach, but accepts that FSR (above) is a big step forward in farmer participation and feedback. Sees the transmission of new technology as a circular process, starting and ending with farmers. Farmers decide the priorities of research, design and conduct on-farm experiments, select and adapt the innovations most useful to them. Scientists act as catalysts, suppliers of ideas and materials, colleagues in the design of experiments, and so on (role reversal of scientists). FFR is specifically resource-poor farmer orientated. Failure of adoption attributed to wrong technology for farmer circumstances. Solution is to develop useful technology via farmer ideas and interaction with researchers.

(e) *Multiple sources of innovation*. Emphasises the non-linear origin of agricultural innovations of all kinds; and the political, economic and institutional context of research policy decisions. Many ideas and genetic materials originate in farmers' fields, from there they follow circuitous routes and diverse adaptations before reappearing as new technology in the same or different places. The spread of innovations likewise follows diverse routes, from research station to farmer, from research station to research station, from farmer to farmer. The policy implication is that far more cross-transfer of genetic materials and cultivation methods should be encouraged within formal research systems. The multiple sources of innovation approach is compatible with FFR, but goes beyond this to look at the broad picture of the determinants of research policy decisions.

5. Farming systems research (FSR) and farmer first research (FFR) are examined and compared in more detail. These two approaches have many points of overlap, and in some cases they would be indistinguishable in practice. The chief conceptual differences lie in (i) the logical sequence of steps in FSR which is not present in FFR, and (ii) the role reversals of scientists in FFR, which is not necessary in the general practice of FSR.

6. The goals and priorities of research policy are examined in the context of the alternative models of the research process. Goals can be specified at a very *general level* (e.g. growth, equity, food security), at an *intermediate level* (e.g. food production, stability, productivity, livelihood intensity, continuity, and equity), or at a *precise level* (e.g. crop variety genetic goals such as adaptability, hardiness, disease-resistance, responsiveness to fertilizers, etc). Goals become priorities when some method is used to rank their importance, and to decide budgetary allocations between activities and topics. In formal research, following the linear transfer group of models, priorities can be decided according to methods such as the commodity congruity index, scoring systems, or *ex-ante* cost–benefit analysis. In farmer-orientated research, priorities are determined by farmer constraints, needs and goals. Decisions still must be made, however, concerning the resources to devote to formal, on-station, research versus the resources to devote to farmer-orientated research, and there is no clear-cut method for deciding the balance between these two types of research.

7. Methods for undertaking the *ex-post* evaluation of research impact are discussed. The most popular of these is *ex-post* cost–benefit analysis, which is based on the concepts of producer and consumer surplus. The stream of net benefits from research is compared with the cost of research in order to calculate an internal rate of return (IRR) to research investment. This is typically found to be very high: in the range of 40 per cent to over 100 per cent per year. However, many doubts surround the

definitions of both costs and benefits in this model, so their results should be viewed with due circumspection.

8. The position of women with respect to research policies is briefly considered, and the reader is referred to Chapter 12 for a summary of the gender dimensions of agricultural policies.

Further reading

There exists a very large literature on the topics of new technology, research, and innovation in developing country agriculture, and the most that can be done here is to cite selected articles or books that are relevant to the different aspects covered in this chapter. Useful papers on the economic approach to research policy (Schultz) and on FSR can be found in Eicher & Staatz (1990). Useful papers on research expenditures (Judd *et al.*, 1986), the CGIAR system (Herdt & Anderson, 1987), and the IARCs more generally (Ruttan, 1987) can be found in Ruttan & Pray (1987). The paper by Biggs & Clay in Ahmed & Ruttan (1988) provides an overview of alternative approaches to research policy. The report by Schuh & Tollini (1979) is good for a wide range of economic issues in research policy. Recommended journal articles in these contexts are Ruttan (1986), Horton (1986), and Norton *et al.* (1987).

On multiple sources of innovation see Biggs & Clay (1981) and Biggs (1990). On farming systems research see Byerlee & Collinson (1980), Collinson (1981), Byerlee *et al.* (1982), Biggs (1985), Merrill-Sands (1986), Maxwell (1986), and Collinson (1988). On farmer first research see Rhoades & Booth (1982), Chambers & Ghildyal (1985), Ashby (1986; 1987), Chambers & Jiggins (1987), Farrington & Martin (1988), and Chambers *et al.* (1989). The classic contemporary work on indigenous research by farmers is Richards (1985).

Reading list

Ashby, J.A. (1986). Methodology for the Participation of Small Farmers in the Design of On-Farm Trials. *Agricultural Administration*, No. 22.

Ashby, J.A. (1987). The Effects of Different Types of Farmer Participation on the Management of On-Farm Trials. *Agricultural Administration and Extension*, No. 25.

Biggs, S.D. (1985). A Farming System Approach: Some Unanswered Questions. *Agricultural Administration*, No. 18.

Biggs, S.D. (1990). A Multiple Source of Innovation Model of Agricultural Research and Technology Promotion. *World Development*, **18**, No. 11.

Biggs, S.D. & Clay, E.J. (1981). Sources of Innovation in Agricultural Technology. *World Development*, **9**, No. 4.

Biggs, S.D. & Clay, E.J. (1988). Generation and Diffusion of Agricultural

Technology: Theories and Experiences. In *Generation and Diffusion of Agricultural Innovations: the Role of Institutional Factors*, eds. I. Ahmed and V.W. Ruttan. Aldershot: Gower.

Byerlee, D. & Collinson, M. (1980). *Planning Technologies Appropriate to Farmers – Concepts and Procedures*. Mexico: CIMMYT.

Byerlee, D., Harrington, L. and Winkelmann, D.L. (1982). Farming Systems Research: Issues in Research Strategy and Technology Design. *American Journal of Agricultural Economics*, **64**, No. 5.

Chambers, R. & Ghildyal, B.P. (1985). Agricultural Research for Resource-Poor Farmers: The Farmer-First-and-Last Model. *Agricultural Administration*, No. 20.

Chambers, R. & Jiggins, J. (1987). Agricultural Research for Resource Poor Farmers: Transfer of Technology and Farming Systems Research. *Agricultural Administration*, No. 27.

Chambers, R., Pacey, A. & Thrupp, L.A. (eds) (1989). *Farmer First – Farmer Innovation and Agricultural Research*. London: Intermediate Technology Publications.

Collinson, M. (1981). A Low Cost Approach to Understanding Small Farmers. *Agricultural Administration*, No. 8.

Collinson, M. (1988). The Development of African Farming Systems: Some Personal Views. *Agricultural Administration and Extension*, No. 29.

Eicher, C.K. & Staatz, J.M. (eds.) (1990). *Agricultural Development in the Third World*, 2nd edn. Baltimore: Johns Hopkins.

Farrington, J. & Martin, A. (1988). *Farmer Participation in Agricultural Research: A Review of Concepts and Practices*. Overseas Development Institute, Agricultural Administration Unit, Occasional Paper No. 9.

Herdt, R.W. & Anderson, J.R. (1987). The Contribution of the CGIAR Centers to World Agricultural Research. In *Policy for Agricultural Research*, eds. V.W. Ruttan and C.E. Pray. Boulder, Colorado: Westview Press.

Horton, D. (1986). Assessing the Impact of International Agricultural Research and Development Programs. *World Development*, **14**, No. 4.

Judd, M.A., Boyce, J.K. & Evenson, R.E. (1986). Investing in Agricultural Supply: The Determinants of Agricultural Research and Extension Investment. *Economic Development and Cultural Change*, **35**, No. 1. Also in *Policy for Agricultural Research*, eds. V.W. Ruttan and C.E. Pray, Ch. 1. Boulder, Colorado: Westview Press (1987).

Maxwell, S. (1986). Farming Systems Research: Hitting a Moving Target. *World Development*, **14**, No. 1.

Merrill-Sands, D. (1986). Farming Systems Research: Clarification of Terms and Concepts. *Experimental Agriculture*, **22**, 87–104.

Norton, G.W., Ganoza, V.G. & Pomareda, C. (1987). Potential Benefits of Agricultural Research and Extension in Peru. *American Journal of Agricultural Economics*, May.

Rhoades, R.E. & Booth, R.H. (1982). 'Farmer-Back-to-Farmer' a Model for Generating Acceptable Agricultural Technology. *Agricultural Administration*, No. 11, 127–37.

Richards, P. (1985). *Indigenous Agricultural Revolution: Ecology and Food Production in West Africa*. London: Hutchinson.

Ruttan, V.W. (1986). Assistance to Expand Agricultural Production. *World Development*, **14**, No. 1.

Ruttan V.W. (1987). Toward a Global Agricultural Research System. In

Policy for Agricultural Research, eds. V.W. Ruttan and C.E. Pray, Ch. 3.
Boulder, Colorado: Westview Press.

Ruttan, V.W. & Pray, C.E. (eds.) (1987). *Policy for Agricultural Research*.
Boulder, Colorado: Westview Press.

Schuh, G.E. & Tollini, H. (1979). *Costs and Benefits of Agricultural Research:
The State of the Arts*. World Bank Staff Working Paper No. 360, October.
Washington D.C.: World Bank.

Schultz, T.W. (1990). The Economics of Agricultural Research. In
Agricultural Development in the Third World, eds. C.K. Eicher and J.M.
Staatz, Ch. 22, 2nd edn. Baltimore: Johns Hopkins.

11

Irrigation policy

Irrigation policy

Irrigation is about the supply and demand for water as a variable input into crop production. Irrigation policy is about the role of the state in promoting or providing irrigation facilities. It is also about policy choices that exist with respect to alternative irrigation technologies, the management of large-scale irrigation schemes, and alternative methods for recouping from farmers the cost of providing them with irrigation.

Irrigation may be defined as the use of human technology to increase and to control the supply of water for crop production. In most cases, irrigation is supplementary to the naturally occurring supply of water to crops from rainfall. However, there are important examples – in arid and desert regions – where there would be no crop production at all in the absence of irrigation. Irrigation works have existed for thousands of years in parts of Asia, the Middle East and North Africa, and are traceable in some locations back to about 6000 BC.

From an economics point of view, irrigation represents a classic example of *market failure*, and thus state involvement of one kind or another has been virtually axiomatic in most kinds of irrigation development. Market failure may be defined in this context as an inability to define private ownership rights to water as a resource, resulting in (i) the non-formation of a market price for water, (ii) the existence of externalities caused by the impact of individual user behaviour on the collective access to water of users as a group, and (iii) a divergence between the private marginal costs and social marginal costs of water provision for irrigation.

These market failures and the policy issues to which they give rise are defined and described in more detail later in this chapter. Here it may be noted, as an example, that the individual owner of a tubewell used for crop irrigation draws water from under the ground without knowledge of the total water supply available or of the impact of his or her actions on other users. Tubewell irrigation thus represents a category of market failure referred to as a *common property resource*. Another example of the same class of problem is the impact of individual fishing vessels, each trying to maximise their catch, on the overall availability of fish in the sea. In both cases the marginal cost – of using additional water, or catching additional fish – to the individual operator is lower than the marginal cost to operators as a group.

There are important links between irrigation policy and other policies examined in this book. Irrigation water is a variable input that exhibits a high degree of *complementarity* with other variable inputs, especially in the context of high yielding crop varieties. The provision of irrigation water on its own, or inadequately supported by access to complementary inputs, is likely to yield poor or even negative results for farm output. This is because farmers may switch from less water-dependent crops to more water-dependent crops, which are unable to achieve their yield potential for lack of other variable inputs.

Irrigation policy is linked to: (i) input policy, due to input complementarity; (ii) credit policy, due to the increased working capital requirements of irrigated crops; (iii) mechanisation policy, because it involves some of the same issues of technology choice; (iv) land reform, because irrigation schemes often involve changes in land tenure or land resettlement; (v) marketing policy, since a workable market infrastructure must exist to handle the sale of output from an irrigation scheme; (vi) price policy, since irrigation may make farmers more responsive to price changes; and (vii) research policy, since the priorities of research are likely to be predicated in part on the overall proportion of irrigated farm land and on future irrigation plans.

Three policy issues dominate contemporary debates on irrigation policy. These are: *first*, the issue of choice of technology in irrigation, especially the relative cost and labour intensity of alternative types of tubewell irrigation; *second*, the issue of institutional choice in the management of large-scale irrigation schemes; and *third*, the issue of farmer charges for irrigation water, which is linked to the economic problem of resource allocation in the presence of market failures. These policy issues are inter-related since the choice of technology determines in part the nature of the management problem in irrigation, and solutions to the irrigation management problem are linked to water pricing issues. In summary, this chapter has the following purposes:

(a) to set out the *objectives* of irrigation policy, including conflicts in objectives, which are sometimes observed;

(b) to describe different *types of irrigation*, and at the same time to identify problems of *technology choice* in irrigation strategy;

(c) to set out some *economic concepts* relevant to the formulation of irrigation policies;

(d) to describe the problems that arise in *irrigation management*, with special emphasis on large-scale state irrigation schemes;

(e) to examine *water charges*, as a policy issue of resource allocation under conditions of market failure;

(f) to consider some special problems of *irrigation in resource-poor environments*, with particular reference to Sub-Saharan Africa;

(g) to consider problems that arise from the neglect of *women* in the design of irrigation projects.

Objectives of irrigation policy

The ultimate objectives of irrigation policy are no different from those of other policies described in this book, viz. objectives of *output* (or resource use efficiency), *equity* in income distribution, long term *sustainability*, and *food security* at micro- and at macro-economic levels. The particular ways that irrigation can serve these objectives differ, however, from other policies. So too does the nature of conflicts between competing objectives in irrigation policy.

Irrigation involves increasing the supply of water to crops and evening out the supply of water over time. Assuming that these functions are achieved, the potential contributions of irrigation towards farm output growth can be summarised as follows:

(a) Irrigation reduces risk by diminishing the adverse impact of rainfall variation on crop growth and yields. This reduction in risk may on its own have a positive impact on output due to the lower probability of the farm household incurring a loss from the purchase of off-farm cash inputs. The incentive to use cash inputs at optimal levels is increased, and so is the ability to forward-plan production.

(b) Irrigation increases crop yields directly, by reducing the incidence of water stress in plants caused by uneven water supply, and by its complementary impact in raising the productivity of other variable inputs.

(c) Irrigation permits farm output to be increased, because the household can switch to a higher value crop mix, or because higher yielding varieties that are more responsive to high levels of complementary inputs can be cultivated.

(d) Irrigation permits a rise in the multiple cropping index – the average number of crops that can be grown sequentially on a given area of land during an annual cycle – by providing a supply of water in dry seasons, and by permitting greater flexibility in the timing of sowing (Tetlay *et al.*, 1990).

(e) Irrigation permits previously uncultivated land to be brought into cultivation, by extending the margin of cultivation into semi-arid or arid regions, provided that soils are capable of sustaining crop production in the presence of sufficient water.

The degree to which irrigation can achieve higher farm output via these effects varies according to both technical and socio-economic constraints. Technical constraints are partly related to side-effects of irrigation itself, including levels of soil salinity, which are increased under certain irrigation conditions, and proneness to waterlogging of soils, which can be important in some irrigated areas. Socio-economic constraints include the availability of sufficient labour at peak periods of labour demand in the agricultural calendar to take advantage of the increased cultivation potential that irrigation makes possible.

The equity impact of irrigation depends on a host of variables associated with the nature of irrigation technology, the organisation of irrigation schemes, the allocation of water rights within schemes, and so on. Where equity is an explicit objective of irrigation investment, then there is no *a priori* reason why the above output impacts of irrigation should not at the same time contribute to equity goals. Many irrigation schemes are set up on a small-farm basis, with existing small farmers or local landless families as the beneficiaries of the scheme, and with complementary provision of inputs and credit designed to permit poor households to make a successful start within the scheme.

When irrigation schemes fail to meet equity criteria for success, it is usually not too difficult to discover the reasons. In tubewell irrigation, governments have sometimes encouraged types of technology that are too costly for poor households to purchase or to maintain. In canal irrigation systems, equity intentions can be subverted by favouritism on the part of state officials in initial land allocations, by consolidation of holdings by larger farmers, by collusion between larger farmers and irrigation officials in the allocation of water, and by the tail-enders problem (farmers near the irrigation outlet of a canal – so-called 'head-enders' – obtain priority water allocations in times of peak demand).

Some authors emphasise *sustainable livelihoods* as an objective for policies such as irrigation, in preference to the economist's usual distinction between output and equity. The potential output effects of irrigation – higher yields, more multiple cropping, more certainty with respect to future output – are consistent with an 'improved livelihoods' goal for irrigation scheme participants. So too is the increase in, and more stable level of, labour demand for landless rural workers created by more multiple cropping. The sustainability of these livelihoods is dependent on the sensitivity of schemes to technological constraints, such as the salinity problem alluded to above, and to management skill in anticipating and correcting for adverse effects. Some irrigation schemes prove doomed to rapid disintegration either due to management failure or due to intractable problems in the wider socio-economic environment.

Irrigation types and choice of technology

A vast array of different technologies can be observed worldwide for increasing the supply of water to crops, and for stabilising the supply across the seasons. These vary from ancient manual methods for raising water from permanent rivers, to high technology dams with an associated network of canals reaching out over an extensive geographical area.

Irrigation methods are classified in the first instance according to whether they make use of available *surface water*, or whether they draw up water that is held in the ground, called *groundwater*. The main technology for utilising surface water is *canal irrigation*, and the main technology for utilising groundwater is *tubewell irrigation*.

Surface water is available in permanent rivers and streams, and the volume that can be accessed for irrigation can be increased by the advent of storage structures such as weirs and dams. Water from rivers or dams is fed into a network of canals, which carries it to the site of cultivation. In the simplest case this may be adjacent to the river, in some cases it may be many kilometres away. The lowest-cost types of canal irrigation are those that involve simple diversion of permanent streams, with minimum attention to the water-retention efficiency and durability of water channels. The highest-cost types of canal irrigation are those fed by big dams, with concrete-lined primary distribution canals, sluice-gates and weirs, extensive networks of secondary canals, and controlled outlets into field distribution channels. Every conceivable variation between these two extremes can be found in irrigated agriculture across the developing countries.

Figure 11.1 depicts the nature of a canal irrigation system by reference

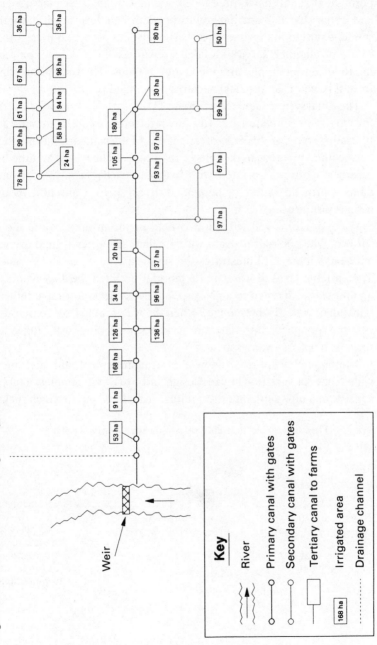

Figure 11.1. Illustration of a canal irrigation system.

to a wetland rice irrigation project in Indonesia. In this example, water is directed into the canal system by means of a weir across a river. The permanent canals have three levels – primary canals, secondary canals, and tertiary canals – and the gravity flow through these levels is regulated by gated outlets at the junctions. Tertiary canals provide outlets into field irrigation channels serving variable sized areas of rice cultivation according to local topography and the layout of fields. The total area irrigated from this weir is about 2300 hectares of wetland rice.

The canal system depicted in Figure 11.1 is at the lower end of the range for the size of cultivated area (usually referred to as the 'command area') typically served by this type of irrigation. Many canal irrigation schemes have command areas in the tens of thousands of hectares, and the larger schemes – often associated with hydroelectricity generation from big dams – provide water for command areas up to a hundred thousand hectares or more.

Water for tubewell irrigation is held in the ground below the land surface. The geological strata within which the water is held are called *aquifers*. Figure 11.2 illustrates the simplest type of aquifer formation. The variable level of water in the aquifer is called the *water table*. The aquifer can be likened to a giant sponge, with the water table indicating how full of water is the sponge. When the water table rises to the surface (i.e. the sponge is saturated), the surface soil becomes waterlogged, and springs, bogs, or swamps arise.

The basic concept of a tubewell is straightforward, although there is wide scope for variation in size, design and cost. At its simplest a tubewell consists of a pipe sunk into the aquifer, and a hand pump which sucks the

Figure 11.2. Illustration of a shallow tubewell irrigation system.

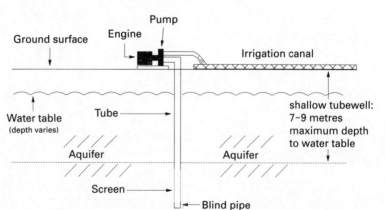

water accumulated in the pipe to the surface. The pipe is perforated over part of its length, or contains a special perforated segment, called a screen. Choices of technology exist with respect to each component of the tubewell system: the pipe and screen, the pump, the power supply, and the distribution system to fields. Some notes on each of these components are as follows:

(a) *Pipe and screen*. The pipe can vary in diameter and in length, and these variations partly define differences between shallow tubewell and deep tubewell technologies. Screens can be made of bamboo, fibreglass, or stainless steel, with large differences in cost associated with each type.

(b) *Pump*. Pump mechanisms vary in cost and complexity, from simple surface-mounted suction pumps, to vertical shaft pumps, and to submersible pumps located deep in the structure of the well.

(c) *Power supply*. The power supply for pumping water to the surface may be human power, animal power, electricity, or an internal combustion engine. The main choice in modern tubewells is between electricity and diesel powered pumps, though the hand pump remains the cheapest type of pump for poor small farmers to buy.

(d) *Distribution system*. The water can be carried to the fields by pipes or canals, the choices between these depending in part on the volume of water flow and the distance to be covered.

Whereas canal irrigation has tended to be a state activity, tubewell irrigation lends itself to individual ownership due to its variable size and cost, and the potential – if sub-surface conditions permit – to locate tubewells close to fields. There exist large-scale tubewell irrigation schemes (e.g. in Pakistan) where groundwater is pumped in large volumes into canal systems. There have also been cases where governments have leased tubewells to farmers or farmer groups rather than encouraging private ownership (e.g. Bangladesh in the 1970s). However, these are exceptions rather than the rule, and private ownership nowadays predominates in the spread of tubewell technologies.

Choice of technology is a central issue in tubewell irrigation, because the state can alter over a wide range the incentives for using alternative components in tubewell design (for a Bangladesh example, see Biggs & Griffith, 1987). Similar considerations apply to irrigation in this context as to mechanisation and to research. In labour-abundant societies, labour-using technologies are preferable to labour-saving technologies, and equity goals are best served by technologies that are low cost, use local materials, are flexible in design according to local needs, and do not require high technology spare parts to be kept in operation.

Surface irrigation and groundwater irrigation are not mutually exclusive alternatives, even though the general tendency is to observe one or
the other as the main type of irrigation in any particular locality. A critical
feature of tubewell irrigation is the rate at which the aquifer recharges its
supply of water relative to the rate of water withdrawal from the system.
Recharging occurs from rainfall and from surface water seepage. Canal
irrigation can be a major source of the surface water seepage required to
recharge aquifers that are being tapped for tubewell irrigation. Farmers
located within canal irrigation areas increasingly use tubewells to supplement water supply from canals in periods of peak demand on the canal
system, or if they are located in disadvantageous positions relative to
canal outlets.

A further important aspect is the salinity of groundwater supplies.
Where groundwater supplies are saline they often need to be combined
with canal irrigation sources in order to avoid the soil salinity rising to
levels damaging for crop production. A host of physical inter-
dependencies between the two types of irrigation apply, and these lead to
parallel socio-economic inter-dependencies in the management and costs
of water as a resource in agricultural production.

Economic concepts for irrigation policy

The purpose of this section is to outline the special economic
features of irrigation that make the supply and demand for water
different from that of other commodities in a market economy.

Reference has already been made to the problem of defining a *market*
for the water used by farmers to irrigate their fields. This problem arises
out of *market failure* in the sense that the equilibrating mechanism of
demand and supply at a market price does not function. Understanding
the nature of these market failures is important for irrigation policy, since
they hold the key to ways of improving the economic efficiency of water
use in irrigation schemes as well as limiting the budgetary costs to the
state of operating such schemes.

The supply and demand for irrigation water display in various combinations the categories of market failure called by economists *public
goods*, *externalities*, and *common property resources*. These are described
in turn in the following paragraphs:

Public goods

A public good is one which, once made available, cannot exclude
individuals from its use, and therefore cannot charge them a price for its

use. Typical examples are street lighting, the police force, national defence, and public roads (except toll roads). For all of these, the extent of their utilisation by individuals cannot be measured, and their use cannot therefore be priced. This is the reason why private businesses would not normally supply such goods, and the cost of them is typically borne by the government budget and is financed by domestic taxation or foreign borrowing.

Canal irrigation can be characterised in part as a public good. Once the canal system is installed, it would cost too much in practice to regulate the amount of water consumed by the individual farmer, and it is often not possible to prevent farmers at the periphery of irrigation schemes from making use of the water made available by the scheme. Most developing-country governments have treated canal irrigation as a public good for policy purposes. Irrigation schemes are state financed and are run by parastatal authorities. No attempt is made to charge farmers for the water they consume, although a land tax may sometimes be used in order to recoup some of the capital or running costs of schemes.

Public goods run into problems of allocation between users when *congestion* occurs, i.e. when demand for the essentially 'free' service outstrips the capacity available. Traffic jams on public roads typify the congestion problem. In irrigation, congestion takes the form of not enough water to go round at peak levels of demand. Due to the absence of a market price to reflect this congestion, non-market mechanisms take over the allocation of scarce resources. These include bribery of irrigation officials, meddling with gates, blocking channels, breaking canal banks, taking water out of turn, and so on.

Externalities

Externalities arise whenever the individual does not have to bear the full costs of side-effects occurring as the result of personal action. The typical example is the factory which poisons a river with pollutants. The private cost to the factory of disposing of its pollutants into a river is lower than the social cost, to downstream river users or to the community at large, of experiencing a clean stream being converted into a poisoned waterway. The market cannot correct this problem because no market signals, in the form of prices, convert the social desire for a clean stream into a private cost that would prohibit the factory from polluting. State regulation is required either in the form of direct prohibition, or fines, or taxes that can be used to cover the cost of post-pollution clean up action.

Irrigation is rife with externalities. Some of these are scheme-wide externalities; some are the result of individual farmer action that causes disbenefit to other farmers or to the group of farmers as a whole. Scheme-wide externalities include (i) the impact of dams or weirs on downstream users of river waters, especially when seasonal patterns of water volume are disrupted and silt previously carried downstream is now held back in the dam, (ii) the impact of dams on the communities that previously lived in the area flooded, and (iii) the increase in water-borne diseases that may occur due to dams, ponds, and irrigation channels.

Farmer-induced externalities include (i) the curtailment of supplies to downstream users due to excessive water use by farmers who are better placed with respect to outlets (the head-enders versus tail-enders problem), (ii) the host of private actions to the detriment of other users already listed under congestion of public goods above, (iii) waterlogging or salinisation of the cultivated area of some users due to the actions of other users. A special class of farmer-induced externality is the common property resource case discussed next.

Common property resource

This is the category of market failure that was already briefly described in the introduction to this chapter. It is also sometimes called a *common pool resource* or *open access* resource, in order to make clear that property ownership *per se* is not necessarily relevant to the types of resource allocation problem which arise. In the irrigation sphere, it applies to tubewell irrigation (Feinerman, 1988), and to many of the externalities of canal irrigation described above. The essential features of a common property resource problem are:

(a) The resource has a finite capacity for utilisation over a given period of time. In other words, the resource is renewable (as distinct to a non-renewable resource such as crude oil), but can only replenish itself at a certain rate. For tubewell irrigation this replenishment rate is the so-called recharge rate of the water holding aquifer. Clearly, sustainable use of the resource requires that over time the demand for water from an aquifer is in balance with the recharge rate of the aquifer.

(b) The individual user, acting in self-interest, uses the resource up to the point where the marginal cost of drawing on the resource (i.e. the operating cost of pumping one more litre of water) equals the marginal revenue obtained by using additional units of the resource in farm production. This is simple production theory (see Ellis, 1988a: Ch. 2).

(c) However, if all users follow this self-interest logic, the aggregate demand for the resource exceeds its replenishment rate, leading to steeply rising marginal cost for the group as a whole as supplies become more difficult to obtain. Furthermore, such action can irreversibly damage or destroy the future availability of the resource, as happens, for example, with overfishing in natural fisheries or the destruction of forests for firewood.

The common property resource problem has been modelled by economists using a game called the Prisoners' Dilemma. A description of the original Prisoners' Dilemma game can be found in Wade (1988: 498 fn 3) or Randall (1988: 25). For an irrigation-type problem, the simplest form of the game can be stated as follows.

There are two individual farmers, call them Farmer 1 and Farmer 2, who do not communicate with each other. Each farmer follows a separate strategy towards the use of irrigation water denominated S_1 (for Farmer 1) and S_2 (for Farmer 2). Each farmer is aware that there is a problem concerning their joint over-use of the water resource, and each pursues a strategy that can take one of two directions: to act selfishly by taking as much water as he or she wishes (strategy with value 0); or to restrain personal use in order to help conserve the resource (strategy with value 1). The joint outcome of their individual choices can be described as $F_i(S_1,S_2)$, where i refers to either Farmer 1 or Farmer 2. The range of possible joint outcomes is shown in Box 11.1.

The optimum joint outcomes for the two farmers, as well as for the sustainability of the common resource, is the cooperative outcome $F_i(1,1)$. However, there are several factors that operate against the occurrence of $F_i(1,1)$. A consequence of the assumption of non-communication between the two farmers is that neither knows in advance how the other is going to act, and each mistrusts the other. For each individual farmer the best outcome is to act selfishly (i.e. to take as much

---

BOX 11.1.

	Farmer 2 (S_2)	
	Be selfish (0)	Cooperate (1)
Farmer 1 (S_1)		
Be selfish (0)	(0, 0)	(0, 1)
Cooperate (1)	(1, 0)	(1, 1)

water as desired) while the other farmer acts cooperatively (i.e. restrains water usage). Concomitantly, for each farmer the worst outcome is to act cooperatively while the other farmer acts selfishly. Outcomes in which both farmers act cooperatively, or both act selfishly, occupy intermediate positions in the preference scale of each farmer. In notation, the different outcomes are ranked by each farmer individually as follows (where the symbol > means that the preceding alternative is preferred to the next):

$$\text{for Farmer 1, } F_1(0,1) > F_1(1,1) > F_1(0,0) > F_1(1,0)$$
$$\text{for Farmer 2, } F_2(1,0) > F_2(1,1) > F_2(0,0) > F_2(0,1)$$

Given these individual preference orderings, the optimum joint outcome $F_i(1,1)$, is not attainable. By each pursuing their own first preferences, the farmers ensure that the worst joint outcome $F_i(0,0)$ occurs.

The Prisoners' Dilemma game demonstrates that under certain conditions the private preferences and actions of atomistic individuals lead to the worst outcome for social welfare. This is the opposite of the predictions of economic theory for markets that work. The conclusion of this model is that forms of cooperation and trust between individuals must be devised in order to overcome the problem of an absent or defective market for a resource such as water. The management failure common in large-scale irrigation schemes can be interpreted in this light as failure by canal officials to enforce the cooperative solution on farmers in the scheme (Wade, 1988).

The Prisoners' Dilemma situation can be shown not to collapse towards the least desirable outcome if certain conditions of interaction between the parties are met (Randall, 1988: 26–7). The main alternatives are (i) coordination of the actions of both parties, (ii) the individual being concerned about his or her reputation within the community of participants, or (ii) users who are harmed by the selfish actions of other users replying by taking selfish action themselves. These findings have implications for irrigation management policy. They show that enhanced interaction, participation, and communication between farmers and with irrigation officials must form the cornerstone of institutional solutions for escaping the Prisoners' Dilemma.

Irrigation management and water charges

The preceding treatment of the public good, externality, and common property resource aspects of irrigation provides an appropriate context within which to locate policy discussion of irrigation management and water charges. Policy issues of management and resource use efficiency apply especially to large-scale public canal irrigation schemes. Private tubewell irrigation, especially dispersed small-scale individual tubewells, raise policy issues more to do with choice of technology (already discussed above) than to do with management. All types of irrigation, including private tubewells, display features of externality and common property, but in the discussion that follows the focus is on large-scale public schemes.

Large-scale irrigation tends to be treated by governments as a public good. The typical institutional context is for a parastatal organisation, with a title like the National Water Authority, to be made responsible for both construction and maintenance of irrigation schemes. The parastatal is administratively located under a parent Ministry, which can sometimes be the Ministry of Agriculture but is often a non-agricultural executive agency such as the Ministry of Public Works. Finance for new construction is obtained from external donors in the form of grants or soft loans which cover the foreign exchange costs of capital works. The budget for recurrent operation and maintenance (henceforth O & M) is provided by central government, and is rarely related to fees paid by farmers.

A number of policy problems have been observed with respect to the management and resource use efficiency of irrigation schemes located under this type of administrative structure. Some main policy issues are as follows:

(a) Public irrigation agencies are rife with corruption and income-seeking (Wade, 1982). Irrigation officials are often poorly paid, remote from central authority, ill-motivated, not sympathetic to farmers, and they are sometimes subject to regular transfers – e.g. every two years – which reduces their commitment to any particular scheme (Wade, 1985).

(b) Partly due to this last reason, such agencies display a high preference for new capital construction over recurrent O & M. Capital construction inflates annual budgets and enhances the opportunities for non-salary gains in personal incomes. The outcomes are cost overruns on capital works, delays in the completion of construction projects, and neglect of O & M such that the canal infrastructure sometimes starts to disintegrate within two or three years of completion.

(c) Also due to the rent-seeking reason, irrigation officials develop a self-interest in disrupting the water supply to farmers, since bribes paid by farmers to ensure water continuity can be an important source of personal income.

(d) The top-down bureaucratic mode of operation of such agencies – coupled with their central financing – is ill-suited to the involvement of

farmers in the management of canal systems. Lack of farmer participation and lack of access to officials are rife in public irrigation schemes.

(e) Farmers themselves have little incentive to contain their water
demand, to comply with rules, or to contribute to scheme maintenance.
Farmers may pay a charge for participation in a scheme – usually a levy or
fee on the area irrigated – but this charge bears no relation to the amount
of water used, and since it is typically not paid directly to the local
irrigation office there is no economic relationship between the costs of
scheme management and farmer use of the water resource. The supply
and demand for water are disconnected in the typical public irrigation
scheme.

One proposed solution to these problems is to privatise irrigation
schemes. The canal infrastructure would be sold to a private operator. It
is argued that the private owner would quickly sort out the problems of
motivation, incentive, and lack of adequate O & M on the supply-side of
water provision. Farmers would be charged a price per litre for the
volume of water used, sufficient to cover operating costs and to provide a
rate of return to capital invested. This in turn would make farmers
efficient in their use of water. They would use water only up to the point
where the marginal return to water use equalled the price per litre that
they were paying for water. A proper market for irrigation water would
be created and efficiency ensured.

This is a fanciful solution which falls apart on close inspection (Moore,
1989). Neither the supply of water nor its demand in a canal irrigation
system can be regulated with the degree of accuracy necessary for the
private solution to be viable for the private operator. The supply of water
in a canal irrigation system is affected by a host of variables that are either
impossible to control or could only be controlled at great cost. These
include the fluctuating level of rivers from which water is drawn, the
seepage and losses from canals, the variable effect on water flows of
rainfall, and the infeasibility of closely monitoring flows over the geographical spread of the scheme.

The demand for water is likewise impossible to control short of
technical solutions that would be so high cost as to make irrigation
schemes non-viable for all parties concerned. Very few farmers obtain
their water in an irrigation scheme directly from an outlet at which the
volume flow can be accurately measured. Most farmers receive their
water indirectly via other farmers' fields (especially in wetland rice
cultivation) or through field channels that are diverted from one field to
another according to local water needs. No measurement of water

wastage, run off, or non-use of supply are possible at the field level. Finally, the private solution ignores the many ways farmers can circumvent controls, e.g. by taking water at night, breaking canal walls, installing private tubewells to take advantage of the groundwater effects of seepage from canals, and so on.

It is clear that viable policy solutions to the management problems of canal irrigation lie somewhere in the middle ground between the pure public good approach and the flawed private ownership proposal (Boyce, 1988: A-19). Any such solution must accept that volumetric water pricing to farmers is economically non-viable even if technically feasible, and that other types of levy must therefore be devised in order to give farmers a better sense of the economic cost of the water resource. Any such solution must also take into account the externality and common property aspects of irrigation provision. This means that methods of cooperation and trust must be built into proposed solutions.

Some main ideas regarding practicable solutions are summarised as follows:

(a)   *Farmer involvement*
        The separation of function and status between irrigation officials and farmers is an artificial one that leads to mistrust between the two parties and causes counter-productive outcomes of their joint behaviour (Wade, 1988). This separation can be broken down by giving farmers more responsibility for certain types of activity 'above the outlet'. One proposal is for groups of farmers to choose from amongst themselves a representative to patrol and to regulate the water flow into secondary and tertiary canals. Failure to discharge this duty to the satisfaction of farmer members results in quick recall and election of a new patrol person. This method is used, with observed beneficial results, in South Korea (*Ibid*: 495) and Taiwan (Moore, 1989: 1742).

(b)   *Farmer participation*
        There is a temptation to believe that farmer irrigation groups or associations could take over most of the O & M functions of bureaucrats, even in large schemes. This neglects conflicts of interest between farmers within schemes (Moore, 1989: 1740). The more unequal the socio-economic status of scheme farmers, the less likely that imposed collaboration between them will be successful (Boyce, 1988: A-13). Irrigation systems based on ancient cultural forms of water management, such as

the *subak* system in Bali (Geertz, 1980), typically involve a high level of participation and cooperation by farmers. However, such traditional cultural methods can seldom, if ever, be transplanted wholesale to other settings. A cautious view must be taken as to which components of O & M can be successfully devolved to farmer management, and this is likely to vary in different settings.

(c)   *Separation of functions*

Separation of the capital and construction side of irrigation from the O & M side is advocated by several writers (Chambers, 1988: Ch. 9; Moore, 1989). This means that quite distinct agencies, with different tasks, and different structures would be created. Several benefits are thought to follow. *First*, conflicts of time allocation and work priority between new projects and recurrent O & M would disappear. *Second*, staff of the new O & M agency would be removed from new projects, and would therefore be less likely to push for them on dubious grounds. *Third*, senior management of the new O & M agency would be more likely to press for more resources for O & M itself, typically under-funded in many irrigation schemes.

(d)   *Water charges*

Finally there is the issue of water charges to farmers. There is general agreement in the literature that farmers should be charged realistically in economic terms for their participation in irrigation schemes. It is also agreed that capital costs need to be separated from recurrent O & M costs in devising and implementing farmer payment methods.

In principle, farmers should be required to repay the capital cost of irrigation, and the most practicable way to do this is to apply a uniform repayment levy – perhaps payable over several years – per hectare of cultivated land irrigated by the scheme. A side-effect of this would be less political pressure from farmers for expensive irrigation schemes, and more awareness from the outset concerning the value of the canal infrastructure that has been created. In practice, it is rare for governments to seek to recoup more than a small fraction of the capital cost of large-scale schemes. For already existing schemes, the issue of capital repayment is academic since the capital is a sunk cost.

Recurrent O & M costs can be met by an irrigation service fee. For a discussion of alternatives see the case-study of Egypt in Bowen & Young

(1986). The reasons this fee cannot in practice take the form of volumetric water pricing have already been discussed. As for capital cost recovery, the most practicably and equitable method of fixing the service fee is to set a rate per irrigated hectare. Some variation in the rate may be desirable to reflect visible differences in water access by farmers at differing distances from outlets. However, this has the disadvantage that some farmers would then feel entitled to receive more water than other farmers, and cooperation between farmers as a group becomes more difficult.

The typical practice of most governments is to collect only a proportion of O & M costs in the form of service fees, and to pay these into central government funds. Sometimes the cost of collection is higher than the income from fees collected. From an economic viewpoint it would be more effective to make the income of the local O & M service agency dependent on the collection of fees from farmers. This creates the necessary link between payment and quality of service that is missing due to the inability to price water. The payment of fees by farmers to the local branch of the O & M agency gives farmers at least a superficial means of registering discontent with the service, for example by withholding fees. Better still if O & M management involves some type of farmer representation, since then a direct interpersonal connection exists between farmers and scheme management.

In summary, many policy problems are associated with the management of canal irrigation schemes and with the lack of farmer awareness of the economic cost of water as a resource. It is widely agreed that these problems could be alleviated by a combination of (i) farmer involvement in some aspects of O & M, (ii) institutional separation of O & M from new construction, (iii) charging farmers the full cost of O & M in the form of area-based irrigation service fees, and (iv) making the operating income of local O & M agencies dependent on the collection of irrigation service fees from farmers.

Some cautionary remarks are also in order. Increased farmer involvement in O & M is not synonymous with total farmer control of these activities, and the amount of farmer involvement that is feasible needs to be approached with caution in the light of local conditions and customs. The slogan of farmer participation is not a panacea for the problems of canal irrigation. The central point is to create conditions of trust (i) between farmers, and (ii) between farmers as a group of irrigation officials, such that the first-best rather than the worst outcome of Prisoners' Dilemma type situations is obtained.

Irrigation in resource-poor environments

It is tempting to consider that irrigation can solve the problems of farm families wherever crop production appears to be technically constrained by inadequate water supply conditions. This is the principle that hydraulic engineers often seem to follow when identifying sites suitable for irrigation schemes. The pressure to seek irrigated solutions is especially strong when the cause of poverty and famine so manifestly appears to be a shortage of water for crops, as in the case of many African famines.

Irrigation is not, however, always the best solution nor even a solution at all under certain ecological and economic conditions. The points that follow have been put forward with reference to the historical experience of irrigation in Sub-Saharan Africa (Moris, 1987). However, most of them also serve as general points about irrigation in resource-poor environments:

(a) Irrigation can fail to increase total output. A substitution may occur from subsistence food crops to marketed cash crops giving an illusion of output growth when none has occurred.

(b) Irrigation schemes involving dams have occasionally been known to displace more farm families above the dam than new farms that they created below the dam.

(c) Irrigation schemes involving dams can reallocate water from more severe to less severe water-short locations. This occurs when a dam located in fairly well-watered highlands reduces the amount of water available in semi-arid zones downstream.

(d) Irrigation schemes can widen the divergence between farm household goals and state goals. The primary farm household goal may be food security involving diversity of crops, extensive cultivation, low use of purchased inputs, and low reliance on unreliable state services. The government goal may be intensive cultivation of a single crop, using high levels of purchased inputs, and highly dependent on state services.

(e) Irrigation may fail to achieve output gains due to a shortage of labour at peak periods in the agricultural calendar. The seasonal labour constraint prevalent in African agriculture makes for a contrast with the typical labour market conditions in Asian agriculture.

(f) Irrigation O & M may prove unsustainable in the face of collapse of supply lines and lack of foreign exchange. Lack of fuel, spare parts, transport, cement, and so on can result in the rapid deterioration of the infrastructure to the point that it becomes unworkable.

(g) Irrigation may fail because similar problems to those listed in (f) above afflict farm production on the scheme. Farmers may confront lack of essential purchased inputs, lack of approved seed, difficulty in crop marketing, poor official prices for output, and a host of other factors resulting in low and deteriorating farm performance.

Irrigation policy and women

Large-scale canal irrigation schemes have tended to neglect the gender dimension. This has perhaps been one of their less severe problems in Asia, although issues of bias towards men in land registration, division of tasks, provision of inputs, extension services, and so on arise there as elsewhere. However, most case-studies highlighting gender flaws in irrigation schemes relate to the African experience. Some relevant points are summarised here:

(a) in several irrigated rice projects in Africa, irrigated plots were handed over to men, even though in all cases women had hitherto been exclusively responsible for rice cultivation (Dey, 1985);

(b) in some of these schemes, women continued to work in swamp rice cultivation thus depriving the irrigation scheme of labour and reducing the intensity of land use significantly below its potential;

(c) more generally, irrigation schemes in Africa have resulted in conflicts between men and women over women's time allocation and control over cash income (Hanger & Moris, 1973; Dey, 1981);

(d) in some cases, these conflicts are never resolved resulting in poor scheme performance, in others they are partially resolved by men paying for women's labour time (Jones, 1986);

(e) in one project, attempts by foreign donors to ensure that irrigated plots were allocated to women were subverted by the local project administration so that plots ended up in men's hands (Carney, 1988; von Braun *et al.*, 1989).

This last point raises some interesting issues. Policy appeals on behalf of women from afar can be ignored or circumvented by local officials, even when large amounts of external funding are involved. The paradoxical situation may arise that outsiders become the champions of women's traditional rights, while national bureaucratic agencies set themselves to erode or rescind those rights.

Summary

1. This chapter is about irrigation policy. Irrigation is defined as the use of human technology to increase and to control the supply of water for crop production. Irrigation policy is about the role of

the state in promoting or providing irrigation technologies, and about policy choices that exist with respect to technology, management of large-scale irrigation schemes, and ways of charging the cost of water as an input to farmers.

2. The objectives of irrigation policy are set out. A main objective is to increase agricultural output and incomes by reducing risk, increasing yields, allowing higher value crops to be grown, raising the degree of multiple cropping, and bringing uncultivated land into production. These impacts can serve equity goals as well as output goals, depending on the way irrigation schemes are implemented and operated. An important issue is the sustainability of irrigation technology once it is in place.

3. There are two main types of irrigation technology: surface water technology associated with canal irrigation, and groundwater technology associated with tubewell irrigation. Some main features of canal irrigation are described, including the nature of the canal infrastructure required in large-scale schemes. Tubewell irrigation encompasses a wide range of technology choices with respect to the size and components of tubewells.

4. Irrigation provision involves several types of market failures, described as public goods, externalities, and common property resources. A public good is one which once made available cannot exclude individuals from its use. Large-scale canal irrigation schemes in developing countries tend to be regarded as public goods: the state provides the irrigation service and farmers are not charged for the volume of water they consume.

5. Irrigation typically involves many externalities. An externality is defined whenever the individual does not have to bear the full cost of side-effects occurring as a result of personal action. Some irrigation externalities apply to schemes as a whole, for example, the impact on downstream river users of dam construction, the impact on upstream dwellers of losing their land and livelihoods, the impact of irrigation works on the incidence in the community of water-borne diseases. Other externalities relate to individual farmer actions, including the impact on tail-end users of excessive water use by head-end users, private actions to secure extra supplies, and waterlogging or salinisation of adjacent plots.

6. Irrigation also involves common property resource type problems. A common property resource is one that has a finite capacity for utilisation over a given period of time, and the

impact of self-interest strategies by individuals is for the aggregate utilisation of the resource to exceed the renewal level of capacity. A simple game shows that the pursuit of self-interest tends to lead to non-sustainable exploitation of a common property resource. Methods of building trust and cooperation between individual users are required in order to overcome this problem.

7. The key policy issues in large-scale canal irrigation are management, operations and maintenance (O & M), and water charges for farmers. Irrigation agencies tend to be rife with rent-seeking, display a high preference for new capital construction over recurrent O & M, disrupt water supplies to farmers in order to gain bribes, and involve top-down bureaucratic procedures for water management. Partly due to these factors, but also related to the lack of a connection between water use and charges, farmers have little incentive to contain water demand, comply with rules, or contribute to scheme maintenance.

8. Privatisation of canal irrigation schemes does not provide a solution to these problems because neither the supply nor the demand for water can be controlled with sufficient accuracy to make such schemes financially viable for the private operator.

9. Public administration of schemes can be improved, however, by involving farmers in selected O & M activities, by separating the construction side of canal irrigation from the O & M side, by making farmers pay the full cost of O & M, and by making O & M agency income dependent on irrigation service fees collected from farmers. There are many alternative ways these proposals can be implemented, but building trust, cooperation, and feedback between farmers and irrigation management agencies are the central objectives in view. In addition, individual schemes need to be made more financially self-reliant, with benefits for cost efficiency in water use.

10. Irrigation schemes confront special difficulties in resource-poor environments. Irrigation may create conditions in which the food security strategies of farm families, the time allocation of their labour, their crop mix, and their independence from unreliable markets and services are all more fragile after the scheme than before the scheme. In countries confronting recurrent macroeconomic and foreign exchange crises, the sustainability of proposed irrigation technologies is a critical issue.

11. The position of women with respect to irrigation policy is briefly considered, and the reader is referred to Chapter 12 for a comparative summary of the gender dimensions of agricultural policies.

Further reading

A useful basic textbook on the economics of irrigation is Carruthers & Clark (1981). Some excellent journal papers covering the issues of market failure and irrigation management are Boyce (1988), Wade (1988), and Moore (1989). Similar issues are also covered by O'Mara (1988b) and Randall (1988). A wide range of issues in the management of canal irrigation in South Asia is covered in Chambers (1988). Also see Goodell (1984) on organisational conflicts in rice irrigation schemes, and Bowen & Young (1986) on the issue of water charges, illustrated by an Egyptian case-study. For examples of gender-related defects of rice irrigation schemes in Africa see Dey (1981; 1985), Jones (1986), and Carney (1988). A useful case-study on choice of technology in tubewell irrigation is Biggs & Griffith (1987). Finally, Moris (1987) provides a good overview of the special problems and prospects of irrigation in Sub-Saharan Africa.

Reading list

Biggs, S.D. & Griffith, J. (1987). Irrigation in Bangladesh. In *Macro-Policies for Appropriate Technology in Developing Countries*, ed. F. Stewart, Ch. 3. Boulder, Colorado: Westview Press.

Bowen, R.L. & Young, R.A. (1986). Appraising Alternatives for Allocating and Cost Recovery for Irrigation Water in Egypt. *Agricultural Economics*, **1**, 35–52.

Boyce, J.K. (1988). Technological and Institutional Alternatives in Asian Rice Irrigation. *Economic and Political Weekly*, March 26th.

Carney, J.A. (1988). Struggles Over Crop Rights and Labour Within Contract Farming Households in a Gambian Irrigated Rice Project. *Journal of Peasant Studies*, **15**.

Carruthers, I. & Clark, C. (1981). *The Economics of Irrigation*. Liverpool: Liverpool University Press.

Chambers, R. (1988). *Managing Canal Irrigation*. Cambridge: Cambridge University Press.

Dey, J. (1981). Gambian Women: Unequal Partners in Rice Development Projects? *Journal of Development Studies*, **17**.

Dey, J. (1985). Women in African Rice Farming Systems. In *Women in Rice Farming*, Ch. 23. International Rice Research Institute (IRRI). Aldershot: Gower.

Goodell, G.E. (1984). Bugs, Bunds, Banks and Bottlenecks: Organizational Contradictions in the New Rice Technology. *Economic Development and Cultural Change*, **33**, No.1.

Jones, C.W. (1986). Intra-Household Bargaining in Response to the Introduction of New Crops: A Case Study from North Cameroon. In *Understanding Africa's Rural Household Farming Systems*, ed. J.L. Moock, Ch. 6. Boulder: Westview Press.

Moore, M. (1989). The Fruits and Fallacies of Neoliberalism: The Case of Irrigation Policy. *World Development*, 17, No. 11.

Moris, J. (1987). Irrigation as a Privileged Solution in African Development. *Development Policy Review*, 5, 99–123.

O'Mara, G.T. (ed.) (1988a). *Efficiency in Irrigation: The Conjunctive Use of Surface and Groundwater Resources*. Washington D.C.: World Bank.

O'Mara, G.T. (1988b). The Efficient Use of Surface Water and Groundwater in Irrigation: An Overview of the Issues. In *Efficiency in Irrigation: The Conjunctive Use of Surface and Groundwater Resources*, ed. G.T. O'Mara, Ch. 1. Washington D.C.: World Bank.

Randall, A. (1988). Market Failure and the Efficiency of Irrigated Agriculture. In *Efficiency in Irrigation: The Conjunctive Use of Surface and Groundwater Resources*, ed. G.T. O'Mara, Ch. 2. Washington D.C.: World Bank.

Wade, R. (1988). The Management of Irrigation Systems: How to Evoke Trust and Avoid Prisoners' Dilemma. *World Development*, 16, No. 4.

Comparative summary

The eight policy topics examined in preceding chapters can usefully be compared and contrasted with respect to some of their salient features. One reason for making such a comparison is that it helps to locate some of the important debates in the literature on agricultural policies in developing countries, for example, the debate between price policy interventions and technology policy interventions. Another reason is that it helps to assess the relevance of the state versus market theme as it applies in different ways to different policies.

Table II.1 makes a comparative summary of selected aspects of agricultural policies. The five aspects that are identified are (i) the economic dimension of the farm system upon which the policy is designed to have an effect, (ii) the categories of instrument that the policy mainly utilises, (iii) the type of efficiency impact the policy is designed to have, (iv) the most common defect observed in policy implementation, and (v) a category designated as the 'deregulation rating', meaning the degree to which the policy area is susceptible to withdrawal of the state and an enhanced role for the market.

The first of these aspects is merely a restatement of the organising principle for the book as a whole, and this does not require further elaboration here. The other four aspects are described in the following paragraphs, with special attention to comparisons between policies:

Policy category

This refers to the distinction made in the first chapter between price, institution, and technology interventions. Some policy instruments act directly or indirectly on the *prices* of farm inputs and outputs. Some instruments are concerned with the *institutions* involved in the marketing

Table II.1. *Comparative summary of agricultural policies*[1]

Policy	Influence upon	Policy categories	Efficiency impact	Common defects	Deregulation rating
Price	Outputs	Price	Allocative	Farmer squeeze	High
Marketing	Outputs	Institutions	Allocative	Parastatal inefficiency	Medium/high
Input	Variable inputs	Price Technology Institutions	Allocative Technical	Delivery failures	High
Credit	Working capital	Institutions (Price) (Technology)	Allocative	Supply bias	Medium
Mechanisation	Fixed capital	Price (Technology)	Allocative (Technical)	Tractor bias	High
Land reform	Land	Institutions	Allocative	Political difficulty	Low
Research	Productivity (all resources)	Technology	Technical	Ignore farmer needs	Low
Irrigation	Water	Technology (Institutions)	Technical	Market and state failures	Low (for canal irrigation)

Note: [1] The meaning of comparative descriptions used in this table is given in the text.

of agricultural commodities and in the delivery of farm inputs, or in the institutional forms of land tenure or credit provision. Some instruments are concerned directly with the creation of new *technology* and its transmission to farmers.

In the comparative table, the main policy category that applies to a particular policy topic is identified. Some policies, like input policy for example, involve more than one policy category. Where a second category is present but is considered subsidiary it is identified by parentheses.

The main purely price policies are output price policy, and price policies for variable inputs. The pace and direction of mechanisation is also predominantly influenced by relative prices which are affected by state actions. Credit policy is a price policy to the extent that the rate of interest is set by the state.

The major institutional policies are those related to crop marketing, input delivery, credit provision, and land reform. With respect to all of these the state moves to create or modify the institutional forms by which commodities or resources are transacted. In the case of land reform, institutions refer to the predominant organisation of land tenure, including legal requirements. Thus sharecropping is regarded as an 'institution' even though it is not a single organisation like a parastatal agency. Irrigation policy also involves institutions in the form of the management systems for large-scale canal irrigation schemes.

The major technology policy is agricultural research policy. Irrigation can also be regarded as being a technology policy since its intention is to achieve a quantum increase in output for given levels of all other resources. Input policies and mechanisation policies also involve dimensions of technological change and technology choice.

Efficiency impact

The efficiency impact refers to the two main ways recognised by economists in which farmers can move to a new position on the production function (see Ellis, 1988a: Chs 2 and 4). Farmers obey allocative efficiency when they adjust their mix of resources, and the allocation of resources between different outputs, according to relative prices. Farmers obey technical efficiency when they operate on the most productive production function open to them in the sense of getting the most output for a given level of resources.

Most agricultural policies are allocative in nature. Even when they are concerned with institutions, their indirect effect is often to change relative prices and thus to influence the operating position of farms in an allocative way. The only policies that rely predominantly on resource productivity effects in order to increase output are research policy and irrigation policy. Improved delivery and information for variable inputs also have these effects, though in practice the technical and allocative effects of input policies are difficult to disentangle.

Mechanisation policy is designated as having technical efficiency as a subsidiary feature. However, only if mechanisation can be proven to raise overall resource productivity does it increase the technical efficiency of farm production. For some main types of mechanisation – tractors, power tillers – an increase in technical efficiency is unproven.

This and the preceding set of comparisons are interesting in the context of the price policies versus technology policies debate. Many economists have concluded that price policies of all kinds are of doubtful merit for raising output in developing country agriculture. According to this perspective, the main emphasis of policy should be towards technology policies that increase the technical potential of farm production. The comparative table serves to highlight that relatively few types of state intervention satisfy the definition of a technology policy in the strict economic sense.

Common defects

This column of the comparative table seeks to capture the single most important defect that has come to be associated with past experience of different agricultural policies. These defects can be interpreted as 'state failures' associated with each policy.

Price policy tends to be associated with low prices to farmers or with adverse rural–urban terms of trade. Sometimes this is due to keeping food prices low for urban consumers, sometimes it is due to high export taxes on export commodities. Marketing policy tends to be associated with the inefficiency and corruption of state marketing institutions. Input policy tends to be associated with the inefficiency and rationing behaviour of state input delivery agencies.

Credit policy is associated with a bias towards credit supply and the neglect of savings, as well as with flaws in credit institutions. Mechanisation policy is associated with the permissive tractorisation that occurred in many countries in the 1960s and 1970s. Land reform policy is associated with the political sensitivity of land redistribution, and with the consequent failures of many land reforms to achieve their original objectives. Research policy has in the past been associated with top-down modes of transfer with high levels of on-farm failure, except in the case of 'Green Revolution' crops. Irrigation policy is associated with failures in the management of canal irrigation schemes.

Deregulation rating

This column of the comparative table refers to the state versus market debate. It attempts to rank policies according to the feasibility and advisability of state withdrawal from that area of economic life, thus giving greater scope to the operation of the market. Policies are ranked according to high, medium, or low susceptibility to state withdrawal. These rankings are relative, not absolute. They do not propose that there are cases where there is no role for the state, nor that there are cases where there is no role for the market.

Policies for which there exists scope for much less state intervention than in the past include output price policy, input price policy, marketing policy, and mechanisation policy. In all these cases allocative efficiency might be improved by a lower profile on the part of the state, though price stabilisation may remain a justifiable type of state intervention for some commodities and inputs.

Policies for which only medium scope exists for state withdrawal include input delivery and credit policies. Input delivery is a difficult case, in which the feasibility of state withdrawal depends on the functioning of the economy as a whole, and in particular on input availability, transport, and communications. Where markets are working well input delivery becomes a candidate for less state intervention. Credit requires state regulation of banking systems and financial markets even if savings and loans are mainly handled by private sector institutions.

Policies for which low scope exists for state withdrawal include land reform, research, and large-scale canal irrigation. Land reform is in some respects an all-or-nothing matter as far as state intervention is concerned. Clearly land redistribution can only be put into effect by the state, assuming political circumstances permit this to happen. If land reform is not in the process of taking place, then the role of the state retreats to one of regulation (e.g. keeping records of land titles, etc.). Both research and large-scale irrigation are public goods, the supply of which is predicated on public provision. Agricultural research is probably the least susceptible to market rather than state provision, although even here there are components of the R & D process, like seed multiplication, that can be devolved to the private sector rather than remain in state hands.

PART III

Cross-cutting themes

12

Women and agricultural policies

Invisible to policy

A subsidiary theme running throughout the policy chapters of this book has been the impact on women of agricultural policies designed to affect the socio-economic environment of farm household production. The existence of this theme does not mean that women are normally taken into account in the formulation and implementation of agricultural policies. On the contrary, most agricultural sector policies, in most countries, are oblivious to gender, and the term 'gender-oblivious' is used here to capture this typical state of affairs. In other words, women are usually *invisible* to agricultural policies.

Policies that ignore gender entirely in their design nevertheless often have important impacts on the lives and livelihoods of women. In addition, such policies sometimes fail to achieve their objectives due to the neglect of the role of women in the processes that they aim to influence.

This distinction between, on the one hand, the impact – positive or negative – on the material welfare of women, and, on the other hand, the success of policies in terms of their own goals, is an important one. The two can be closely related, but this is not always the case. Sometimes a policy fails precisely because of its adverse impact on the role and status of women. Sometimes a policy succeeds in its own terms but has adverse side-effects on women, to a degree that is unacceptable from the viewpoint of the goal of equality of participation in development of women and men.

The aims of this chapter are (i) to identify the critical aspects of women's lives that determine the impact of gender-oblivious policies on women, (ii) to provide a comparative summary of policy side-effects on women, drawing on points already made in previous chapters, and (iii) to put forward some ideas concerning the design and implementation of gender-aware agricultural policies.

Determinants of policy impacts on women

The ways in which gender-oblivious agricultural policies affect, and are affected by, women's role in farm household production are very diverse, and often seem contradictory when empirical evidence is compared from different sources. This is not surprising given the diversity of cultural and economic settings in which given types of policy have their impact.

A classic example of this diversity of policy outcomes is the impact of irrigated high-yielding rice projects on the employment and incomes of women. Irrigated high-yielding rice increases employment in rice production due to the higher labour-intensity of operations like transplanting, weeding, input application, and harvesting, and due to the increased potential for multiple cropping. The extent to which women gain from this change in technology depends, *inter alia*, on (i) the types of farm and post-harvest task that they normally undertake, (ii) the impact of higher household incomes on use of family versus hired labour, (iii) the role of women as members of farm-owning households versus their role as hired labour, (iv) the pace and direction of changes in post-harvest technology that may accompany the change in farm technology, and (v) crop-specific divisions of resource ownership and control, between women and men, that may have preceded the advent of new rice technology.

These factors produce variable outcomes in different settings. Where women engage in labour-intensive tasks of transplanting, weeding, and harvesting, as in many parts of South and South-East Asia, their employment is increased (Agarwal, 1985; Sen, 1985). Where they do not engage in field tasks, as in Bangladesh, their relative level of employment in the rice sector compared to men is decreased (Begum, 1985). Where post-harvest technology changes, for example from manual to mechanical threshing, or from hand pounding to mechanised milling, this more than offsets the gains in farm employment, reducing women's employment overall (Res, 1985; MacPhail & Bowles, 1989). There may be a switch from farm women to hired women in rice employment (White, 1985). In West Africa, the new technology has been observed to fail to achieve its potential for high yields or multiple cropping due to conflicts between men and women over land and over women's labour time (Dey, 1981; Carney, 1988).

This variability of outcomes of one category of policy change reveals the importance of possessing a framework within which the impacts of policies on women can be interpreted. In the absence of such a framework, empirical evidence tends to float about as a set of apparently unrelated facts, and this is not helpful for advancing the cause of a gender dimension in policy design. The components of such a framework are set out below. They encompass both household and wider economy dimensions of women's role in the farm sector of developing countries:

1.   *Social status of the household*
        Confusion over policy impacts for women immediately arise when the type of rural household is not specified (White, 1985). It is useful in the first instance to distinguish households according to whether they are (i) more than food self-sufficient, (ii) less than food self-sufficient, (iii) landless, and (iv) headed by women rather than men. The impact of policies on households that hire out labour (categories (ii) and (iii)) is likely to be quite different from the impact on households that hire in labour. Likewise, policy impacts will vary between male-headed households and households with female heads.

These distinctions help to avoid the confusion that sometimes arises between policy requests to reduce the drudgery of women (e.g. by introducing labour-saving devices) and appeals for policies to create more employment for women. The material welfare of women in food self-sufficient households may be improved by the labour-saving effects of certain types of state intervention, but the reverse is true for women in landless households. The target type of household for policy impacts must be specified.

2.   *Time allocation*
        The ability of many different types of policy to achieve stated goals, as well as their effects on women, are determined by the nature of time allocation between men and women within the farm household. A key consideration is the substitutability of male and female time in reproductive and productive tasks (Beneria, 1979; Ellis, 1988a: 166–74). It is commonplace for this substitutability to be very low for reproductive tasks (childcare and the daily maintenance of the household), thus constraining absolutely the capacity of women to respond to new opportunities in the productive sphere.

An extreme example of this problem occurs where men are absent from the farm, participating in distant wage work (as is common in

Southern African countries). In this case, women's obligations in repro-
ductive tasks may prohibit advances in farm productivity that require
more intensive labour on the farm (Chipande, 1987). This has been held
to explain agricultural stagnation in some parts of Southern Africa (Low,
1986).

3.   *Resource ownership and control*
      It is not safe to assume that the ownership and control of
resources is always vested in the male head of the farm household, or in
the household as a joint decision-making unit. In many rural societies,
especially in Africa, women have different spheres of obligation, resource control, and decision-making from men. A failure to take into
account these separate spheres of responsibility can spell failure for
policy initiatives and irreversible damage to the economic status of
women.
      A good example of this consideration is the experience of irrigated rice
projects in Africa as described in Dey (1981), Dey (1985), Jones (1986),
Carney (1988), and von Braun *et al*. (1989). In several instances irrigated
rice projects were designed in complete neglect of rice as a crop under
women's control over labour and land use, the nature of reciprocal labour
and output obligations between men and women, and customary rights of
land access between men and women. Irrigated rice plots were allocated
to men. When, in one case, an attempt was later made to allocate them to
women, they still ended up under men's control. Outcomes included
failure of projects to achieve output targets, failure to achieve multiple
cropping, abandonment or under-utilisation of irrigated areas, and conflicts between men and women over women's labour time.

4.   *Control over income and its distribution*
      It is also not safe to assume that income is under the control of a
single household head, or that increasing income for the household is
synonymous with rising living standards for all members of the household. In societies such as those referred to in the preceding example, the
separate access of women to productive activity is also often the only way
that women obtain cash incomes over which they have some control. In
some cases, the care of children, their clothing and education, is the
responsibility of women from their own sources of funds, and men do not
contribute to these expenses. Policies that inadvertently remove cash
income sources from women also then have the effect of depriving
women and children of resources for consumption or for education.

More generally, increasing control by men over cash income, often the result of the increased integration of peasant households into the market economy promoted by government policies, by no means ensures rising living standards for women and children. It is for this reason that many writers advocate the adoption of policies that seek to raise women's incomes directly. Gender-oblivious policies cannot be guaranteed to improve the conditions of women, even if they generate more income for the household.

5.   *Marketing and processing*
        The gender division of labour in the processing and marketing of crops is an important feature determining the outcome for women of diverse agricultural policies. In societies in which women have a long-established role in crop marketing, their command over cash income is more assured, and their ability to capture a proportion of the benefit of rising farm productivity is also enhanced. This applies especially for women members of farm households, although a generally widespread involvement of women in marketing also provides potential livelihoods for landless women.
        In some societies, a major task of women lies in the post-harvest processing of food. This type of work is often onerous, time-consuming and repetitive, as in the hand pounding of grain. Technology that reduces the drudgery of food processing can be beneficial to women, by releasing labour time for other activities. On the other hand, the same technology can greatly reduce the employment prospects for women from landless households in societies where post-harvest processing involves extensive hiring of labour. The impact of technical change in food processing, like so many other changes, cannot be discussed in isolation from the social conditions in different places.

6.   *Markets and relative prices*
        The categories listed so far refer mainly to household level determinants of policy impacts on women. Households participate to a greater or lesser degree in markets for inputs and outputs, and the working of markets thus influences to an important degree these household outcomes. Moreover, markets can have more immediate and direct impacts on women than those mediated through the agency of the household. For example, the labour market sets the market wage for men and for women; output markets set the prices for crops produced by

women, men or both jointly; input markets determine the availability and costs of variable inputs; and so on.

Many state policies are designed to improve the way markets work or to control the level and stability of prices in those markets. These interventions can have a direct effect on women, for example if the price of small-scale rice mills is subsidised, or if the farm-gate price of a crop mainly grown by women is increased. However, the key aspect of markets and prices, is how *relative* prices are influenced by policies. It is the relative price of mechanical driers compared to the wage of women that determines whether mechanical driers replace women in drying a crop. It is the relative price of an export crop compared to a food crop that may determine whether the household switches resources from a crop that is more advantageous to women to one that is less advantageous to women.

In summary, this section sets out a framework of six categories that between them determine the impact of general agricultural policies on women. These six categories are: household status; time allocation; control over resources; control over incomes; participation in post-harvest activities; and relative prices in labour, input, and output markets. These categories are not only useful for tracing why similar types of policy have different impacts on women in different places. They are also useful as an organising principle for taking women properly into account in the design of policies. We return to this in due course.

Comparative summary of policy effects on women

The purpose of this section is to bring together in one place the points that have been made about policies and women in preceding policy chapters. While this involves some repetition of previous arguments, some wider and comparative issues are also examined in the present context. Policies are discussed in sequence as follows:

Price policy

Price policies seldom, if ever, take gender into account. But the effectiveness of price policy in achieving stated goals may be influenced by gender considerations at the level of the household. Moreover, price policy may have impacts on the livelihoods of women that are unanticipated in gender-oblivious policy formulation. Several different possibilities can be distinguished:

(a) women's time allocation can be a constraint on the price responsiveness of output where there is limited substitutability of male and female labour time;

(b) low farm prices cause households to use less hired labour, thus reducing employment for women from landless households, and vice versa for high farm prices;

(c) price-induced switches in cropping patterns may change the balance of labour inputs, or land use, or incomes, between men and women;

(d) price policy is often used to promote crops, for example export crops, for which men may have greater control over resources and incomes than women, thereby reducing the economic independence and options of women.

The existence of gender-related impacts in the price policy arena does not necessarily mean that these can be taken into account in price policy. For one thing, price policies usually apply countrywide, and many different – perhaps even opposing – gender effects may occur for the same price policy in different peasant communities within a country. For another, there may be overriding economic criteria in the approach to farm prices (e.g. border pricing), that make gender an issue that it is not possible to address in price policy. Nevertheless, examples can arise where the gender effects of a proposed change in relative prices are inescapable.

Marketing policy

Agricultural marketing in developing countries is an example of an activity in which women often have high levels of participation. There are many instances where marketing has traditionally been considered more of a female than a male activity. Women can engage in marketing in several different ways, for example, (i) as private traders whose chief source of income is trading, (ii) as stallholders in village and town markets, (iii) as the person in the farm household chiefly responsible for selling selected outputs or all outputs, (iv) as the processor of farm outputs prior to their consumption or sale in markets.

Marketing policies typically neglect gender despite the importance of women in marketing roles. A few examples will suffice:

(a) monopoly state marketing boards by-pass and substitute for private forms of marketing altogether, and by doing this they may exclude women from diverse levels of marketing activity in which they were formerly engaged;

(b) other state-sponsored marketing agencies, such as cooperatives, tend to be dominated by male officials and bureaucrats, even when operating in places where women have a tradition of marketing;

(c) men rather than women may be favoured recipients of trading licences, in cases where private marketing activity is regulated by a licencing system.

Women's role in marketing is not only affected by gender-oblivious marketing policies, it is also affected by state policies towards new processing technology. In many societies women have chief responsibility for the post-harvest processing of food, whether for home consumption or sale, and this can be classified as a marketing activity when the output is for sale. A classic example is the fall in employment for women in the hand-pounding of rice due to the spread of small rice mills in Asia in the 1960s and 1970s (several studies are collected in IRRI, 1985). While data on this vary between sources, it seems that the labour time of small rice mills is about one twentieth or lower than that of hand pounding for a given volume of throughput.

Unlike price policy, the role of women in agricultural marketing is readily perceived, and not conceptually difficult to take into account in policy formulation (the politics of so doing is another matter).

Input policy

Input policies seldom, if ever, take women into account. This is perhaps understandable where price interventions in inputs are concerned, for the same reason that it is difficult to account for gender in price policy. However, the type, delivery, advice, and crop-specific aspects of inputs have evident gender dimensions, and a sample of these is cited as follows:

(a) intensive input application requires more labour time, and this may or may not be feasible within the constraints of time allocation procedures within the household;

(b) one particular input, herbicides, saves time in weeding, and this may be women's time saved when women do the weeding;

(c) information and safety precautions concerning the use of chemical inputs may be communicated to men, rather than women, with obvious implications for women's health and safety;

(d) more generally, women may not be taught how to use fertilizers and other chemical inputs properly, resulting in waste, incorrect use, use on wrong crops, and so on (Dey, 1981).

Input policy covers a diverse bundle of policy issues with respect to prices, access, and information on variable inputs. It is difficult to generalise about gender impacts. An obvious requirement is for extension workers to advise women rather than men, when it is women undertaking the tasks where new technology and new inputs are involved.

Credit policy

Formal credit schemes are typically gender-oblivious, and they are in practice gender-biased towards men when it is the male head of household who is approached and registered for the provision of institutional credit. It is becoming more widely recognised that women can make good use of credit in their own right for activities that improve their own livelihoods and the income security of their families (Berger, 1989). Some negative aspects of male-biased provision are as follows:

(a) it reinforces other trends whereby women become excluded from activities in which they formerly had economic control, this control being passed to men (food processing and produce marketing are other relevant examples);

(b) credit for labour-saving equipment and machines may displace more women than men in farm and non-farm operations;

(c) credit for cash crop production in which men are engaged may result in increasing conflicts of land and labour use between men and women;

(d) in some cases formal credit schemes directed to men may replace informal credit systems controlled by women (White, 1985: 123).

There is no defensible reason for credit policies to be biased towards men. Women have great potential for the productive use of credit, as demonstrated by experiments such as the Grameen Bank in Bangladesh (Hossain, 1988) and many non-government credit programmes (Berger, 1989: 1025). It is possible that women are more reliable than men at using credit for the purposes for which it was designated, and at repaying loans.

Mechanisation policy

As discussed in Chapter 8, farm mechanisation in developing countries has tended to proceed more in the absence of a coherent policy than with consistent aims in view. Permissive tractorisation has occurred due to misconceived projects of foreign donors, manufacturing sector interests, overvalued exchange rates, and cheap credit. It goes without saying that the differential impacts on men and women of farm mechanisation have been scarcely considered.

In recent history, women appear to have been most strongly affected by mechanised post-harvest technologies in the threshing and milling of grain. This has already been described under marketing policy above, and there are many examples cited in IRRI (1985). Mechanisation of paddy threshing and rice milling causes a substantial fall in the employment opportunities of women from landless families in the labour-abundant societies of South and South-East Asia.

Other gender consequences of mechanisation are more diverse and mixed. It is sometimes argued for Sub-Saharan Africa that seasonal labour is a binding constraint on increasing output, and that selective mechanisation could help to remove this constraint. Since a high proportion of farm labour is contributed by women, it is often the time allocation of women that is the operative constraint in this argument. The difficulty is that power-tillers and related types of equipment which are suitable to small-scale farming are often unsuitable for the soil and climatic conditions that prevail in much of Sub-Saharan Africa.

Mechanisation is a policy area where it is feasible to consider the differential impact on men and women of proposed farm or post-harvest technologies. Mechanisation is sometimes advocated for its reduction in the drudgery of women's lives, but this needs to be set within a context of existing patterns of activity between households of different types, and employment alternatives for women who may otherwise have few options for family survival.

Land reform policy

Land reforms typically take place under conditions of social and political upheaval, and their preoccupation is often with the difficult task of expropriating land belonging to landowners and distributing it to tenants, landless households, or cooperatives. The independent rights of women to land have tended to receive little, if any, attention in land reform policies and debates. Land reform is gender-oblivious or male biased, the latter especially with respect to the registration of ownership title to land following the reform (Deere, 1985).

If the definition of land reform is momentarily widened to include all policies governing the re-registration of land titles, the privatisation of common or community land, and the distribution of public lands, then women are often deprived of long established rights of land access in the process of reform (Agarwal, 1988; Kandiyoti, 1990). This also at a stroke can remove women from independence of resource allocation decisions, control over the product of the land, and bargaining strength against men concerning women's labour time. In short, male-biased land registration decisions can sharply and irreversibly worsen the social subordination of women to men. Some examples are as follows:

(a) redistributive land reform may register new holdings in the name of men, even though women used to have independent access to a plot on the landowners land;

(b) tenancy reform may result in lease contracts being drawn up in the names of male tenants, when previously women as well as men possessed sharecropping rights and obligations;

(c) traditional rights of female land inheritance may be ignored in the design of laws for the registration of communal or village lands in private ownership, and the land then becomes the freehold property of male household heads, thus also switching to male inheritance;

(d) land re-registration laws designed to remove anomalies and ambiguities from existing ownership records can ignore custom- ary female land use rights, and pass ownership of female lands to male household heads;

(e) land improvement projects – including irrigation schemes, area- based agricultural development projects, and resettlement schemes – often deliver ownership of improved plots to men, even though previous land access in that area involved extensive customary use rights by women.

A comparative review of 13 Latin American agrarian reforms (Deere, 1985) concluded that they overwhelmingly benefited men, even when cooperative or communal post-reform land use was instituted. The chief reason for this was that male household heads were almost always treated as the beneficiaries of reform, and therefore all supporting measures (inputs, credit, extension information, and so on) were also channelled to male household heads. Even in post-reform cooperatives, women became excluded and alienated from subsequent organisation and decision-making on reform lands.

The tendency to register land in male names reflects deep-seated male-dominance in all societies. Since bureaucracies and legal systems tend to be dominated by men, appeals for recognition of the rights of women are regarded as minority views or are simply ignored by decision-making bodies. Yet on the face it, land reform policies perhaps more so than other policies in this book, should lend themselves to taking account of women's land rights in policy implementation.

Research policy

The orthodox model of research policy – variations on the theme of technology transfer – is usually gender-oblivious. Research priorities are determined mainly by criteria of raising output, irrespective of women's role in farming systems. The same is not true, or should not be true, for the research policy models denominated as farming systems research (FSR) and farmer first research (FFR) in Chapter 10. Research that involves close observation of farming systems, interaction with farmers, on-farm trials, feedback between farmers and research stations, and so on should incorporate the role, needs, and objectives of women into its method.

The conventional approach to research policy has flaws where gender is concerned. Some relevant issues are as follows:

(a) the historical bias in some parts of the world towards research on export crops or major food staples often resulted in the neglect of crops cultivated by women;

(b) new crops or cropping systems are imposed on farmers without taking into account the gender division of labour in the farm household, and the allocation of women's time, thus resulting in innovation failures;

(c) extension officers have a well-known and documented bias towards communicating with male household heads, even concerning crops or practices that are within the domain of women.

The need to take gender into account in research policy has been recognised and discussed in the literature on FSR and FFR (Moock & Okigbo, 1986; Chambers *et al.*, 1989). There have also been research initiatives on the role of women in farming systems by CGIAR centres (e.g. IRRI, 1985, 1988). Of course there is always a big gap between the theory and reality of these efforts to integrate the gender dimension into the practice of agricultural research. Research systems have a long way to go in this regard.

Irrigation policy

Large-scale canal irrigation schemes have tended to neglect gender dimensions. This has perhaps been one of their less severe problems in Asia, although issues of bias towards men in land registration, division of tasks, provision of inputs, extension services, and so on arise there as elsewhere. However, most case-studies highlighting gender flaws in irrigation schemes relate to the African experience. Some relevant points are summarised here:

(a) in several irrigated rice projects in Africa, irrigated plots were handed over to men, even though in all cases women had hitherto been exclusively responsible for rice cultivation (Dey, 1985);

(b) in some of these schemes, women continued to work in swamp rice cultivation thus depriving the irrigation scheme of labour and reducing the intensity of land use significantly below its potential;

(c) more generally, irrigation schemes in Africa have resulted in conflicts between men and women over women's time allocation and control over cash income (Hanger & Moris, 1973; Dey, 1981);

(d) in some cases, these conflicts are never resolved resulting in poor scheme performance, in others they are partially resolved by men paying for women's labour time (Jones, 1986);

(e) in one project, attempts by foreign donors to ensure that irrigated plots were allocated to women were subverted by the local project administration so that plots ended up in men's hands (Carney, 1988; von Braun *et al.*, 1989).

This last point raises some interesting issues. Policy appeals on behalf of women from afar can be ignored or circumvented by local officials, even when large amounts of external funding are involved. The paradoxical situation may arise that outsiders become the champions of traditional women's rights, while national bureaucratic agencies set themselves to erode or rescind those rights. The same circumstances can apply to any of the policies we have considered here.

Towards gender-aware agricultural policies

The reasons for taking the role and status of women seriously in the formulation of agricultural policies are not just ones of moral indignation concerning the subordinate status of women or the erosion of their dignity in the development process, though many would argue that these were grounds enough. The neglect of gender sometimes results in policy outcomes that fall short of their intentions, and may even be negative in the sense that policy reduces rather than increases the living standards of those it is designed to assist (Kandiyoti, 1990).

The fundamental requirement of policies that take women properly into account is to find out in advance of policy design the way in which women are likely to be influenced by policy action. A framework within which to organise this task of 'finding out' has already been suggested. It includes the six components:

(a) livelihood status of the farm or rural household

(b) time allocation between men and women

(c) control over resources between men and women
(d) control over income between men and women
(e) post-harvest and marketing activities of women
(f) prices and markets for labour, inputs, and outputs

The farming systems research approach, and its close allies, seems the most obvious means of accumulating knowledge about farm women, their circumstances, constraints, and goals. It is doubtful, however, under current schemes for organising FSR, that its findings are ever synthesised in forms that would be accessible for more general policy makers (see Chapter 10). The amount of information needed in order to incorporate women's needs in policy formulation varies with the type of policy, its scope (local or national), and the complexity of issues under consideration. Protection of women's rights under land registration, for example, is more a matter of political will than deep research. Women's traditional rights to land are typically well understood in local communities.

A critical aspect of discovering the impact of policies on women is to *ask* the women who are likely to be affected by a policy initiative. It is no good asking just any women about their views on a policy. Asking women can be more difficult than it first appears (Sen, 1987: 6–10): women's responses to outsiders' questions are conditioned by their cultural perceptions of what they think outsiders want to hear, or sometimes what they think they *ought to say* according to pressures of social conformity. Nevertheless, asking women can sometimes dispel false inferences about women's needs. For example, an extension project in one African country assumed that women farmers would prefer female extension officers, but when the women were asked about this they unanimously expressed a preference for male extension officers.

The integration of women's needs into mainstream agricultural policies would constitute a large step forward in the more general elevation of women in development strategy. While many developing countries created some capacity to handle the policy needs of women during the 1980s, by the end of the decade most projects for women were still microlevel women-specific projects (e.g. village water projects) implemented by non-governmental organisations (NGOs), not women-orientated dimensions in macro or sectoral level policies (Grown & Sebstad, 1989; McKee, 1989).

A useful typology of policy approaches to women is contained in Moser (1989: 1808). Policies are characterised across a spectrum ranging from welfare, to equity, to poverty-orientated, to efficiency, and to empowerment. Many projects for women are pure welfare projects or disintegrate into welfare even though starting with different intentions (Buvinic, 1986). The ultimate aim should be to increase women's productivity and self-reliance, which means moving towards the efficiency and empowerment end of the policy spectrum.

The integration of women into the concerns of mainstream policy formulation and integration does not mean that women lose their social and economic identity. On the contrary, the whole point is to identify women's needs that differ from those of men, so that policies are devised to take into account the different circumstances of women and men. This policy process has been called 'gender planning' (Moser, 1989). Agricultural policies vary in the degree to which they are susceptible to this idea of gender planning, but the main point is that impacts on women should have high status across the range of policies, and should be accorded special emphasis with respect to policies that can have a direct impact on living standards, dignity, and self-reliance of farm women.

Summary

1. This chapter is about the impacts of agricultural policies on women. Policies may be successful in their own terms yet have negative side-effects on the material welfare of women. Sometimes policies fail due to the neglect of gender issues in their design. The term 'gender-oblivious' is used to describe policies that are formulated without heed to their differing impacts on men and women.

2. A dual purpose framework is set out for organising ideas about women and agricultural policies. One purpose is to trace why similar types of policy have different impacts on women in different places. The other purpose is to provide an organising principle for taking women properly into account in the design of policies. The six components of this framework are as follows:
   - (a) livelihood status of the farm or rural household
   - (b) time allocation between men and women
   - (c) control over resources between men and women
   - (d) control over income between men and women
   - (e) post-harvest and marketing activities of women
   - (f) prices and markets for labour, inputs, and outputs

3. A comparative summary is provided of gender issues which can arise with respect to each of the policies covered so far in this book: price policy, marketing policy, input policy, credit policy,

mechanisation policy, land reform policy, research policy, irrigation policy. It is observed that all such policies are typically formulated and implemented without heed to gender differences in policy impacts. Policies vary, however, in the degree to which scope exists for incorporating gender issues in their design.

4. Policies with high potential for taking into account the separate needs of women and men are marketing policy, credit policy, research policy, and irrigation policy. The critical issue of women's rights of access to land is discussed under the rubric of land reform policy, but in reality there is a separate issue here of registration of freehold land titles in women's names where there is a tradition of hereditary female land rights. Input policy and mechanisation policy represent intermediate potential for gender awareness, with the main issue in input policy being provision of information to women on inputs where it is women who are chiefly responsible for their application. Price policy has low potential for gender awareness since output prices are either market prices involving no intervention, or are prices set countrywide for all market participants, women or men.

5. The fundamental requirement of policies that take women properly into account is to find out in advance of policy design the ways in which women are likely to be influenced by policy action. For farm and household level impacts, data deriving from FSR surveys would seem a useful source of relevant information. Women likely to be affected by a policy initiative must be asked their views on what is proposed. Integrating women's needs into mainstream policies is an important step in moving away from purely welfare orientated projects for women.

Further reading

There is not a great deal of published material that is centrally on women and agricultural policies. An exception is the collection of papers by the International Rice Research Institute (IRRI, 1985) on women in rice farming, which is an excellent source for many different aspects of women's lives in rice cultivation and processing. The fascinating story of women in rice irrigation projects in Africa can be traced through a series of published papers or reports (Dey, 1981; Dey, 1985; Jones, 1986; Carney, 1988; and von Braun *et al.*, 1989). A useful paper on women and credit policy is Berger (1989), and several relevant papers on women and farming systems research are contained in Moock & Okigbo (1986). For women and land reform in Latin America see Deere (1985). More general overview papers are Kandiyoti (1990) on rural women policies, Buvinic (1986) on welfarist tendencies in women policies, Moser (1989) on gender planning, and Grown & Sebstad (1989) on livelihood strategies for poor women.

Reading list

Berger, M. (1989). Giving Women Credit: The Strengths and Limitations of Credit as a Tool for Alleviating Poverty. *World Development*, **17**, No. 7.

Buvinic, M. (1986). Projects for Women in the Third World: Explaining their Misbehaviour. *World Development*, **14**, No. 5.

Carney, J.A. (1988). Struggles Over Crop Rights and Labour Within Contract Farming Households in a Gambian Irrigated Rice Project. *Journal of Peasant Studies*, **15**.

Deere, C.D. (1985). Rural Women and State Policy: The Latin American Agrarian Reform Experience. *World Development*, **13**, No. 9, 1037–53.

Dey, J. (1981). Gambian Women: Unequal Partners in Rice Development Projects? *Journal of Development Studies*, **17**.

Dey, J. (1985). Women in African Rice Farming Systems. In *Women in Rice Farming*, Ch. 23. International Rice Research Institute (IRRI). Aldershot: Gower.

Grown, C.A. & Sebstad, J. (1989). Introduction: Toward a Wider Perspective on Women's Employment. *World Development*, **17**, No. 7.

International Rice Research Institute (IRRI) (1985). *Women in Rice Farming*, Aldershot: Gower.

Jones, C.W. (1986). Intra-Household Bargaining in Response to the Introduction of New Crops: A Case Study from North Cameroon. In *Understanding Africa's Rural Household Farming Systems*, eds. J.L. Moock and B.N. Okigbo, Ch. 6. Boulder: Westview Press.

Kandiyoti, D. (1990). Women and Rural Development Policies: The Changing Agenda. *Development and Change*, **21**, No. 1.

Moock, J.L. & Okigbo, B.N. (eds) (1986). *Understanding Africa's Rural Households and Farming Systems*. Boulder: Westview Press.

Moser, C.O.N. (1989). Gender Planning in the Third World: Meeting Practical and Strategic Gender Needs. *World Development*, **17**, No. 11.

von Braun, J., Puetz, D. & Webb, P. (1989). *Irrigation Technology and Commercialization of Rice in the Gambia: Effects on Income and Nutrition*. International Food Policy Research Institute, Research Report 75, August.

13

Food policy and food security

Scope and definition of food policy

The previous policy chapters of this book have not been exclusively about food commodities. Policy instruments are discussed in terms
of their intended impact on the farming system, rather than in terms of
crop-specific goals and effects. Nevertheless, the balance of discussion,
and the examples cited, are inevitably weighted towards the staple grains.
This reflects the strategic importance of staple foods in the agricultural
policies of most developing countries, as well as the prevalence of food
cultivation in peasant farming systems.

All the groups of policy instruments set out in preceding chapters have
one feature in common. They are predominantly concerned with
influencing the *domestic production* of agricultural commodities and are
less concerned with the demand or consumption side of agricultural
markets. This bias towards production is not surprising since the middle
part of the book is structured around the concept of policy influences on
the peasant farm as a production system.

Food policy as a topic cuts across the approach and emphasis of the
preceding chapters. *First*, food policy is specific in its focus on food, and
especially on the staple foods essential for the survival of people. *Second*,
food policy is ultimately concerned with the adequacy of food consumption by the population of a country, not just with food production. *Third*,
food policy is concerned with correcting imbalances between food availability, on the one hand, and the differing capability of people (or
countries) to obtain access to food, on the other. *Fourth*, food policy
views the problems of poverty and unequal incomes in terms of the risks
they represent for the incidence of undernutrition or starvation in
different sectors of the population.

A working definition of food policy can be stated as follows (see also Timmer *et al.*, 1983: 9–10; Gittinger *et al.*, 1987: 1–4):

Definition
Food policy concerns the integration of state actions affecting the supply, distribution, and consumption of food in order to ensure continuity of access to enough food for all the people in a country.

In this context, supply refers not just to domestic production, but also to the potential that exists for supplementing food production by commercial imports or by food aid. Distribution refers to the way food marketing channels work, and to the effectiveness of the time, place and form functions of domestic marketing systems described in Chapter 5. Consumption refers not just to the aggregate volume of staple foods consumed by the population at large, but to the distribution of this volume between people, and to the ability of different groups of people to acquire staple foods given their patterns of employment and incomes, and the levels and trends of food prices.

In the light of this definition, it is helpful to think about food policy in terms of the equation of food availability to food requirements. This can also be stated as the equation of food supply to food demand, on the understanding that supply and demand refer to the foods needed to satisfy the fundamental nutritional requirements of the population.

On the supply side, food policy is concerned with food production and its rate of growth, with food imports, and with food aid. Food production encompasses all those facets that have formed the main body of this book: the inputs, outputs, and technology of farm production, as well as instruments aiming to change the size and composition of food output. Food imports provide an alternative to domestic production for the achievement of a given level of total supply. The use made of imports for this purpose depends on both efficiency criteria (world prices versus domestic production cost) and macroeconomic feasibility (availability of foreign exchange). Food aid provides yet a third alternative source of food supplies, and its role is examined in a later section of this chapter.

On the demand side, food policy is concerned with the adequacy of food consumption across all groups of people and individuals in society. It is concerned with the aggregate and average nutritional status of the population, with identifying those groups and individuals whose nutritional status is below the minimum required for healthy survival, with the purchasing power of different groups of people over food, and with policy instruments designed to improve the access to food of sections of the population that are vulnerable to inadequate levels of food consumption.

Food policy is also concerned with the ability of the food marketing system to achieve efficiently the required spatial and temporal distribution of food, including interseasonal stabilisation of volumes and prices. Stability of prices and supplies is a crucial integrating concept in food policy (Timmer, 1989).

The equation of food availability to food requirements has international, national, household and individual levels. The international level of food policy is concerned with food supply and demand on a global scale, as well as with patterns of food trade between countries, and trends in world prices for staple foods. A central issue is the degree to which world food output keeps pace with world population growth. A related concern is geographical variation in food surpluses and deficits.

It has become commonplace to observe that at a global level food availability has tended to outstrip population growth since the mid-1970s (Mellor & Johnston, 1984; Falcon *et al.*, 1987). Major regions of the world (South and South-East Asia) have moved into food self-sufficiency from a previous food deficit, while the Western industrial countries (North America and Western Europe) have exhibited a strong secular tendency to food surpluses. Even if the global food balance were to become more precarious in the future, the *potential* exists for global output to outstrip consumption, as evidenced by the active discouragement of growth in output in the West (such as payments to persuade farmers to take land out of production).

This tendency for supply at a global level to outstrip demand has implications for the conduct of a national food policy in food-deficit countries. World prices for staple grains have tended to decline in real terms. The option of importing food in order to supplement domestic output has become a valid alternative to the pursuit of food self-sufficiency (Donaldson, 1984; World Bank, 1986a: 31). However, for poor Sub-Saharan African countries this option is less viable than is sometimes proposed. This is due to their acute shortage of foreign exchange, and the logistical problems of moving imported food from points of entry to deficit zones.

The national dimension of food policy is the main focus of this chapter, as also is the necessity to distinguish the national food balance from the food balance at household and individual levels. A country may exhibit equilibrium in the aggregate supply and demand for food, yet have many families or households that for different reasons are unable to command adequate food for healthy survival. Similarly, households may appear to have adequate food, yet individuals within households are observed to suffer from nutritional deficiencies.

Inequalities of food distribution within households remain a debatable issue in the food policy literature (Payne, 1990). The distinction between households and individuals remains important for food policy in any case because women and children have special nutritional needs that may not be met by household adequacy in the provision of basic calories. Nutrition programs designed to provide women and children with nutritional supplements are a part of food policy that involves the targeting of individuals, rather than households or larger categories of the population.

In summary, food policy is ultimately about the stable access to sufficient food for all the people in a country. It is thus about the avoidance of famine, malnutrition, or undernutrition which deprive individual human beings of the basic needs of health and energy. At the centre of food policy is the balance between food availability and requirements. This balance can be described at international, national, household, and individual levels. The chapter proceeds according to the following objectives:

(a) to describe the *evolution of concepts* surrounding food and nutrition that have contributed to the contemporary approach to food policy;
(b) to define and discuss *food security* as an integrated approach to food policy;
(c) to set out the main *instruments* of food policy, taking into account past and current ideas about food security;
(d) to examine the role of *food aid* in food security strategies.

Evolution of concepts

Ideas about food and nutrition in developing countries have changed considerably over the past two decades, and current approaches to food problems reflect these changes. At the centre of this evolution of ideas is the distinction between *food availability*, on the one hand, and *food entitlement*, on the other.

Food availability refers to the supply of food available at international, national, or local levels. The previous orthodoxy in food policy interpreted food availability as the central policy problem, whether long term or short term, national or local. The idea that food availability tends to fall short of long-term food requirements is an old one and is often associated with the doctrine of Thomas Malthus (1766–1834) that agricultural output tends to grow arithmetically, i.e. in a linear fashion, while population grows geometrically, i.e. on an exponential growth curve. This results in a tendency for the gap between food supply and food needs to widen over historical time, with famine acting as the mechanism to close the gap.

Moving to more recent times, the FAO World Food Conference in 1974 placed primary emphasis on the problems of food supply deficits and methods for overcoming them. This conference took place in a period of severe short-term shortages of food commodities in international trade, and high world prices for staple grains. The conference helped to set the tone for international and national responses to food problems in developing countries during the following decade.

An interlocking set of propositions and policy responses follows from an underlying belief in food shortage as the cause of inadequate nutrition at the different levels of geographical aggregation. Short supplies and unstable prices in world markets mean that national food security must depend on domestic production. This results in a push for national self-sufficiency as the prime policy goal, and policies are put in place to encourage rapid growth in domestic production of food staples. At the national level, seasonal shortages and unstable prices are handled by the advent of public food security stocks. Prices for producers and consumers may be fixed (see Chapter 4). Localised shortages and uneven prices are laid at the door of malfunctioning food marketing systems. The solution is for the state to intervene in order to ensure continuous supplies and stable prices across the national territory.

Developing country food policies in the 1970s reflected these connections to a food shortage orthodoxy. Many countries pursued food self-sufficiency as a prime objective. Many also instituted parastatal grain agencies either to carry out buffer stock operations or to act as sole purchasing and distribution agents for food at fixed prices. Moreover, other types of farm policy obeyed the same kind of logic. The advent of state farms in order to attempt to produce high marketed surpluses of grain for delivery to towns and cities is a relevant example. This is not to say that food policies always pulled in the same direction or were free of logical inconsistencies. The organisational failings of state agencies in the production or procurement of staple grains may have sometimes exacerbated rather than alleviated local and national food shortage situations.

Contrasting the orthodox emphasis on supply or production, *food entitlement* refers to the command over food of households or individuals. The concept of food entitlement originates in a celebrated series of writings on the causes of famine by Amartya Sen (Sen, 1980; 1981a; 1981b). Related ideas about the causes of malnutrition and starvation also appeared in other writings at around the same time (e.g. Reutlinger, 1977). The essence of the entitlement approach is that people do not necessarily or even mainly starve due to an insufficient supply of food, they starve because they possess insufficient command over, or access to, food. Sen distinguishes four different types of entitlement that individuals or households in a market economy may possess or acquire (modified from Sen, 1981b: 4):

(a) *trade-based entitlement*: ownership of goods or resources obtained by trading something a person or household owns with another party;

(b) *production-based entitlement*: ownership of output produced using personal or household resources, or using resources willingly hired by others;

(c) *own-labour entitlement*: ownership of personal labour power, thus enabling the person or household to obtain trade or production based entitlement in exchange for their own labour power;

(d) *inheritance and transfer entitlements*: ownership of goods or resources bequeathed or freely given to the person or household.

As suggested by this list, the concept of entitlement encompasses both non-monetary and monetary command over food and other commodities. Non-monetary command over food occurs with respect to subsistence production, payments in kind, gifts and physical transfers within the community, and intra-household food distribution. Monetary command over food is described by the concept of *exchange entitlement*. This is the household or individual's purchasing power over food, given prevailing market prices of food and other commodities.

The food entitlement of an individual or household clearly has long-run and short-run dimensions, as well as being susceptible to rapid changes of fortune for people living at the margin of poverty. The following examples are designed to clarify the concept, with special reference to personal or household food security. The first two examples refer to non-monetary food entitlement, the last three refer to exchange entitlement expressed as purchasing power over food:

(a) A semi-subsistence farm household is accustomed to meeting its own food needs as first priority, only selling output in excess of household requirements. A flood destroys its food crop just before harvest, resulting in an immediate and substantial fall in household food entitlement.

(b) A household possesses just sufficient food, but this food is distributed unequally between household members so that some individuals suffer nutritional deficiencies. This occurs in some rural societies where males are given preferential access to food over female members of the family. In this case women and female children experience a failure of food entitlement due to the non-monetary procedure for allocating food within the household.

(c) A household lacking its own or inherited resources depends on the wage employment (own-labour entitlement) of its members for survival. Persistent lack of employment opportunities for such a family implies chronic lack of food entitlement, and hence long-term inability to obtain enough to eat.

(d) A farm family sells most of its crop immediately after harvest in order to pay off debts to a landlord or moneylender. In the meantime, drought occurs elsewhere in the country, and food prices rise steeply. The family finds it is unable to maintain normal food consumption. Its food entitlement is reduced by the widening gap between its sale price and purchase price of food, leading to a temporary inability to buy enough to eat.

(e) A farm family cultivating coffee buys expensive cash inputs on the advice of an extension officer in order to raise crop yield. However, a glut of coffee on the world market develops so that when harvest time arrives the family receives insufficient cash for food purchases during the next year. The food entitlement of the family declines due to the adverse terms of trade between farm input and farm output prices.

The concept of food entitlement causes a significant shift in the emphasis and focus of food policy. *First*, an aggregate shortage of food becomes only one amongst several factors that can cause short-term or long-term inadequacy of food consumption. Food shortage affects entitlements primarily via a rise in the market price of food. This diminishes the purchasing power of sectors of the population that are dependent on market purchases of food for their survival. For farmers and for farm labour the effect of such a price rise may be positive or negative for their food entitlement depending on whether they are food producers, whether they produce output surplus to household requirements, and whether it is a fall in output on their own farms that has caused the food shortage and price rise.

Second, a number of adverse price changes originating in events other than food shortage can cause a fall in the exchange entitlement over food of different groups in the population. Some examples are (i) a rise in food prices caused by an exchange rate devaluation, (ii) a fall in the farmers terms of trade, (iii) a widening of the marketing margin between farm-gate sales prices and food retail prices, and (iv) a rise in consumer prices not compensated by an equivalent rise in wages.

Third, food entitlement shifts the focus away from the aggregate economic level towards a disaggregated view of the circumstances of social groups vulnerable to inadequate access to food. Such groups may be urban or rural. They are likely to be unemployed or to depend on casual labour for their survival. They may own some land, but barely sufficient for family subsistence. They may be farmers in drought prone zones who regularly confront the borderline between survival and starvation in pursuit of a livelihood. They will certainly in most cases be amongst the poorest groups in the population. The food entitlement approach makes a direct and obvious link between poverty and food insecurity.

Fourth, and closely related, the food entitlement approach makes it clear that enough food at the aggregate level is not a sufficient condition for all people in society to have adequate access to food. What matters at the household or individual level is the command of people over food, and this varies according to the nature and strength of their food entitlements. In countries with highly unequal income distributions, widespread unemployment or underemployment, and extensive poverty, there can be a high incidence of inadequate nutrition despite the existence of enough food at the aggregate level.

Another less prominent but nevertheless important shift in ideas related to food policy over the past two decades concerns nutrition.

It used to be considered that the chief problem of malnutrition in developing countries was not a deficiency in the consumption of energy or calories, but was lack of dietary protein, essential minerals, and vitamins. The policy response that followed from this was to encourage people to diversify their diets, and to provide dietary supplements in food distribution schemes.

It is nowadays recognised that provided there is adequate energy in the diet, protein and other dietary requirements tend largely to look after themselves. Exceptions to this can occur, such as iron, iodine, or vitamin A deficiencies. However, the fundamental nutritional problem in food policy is *undernutrition*, i.e. insufficient dietary energy or calories, rather than *malnutrition*, i.e. defective combinations of energy, protein, vitamins, and other dietary elements.

Space does not permit elaboration of these nutritional aspects of food policy here. A useful review of evolving ideas about minimum daily requirements of dietary energy is given in Payne (1990). Recent writing in this area suggests that determining relevant guidelines for the minimum acceptable energy intake of men, women and children is not as straightforward as it sometimes appears in publications dealing with such guidelines. This means that data on the numbers and proportions of undernourished people in developing countries, calculated according to fixed minimum calorie levels (for example, the 2500 kcals/day for an adult male that is often used as a rough guide), are prone to wide margins of error.

Food security

The concept that helps to foster an integrated approach to food and nutrition problems is that of *food security*. This places stress on the avoidance of undernutrition or starvation as the fundamental food policy goal. It implies putting in place a set of instruments and mechanisms that seek (i) to overcome existing long-term nutritional deprivation in vulnerable groups of the population, and (ii) to avert short-term nutritional deprivation resulting from adverse natural events or sudden changes in the capacity of people to acquire enough food.

There have been many definitions of food security in the literature over the years. However, the definition that is nowadays widely accepted as capturing the spirit of the concept is that advanced by the World Bank (1986a: 1):

Definition
[*Food security*] *is . . . access by all people at all times to enough food for an active, healthy life. Its essential elements are the availability of food and the ability to acquire it. Food insecurity, in turn, is the lack of access to enough food.*

Several variations on this definition are set out and compared in Maxwell (1990: 2–3). These tend to produce small differences in interpretation, but general consensus on the basic principles of food security seems to prevail. As embodied in the World Bank definition, these principles may be distinguished as follows.

First, the definition emphasises access to food rather than the supply of food. This is consistent with the concept of food entitlement, and it focuses on whether people have sufficient command over food, and thus on methods to supplement this entitlement where it is deficient or absent. *Second*, the definition emphasises the access to food by *all* people, implying that an aggregate view is insufficient, the situation of individuals and social groups at risk is of critical importance. *Third*, the definition refers to both 'availability of food' and 'ability to acquire food', corresponding to the food availability versus food entitlement distinction made in the preceding section. This definition of food security owes much to the shift away from thinking about food problems solely in terms of available food supply.

The World Bank definition of food security also makes an important distinction between *chronic food insecurity* and *transitory food insecurity* (World Bank, 1986a: 1). Chronic food insecurity is defined as a continuously inadequate diet caused by the persistent inability to acquire enough food. Transitory food insecurity is defined as a temporary decline in a household's access to enough food. Both these concepts are based on a food entitlement perspective on food policy, and both focus on the situation of the household or the individual rather than on macroeconomic aggregates.

The distinction between chronic food insecurity and transitory food insecurity has become an accepted part of food policy analysis, and it provides a useful organising scheme for discussing food policy instruments. It has been argued, however, that for assessing the severity of any given food policy problem, the distinction needs to be supplemented by an index of the intensity of food insecurity under review (Maxwell *et al.*, 1990: 53). The citizens of a country may exhibit transitory food insecurity, but of an isolated, scattered, and relatively mild kind that does not justify costly and dramatic measures of relief. On the other hand, famine is a type of transitory food insecurity, the occurrence of which requires large-scale, urgent, and coordinated relief.

A complementary view of food insecurity is in terms of the *risk* that certain social groups will confront starvation (Anderson & Scandizzo, 1984). *Food risk* is measured as the probability that a given population, defined for example by geographical location, may experience inadequate access to food. This probability is, in turn, the product of environmental risk (i.e. the probability of crop failure), on the one hand, and income risk (i.e. the probability of failing to earn enough), on the other. The task of food security policy is to reduce the level of these probabilities, and by posing them in risk terms it is evident that stabilising supply and reducing the incidence of poverty *both* have an important role to play.

Food policy instruments

The shift in emphasis from a food availability to a food entitlement view of food security leads also to a shift in the combination of policy instruments that are considered appropriate for an integrated food strategy. In what follows, policy instruments related to food supply are considered separately from policy instruments related to food demand. In addition, attention is given to whether instruments operate to alleviate chronic as opposed to transitory food insecurity, and whether they are general or targeted in scope.

Food supply

Previous mainstream ideas about food policy emphasised the supply side of food markets, and placed priority on domestic production rather than trade. In addition, price stability for consumers and producers has always featured strongly in conventional food policies. In the following paragraphs these features and policy instruments are examined under the sub-headings of self-sufficiency and price instability.

(a)   *Self-sufficiency*

The focus on domestic self-sufficiency in staple foods is based in part on avoiding undue reliance on unstable and unpredictable world food markets. Domestic food production is promoted by the range of policies discussed earlier in this book, including producer price policy, input policy, credit policy, research policy and irrigation policy.

Growth of domestic food production towards self-sufficiency mainly addresses the problem of aggregate food availability. It has some impact on chronic food insecurity to the extent that the employment and income prospects of poor farmers and landless labourers are improved. It may also help overcome some types of transitory food insecurity. For example, irrigation does this by reducing the seasonality of output for participating farmers.

(b)   *Price stability*

In conjunction with food self-sufficiency, price stability is typically approached by the creation of a national food security stock, built up from domestic production. The food security stock is used to stabilise consumer prices by releasing grain out of stock to defend a ceiling retail price. Many different ways of operating such a stock can be found across the developing countries, some based on floor and ceiling prices – which is the conventional buffer stock model – and some based on fixed producer and consumer prices.

Price stability based on domestic production and domestic stocks requires the existence of a parastatal authority with wide-ranging, sometimes monopoly, powers to buy and sell grain, and to regulate the quantity and price of imported supplies in years when there is a shortfall in the domestic market.

(c)   *Further points on the food supply approach*
        The conventional food policy model is aggregative in nature. It interprets food security as the national balance of supply and demand, with the main objective being to bring the growth in domestic production into line with the growth in domestic food demand. A successful example of this model is the food strategy followed by Indonesia in the 1970s and 1980s (Ellis, 1990). Interpersonal inequalities of consumption are relatively down-played in this model. However, concern for political stability and the avoidance of urban unrest means that keeping consumer prices low in urban areas is sometimes given priority in the conventional model.

The pursuit of domestic self-sufficiency is regarded nowadays as a potentially high cost and socially inefficient method for achieving the supply side of food security. It is pointed out that self-sufficiency is neither a *necessary* nor a *sufficient* condition for the achievement of food security (World Bank, 1986a: 31). It is not a necessary condition, since imported supplies can be used to cover the varying gap between domestic production and consumption. It is not a sufficient condition because even with self-sufficiency there may be significant categories of the population facing chronic or transitory food insecurity due to lack of food entitlement.

Even if broad self-sufficiency can be justified in comparative advantage terms, i.e. it is cheaper to produce domestic food than to import food, the cost of balancing supply and demand at the margin can be reduced considerably by making more use of the world market rather than depending entirely on domestic stocks. This is because the size of stock required to balance the domestic market using only domestic supplies is many times larger than the size of stock needed if imports are utilised to assist with balancing the market. The food security document of the World Bank (1986a: 42–8) contains a concise and useful statement of these issues.

Food demand

The contemporary approach to food security emphasises the demand side of food markets, and the disaggregated access of people to food. This leads to emphasis on a different set of policy instruments from those associated with the aggregate production model, although it should be understood that these are matters of emphasis and degree, not the wholesale abandonment of one set of policies in favour of another.

In the following paragraphs the major features and instruments of demand side food policy are examined under the sub-headings of nutritional status and policy instruments.

(a)   *Nutritional status*

The nutritional status of the population at large, and of major sub-categories within the population needs to be regularly monitored. There are various methods for doing this which are discussed in the literature (Timmer *et al.*, 1983: Ch. 2). Some common components are (i) the construction of a national food balance sheet in order to obtain an overall picture of the nutritional status of the country, (ii) use of household income and expenditure surveys or more specialised surveys to estimate the proportion of the population falling below minimum standards of food consumption, (iii) use of similar sources to identify the type of population category, income class, and location of vulnerable groups, (iv) more specific investigations of vulnerable groups to assess the degree, nature, and intensity of their inability to acquire sufficient food.

These methods are individually prone to wide margins of error. However, the pursuit of accuracy must be weighed against the costs of obtaining additional information. In the end, the important task is to obtain orders of magnitude as far as numbers of people are concerned, and to identify the geographical location and occupational situation of food-deficit or vulnerable groups.

(b)   *Policy instruments*

Instruments for tackling lack of entitlement over food can take two forms: either lowering the price of food to improve exchange entitlement (food subsidies), or increasing command over food (by employment creation, food-for-work programmes, or cash transfers). These instruments can be general in scope, i.e. they apply to all food consumers, or can be targeted as precisely as possible to the social groups in need.

General consumer subsidies on food have been favoured by some countries (Egypt is a frequently cited example). This means that the problem of identifying vulnerable groups is avoided. However, it also means that all consumers, whether rich or poor, benefit from the subsidies.

One problem with general consumer subsidies is that they have high budgetary costs which are also open-ended – the subsidy must cover the growth in demand induced by the low prices. This includes the substitution by consumers (including richer consumers) of the subsidised food for higher priced foods. Another problem is the impact on farm prices, and thus on the incentive to produce. Consumer prices can to some degree be insulated from farm prices where the subsidy is applied to the processed product, for example, wheat flour. However, for a commodity like rice, this insulation is minor, and low urban food prices soon translate themselves into low farm-gate producer prices.

The costs of general consumer subsidies vary according to the degree of self-sufficiency in the country, and the way the subsidy is implemented. The highest cost would be incurred for a self-sufficient country in which the subsidy is applied to every single kilogram sold. An alternative, lower cost, mechanism is to subsidise the price of imported supplies so that domestic prices are forced down, but this runs into the problem of adverse effects on producer prices and incentives.

The alternative to general consumer subsidies is to target relief to groups known to be at risk. Various instruments can be found in different countries including 'fair price' shops, food stamps, public employment programmes, food-for-work schemes, and so on. Targeting that depends on providing low-cost food to eligible groups suffers from high administrative costs and inevitable leakages and abuses. This category may be described as 'administered targeting', and it includes any type of scheme where the rules of exclusion or inclusion are determined and administered by specialised bureaucratic agencies.

An alternative type of targeting – 'self-regulating targeting' – is to choose commodities for subsidy, locations for subsidy, or employment programmes such that anyone is eligible to participate. An example would be to subsidise the price of an inferior staple food only consumed by poor people. Another example would be to create a food-for-work programme in a location where the number of people requiring relief more or less corresponded to the amount of work that can be offered.

The consensus on policy instruments designed to alter the food entitlement of people is that targeted interventions are preferable to generalised interventions, and that self-regulating targeting is preferable to administered targeting. Aside from bureaucratic feasibility, government budgetary cost, and so on, the economic reason for preferring targeting to generalised interventions is that the former avoids the creation of economy-wide price distortions.

These demand-side interventions in food markets are mainly aimed at alleviating the chronic, long-term, food insecurity of vulnerable groups. It is rarely feasible to implement instruments such as subsidies and targeting for temporary or seasonal changes in food entitlement, due to the inevitable slowness of the political and administrative processes by which they are established. An exception might be seasonal food-for-work projects conducted in locations known to suffer from nutritional deprivation at certain times of each year.

Integration of policy instruments

Ideally, both supply side and demand side instruments of food security should be integrated in order to form a coherent and integrated food policy. This rarely occurs in practice, not the least because different components of the overall food and nutrition picture are often handled by different state agencies at central government level. Domestic agricultural production is almost always handled by the Ministry of Agriculture. Nutrition, on the other hand, may be located in the Ministry of Health. Public employment schemes or food-for-work projects may be in the domain of the Ministry of Labour or the Ministry of Public Works. The effort of coordinating the food security activities of all these agencies is considerable and seldom achieved except, perhaps, in food disaster situations.

There is general agreement in the literature that as far as the demand side of food policy is concerned, the ultimate long-run objective is to eliminate poverty via a combination of overall growth, and attention to the income distribution dimensions of alternative growth strategies. For example, one of the leading writers in the food policy area sees the solution to the food entitlement problem to lie in employment-intensive development, especially of the small-farm sector; leading to patterns of rising demand for labour-intensive consumer goods, self-reinforcing growth of small-scale activity, and rising employment and incomes for previously vulnerable social groups (Mellor, 1988a; 1988b).

Food aid

The role of food aid in food policy and food security has long been a debatable issue, and it is appropriate to review some of the main points arising in this chapter.

Food aid is a method for disposing of food surpluses produced in the industrialised countries. Historically, the chief source of food aid has been the USA, although in more recent years its share of total food aid flows to developing countries has fallen to nearly half, and the EEC has become a major participant in food aid. The total volume of food aid fluctuates around 10 million tons of food grains per year, and, depending on how this is valued, it is equivalent to roughly 10 per cent of official development assistance from the industrialised to developing countries. About 20 per cent of food aid is delivered to developing countries as multilateral food aid through the FAO World Food Program.

For the purposes of food policy discussion, four main categories of food aid can be distinguished (Ezekiel, 1988: 1377). These categories are:

(a) *Program food aid*. This is the largest category of food aid in quantitative terms, and is food aid delivered for purposes of sale by recipient governments.

(b) *Project food aid*. This is food aid designed for use in specific food-related projects in developing countries, including nutrition projects, food-for-work schemes, other types of employment creation scheme, and rural development projects.

(c) *Emergency food aid*. This is urgent food aid delivered in order to overcome acute local or national food deficits, such as occur in famines, or as a consequence of natural disasters and wars.

(d) *Adjustment food aid*. This is food aid delivered as part of a structural adjustment package, and designed to mitigate the effects on social groups whose access to food is adversely affected by policy reform packages.

These categories of food aid evidently fit into the food policy framework in different ways. Adjustment food aid is concerned with compensating people affected by transitory loss of food entitlement, caused by changes in macroeconomic or sectoral policies. It might be provided, for example, where an adjustment package involves the removal of a consumer subsidy on an imported grain sold in urban centres. Emergency food aid is concerned with increasing food availability in a situation of localised or national food availability decline. Project food aid is mainly concerned with the alleviation of chronic food insecurity. It is therefore complementary to the targeted food entitlement interventions discussed in the previous section.

Program food aid, as well as being the largest of these food aid categories, is also the most contentious. This is because it is not about delivery of food to poor people *per se*, but about macroeconomic effects on the balance of payments, government budget, general level of food prices, and so on. Program food aid is provided explicitly as balance of payments support to food-deficit countries that otherwise would have to import food at commercial prices. However, its ramifications go beyond the simple substitution of food aid for commercial food imports, as the discussion that follows demonstrates.

Program food aid is typically conceived as conveying several benefits to food-deficit countries. It provides food at no cost, or at greatly subsidised cost, to assist in covering the gap between domestic food production and domestic food consumption. This food is sold by recipient governments at prevailing market prices, or at the level of retail food prices determined by food price policy. The positive effects of this type of food aid are thus:

(a) to release foreign exchange, which can then be used to import other commodities required for the fulfilment of development objectives;

(b) to generate government budgetary income, which can be used to support the recurrent or capital costs of development activities, including employment-creation schemes, rural development projects, or poverty alleviation schemes;

(c) to assist in the operation and management of food price stabilisation schemes, such as buffer stocks, by providing low-cost supplies to supplement domestic purchases;

(d) to create a higher general level of food consumption, and thus higher nutritional status for the population as a whole, due to the enhanced ability to stabilise the retail prices of food at levels beneficial to consumers;

(e) to act as an addition to the financial aid resources that developing countries would otherwise receive from donor countries, since food aid decisions tend to be separate from financial aid decisions.

The point made under (d) above is strengthened when project food aid is taken into account, since project food aid often directly expands the food consumption possibilities of society as a whole by addressing the food entitlement problems of vulnerable social groups.

This list of the alleged advantages of food aid can be counter-posed to a set of potential disadvantages of food aid that have been identified in past food policy literature. The defects of program-type food aid have been posed variously as follows:

(a) by increasing domestic supply, food aid depresses domestic market prices for food grains, and this results in a reduction of domestic output (the disincentive effects on production argument);

(b) food aid causes a substitution of imported grains (e.g. wheat) for locally produced food staples (e.g. cassava, sorghum, millet), thus causing a decline in their demand, and long-term consumer dependence on imported food supplies;

(c) food aid is erratic in volume due to its reliance on the fluctuating surpluses of developed countries, and the state of world food markets; when surpluses are low or world prices are high food aid dwindles just at the same time that recipient countries are most in need of assistance for balancing domestic markets.

The last of these is less of a problem nowadays than it was in the past, due to firm commitments by the donor countries to maintain agreed minimum levels of food aid flows irrespective of events in world markets. The domestic food market impacts of food aid are a more serious potential problem, though there is little evidence to support the idea that food aid, on its own, has been responsible for low producer prices of foods in any particular country. Domestic policies, including macro-economic policies such as overvalued exchange rates, have been the principle reason for low farm-gate food prices in some developing countries. The evidence on food aid is that it is usually managed rather carefully to avoid this problem. Consumer substitution and long-term changes in tastes may be a valid disadvantage of food aid, although there is not a lot of firm evidence to support this point of view.

These arguments concerning food aid were reviewed in the late 1970s (Maxwell & Singer, 1979), and are also considered in more recent papers (Singer, 1987; Ezekiel, 1988). The consensus is that the benefits of food aid, especially in assisting countries to carry out food entitlement based food policies, outweigh the potential disadvantages. These disadvantages anyway remain 'potential' rather than proven for those developing countries that have been large recipients of food aid over the past two decades. The alleviation of chronic food insecurity using targeted interventions makes particular use of food aid, and many such targeted schemes would disappear if they had to depend for their implementation solely on domestic or world market commercial food supplies.

Summary

1. This chapter provides a brief overview of food policy and food security, especially with respect to aspects of food policy that are not covered in the preceding policy chapters of the book. The

chapter sets out the scope of food policy, the changing ideas about food and nutrition in developing countries, the concept of food security, the instruments of food policy, and some basic ideas about food aid.

2. Food policy is defined as the integration of state actions affecting the supply, distribution and consumption of food in order to ensure continuity of access to enough food for all the people in a country. In this context, supply refers to total food availability, including domestic production, commercial imports and food aid. Distribution refers to the operation of food marketing systems. Consumption refers to the ability of people to acquire food given their patterns of employment and incomes, and the levels and trends of food prices.

3. Food policy is essentially about the balance between food availability and food requirements. This balance has international, national, household, and individual dimensions. A surplus of food at the international level does not guarantee that all countries possess sufficient food for their populations to obtain an adequate diet. Likewise, self-sufficiency in food at the national level does not guarantee access to food for social groups and households who lack the purchasing power to buy the food.

4. Ideas about food policy have changed, especially in the relative emphasis that is placed on food availability versus food entitlement. While in the past, attention was focused on lack of food availability, and on increasing domestic production, the current emphasis is on the command of people over food. The term food entitlement focuses on the non-monetary and monetary command of people over food. It also focuses on the kinds of change, such as natural disasters or adverse price movements, that can reduce food entitlement to below a minimum acceptable level in terms of nutrition.

5. The concept of food security helps to bring together and to integrate contemporary ideas about food policy. A widely accepted definition of food security is . . . 'access by all people at all times to enough food for an active, healthy life' (World Bank, 1986a: 1). Food insecurity is a lack of access to enough food, and we can distinguish between chronic food insecurity and transitory food insecurity. Chronic food insecurity is defined as a continuously inadequate diet caused by the persistent inability to acquire enough food. Transitory food insecurity is defined as a

temporary decline in a household's access to enough food. All these concepts of food security are based on the food entitlement perspective on food policy.

6. Food policy instruments may be divided between those concerned with supply and those concerned with demand. Orthodox food policies are concerned mainly with supply, and within that they focus on domestic self-sufficiency and price stability. Domestic food growth addresses some aspects of chronic food insecurity, although not the main ones related to food entitlement. Price stabilisation is the main instrument designed to address transitory food insecurity.

7. The contemporary emphasis of food policy is on food access, and is concerned with the alleviation of chronic food insecurity via general or targeted food subsidy and employment creation schemes. Food security targeting may be subdivided between administrative targeting (bureaucratic decisions concerning eligible recipients) and self-regulating targeting (choosing commodities or locations for which access by the target group defines itself).

8. A brief review of food aid and its role in food policy is provided. Food aid is distinguished between program food aid, project food aid, emergency food aid, and adjustment food aid. These play different food policy roles either on the demand or supply side of food markets. Program food aid is quantitatively the most important type of food aid, and is also the category that has been most debated over the years in the food policy literature. The conclusion here is that food aid of all types has a potentially positive role to play in food entitlement orientated food policies.

Further reading

There exists a large literature on food policy and food security in developing countries. The best starting point for the contemporary approach is the World Bank publication *Poverty and Hunger* (World Bank, 1986a). An earlier textbook orientated towards the economic approach to food supply and demand is Timmer *et al*. (1983). Useful collections are the food policy volume edited by Gittinger *et al*. (1987), the food subsidies volume edited by Pinstrup-Andersen (1988), the special issue of *World Development* on food security (Kumar & Lipton, 1988), and the special issue of *IDS Bulletin* on food security (Maxwell, 1990). Relevant chapters on food policy can also be found in Eicher &

Staatz (1990: Chs. 10–12) and Mellor & Ahmed (1988: Chs. 14 and 15). On the underlying concepts of the food entitlement approach to food security see Sen (1981b) on famines. Related ideas are contained in Reutlinger (1977). On food aid see the earlier survey by Maxwell & Singer (1979) as well as more recent papers by Singer (1987) and Ezekiel (1988). Material on food aid can also be found in several of the books and collections cited above.

Reading list

Eicher, C.K. & Staatz J.M. (eds) (1990). *Agricultural Development in the Third World*, 2nd edn. Baltimore: Johns Hopkins.

Ezekiel, H. (1988). An Approach to a Food Aid Strategy. *World Development*, **16**, No. 11.

Gittinger, J.P., Leslie, J. & Hoisington, C. (eds) (1987). *Food Policy: Integrating Supply, Distribution, and Consumption*. Baltimore: Johns Hopkins.

Kumar, S.K. & Lipton, M. (eds) (1988). Current Issues in Food Security. *World Development*, **16**, No. 9.

Maxwell, S. (ed.) (1990). Food Security in Developing Countries. *IDS Bulletin*, **21**, No. 3.

Maxwell, S. & Singer, H. (1979). Food Aid to Developing Countries: A Survey. *World Development*, **7**.

Mellor, J.W. & Ahmed, R.U. (1988). *Agricultural Price Policy for Developing Countries*. Baltimore: Johns Hopkins.

Pinstrup-Andersen, P. (ed.) (1988). *Food Subsidies in Developing Countries*. Baltimore: Johns Hopkins.

Reutlinger, S. (1977). Malnutrition: A Poverty or a Food Problem? *World Development*, **5**, No. 8.

Sen, A.K. (1981b). *Poverty and Famines: An Essay on Entitlements and Deprivation*. Oxford: Clarendon Press.

Singer, H.W. (1987). Food Aid: Development Tool or Obstacle to Development? *Development Policy Review*, **5**, 323–39.

Timmer, C.P., Falcon, W.P. & Pearson, S.R. (1983). *Food Policy Analysis*. Baltimore: Johns Hopkins.

World Bank (1986a). *Poverty and Hunger: Issues and Options for Food Security in Developing Countries*. Washington D.C.: World Bank.

14

Policies in perspective

This book has examined the main policies by which governments in developing countries seek to influence the growth rate and composition of agricultural production, as well as to achieve income distribution and food security goals. The policies described in the book apply especially to the peasant or small-farm sector in developing countries, although their scope may often be such as to affect the agricultural sector as a whole.

The book is organised around a central set of eight policy chapters, covering the topics of price policy, marketing policy, input policy, credit policy, mechanisation policy, land reform policy, research policy, and irrigation policy. These chapters are preceded by material covering the nature of policy, a framework for policy analysis, and methods and tools used by economists to undertake agricultural policy analysis. They are followed by chapters that discuss the status of women in agricultural policies, and features of food policy and food security that are not covered in the main policy chapters.

There are several themes running through the book, which are referred to as cross-cutting themes. Gender and food policy are two such themes. The roles of markets and the state in agricultural development is another. A final theme is the relationship of policy to the socio-economic concept of the peasant household. Policies are important determinants of the long-run fate of peasants. However, also, the short-run success or failure of policies can be significantly influenced by peasant household decision-making, which differs from that of the purely market-orientated farm enterprise.

This chapter provides a brief summary of some major strands arising from the content of the book. The aim is to bring out some key points and

ideas, and to make connections between them. This is done according to the following sub-headings: .
 - market, state and policies
 - framework and methods of analysis
 - agricultural policies
 - women and policies
 - food policy and food security

Market, state and policies

Most policies are predicated on the premise that the state can do better than the market in achieving specific outcomes for society. This notion held powerful sway in developing countries over roughly three decades from the early 1950s to the early 1980s. Widespread state intervention was also consistent with the emergence of new nation states in this period, and the assertion of state power and nationalism in the newly independent countries. For this reason it is superficial to associate state controls with political labels like 'left-wing' or 'socialist', because countries with widely differing official ideologies have had similarly high levels of state involvement in the economy.

In the 1980s, the prevalent belief in the wisdom of state-led solutions to economic problems began to be placed in serious doubt. It was observed that the outcomes of state actions could sometimes be much worse for the livelihoods of a country's citizens than the outcomes of market defects that governments had attempted to rectify. The contemporary assessment of policy therefore requires questioning the nature and scale of state controls, and weighing in the balance the roles that are played by the market and the state in different spheres of economic activity.

In this context, 'market failures' can be compared and contrasted with 'state failures'. Market failures may result from monopoly, non-provision (of public goods), externalities, common property resources, transaction costs, moral hazard problems, and insufficient information. State failures may occur due to defective information, unpredicted side-effects, second-best outcomes, poor implementation, poor motivation, impropriety, and inefficiency.

The occurrence of widespread – even catastrophic – state failure is nowadays a widely recognised feature of the development process in some countries and regions. This encompasses not just minor instances of bureaucratic inefficiency and mismanagement, but also personal rule systems, coercion, nepotism, income-seeking, and generalised corruption. These problems do not have purely economic connotations. They are also associated with highly centralised power, lack of popular partici-pation, inflexibility, and problems of access to state commodities and services.

This book does not advocate an extreme view in either direction with respect to the state versus market debate. It recognises that there are some types of intervention which the state is likely to prove more competent to undertake than other types of intervention. Each case must be taken on its merits. However, one conclusion is that it is almost always advisable to have non-intervention as an alternative on the table in policy discussion. This is not because non-intervention is necessarily the most appropriate course of action to take, but rather because it permits a much wider range of possible mixes between market and state roles to be reviewed.

States have proved especially incompetent in monopoly crop market-ing, in fixing rigid farm-gate prices for farmers, and in creating monolithic institutions for the delivery of inputs or credit to farmers. In many countries, the prices and the marketing or delivery of farm outputs and inputs could certainly be left much more to private actors and to market forces of supply and demand than has hitherto been the norm. On the other hand, price stabilisation for major strategic commodities, like food staples, has proved fairly successful in some countries. The point then is how to stabilise prices using minimum rather than maximum degrees of state intervention.

Framework and methods of analysis

The book provides a framework and some basic analytical tools for the economic analysis of agricultural policies. The framework is the objectives–constraints–instruments model of policy analysis originally devised by Tinbergen in the 1950s. In the light of concepts of 'state failure', this framework cannot be based on the assumption that the state is always trying to act in the best interest of society as a whole. Nevertheless, it provides a logically coherent way of organising ideas about policies, and for comparing alternative policy instruments.

The analytical tools provided in the book are those of partial equilib-rium analysis which permit the quantitative and welfare effects of policies to be examined in the markets most directly affected by policy action. Key concepts and methods that are set out in the early chapters of the book can be summarised as follows:

(a) the economic concept of social welfare is defined as the total volume of material goods and services available for consumption in society;

(b) policy analysis is based in part on the concept of the Pareto optimum, defined as a situation for society as a whole in which it is not possible to make one person better off without making another person worse off;

(c) almost all policies violate the Pareto optimum, since there are always losers as well as gainers from policy interventions;

(d) for this reason, policy analysis is based on the compensation criterion, which states that a policy change may be worth considering provided that the gainers could potentially compensate the losers and still be better off than they were before the change;

(e) the concepts in partial equilibrium analysis that enable the compensation criterion to be made operational are those of producer surplus and consumer surplus, and these can be calculated with knowledge of the elasticities of supply and demand in markets affected by the policy, as well as the changes in economic variables (prices, yields, etc.) which the policy intends to bring about;

(f) the gains and losses of policies can be measured both in private prices – the actual prices faced by consumers and producers – and in economic prices that represent the opportunity cost to society of farm inputs and outputs;

(g) various measures are commonly used to try to capture in a single figure the divergence between the private prices induced by policy interventions, and the economic prices represented by world prices for tradeable outputs and inputs: examples are the domestic resource cost (DRC), the effective rate of protection (ERP), and the subsidy ratio to producers (SRP).

Agricultural policies

The treatment of agricultural policies in this book is based on the principle of linking policy topics to their intended impact on the inputs and outputs of the farm system. Policy instruments are observed to fall into three main categories, with more than one category sometimes applicable to a particular policy topic. These categories are price, institution, and technology interventions.

As far as the efficiency of farm production is concerned, policy interventions can work in one of two underlying ways in economic terms: they can attempt to alter the allocative position of farmers by changing the relative prices of inputs and outputs; or they can attempt to alter the technical production frontier by raising the productivity of existing resources. When economists speak of price versus technology policies, it is this analytical distinction that they have in mind.

Price policies are nowadays regarded with suspicion by economists. This includes institutional interventions (e.g. marketing boards or state credit agencies) that seek to cause allocative rather than technical changes in farm output. There are several reasons for this anti-price-policy stance, aside from the wide-spread observation of practical implementation failures:

(a) farm households are observed to be highly responsive to relative prices, and they do not require the state to help them in this;

(b) state prices may begin by being broadly related to underlying supply and demand, but they can quickly diverge from this, resulting in unpredicted surpluses or shortages, mistaken resource allocation, and adverse budgetary and trade effects;

(c) state institutions established to implement or support price policies are prone to a range of commonplace bureaucratic defects, such as low salaries, poor motivation, inflexible rules, lack of back-up equipment and resources, and pervasive management improprieties.

The agricultural policies described in this book are reviewed in the following paragraphs with reference in particular to the two oppositions of state versus market and allocative versus technical impacts.

Price policy

Farm output prices perform the three functions of allocating farm resources between outputs, affecting income distribution especially between producers and consumers of staple foods, and affecting the rate of return to capital in agriculture compared to other sectors of the economy. Governments have sought to influence all these roles, and have often been observed in practice to depress farm prices in order to favour domestic industry and to keep urban consumers happy.

The least successful types of price policy have been those that have imposed fixed farm-gate prices on farmers, necessitating state control of marketing channels in order to be effective. These have been prone to (i) cumulative divergence between state fixed prices and the underlying demand and supply situation, (ii) mistakes in relative prices between crops, resulting in shortages of some outputs and surpluses of others, (iii) neglect of inflation, resulting in declining farm-gate prices in real terms,

(iv) cumulative divergence between domestic and world prices, and (v) extensive marketing system failures (see also below).

More successful have been policies that seek to stabilise prices for just a few key crops, by the setting of floor prices and ceiling prices supported by state purchases or sales. Such policies can be costly to implement, however, especially if the entire burden of smoothing out inter-seasonal or inter-year fluctuations in output is placed on the domestic market. The conclusions for price policy are:

(a) intervention should be restricted to a few crops of over-riding strategic importance such as the staple food(s) of the country;

(b) intervention should be restricted to stabilisation around a long-run trend indicated by the moving average trend of the world price for that commodity;

(c) stabilisation for food crops should make flexible use of imports to supplement domestic buffer stocks, thus reducing the required size of public stocks, minimising storage losses, and reducing the scale of domestic procurement by state agencies.

Marketing policy

Governments have a tendency to intervene massively in agricultural marketing channels, especially if they are also trying to fix farm-gate producer prices. While the reasons for this intervention are ostensibly to solve defects in the working of private trade, they are quite often to try to exclude an ethnic minority from agricultural marketing or to enable the state to generate more resources for its own maintenance.

The least successful form of marketing intervention has been the creation of monopoly marketing parastatals. This is closely followed by state-sponsored cooperatives imposed on farmers from above. Parastatals have proved prone to (i) high overhead unit costs, (ii) duplication of infrastructural facilities across crops, (iii) poor capacity utilisation of godowns, transport, and processing facilities, (iv) unsuitable tasks and functions, (v) residual determination of producer prices, and (vi) the usual array of state institution failures already mentioned elsewhere.

Amongst the policies covered in this book, marketing is perhaps the most susceptible to withdrawal of direct participation by the state, and replacement by indirect encouragement of a diverse and competitive private trade. An important residual role for the state is to provide price monitoring and market information services of a kind that the private trade would not supply.

Input policy

State intervention in input markets has taken two main forms: price subsidies on key purchased inputs such as fertilizer, and state delivery systems to replace private trade in farm inputs.

Economists continue to debate the wisdom of input subsidies, though in practice many governments have been forced to abandon them under structural adjustment programmes. In some countries, fertilizer subsidies have been successful in causing rapid and widespread increases in fertilizer use. However, this has been contingent on unlimited supply being available at the subsidised price, for otherwise rationing occurs with many detrimental side-effects. Moreover, a distinction must be made between the high output gains of increased fertilizer use under irrigated conditions for rice and wheat, and the much less dramatic gains to be made in resource-poor agricultural environments.

State delivery systems for variable inputs have been prone to the same kinds of defect as those observed for parastatal marketing agents. The quantity and timeliness of supply are critical features. Methods for improving the delivery of variable inputs, and for encouraging their more rapid uptake by farmers, remain unresolved in the literature. An unavoidable role for the state exists in the market regulation of agricultural chemicals, which can be hazardous to health or damaging to the environment. In addition, the use of new inputs by farmers requires the transmission of accurate information in order to avoid mistakes and waste of scarce resources.

Credit policy

The traditional approach to credit has been for the state to undertake to supply credit to farmers, usually at subsidised rates of interest. State credit provision is a response to the absence of fully formed rural financial markets, and this situation is caused in turn by the high costs of acquiring information about borrowers (transaction costs) and lack of borrower collateral. The activities of moneylenders do not constitute a market in loanable funds, because each moneylender transaction is unique and there is no market rate of interest.

State credit provision has been criticised on several grounds, the main drift of the argument being that it fails in the end to create sustainable rural financial markets. Credit has tended to be supply led, to depend on external funds, to neglect savings, to neglect fungibility, to rely on rationing, to experience low loan repayments, and so on. State credit institutions are no less prone than marketing parastatals or input delivery agencies to a range of commonplace bureaucratic failings.

The emphasis of the credit policy debate has been on the creation of viable credit institutions, whether these are public, private, or a mixture of both. Experimentation in institutional forms is encouraged, and several case studies exist of creative solutions to the problem of providing sustainable savings and credit facilities for poor farmers and landless labourers. Essential components are the use of economic levels of interest rate – reflecting the opportunity cost of funds – and the encouragement of savings as well as loans.

Mechanisation policy

Farm mechanisation in developing countries has in the past been characterised more by the lack of coherent policy, than by coordinated state action. In many of the large developing countries that were undergoing import-substituting industrialisation in the 1960s and 1970s, rapid rates of tractorisation occurred as the result of price distortions created for other purposes (e.g. overvalued exchange rates, subsidised credit), or in order to support domestic machinery manufacturers.

The key issue in farm mechanisation is that prices should fully reflect social opportunity costs. The pace of mechanisation should reflect true underlying changes in resource scarcities in agriculture, not the artificial lowering of machinery prices resulting in the inefficient substitution of machines for labour. Many studies have demonstrated that the purported output gains of mechanised farming are more imaginary than real. Mechanisation often results in the straight substitution of capital for labour with negligible or negative changes in overall resource productivity.

However, the income distribution effects of mechanisation are far from negligible. Income flows to rural labour become income flows to urban machinery manufacturers, and dramatic changes in farm size distribution may take place as machinery owners seek to adapt farm sizes to machine capacity.

The role of the state with respect to mechanisation is ultimately relatively minor. Two valid functions are, however, first, to ensure that machinery and equipment is not made artificially cheap by the operation of other policies (e.g. credit policy), and, second, to encourage the development of a much wider range of mechanical technologies at the labour-using end of the range of technical alternatives.

Land reform policy

The treatment of land reform in this book emphasises the unique character of land reform compared to other price and technology policies. This uniqueness is found in the multiple social and economic roles of land as a resource. Full scale land reform involves dispossessing landowners of their private property in law, and redistributing this land for improved social equality and higher agricultural production.

Land reform tends to occur in discrete and unpredictable jumps in the history of a country. It depends on a conjunction of political forces and pressures that rarely come together with sufficient strength to carry through a systematic change in the ownership distribution of land. Economists have an ambivalent view of land reform. On the one hand, they recognise both efficiency and equity gains to be obtained from a more equal size distribution of farms. On the other hand, the violation of property rights involved in land reforms runs counter to the fundamental precepts of neoclassical economics.

The most effective land reforms appear to be those that create a freehold or leasehold small-farm structure as a result of the reform. Experiences with cooperative, communal, and state farms have not been encouraging, though they have worked moderately well in some places. The central economic point is whether economies of scale can be achieved in larger units of agricultural production. To date, the existence of such economies remains doubtful and unproven from available evidence.

Aside from full-scale land reform, governments can influence the access of farmers to land in many different ways, and some of these are ongoing initiatives rather than major political events. The institution of freehold land ownership in place of previous village or community land allocation is a continuing process in many countries, and it is a process rather prone to abuse by the richer and more powerful members of rural communities.

Research policy

Research policy is about the generation and diffusion of new technology for farmers. As such, it comes closest to being concerned exclusively with technical rather than allocative efficiency at the farm level. A strong case exists for viewing agricultural research as a public good to be funded and conducted under state or international auspices.

The returns to state investment in agricultural research appear to be high, though experience in developing countries is uneven in this respect.

As for several other agricultural policies, there is a contrast between Asia and Africa in this regard. In general, it is a mistake to infer lessons from the Green Revolution in Asia and apply them to entirely different agricultural environments.

Research policy has undergone major changes in fashion over the past two decades, although the degree to which this has changed the success rate of research projects remains to be assessed. Strong emphasis is placed on participation and interaction with farmers, exemplified by the increasing popularity of farming systems research (FSR), and the closely allied ideas of farmer first research (FFR). These concepts and procedures mirror what has always been good research practice by keen and inquisitive agricultural scientists. It is wrong to think that they are entirely new, and they can perhaps be more accurately interpreted as a counterbalance to tendencies for research to become more office and laboratory bound, especially when insufficient resources are allocated for field visits.

The overall validity of state and donor funding to agricultural research is not in doubt. However, the contemporary focus of external aid donors towards funding massive FSR projects within developing country research systems raises issues of sustainability similar to those that arise in the context of donor-dependent credit institutions.

Irrigation policy

The role of the state towards irrigation varies between private tubewell irrigation and public canal irrigation. Private tubewell irrigation raises issues of appropriate technology and relative prices similar to those that arise for mechanisation. Canal irrigation is a public good, and its operation involves certain types of market failure that in practice rule out organisation along private lines. The necessity for state involvement in the management of large-scale canal irrigation is accepted, even if sometimes reluctantly, by most economists.

The chief issues in canal irrigation are how to improve the recurrent operation and maintenance (O & M) of canal schemes, and how to make farmers more aware of the social opportunity cost of the water they utilise.

Irrigation authorities are prone to all the same institutional failures as marketing or credit authorities. It is possible that these can be overcome by making them more accountable to their clients, the farmers. At the same time, farmers should meet the full O & M costs of water provision. The volumetric pricing of water to individual farmers remains infeasible on technical and cost grounds. However, scope exists for institutional experimentation in making the income of water management agencies dependent on area service fees paid by farmers, with mechanisms for increasing the interdependence and trust between both parties.

Women and policies

Agricultural policies have traditionally ignored the gender dimension in their design and implementation. Policies may be successful in their own terms yet have negative side-effects on the material welfare of women. Sometimes policies fail due to the neglect of gender issues in their formulation.

This book suggests a framework for organising ideas about women and agricultural policies. The main purpose of such a framework is to provide an organising principle by which women can be taken properly into account in the design of policies. The six components of this framework are:

(a) livelihood status of the farm or rural household
(a) time allocation between men and women
(b) control over resources between men and women
(d) control over income between men and women
(e) post-harvest and marketing activities of women
(f) prices and markets for labour, inputs, and outputs

Policies vary in their potential for taking into account the rights and needs of women. Price policy has low potential in this regard since output prices are either market prices involving no intervention, or are prices set countrywide for all market participants, women or men.

Input policy and mechanisation policy represent intermediate potential for taking gender into account, with the main issue in input policy being provision of information to women on inputs when it is women who are chiefly responsible for their application on the farm. Policies with high potential for taking into account the separate needs of women and men are marketing policy, credit policy, research policy, and irrigation policy. A critical issue with respect to land policy is that women should not lose customary and hereditary land rights when freehold land registration occurs, whether or not this involves the larger issue of land reform.

Food policy and food security

The agricultural policies that form the core of this book are mainly orientated towards the domestic production of agricultural commodities, of which food production is a major but not the only component. This orientation towards production is not surprising, since the choice was made to structure the book around the concept of policy influences on the peasant farm as a production system.

Food policy as an integrated set of concerns about food and nutrition in developing countries differs from this emphasis on domestic production. Food policy concerns both food availability and the ability of people to obtain access to enough food. Food policy is defined in the book as the integration of state actions affecting the supply, distribution, and consumption of food in order to ensure continuity of access to enough food for all the people in a country.

The main departure for the contemporary approach to food policy is the distinction between food availability and food entitlement. There may be sufficient food in terms of aggregate supply, but social groups, households, or individuals may not be able to obtain enough food due to lack of command over food. The term food entitlement focuses attention on this problem of command over food. It also shifts the centre of food policy discussion away from aggregate food availability towards the disaggregated and variable capability of people to acquire enough food in order to maintain acceptable minimum levels of nutrition.

The concept of food security is useful for capturing these ideas about food entitlement. A widely accepted definition of food security is . . . 'access by all people at all times to enough food for an active healthy life'. Food insecurity is lack of access to enough food, and we can distinguish between chronic food insecurity, reflecting a persistent inability to acquire enough food, and transitory food insecurity, reflecting a temporary decline in a household's food entitlement.

In accordance with these changes in perception about food problems, the orientation of food policy instruments has undergone changes in emphasis. The previous concerns with adequate total food supply and food price stability remain valid, although greater use of world markets to achieve these aims is advocated nowadays, compared to the previous preoccupation with domestic food self-sufficiency. Much more attention is given nowadays to the consumption side of food security, and particularly to methods for increasing the command over food of people who are vulnerable to inadequate nutrition.

Instruments on the consumption side of food policy include general and targeted food subsidies, as well as employment creation and income generation schemes. Targeted food policy interventions may be subdivided into administrative targeting (bureaucratic decisions concerning eligible recipients) and self-regulating targeting (where the population that is targeted is self-defined by its geographical location, food consumption patterns, or socio-economic status). The current preference in the food policy literature is for targeted interventions over general interventions, and for self-regulating over administrative forms of targeting.

Conclusion

Agricultural policy is a complex matter. The way it is conducted varies tremendously across the developing countries. The scope and form of state controls owe as much to history and politics as they do to economics. At the academic level it is subject to swings of fashion. At the level of aid donors and international agencies these swings are reflected in changes in their allocation of grants and loans.

This book has tried to avoid taking a dogmatic position with respect to appropriate types and levels of state intervention in the agricultural economy. Policies sometimes speak for themselves in that their negative or damaging effects are plain for all to see. It does not take an economist to recognise a disaster when it is staring one in the face.

The main conclusion of this book is that policies vary in the degree to which it is feasible or advisable for the state to step back and let the market go. Moreover, the same category of policy is likely to vary in its susceptibility to deregulation across different countries, at different levels of development, and with different kinds of economic problems.

Ultimately the market versus state debate is not just about the economic superiority of free markets. Policies mean state controls, and the greater the interventionist scope of policies, the wider and deeper the degree of state control over people's lives and livelihoods. Many policies could be improved not solely by withdrawing the state in a purely economic sense, but by making the agencies of policy genuinely accountable to the people they are supposed to assist. Policies should not serve the ends of monumental state bureaucracies; policies should serve the people.

References

Abbott, J.C. (1987). *Agricultural Marketing Enterprises for the Developing World.* Cambridge University Press.

Abercrombie, K.C. (1972). Agricultural Mechanisation and Employment in Latin America. *International Labour Review*, **106**, No. 1.

Adams, D.W. (1988). The Conundrum of Successful Credit Projects in Floundering Rural Financial Markets. *Economic Development and Cultural Change*, **36**, No. 2.

Adams, D.W. & Graham, D.H. (1981). A Critique of Traditional Agricultural Credit Projects and Policies. *Journal of Development Economics*, **8**.

Adams, D.W., Graham, D.H. & von Pischke, J.D. (eds) (1984). *Undermining Rural Development with Cheap Credit.* Boulder, Colorado: Westview Press.

Adams, D.W. & Nehmann, G.I. (1979). Borrowing Costs and Demand for Rural Credit. *Journal of Development Studies*, **15**, No. 2.

Adams, D.W. & Vogel, R.C. (1986). Rural Financial Markets in Low-Income Countries: Recent Controversies and Lessons. *World Development*, **14**, No. 4.

Agarwal, B. (1981). Agricultural Mechanisation and Labour Use: A Disaggregated Approach. *International Labour Review*, **120**, No. 1, January.

Agarwal, B. (1985). Rural Women and High Yielding Rice Technology in India. In *Women in Rice Farming*, International Rice Research Institute (IRRI), Ch. 17. Aldershot: Gower.

Agarwal, B. (1988). Who Sows? Who Reaps? Women and Land Rights in India. *Journal of Peasant Studies*, **15**.

Ahmed, I. & Ruttan, V.W. (eds) (1988). *Generation and Diffusion of Agricultural Innovations: the Role of Institutional Factors.* Aldershot: Gower.

Ahmed, R.U. (1987). Structure and Dynamics of Fertilizer Subsidy: The Case of Bangladesh. *Food Policy*, February.

Ahmed, R.U. (1988a). Pricing Principles and Public Intervention in Domestic Markets. In *Agricultural Price Policy for Developing Countries,* eds. J.W. Mellor and R.U. Ahmed, Ch. 4. Baltimore: Johns Hopkins.

Ahmed, R.U. (1988b). Rice Price Stabilization and Food Security in Bangladesh. *World Development*, **16**, No. 9.

Ahmed, R.U. (1989). Effective Costs of Rural Loans In Bangladesh. *World Development*, **17**, No. 3.

Ahmed, R.U. & Rustagi, N. (1985). *Agricultural Marketing and Price Incentives: A Comparative Study of African and Asian Countries.* Washington: International Food Policy Research Institute.

Anderson, J.R., Hazell, P.B.R. & Evans, L.T. (1987). Variability of Cereal Yields: Sources of Change and Implications for Agricultural Research and Policy. *Food Policy*, August.

Anderson, J.R. & Scandizzo, P.L. (1984). Food Risk and the Poor. *Food Policy*, **9**, No. 1.

Arhin, K., Hesp, P. & van der Laan, L. (eds) (1985). *Marketing Boards in Tropical Africa*. London: Kegan Paul International.

Ashby, J.A. (1986). Methodology for the Participation of Small Farmers in the Design of On-Farm Trials. *Agricultural Administration*, No. 22.

Ashby, J.A. (1987). The Effects of Different Types of Farmer Participation on the Management of On-Farm Trials. *Agricultural Administration and Extension*, No. 25.

Askari, H. & Cummings, J.T. (1976). *Agricultural Supply Response: a Survey of the Econometric Evidence*. Praeger.

Atkins, F. (1988). Land Reform: A Failure of Neoclassical Theorization? *World Development*, **16**, No. 8.

Bale, M.D. & Lutz, E. (1981). Price Distortions in Agriculture and their Effects: An International Comparison. *American Journal of Agricultural Economics*, **63**, No. 1.

Barker, R. & Hayami, Y. (1976). Price Support Versus Input Subsidy for Food Self-Sufficiency in Developing Countries. *American Journal of Agricultural Economics*, November.

Barker, R., Herdt, R.W. & Rose, B. (1985). *The Rice Economy of Asia*. Washington D.C.: Resources for the Future.

Barraclough, S.L. & Domike, A.L. (1970). Agrarian Structure in Seven Latin American Countries. In *Agrarian Problems and Peasant Movements in Latin America*, ed. R. Stavenhagen. New York: Doubleday.

Bates, R.H. (1981). *Markets and States in Tropical Africa*. University of California Press.

Beckman, B. (1988). The Post-Colonial State: Crisis and Reconstruction. *IDS Bulletin*, **19**, No. 4.

Begum, S. (1985). Women and Technology: Rice Processing in Bangladesh. In *Women in Rice Farming*, International Rice Research Institute (IRRI), Ch. 13. Aldershot: Gower.

Beneria, L. (1979). Reproduction, Production and the Sexual Division of Labour. *Cambridge Journal of Economics*, No. 3.

Benor, D. & Harrison, J.Q. (1977). *Agricultural Extension: The Training and Visit System*. Washington D.C.: World Bank.

Berger, M. (1989). Giving Women Credit: The Strengths and Limitations of Credit as a Tool for Alleviating Poverty. *World Development*, **17**, No. 7.

Berry, R.A. & Cline, W.R. (1979). *Agrarian Structure and Productivity in Developing Countries*. Baltimore: Johns Hopkins.

Bhagwati, J.N. (1982). Directly Unproductive, Profit-Seeking (DUP) Activities. *Journal of Political Economy*, **90**, No. 5.

Bhatt, V.V. (1988). On Financial Innovations and Credit Market Evolution. *World Development*, **16**, No. 2.

Biggs, S.D. (1984). Awkward but Common Themes in Agricultural Policy. In *Room for Manoeuvre: An Exploration of Public Policy in Agriculture and Rural Development*, eds. E.J. Clay and B.B. Schaffer, Ch. 5. London: Heinemann.

Biggs, S.D. (1985). A Farming System Approach: Some Unanswered Questions. *Agricultural Administration*, No. 18.

Biggs, S.D. (1990). A Multiple Source of Innovation Model of Agricultural Research and Technology Promotion. *World Development*, **18**, No. 11.

Biggs, S.D. & Clay, E.J. (1981). Sources of Innovation in Agricultural Technology. *World Development*, **9**, No. 4.

Biggs, S.D. & Clay, E.J. (1988). Generation and Diffusion of Agricultural Technology: Theories and Experiences. In *Generation and Diffusion of Agricultural Innovations: the Role of Institutional Factors*, eds. I. Ahmed and V.W. Ruttan, Ch. 2. Aldershot: Gower.

Biggs, S.D. & Griffith, J. (1987). Irrigation in Bangladesh. In *Macro-Policies for Appropriate Technology in Developing Countries*, ed. F. Stewart, Ch. 3. Boulder, Colorado: Westview Press.

Binswanger, H.P. (1978). *The Economics of Tractors in South Asia*. New York: Agricultural Development Council.

Binswanger, H.P. (1984). *Agricultural Mechanization: A Comparative Historical Perspective*. World Bank Staff Working Paper No. 673. Washington D.C.: World Bank.

Bohm, P. (1987). Second Best. In *The New Palgrave: A Dictionary of Economics*, Vol. 4, eds. J. Eatwell, M. Milgate and P. Newman. Macmillan.

Bowen, R.L. & Young, R.A. (1986). Appraising Alternatives for Allocating and Cost Recovery for Irrigation Water in Egypt. *Agricultural Economics*, 1, 35–52.

Boyce, J.K. (1988). Technological and Institutional Alternatives in Asian Rice Irrigation. *Economic and Political Weekly*, March 26th.

Boyce, J.K. & Evenson, R.E. (1975). *Agricultural Research & Extension Programs*. New York: Agricultural Development Council.

Braverman, A. & Guasch, J.L. (1986). Rural Credit Markets and Institutions in Developing Countries: Lessons for Policy Analysis from Practice and Modern Theory. *World Development*, 14, No. 10/11.

Brett, E.A. (1986). State Power and Economic Efficiency: Explaining Political Failure in Africa. *IDS Bulletin*, 17, No. 1.

Brett, E.A. (ed.) (1988). Adjustment and the State: The Problem of Administrative Reform. *IDS Bulletin*, 19, No. 4, October.

Bromley, D.W. (1989). Property Relations and Economic Development: The Other Land Reform. *World Development*, 17, No. 6.

Buvinic, M. (1986). Projects for Women in the Third World: Explaining their Misbehaviour. *World Development*, 14, No. 5.

Byerlee, D. & Collinson, M. (1980). *Planning Technologies Appropriate to Farmers – Concepts and Procedures*. Mexico: CIMMYT.

Byerlee, D., Harrington, L. and Winkelmann, D.L. (1982). Farming Systems Research: Issues in Research Strategy and Technology Design. *American Journal of Agricultural Economics*, 64, No. 5.

Carney, J.A. (1988). Struggles Over Crop Rights and Labour Within Contract Farming Households in a Gambian Irrigated Rice Project. *Journal of Peasant Studies*, 15.

Carruthers, I. & Clark, C. (1981). *The Economics of Irrigation*. Liverpool: Liverpool University Press.

Chambers, R. (1982). Guiding Research Toward Technologies to Meet Regional Rural Needs. *Development Digest*, XX, No. 2.

Chambers, R. (1988). *Managing Canal Irrigation*. Cambridge: Cambridge University Press.

Chambers, R. & Ghildyal, B.P. (1985). Agricultural Research for Resource-Poor Farmers: The Farmer-First-and-Last Model. *Agricultural Administration*, No. 20.

Chambers, R. & Jiggins, J. (1987). Agricultural Research for Resource Poor Farmers: Transfer of Technology and Farming Systems Research. *Agricultural Administration*, No. 27.

Chambers, R., Pacey, A. & Thrupp, L.A. (eds) (1989). *Farmer First – Farmer Innovation and Agricultural Research*. London: Intermediate Technology Publications.

Chipande, G.H.R. (1987). Innovation Adoption among Female-headed Households: The Case of Malawi. *Development and Change*, **18**.

Christiansen, R.E. (ed.) (1989). *Privatization.* Special Issue of *World Development*, **17**, No. 5.

Clay, E.J. & Schaffer, B.B. (1984). *Room for Manoeuvre: An Exploration of Public Policy in Agriculture and Rural Development*. London: Heinemann.

Clayton, E.S. (1983). *Agriculture, Poverty and Freedom in Developing Countries*. London: Macmillan.

Colander, D.C. (ed.) (1984). *Neo-Classical Political Economy: An Analysis of Rent-Seeking and DUP Activities*. Cambridge MA: Ballinger.

Collinson, M. (1981). A Low Cost Approach to Understanding Small Farmers. *Agricultural Administration*, No. 8.

Collinson, M. (1988). The Development of African Farming Systems: Some Personal Views. *Agricultural Adminstration and Extension*, No. 29.

Colman, D. & Young, T. (1989). *Principles of Agricultural Economics.* Cambridge: Cambridge University Press.

Cramb, R.A. & Wills, I.R. (1990). The Role of Traditional Institutions in Rural Development: Community-Based Land Tenure and Government Land Policy in Sarawak, Malaysia. *World Development*, **18**, No. 3.

Crow, B. (1989). Plain Tales from the Rice Trade: Indications of Vertical Integration in Foodgrain Markets in Bangladesh. *Journal of Peasant Studies*, **16**, No. 2.

de Janvry, A. (1975). The Political Economy of Rural Development in Latin America: An Interpretation. *American Journal of Agricultural Economics*, **57**, No. 3.

de Janvry, A. (1981a). *The Agrarian Question and Reformism in Latin America*. London: Johns Hopkins.

de Janvry, A. (1981b). The Role of Land Reform in Economic Development: Policies and Politics. *American Journal of Agricultural Economics*, **63**, No. 2.

Dearlove, J. (1987). Economists on the State. *IDS Bulletin*, **18**, No. 3.

Dearlove, J. & White, G. (eds) (1987). The Retreat of the State? *IDS Bulletin*, **18**, No. 3.

Deere, C.D. (1985). Rural Women and State Policy: The Latin American Agrarian Reform Experience. *World Development*, **13**, No. 9.

Desai, G. (1988). Policy for Rapid Growth in Use of Modern Agricultural Inputs. In *Agricultural Price Policy for Developing Countries*, eds. J.W. Mellor and R.U. Ahmed, Ch. 12. Baltimore: Johns Hopkins.

Dey, J. (1981). Gambian Women: Unequal Partners in Rice Development Projects? *Journal of Development Studies*, **17**.

Dey, J. (1985). Women in African Rice Farming Systems. In *Women in Rice Farming*, International Rice Research Institute (IRRI), Ch. 23. Aldershot: Gower.

Donald, G. (ed.) (1976). *Credit for Small Farmers in Developing Countries*. Boulder, Colorado: Westview Press.

Donaldson, G. (1984). *Food Security and the Role of the Grain Trade.* World Bank Reprint Series, No. 304.

Dorner, P. (ed.) (1971). *Land Reform in Latin America: Issues and Cases*. Madison: University of Wisconsin.

Dorner, P. & Kanel, D. (1971). The Economic Case for Land Reform: Employment, Income Distribution and Productivity. In *Land Reform in Latin America: Issues and Cases*, ed. P. Dorner. Madison: University of Wisconsin.

Eckstein, S., Donald, G., Horton, D. & Carroll, T. (1978). *Land Reform in Latin America: Bolivia, Chile, Mexico, Peru and Venezuela*. World Bank Staff Working Paper No. 275. Washington D.C.: World Bank.

Egger, P. (1986). Banking for the Rural Poor: Lessons from some Innovative Savings and Credit Schemes. *ILO Review*, **125**, No. 4.

Eicher, C.K. & Staatz, J.M. (eds) (1990). *Agricultural Development in the Third World*, 2nd edn. Baltimore: Johns Hopkins.

Ellis, F. (1982). Agricultural Price Policy in Tanzania. *World Development*, **10**, No. 4.

Ellis, F. (1983a). Agricultural Marketing and Peasant-State Transfers in Tanzania. *Journal of Peasant Studies*, **10**, No. 4.

Ellis, F. (1983b). *Las Transnacionales del Banano en Centroamerica*. San Jose, Costa Rica: EDUCA.

Ellis, F. (1984). Relative Agricultural Prices and the Urban Bias Model: A Comparative Analysis of Tanzania and Fiji. *Journal of Development Studies*, **20**, No. 3.

Ellis, F. (1988a). *Peasant Economics: Farm Households and Agrarian Development*. Cambridge: Cambridge University Press.

Ellis, F. (1988b). Tanzania. In *Agricultural Pricing Policy in Africa*, ed. C. Harvey, Ch. 3. London: Macmillan.

Ellis, F. (1988c). Small-Farm Sugar Production in Fiji: Employment and Distribution Aspects. *IDS Bulletin*, **19**, No. 2.

Ellis, F. (1989). Future Rice Strategy in Indonesia: Rice Self-Sufficiency and Rice Price Stability. *Indonesian Food Journal*, **1**, No. 1.

Ellis, F. (1990). The Rice Market and its Management in Indonesia. *IDS Bulletin*, **21**, No. 3.

Evenson, R.E. (1981). Benefits and Obstacles to Appropriate Agricultural Technology. *Annals of the American Academy of Political and Social Science*, No. 458.

Evenson, R.E. & Flores, P.M. (1978). Social Returns to Rice Research. In *Economic Consequences of the New Rice Technology*, International Rice Research Institute (IRRI), pp. 243–65. Los Banos, Philippines.

Ezekiel, H. (1988). An Approach to a Food Aid Strategy. *World Development*, **16**, No. 11.

Falcon, W.P. *et al.* (1987). The World Food and Hunger Problem: Changing Perspectives and Possibilities, 1974–84. In *Food Policy: Integrating Supply, Distribution, and Consumption*, eds. J.P. Gittinger, J. Leslie and C. Hoisington, Ch. 1, pp. 15–38. Baltimore: Johns Hopkins.

FAO (1986). *The World Banana Economy 1970–1984: Structure, Performance and Prospects*. Economic and Social Development Paper, No. 57. Rome: FAO.

Farrington, J. & Martin, A. (1988). *Farmer Participation in Agricultural Research: A Review of Concepts and Practices*. Overseas Development Institute, Agricultural Administration Unit, Occasional Paper No. 9.

Feder, E. (1970). Counterreform. In *Agrarian Problems and Peasant Movements in Latin America*, ed. R. Stavenhagen. New York: Doubleday.

Feinerman, E. (1988). Groundwater Management: Efficiency and Equity Considerations. *Agricultural Economics*, **2**, 1–18.

Fry, M.J. (1982). Models of Financially Repressed Developing Economies. *World Development*, **10**, 731–50.

Geertz, C. (1980). Organisation of the Balinese *Subak*. In *Irrigation and Agricultural Development in Asia*, ed. E.W. Coward, pp. 70–90. Ithaca: Cornell University Press.

Ghai, D., Khan, A.R., Lee, E. & Radwan, S. (1979). *Agrarian Systems and Rural Development*. London: Macmillan.

Gill, G.J. (1983). Mechanised Land Preparation, Productivity and Employment in Bangladesh. *Journal of Development Studies*, **19**, No. 3.

Gittinger, J.P. (1982). *Economic Analysis of Agricultural Projects*, 2nd edn. Baltimore: Johns Hopkins University Press.

Gittinger, J.P., Leslie, J. & Hoisington, C. (eds) (1987). *Food Policy: Integrating Supply, Distribution, and Consumption*. Baltimore: Johns Hopkins.

Goetz, S. & Weber, M.T. (1986). Fundamentals of Price Analysis in Developing Countries' Food Systems. *MSU International Development Papers*, Working Paper No. 29.

Gonzalez-Vega, C. (1977). Interest Rate Restrictions and Income Distribution. *American Journal of Agricultural Economics*, **59**, 973–6.

Goodell, G.E. (1984). Bugs, Bunds, Banks and Bottlenecks: Organizational Contradictions in the New Rice Technology. *Economic Development and Cultural Change,* **33**, No. 1.

Griffin, K. (1979). *The Political Economy of Agrarian Change: An Essay on the Green Revolution*, 2nd edn. London: Macmillan.

Grown, C.A. & Sebstad, J. (1989). Introduction: Toward a Wider Perspective on Women's Employment. *World Development*, **17**, No. 7.

Hakimian, H. (1990). *Labour Transfer and Economic Development: Theoretical Perspectives and Case-Studies from Iran*. Hemel Hempstead: Harvester Wheatsheaf.

Hanger, E.J. & Moris, J. (1973). Women and the Household Economy. In *MWEA: An Irrigated Rice Settlement in Kenya*, eds. R. Chambers and J. Moris, pp. 209–44. Munich: Weltforum Verlag.

Harrigan, J. (1988). Malawi: The Impact of Pricing Policy on Smallholder Agriculture 1971–1988. *Development Policy Review*, **6**, 415–33.

Harriss, B. (1979). There is Method in My Madness: Or is it Vice Versa? Measuring Agricultural Market Performance. *Food Research Institute Studies*, **XVII**, No. 2.

Harvey, C. (ed.) (1988). *Agricultural Pricing Policy in Africa*. London: Macmillan.

Harvey, C., Jacobs, J. & Schaffer, B. (1979). *Rural Employment and Administration in the Third World*. Saxon House.

Hedley, D.D. & Tabor, S.R. (1989). Fertilizer in Indonesian Agriculture: the Subsidy Issue. *Agricultural Economics*, **3**, 49–68.

Heinemann, E. & Biggs, S.D. (1985). Farming Systems Research: An Evolutionary Approach to Implementation. *Journal of Agricultural Economics*, **XXXVI**, No. 1.

Helleiner, G.K. (1975). Smallholder Decision Making: Tropical African Evidence. In *Agriculture in Development Theory*, ed. L.G. Reynolds, Ch. 2. London: Yale University Press.

Herdt, R.W. & Anderson, J.R. (1987). The Contribution of the CGIAR Centers to World Agricultural Research. In *Policy for Agricultural Research*, eds. V.W. Ruttan and C.E. Pray, Ch. 2. Boulder, Colorado: Westview Press.

Herring, R.J. (1983). *Land to the Tiller: The Political Economy of Agrarian Reform in South Asia*. New Haven: Yale University Press.

Heytens, P.J. (1986). Testing Market Integration. *Food Research Institute Studies*, **20**, No. 1.

Holtzman, J.S. (1986). *Rapid Reconnaissance Guidelines For Agricultural Marketing and Food System Research in Developing Countries*. Michigan State University, International Development Working Paper No. 30.

Hoos, S. (ed.) (1979). *Agricultural Marketing Boards: An International Perspective*. Cambridge, MA: Ballinger.

Horton, D. (1986). Assessing the Impact of International Agricultural Research and Development Programs. *World Development*, **14**, No. 4.

Hossain, M. (1988). *Credit for Alleviation of Rural Poverty: The Grameen Bank in Bangladesh*. International Food Policy Research Institute, Research Report 65, February.

Howell, J. (ed.) (1980). *Borrowers and Lenders: Rural Financial Markets and Institutions in Developing Countries*. London: ODI.

Hyden, G. (1980). *Beyond Ujamaa in Tanzania: Underdevelopment and an Uncaptured Peasantry*. London: Heinemann.

Hyden, G. (1983). *No Shortcuts to Progress: African Development Management in Perspective*. London: Heinemann.

Indonesia, BIMAS (1987). *Pelestarian Swasembada Pangan Pada Tahun 2000 Dan Seterusnya*. Jakarta: BIMAS Sekretariat.

International Rice Research Institute (IRRI) (1983). *Consequences of Small-Farm Mechanisation*. Los Banos, Philippines: IRRI.

International Rice Research Institute (IRRI) (1985). *Women in Rice Farming*. Aldershot: Gower.

International Rice Research Institute (IRRI) (1986). *Small Farm Equipment for Developing Countries*. Los Banos, Philippines: IRRI.

International Rice Research Institute (IRRI) (1988). *Filipino Women in Rice Farming Systems*. Laguna, Philippines: IRRI.

Jabara, C.L. (1985). Agricultural Pricing Policy in Kenya. *World Development*, **13**, No. 5.

Jackson, R.H. & Rosberg, C.G. (1984). Personal Rule: Theory and Practice in Africa. *Comparative Politics*, **16**, No. 4.

Jones, C.W. (1986). Intra-Household Bargaining in Response to the Introduction of New Crops: A Case Study from North Cameroon. In *Understanding Africa's Rural Household Farming Systems*, ed. J.L. Moock & B.N. Okigbo, Ch. 6. Boulder: Westview Press.

Jones, W.O. (1972). *Marketing Staple Food Crops in Tropical Africa*. New York, Cornell University Press.

Judd, M.A., Boyce, J.K. & Evenson, R.E. (1986). Investing in Agricultural Supply: The Determinants of Agricultural Research and Extension Investment. *Economic Development and Cultural Change*, **35**, No. 1. Also in *Policy for Agricultural Research*, eds. V.W. Ruttan and C.E. Pray, Ch. 1. Boulder, Colorado: Westview Press (1987).

Just, R.E., Hueth, D.L. & Schmitz, A. (1982). *Applied Welfare Economics and Public Policy*. Englewood Cliffs, New Jersey: Prentice Hall.

Kahlon, A.S. & Tyagi, D.S. (1983). *Agricultural Price Policy in India*. New Delhi: Allied Publishers.

Kandiyoti, D. (1990). Women and Rural Development Policies: The Changing Agenda. *Development and Change*, **21**, No. 1.

Killick, T. (1981). *Policy Economics: A Textbook of Applied Economics on Developing Countries*. London: Heinemann.

Killick, T. (1989). *A Reaction Too Far: Economic Theory and the Role of the State in Developing Countries*. Overseas Development Institute.

King, R. (1977). *Land Reform: A World Survey*. London: Bell & Sons.

Knudsen, O. & Nash, J. (1990). Domestic Price Stabilization Schemes in Developing Countries. *Economic Development and Cultural Change*, **38**, No. 3.

Koester, U. (1986). *Regional Cooperation to Improve Food Security in Southern and Eastern African Countries*. International Food Policy Research Institute, Research Report 53.

Krishna, R. (1967). Agricultural Price Policy and Economic Development. In *Agricultural Development and Economic Growth*, eds. H.M. Southworth and B.F. Johnston, Ch. 13. New York: Cornell.

Krishna, R. (1990). Price and Technology Policies. In *Agricultural Development in the Third World*, eds. C.K. Eicher and J.M. Staatz, Ch. 9, 2nd edn. Baltimore: Johns Hopkins.

Krishna, R. & Raychaudhuri, G.S. (1980). *Some Aspects of Wheat and Rice Price Policy in India*. World Bank Staff Working Paper No. 381. Washington D.C.: World Bank.

References

343

Krueger, A.O. (1974). The Political Economy of the Rent-Seeking Society. *American Economic Review*, **64**, No. 3.

Kumar, S.K. & Lipton, M. (eds) (1988). Current Issues in Food Security. *World Development*, **16**, No. 9.

Laidler, D. & Estrin, S. (1989). *Introduction to Microeconomics*, 3rd edn. Oxford: Philip Allan.

Lamb, G. & Muller, L. (1982). *Control, Accountability, and Incentives in a Successful Development Institution: The Kenya Tea Development Authority*. World Bank Staff Working Paper No. 550. Washington D.C.: World Bank.

Lehmann, D. (ed.) (1974). *Agrarian Reform and Agrarian Reformism: Studies of Peru, Chile, China and India*. London: Faber and Faber.

Lehmann, D. (1978). The Death of Land Reform: A Polemic. *World Development*, **6**, No. 3.

Lele, U.J. (1971). *Food Grain Marketing in India: Private Performance and Public Policy*. Ithaca, New York: Cornell University Press.

Lingard, J. (1984). Mechanisation of Small Rice Farms in the Philippines: Some Income Distribution Aspects. *Journal of Agricultural Economics*, **XXXV**, No. 3.

Lingard, J. & Sri Bagyo, A. (1983). The Impact of Agricultural Mechanisation on Production and Employment in Rice Areas of West Java. *Bulletin of Indonesian Economic Studies*, **XIX**, No. 1.

Lipton, M. (1974). Towards a Theory of Land Reform. In *Agrarian Reform and Agrarian Reformism: Studies in Peru, Chile, China and India*, ed. D. Lehmann. London: Faber and Faber.

Lipton, M. (1980). Farm Price Stabilisation in Underdeveloped Agricultures: Some Effects on Income Stability and Income Distribution. In *Unfashionable Economics*, ed. P. Streeten. London: Weidenfeld & Nicholson.

Low, A. (1986). *Agricultural Development in Southern Africa: Farm Household Theory & the Food Crisis*. London: James Currey.

Lutz, E. & Scandizzo, P.L. (1980). Price Distortions in Developing Countries: A Bias against Agriculture. *European Review of Agricultural Economics*, **7**.

MacPhail, F. & Bowles, P. (1989). Technical Change and Intra-Household Welfare: A Case Study of Irrigated Rice Production in South Sulawesi, Indonesia. *Journal of Development Studies*, **26**, No. 1.

Mars, T. & White, G. (eds) (1986). Developmental States and African Agriculture. *IDS Bulletin*, **17**, No. 1.

Maurya, D.M. (1989). The Innovative Approach of Indian Farmers. In *Farmer First – Farmer Innovation and Agricultural Research*, eds. R. Chambers, A. Pacey and L.A. Thrupp, pp. 9–14. London: Intermediate Technology Publications.

Maxwell, S. (1986). Farming Systems Research: Hitting a Moving Target. *World Development*, **14**, No. 1.

Maxwell, S. (ed.) (1990). Food Security in Developing Countries. *IDS Bulletin*, **21**, No. 3.

Maxwell, S. & Singer, H. (1979). Food Aid to Developing Countries: A Survey. *World Development*, **7**.

Maxwell, S. *et al.* (1990). Is Food Security Targeting Possible in Sub-Saharan Africa?: Evidence from North Sudan. *IDS Bulletin*, **21**, No. 3.

McCalla, A.F. & Josling, T.E. (1985). *Agricultural Policies and World Markets*. London: Macmillan.

McInerney, J.P. & Donaldson, G.F. (1975). *The Consequences of Farm Tractors in Pakistan*. World Bank Staff Working Paper No. 210. Washington D.C.: World Bank.

McKee, K. (1989). Microlevel Strategies for Supporting Livelihoods, Employment, and

344   *References*

Income Generation of Poor Women in the Third World: The Challenge of Significance. *World Development*, **17**, No. 7.

McKinnon, R.I. (1973). *Money and Capital in Economic Development.* Washington D.C.: Brookings Institution.

Mears, L.A. (1981). *The New Rice Economy of Indonesia.* Yogyakarta, Indonesia: Gadjah Mada University Press.

Mellor, J.W. (1966). *The Economics of Agricultural Development.* New York: Cornell University Press.

Mellor, J.W. (1968). The Functions of Agricultural Prices in Economic Development. *Indian Journal of Agricultural Economics*, No. 1.

Mellor, J.W. (1978). Food Price Policy and Income Distribution in Low-Income Countries. *Economic Development and Cultural Change*, No. 1.

Mellor, J.W. (1988a). Food Policy, Food Aid and Structural Adjustment Programmes. *Food Policy*, **13**, February.

Mellor, J.W. (1988b). Global Food Balances and Food Security. *World Development*, **16**, No. 9.

Mellor, J.W. & Ahmed, R.U. (1988). *Agricultural Price Policy for Developing Countries.* Baltimore: Johns Hopkins.

Mellor, J.W. & Johnston, B.F. (1984). The World Food Equation: Interrelations among Development, Employment, and Food Consumption. *Journal of Economic Literature*, Vol. 22, June.

Merrill-Sands, D. (1986). Farming Systems Research: Clarification of Terms and Concepts. *Experimental Agriculture*, **22**, 87–104.

Meyer, C.A. (1989). Agrarian Reform in the Dominican Republic: An Associative Solution to the Collective/Individual Dilemma. *World Development*, **17**, No. 8.

Mishan, E.J. (1988). *Cost–Benefit Analysis*, 4th edn. London: Unwin Hyman.

Monke, E.A. & Pearson, S.R. (1989). *The Policy Analysis Matrix for Agricultural Development.* Ithaca: Cornell University Press.

Moock, J.L. & Okigbo, B.N. (eds) (1986). *Understanding Africa's Rural Households and Farming Systems.* Boulder: Westview Press.

Moore, M. (1989). The Fruits and Fallacies of Neoliberalism: The Case of Irrigation Policy. *World Development*, **17**, No. 11.

Moris, J. (1987). Irrigation as a Privileged Solution in African Development. *Development Policy Review*, **5**, 99–123.

Moser, C.O.N. (1989). Gender Planning in the Third World: Meeting Practical and Strategic Gender Needs. *World Development*, **17**, No. 11.

Nakajima, C. (1986). *Subjective Equilibrium Theory of the Farm Household.* Amsterdam: Elsevier.

Newbery, D.M.G. & Stiglitz, J.E. (1981). *The Theory of Commodity Price Stabilization.* Oxford: Oxford University Press.

Nguyen, D.T. & Martinez-Salvidar, M.L. (1979). The Effects of Land Reform on Agricultural Production, Employment and Income Distribution: A Statistical Study of Mexican States, 1959–69. *Economic Journal*, **89**.

Norton, G.W., Ganoza, V.G. & Pomareda, C. (1987). Potential Benefits of Agricultural Research and Extension in Peru. *American Journal of Agricultural Economics*, May.

O'Mara, G.T. (ed.) (1988a). *Efficiency in Irrigation: The Conjunctive Use of Surface and Groundwater Resources.* Washington D.C.: World Bank.

O'Mara, G.T. (1988b). The Efficient Use of Surface Water and Groundwater in Irrigation: An Overview of the Issues. In *Efficiency in Irrigation: The Conjunctive Use of Surface and Groundwater Resources*, ed. G.T. O'Mara, Ch. 1. Washington D.C.: World Bank.

Oldenburg, P. (1990). Land Consolidation as Land Reform, in India. *World Development*, **18**, No. 2.

Padmanabhan, K.P. (1988). *Rural Credit: Lessons for Rural Bankers and Policy Makers*. London: Intermediate Technology Publications.

Parikh, A. (1990). *The Economics of Fertilizer Use in Developing Countries*. Aldershot: Gower.

Payne, P.R. (1990). Measuring Malnutrition. *IDS Bulletin*, **21**, No. 3.

Pinstrup-Andersen, P. (ed.) (1988). *Food Subsidies in Developing Countries*. Baltimore: Johns Hopkins.

Pletcher, J. (1989). Rice and Padi Market Management in West Malaysia, 1957–1986. *The Journal of Developing Areas*, **23**, 363–84.

Prosterman, R.L. & Riedinger, J.M. (1987). *Land Reform and Democratic Development*. Baltimore: Johns Hopkins.

Putzel, J. & Cunnington, J. (1989). *Gaining Ground: Agrarian Reform in the Philippines*. London: War on Want.

Randall, A. (1988). Market Failure and the Efficiency of Irrigated Agriculture. In *Efficiency in Irrigation: The Conjunctive Use of Surface and Groundwater Resources*, ed. G.T. O'Mara, Ch. 2. Washington D.C.: World Bank.

Ravallion, M. (1986). Testing Market Integration. *American Journal of Agricultural Economics*, February.

Res, L. (1985). Changing Labor Allocation Patterns of Women in Rice Farm Households: A Rainfed Rice Village, Iloilo Province, Philippines. In *Women in Rice Farming*, International Rice Research Institute (IRRI), Ch. 7. Aldershot: Gower.

Reutlinger, S. (1977). Malnutrition: A Poverty or a Food Problem? *World Development*, **5**, No. 8.

Reynolds, L.G. (ed.) (1975). *Agriculture in Development Theory*. London: Yale University Press.

Rhoades, R.E. & Booth, R.H. (1982). 'Farmer-Back-to-Farmer': a Model for Generating Acceptable Agricultural Technology. *Agricultural Administration*, No. 11, 127–37.

Richards, P. (1985). *Indigenous Agricultural Revolution: Ecology and Food Production in West Africa*. London: Hutchinson.

Roberts, H. (ed.) (1987). Politics in Command? *IDS Bulletin*, **18**, No. 4.

Rudra, A. (1987). Technology Choice in Agriculture in India over the Past Three Decades. In *Macro-Policies for Appropriate Technology in Developing Countries*, ed. F. Stewart, Ch. 2. Boulder, Colorado: Westview Press.

Ruttan, V.W. (1986). Assistance to Expand Agricultural Production. *World Development*, **14**, No. 1.

Ruttan, V.W. (1987). Toward a Global Agricultural Research System. In *Policy for Agricultural Research*, eds. V.W. Ruttan and C.E. Pray, Ch. 3. Boulder, Colorado: Westview Press.

Ruttan, V.W. & Pray, C.E. (eds) (1987). *Policy for Agricultural Research*. Boulder, Colorado: Westview Press.

Sandbrook, R. (1986). The State and Economic Stagnation in Tropical Africa. *World Development*, **14**, No. 3.

Sarap, K. (1990). Factors Affecting Small Farmers' Access to Institutional Credit in Rural Orissa, India. *Development and Change*, **21**, No. 2.

Sarma, J.S. (1988). Determination of Administered Prices of Foodgrains in India. In *Agricultural Price Policy for Developing Countries*, eds. J.W. Mellor and R.U. Ahmed, Ch. 9. Baltimore: Johns Hopkins.

Scandizzo, P.L. & Bruce, C. (1980). *Methodologies for Measuring Agricultural Price*

Intervention Effects. World Bank Staff Working Paper No. 394, April. Washington D.C.: World Bank.

Schaefer-Kehnert, W. & von Pischke, J.D. (1986). Agricultural Credit Policy in Developing Countries. *Savings and Development*, **10**, No. 1.

Schmitz, A. (1984). *Commodity Price Stabilization: The Theory and Its Application*. World Bank Staff Working Paper No. 668. Washington D.C.: World Bank.

Schmitz, A. & Seckler, D. (1970). Mechanized Agriculture and Social Welfare: The Case of the Tomato Harvester. *American Journal of Agricultural Economics*, **52**, 569–77.

Schuh, G.E. & Tollini, H. (1979). *Costs and Benefits of Agricultural Research: The State of the Arts*. World Bank Staff Working Paper No. 360, October. Washington D.C.: World Bank.

Schultz, T.W. (1990). The Economics of Agricultural Research. In *Agricultural Development in the Third World*, eds. C.K. Eicher and J.M. Staatz, Ch. 22, 2nd edn. Baltimore: Johns Hopkins.

Sen, A.K. (1980). Famines. *World Development*, **8**, No. 9.

Sen, A.K. (1981a). Ingredients of Famine Analysis: Availability and Entitlements. *Quarterly Journal of Economics*, **96**.

Sen, A.K. (1981b). *Poverty and Famines: An Essay on Entitlements and Deprivation*. Oxford: Clarendon Press.

Sen, A.K. (1987). Gender and Cooperative Conflicts. *WIDER Working Paper*, No. WP18.

Sen, G. (1985). Paddy Production, Processing and Women Workers in India – The South versus the Northeast. In *Women in Rice Farming*, International Rice Research Institute (IRRI), Ch. 21. Aldershot: Gower.

Shaw, E.S. (1973). *Financial Deepening in Economic Development*. New York: Oxford University Press.

Shepherd, A. (1989). Approaches to the Privatization of Fertilizer Marketing in Africa. *Food Policy*, May.

Shivji, I.G. (1976). *Class Struggles in Tanzania*. Dar es Salaam, Tanzania: Tanzania Publishing House.

Singer, H.W. (1987). Food Aid: Development Tool or Obstacle to Development? *Development Policy Review*, **5**, 323–39.

Singh, I., Squire, L. & Strauss, J. (eds) (1986). *Agricultural Household Models*. Baltimore: Johns Hopkins.

Southworth, V.R., Jones, W.O. & Pearson, S.R. (1979). Food Crop Marketing in Atebubu District, Ghana. *Food Research Institute Studies*, **XVII**, No. 2.

Squire, L. & van der Tak, H.G. (1975). *Economic Analysis of Projects*. London: Johns Hopkins.

Stavenhagen, R. (ed.) (1970). *Agrarian Problems and Peasant Movements in Latin America*. New York: Doubleday.

Stewart, F. (ed.) (1987). *Macro-Policies for Appropriate Technology in Developing Countries*. Boulder, Colorado: Westview Press.

Stiglitz, J.E. (1986a). *The Economics of the Public Sector*. New York: Norton and Co.

Stiglitz, J.E. (1986b). The New Development Economics. *World Development*, **14**, No. 2.

Streeten, P. (1987). *What Price Food? Agricultural Price Policies in Developing Countries*. London: Macmillan.

Tarrant, J.R. (1982). Food Policy Conflicts in Bangladesh. *World Development*, **10**, No. 2.

Tetlay, K., Byerlee, D. & Ahmad, Z. (1990). Role of Tractors, Tubewells and Plant Breeding in Increasing Cropping Intensity in Pakistan's Punjab. *Agricultural Economics*, **4**, 13–25.

Thorbecke, E. & Hall, I. (eds) (1982). *Agricultural Sector Analysis and Models in Developing Countries*. Rome: FAO, ESD Paper No. 5.

Timmer, C.P. (1974). A Model of Rice Marketing Margins in Indonesia. *Food Research Institute Studies*, **13**, No. 2.

Timmer, C.P. (1986a). *Getting Prices Right: The Scope and Limits of Agricultural Price Policy*. New York: Cornell University Press.

Timmer, C.P. (1986b). The Role of Price Policy in Rice Production in Indonesia 1968–1982. In *Research in Domestic and International Agribusiness Management*, ed. R.A. Goldberg, pp. 55–106. Greenwich, Conn: JAI Press.

Timmer, C.P. (1987). Corn Marketing. In *The Corn Economy of Indonesia*, ed. C.P. Timmer, Ch. 8, pp. 201–34. Ithaca, New York: Cornell University Press.

Timmer, C.P. (1989). Food Price Policy: The Rationale for Government Intervention. *Food Policy*, **14**, February.

Timmer, C.P. & Falcon, W.P. (1975). The Political Economy of Rice Production and Trade in Asia. In *Agriculture in Development Theory*, ed. L.G. Reynolds, Ch. 14. London: Yale University Press.

Timmer, C.P., Falcon, W.P. & Pearson, S.R. (1983). *Food Policy Analysis*. Baltimore: Johns Hopkins.

Tinbergen, J. (1952). *On the Theory of Economic Policy*. Amsterdam: North Holland.

Tinbergen, J. (1956). *Economic Policy: Principles and Design*. Amsterdam: North Holland.

Tolley, G.S., Thomas, V. & Wong, C.M. (1982). *Agricultural Price Policies and the Developing Countries*. Baltimore: Johns Hopkins.

Tomek, W.G. & Robinson, K.L. (1981). *Agricultural Product Prices*. Ithaca and London: Cornell University Press.

Tsakok, I. (1990). *Agricultural Price Policy: A Practitioner's Guide to Partial Equilibrium Analysis*. New York: Cornell University Press.

Tweeten, L. (ed.) (1989). *Agricultural Policy Analysis Tools for Economic Development*. London: Intermediate Technology Publications.

Vogel, R.C. (1984). Savings Mobilization: The Forgotten Half of Rural Finance. In *Undermining Rural Development with Cheap Credit*, eds. D.W. Adams, D.H. Graham and J.D. von Pischke, pp. 248–65. Boulder, Colorado: Westview Press.

von Braun, J. & Puetz, D. (1987). An African Fertilizer Crisis: Origin and Economic Effects in the Gambia. *Food Policy*, November.

von Braun, J., Puetz, D. & Webb, P. (1989). *Irrigation Technology and Commercialization of Rice in the Gambia: Effects on Income and Nutrition*. International Food Policy Research Institute, Research Report 75, August.

von Pischke, J.D. & Adams, D.W. (1980). Fungibility and the Design and Evaluation of Agricultural Credit Projects. *American Journal of Agricultural Economics*, **62**, No. 4.

von Pischke, J.D., Adams, D.W. & Donald, G. (eds) (1983). *Rural Financial Markets in Developing Countries*. Baltimore: Johns Hopkins.

von Pischke, J.D., Heffernan, P.J. & Adams, D.W. (1981). *The Political Economy of Specialized Farm Credit Institutions in Low-Income Countries*. World Bank Staff Working Paper No. 446. Washington D.C.: World Bank.

von Pischke, J.D. & Rouse, J. (1983). Selected Successful Experiences in Agricultural Credit and Rural Finance in Africa. *Savings and Development*, **7**, No. 1.

Wade, R. (1982). The System of Administrative and Political Corruption: Canal Irrigation in South India. *Journal of Development Studies*, **18**, No. 3.

Wade, R. (1985). The Market for Public Office: Why the Indian State is not Better at Development. *World Development*, **13**, No. 4.

Wade, R. (1988). The Management of Irrigation Systems: How to Evoke Trust and Avoid Prisoners' Dilemma. *World Development*, **16**, No. 4.

Walinsky, L.J. (ed.) (1977). *Agrarian Reform as Unfinished Business: The Selected Papers of Wolf Ladejinsky*. Oxford: Oxford University Press.

Warriner, D. (1969). *Land Reform in Principle and Practice*. Oxford: Clarendon Press.

Westlake, M.J. (1987). The Measurement of Agricultural Price Distortion in Developing Countries. *Journal of Development Studies*, **23**, No. 3.

White, B. (1985). Women and the Modernization of Rice Agriculture: Some General Issues and a Javanese Case Study. In *Women in Rice Farming*, International Rice Research Institute (IRRI), Ch. 8. Aldershot: Gower.

Willig, R.D. (1976). Consumer's Surplus Without Apology. *American Economic Review*, **66**, No. 4.

World Bank (1974). *Land Reform*. Washington D.C.: World Bank, Rural Development Series Paper.

World Bank (1975). *Agricultural Credit*. Sector Policy Paper, Washington D.C.

World Bank (1986a). *Poverty and Hunger: Issues and Options for Food Security in Developing Countries*. Washington D.C.: World Bank.

World Bank (1986b). *World Development Report 1986*. Oxford: Oxford University Press.

Author index

Subject index